ORDNANCE SURVEY

STREET ATLAS
Bristol and Avon

Contents

IV Key to maps

VI Administrative boundaries

1 Street maps

140 Index explanation and abbreviations

141 Index of towns, villages and rural localities

142 Index of street names

PHILIP'S

First edition published 1995 by

Ordnance Survey	and	Philip's
Romsey Road		an imprint of Reed Books
Maybush		Michelin House, 81 Fulham Road, London, SW3 6RB
Southampton SO16 4GU		and Auckland, Melbourne, Singapore and Toronto

ISBN 0-540-06140-9 (Philip's, hardback)
ISBN 0-540-06141-7 (Philip's, softback)
ISBN 0-319-00581-X (Ordnance Survey, hardback)
ISBN 0-319-00582-8 (Ordnance Survey, softback)

To the best of the Publishers' knowledge, the information in this atlas was correct at
the time of going to press. No responsibility can be accepted for any errors or their
consequences.

The representation in this atlas of a road, track or path is no evidence of the existence
of a right of way.

Printed and bound in Great Britain by
Bath Press, Bath

Key to map symbols

⇌	**British Rail station**
🚂	**Private railway station**
⬛	**Bus or coach station**
Ⓗ	**Heliport**
◆	**Police station** (may not be open 24 hours)
✚	**Hospital with casualty facilities** (may not be open 24 hours)
☐	**Post office**
+	**Place of worship**
⬛	**Important building**
P	**Parking**
174	**Adjoining page indicator**
✕	**No adjoining page**
═══	**Motorway**
═══	**Dual carriageway**
──	**Main or through road**
A27	**Road numbers** (Department of Transport)
─┬─	**Gate or obstruction to traffic** (restrictions may not apply at all times or to all vehicles)
- - - -	**All paths, bridleways, BOAT's, RUPP's, dismantled railways, etc.**
═══	**Track**

The representation in this atlas of a road, track or path is no evidence of the existence of a right of way

Amb Sta	**Ambulance station**	LC	**Level crossing**
Coll	**College**	Liby	**Library**
FB	**Footbridge**	Mus	**Museum**
F Sta	**Fire station**	Sch	**School**
Hospl	**Hospital**	TH	**Town hall**

0	¼	½	¾	1 mile
0	250 m	500 m	250 m	1 Kilometre

The scale of the maps is 3½ inches to 1 mile (1:18103)

The small numbers around the edges of the maps identify the 1 kilometre National Grid lines

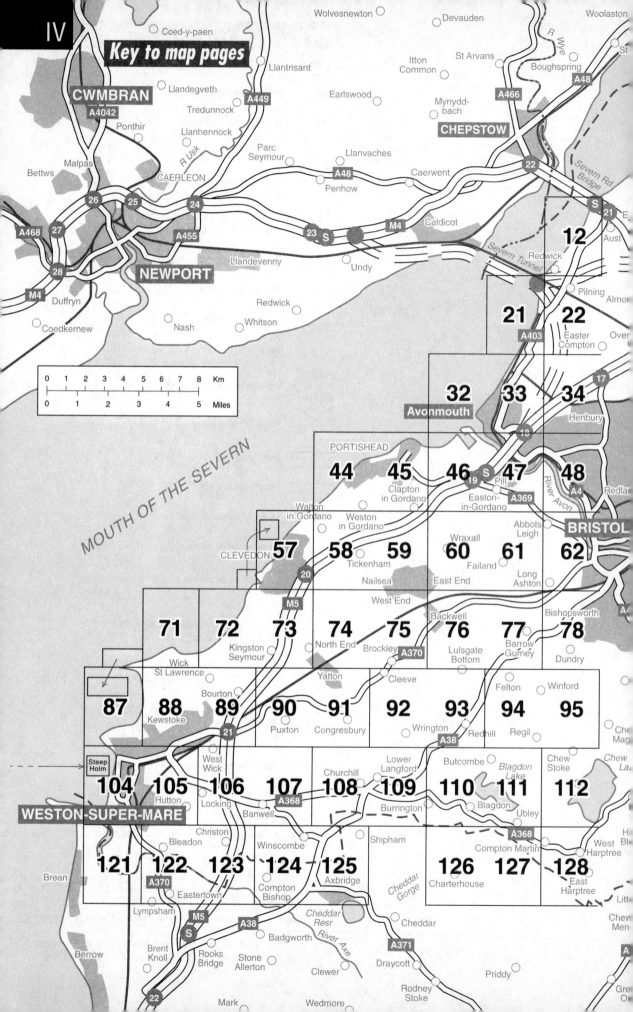

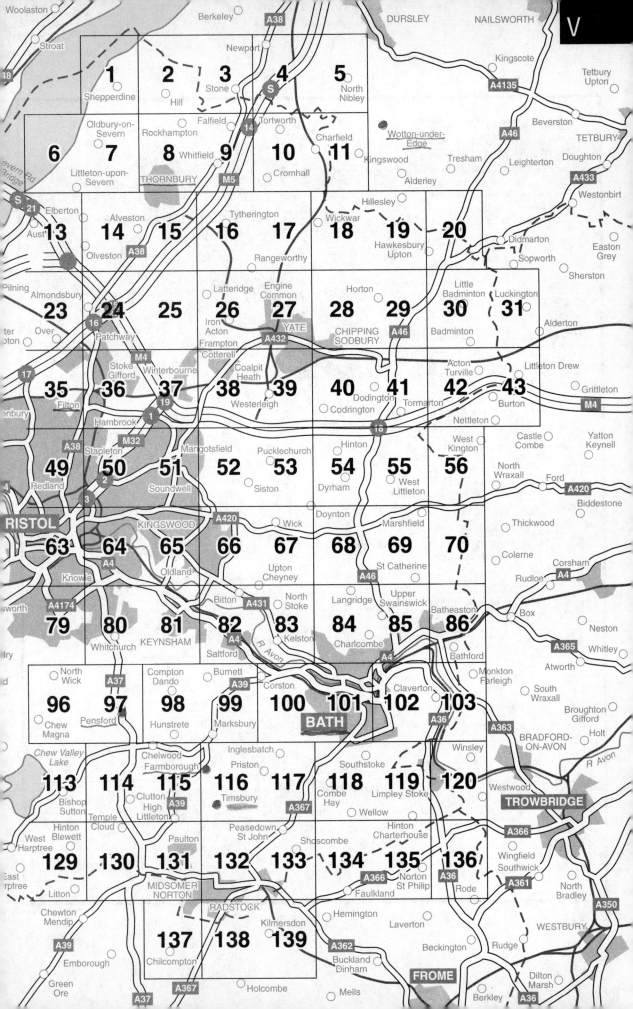

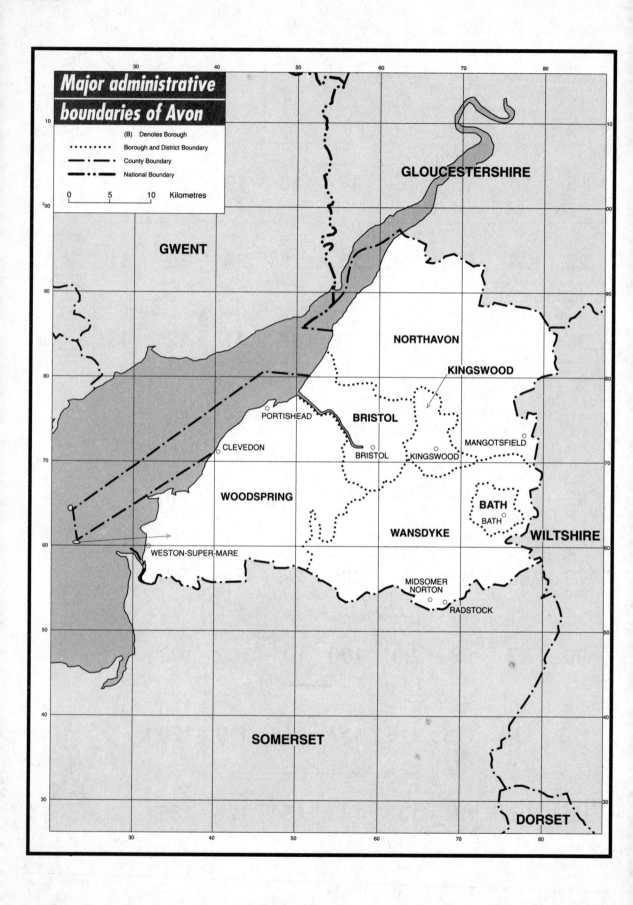

Major administrative boundaries of Avon

(B) Denotes Borough

········ Borough and District Boundary

—·—·— County Boundary

—··—··— National Boundary

0   5   10   Kilometres

GLOUCESTERSHIRE

GWENT

NORTHAVON

KINGSWOOD

PORTISHEAD

BRISTOL

CLEVEDON

MANGOTSFIELD

BRISTOL

KINGSWOOD

WOODSPRING

BATH

BATH

WANSDYKE

WILTSHIRE

WESTON-SUPER-MARE

MIDSOMER
NORTON

RADSTOCK

SOMERSET

DORSET

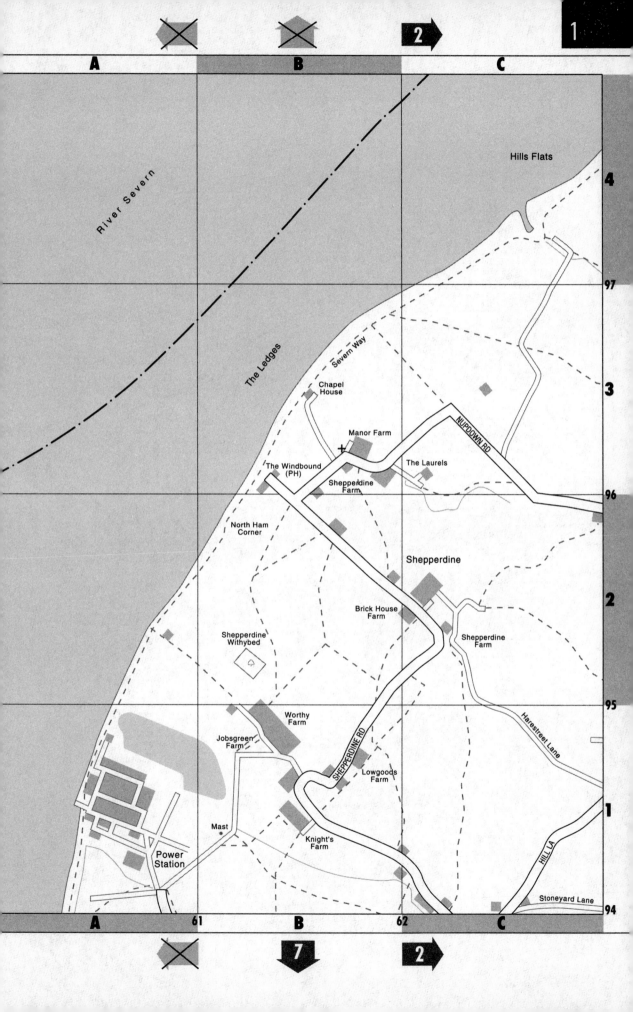

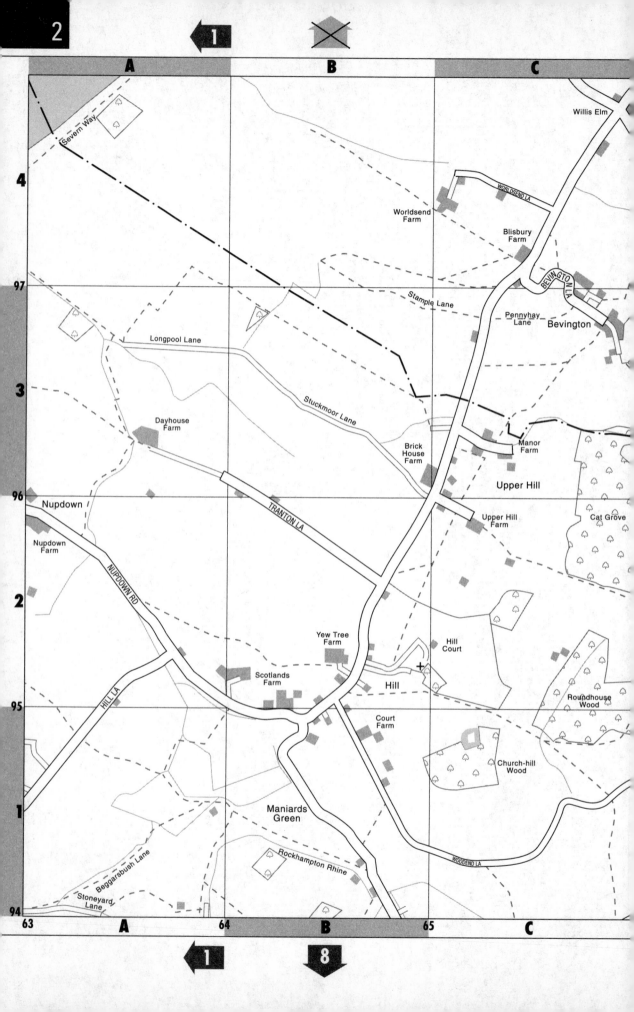

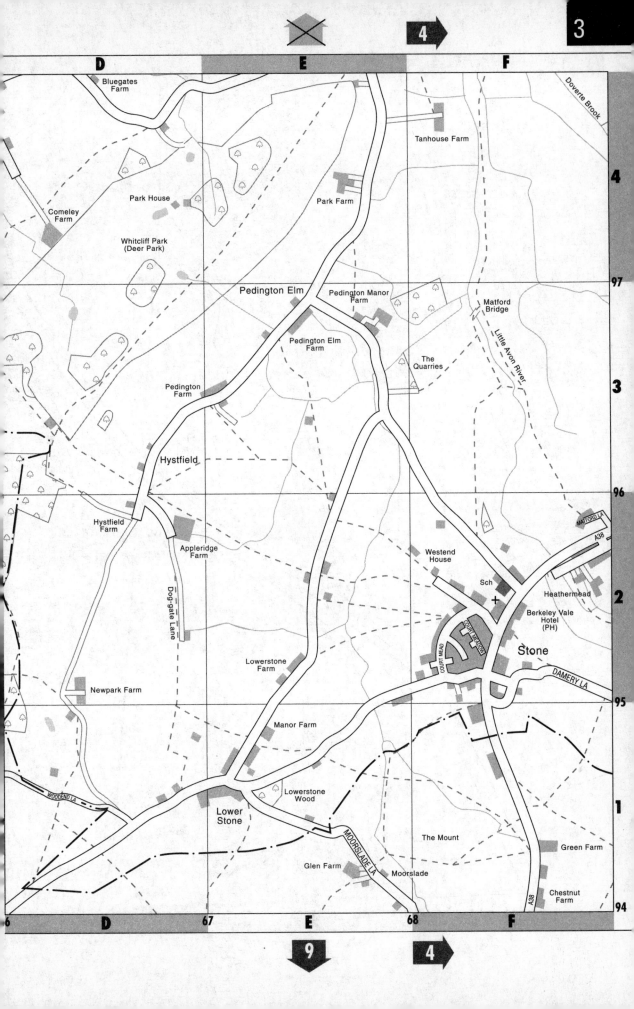

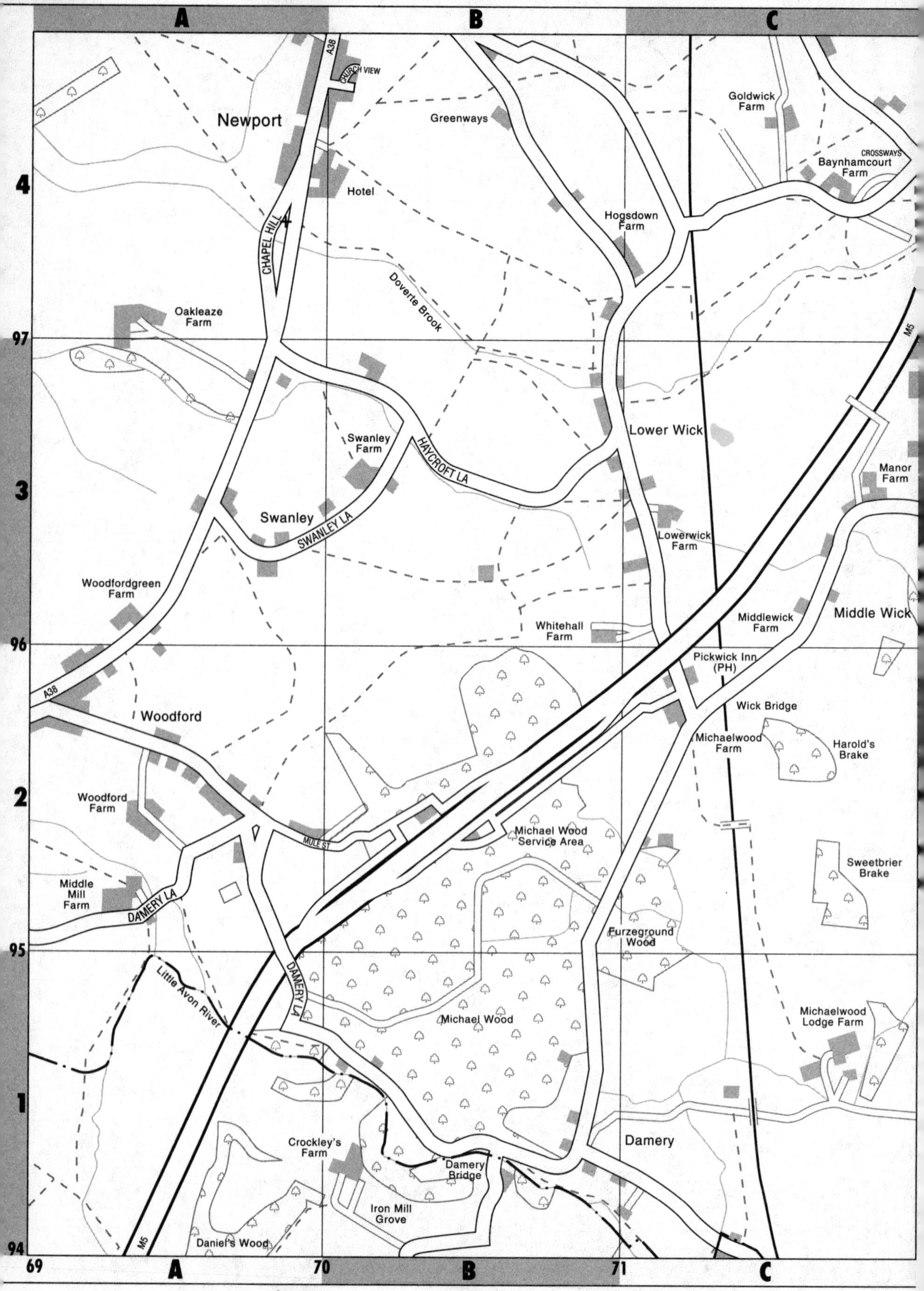

A　　　　　　　B　　　　　　　C

Newport

CHURCH VIEW

A38

Greenways

Goldwick Farm

CROSSWAYS

Baynhamcourt Farm

Hotel

Hogsdown Farm

4

CHAPEL HILL

Doverte Brook

Oakleaze Farm

97

Lower Wick

M5

Swanley Farm

HAYCROFT LA

Manor Farm

3

Swanley

SWANLEY LA

Lowerwick Farm

Woodfordgreen Farm

Middlewick Farm

Middle Wick

Whitehall Farm

96

Pickwick Inn (PH)

A38

Wick Bridge

Woodford

Harold's Brake

Michaelwood Farm

2

Woodford Farm

MULE ST

Michael Wood Service Area

Sweetbrier Brake

Middle Mill Farm

DAMERY LA

Furzeground Wood

95

Little Avon River

DAMERY LA

Michael Wood

Michaelwood Lodge Farm

1

Crockley's Farm

Damery

Damery Bridge

M5

Iron Mill Grove

Daniel's Wood

94

69　　　　A　　　70　　　B　　　71　　　C

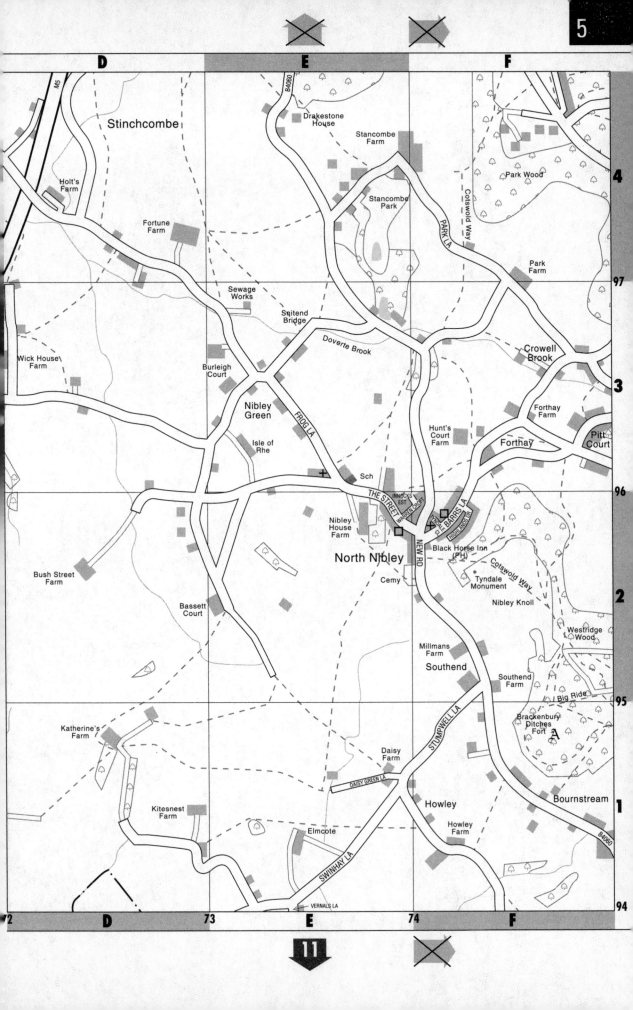

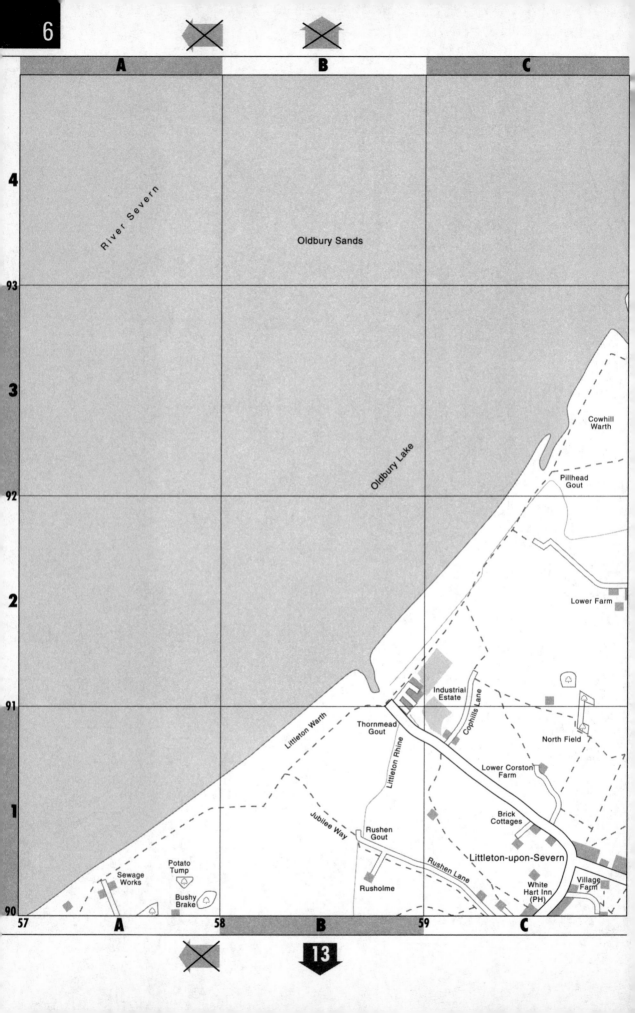

A

B

C

River Severn

Oldbury Sands

Cowhill
Warth

Oldbury Lake

Pillhead
Gout

Lower Farm

Industrial
Estate

Littleton Warth

Thornmead
Gout

Cophills Lane

North Field

Littleton Rhine

Lower Corston
Farm

Jubilee Way

Brick
Cottages

Rushen
Gout

Littleton-upon-Severn

Sewage
Works

Potato
Tump

Rushen Lane

Bushy
Brake

Rusholme

White
Hart Inn
(PH)

Village
Farm

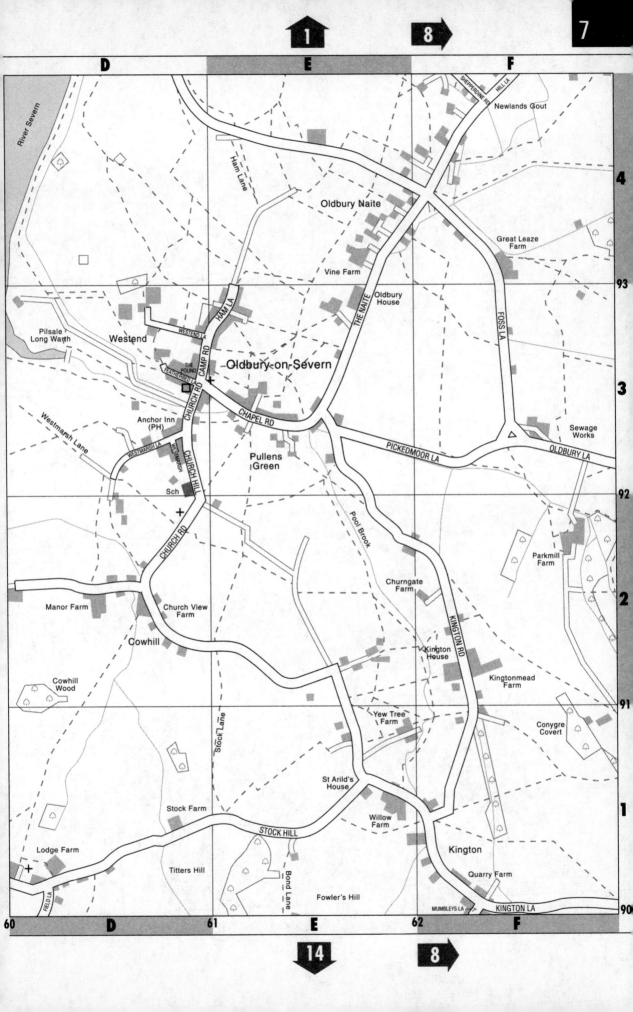

4

River Severn

Newlands Gout

Oldbury Naite

Great Leaze
Farm

93

Vine Farm

Ham Lane

Oldbury
House

Pilsale
Long Warth

Westend

WESTEND LA

HAM LA

THE NAITE

FOSS LA

Oldbury-on-Severn

THE POUND

CAMP RD

FEATHERBED LA

CHURCH RD

3

Anchor Inn
(PH)

CHAPEL RD

PICKEDMOOR LA

Sewage
Works

OLDBURY LA

Westmarsh Lane

WESTMARSH LA

WESTMARSH

CHURCH HILL

Pullens
Green

92

Sch

Pool Brook

Parkmill
Farm

CHURCH RD

Churngate
Farm

2

Manor Farm

Church View
Farm

Cowhill

KINGTON RD

Kington
House

Kingtonmead
Farm

Cowhill
Wood

91

Stock Lane

Yew Tree
Farm

Conygre
Covert

St Arild's
House

1

Stock Farm

STOCK HILL

Willow
Farm

Kington

Lodge Farm

Bond Lane

Quarry Farm

FIELD LA

Fowler's Hill

MUMBLEYS LA

KINGTON LA

90

Titters Hill

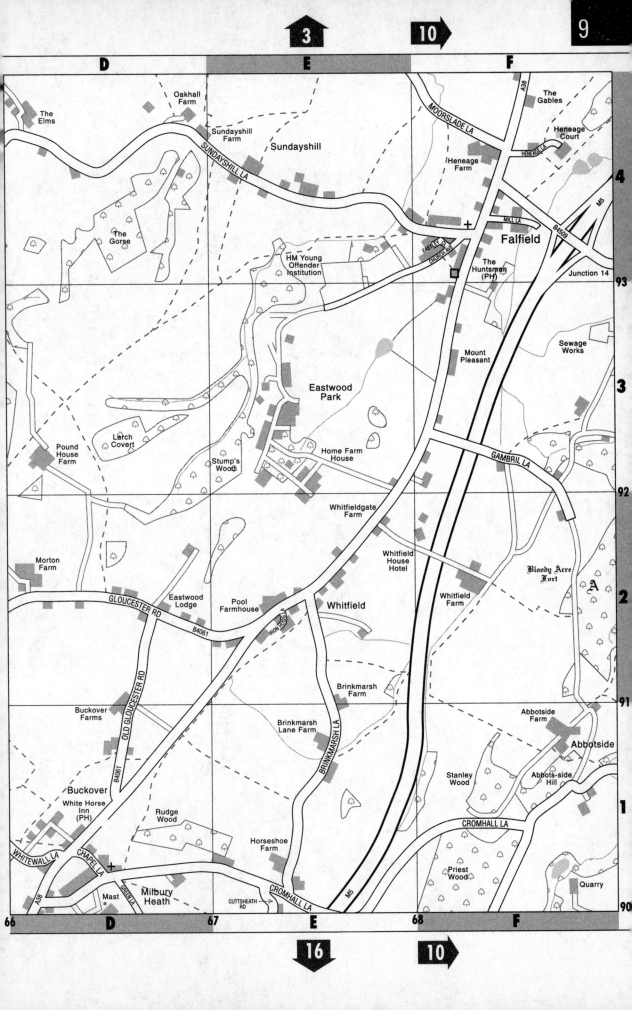

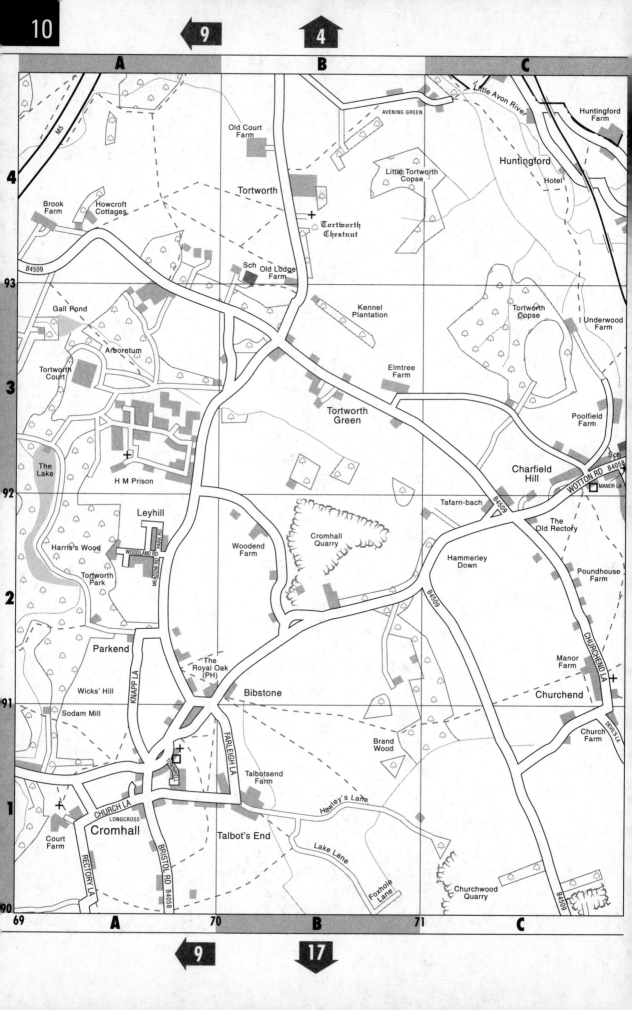

A   B   C

4

Brook Farm

Howcroft Cottages

Old Court Farm

Tortworth

Avening Green

Little Avon River

Huntingford Farm

Huntingford

Hotel

Tortworth Chestnut

Little Tortworth Copse

B4509

Sch   Old Lodge Farm

93

Gall Pond

Kennel Plantation

Tortworth Copse

Underwood Farm

Arboretum

Elmtree Farm

Poolfield Farm

Tortworth Court

3

Tortworth Green

Charfield Hill

Sch B4058

The Lake

H M Prison

Tafarn-bach

B4509

WOTTON RD   MANOR LA

92

Leyhill

Woodend Farm

Cromhall Quarry

The Old Rectory

PARK RD

WOODLAND RD

Harris's Wood

Hammerley Down

Poundhouse Farm

Tortworth Park

MEADOW RD

2

B4509

Parkend

KNAPP LA

Wicks' Hill

The Royal Oak (PH)

Bibstone

Manor Farm

CHURCHEND LA

Churchend

91

Sodam Mill

Brand Wood

Church Farm

DEVIL'S LA

FARLEIGH LA

RANDWELL

Talbotsend Farm

Hawley's Lane

1

Court Farm

CHURCH LA

LONGCROSS

Cromhall

Talbot's End

Lake Lane

Foxhole Lane

Churchwood Quarry

B4509

RECTORY LA

BRISTOL RD

B4058

90

69   A   70   B   71   C

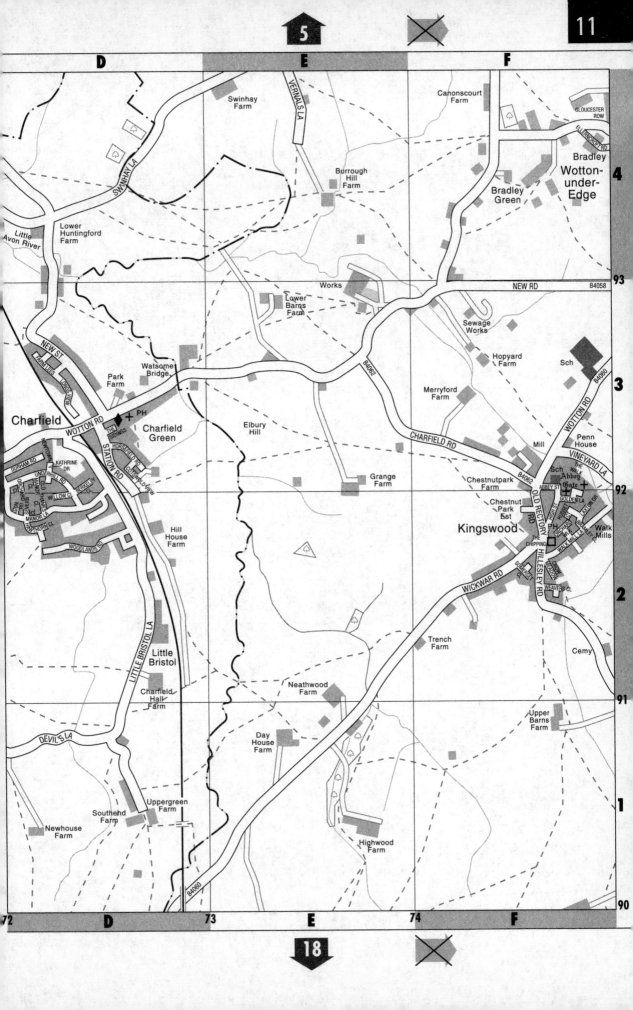

A   B   C

4

M4
Severn Road Bridge (Toll)
Jubilee Way
Toll
Aust Cliff
Pier

89

River Severn

Old Passage
New House Farm
Old Passage House

A403

3

Northwick Oaze

Cake Pill Gout

88

Asnum Copse
Lords Rhine

2

Northwick Warth
Bilsham Rhine
Bilsham Farm
Eastfield Lane

87

Warth Lane
AUST RD
Greenfield Farm
Church Farm
Sch
Church Tower
Mill Farm
B4055
BILSHAM LA
HOLM LA

DANGER AREA

Sugarhole Sand

1

Rifle Range
SEVERN RD
Northwick
Manor Farm
Ballstreet Lane
North Worthy Farm
Holm Rhine
NORTHWICK RD
B4055

Severn Lodge Farm
New Passage
REDWICK RD B4055
A403
Road under construction

86

54   A   55   B   56   C

22

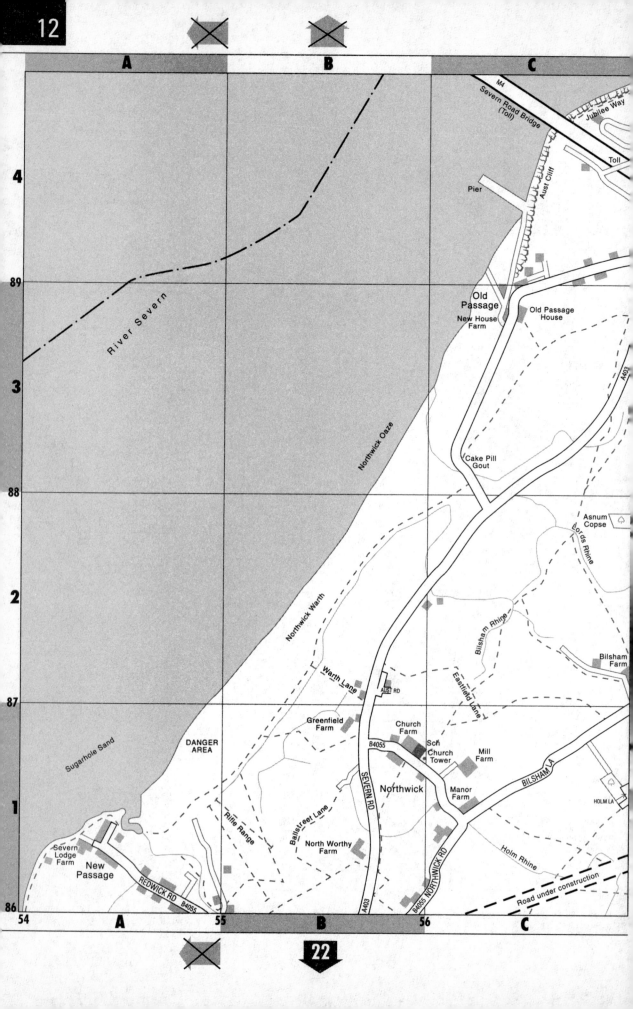

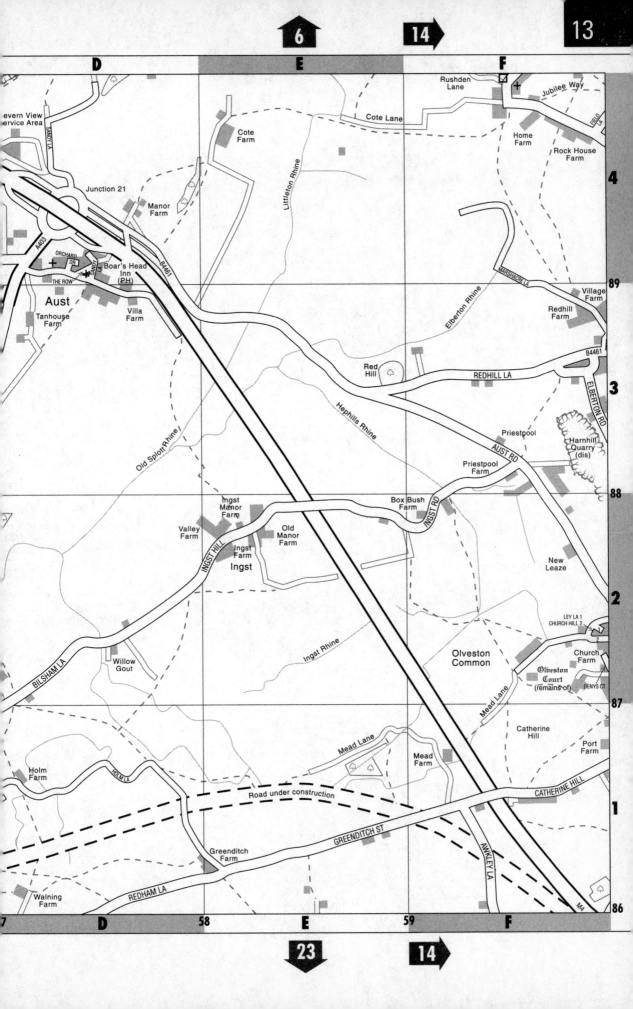

D
E
F

Rushden Lane
Jubilee Way
FIELD LA

Cote Lane
Home Farm
Rock House Farm

4

Severn View Service Area
SANDY LA

Cote Farm

Littleton Rhine

Junction 21
Manor Farm

MARSHACRE LA
Village Farm

89

A403
ORCHARD DR
SANDY LA
Boar's Head Inn (PH)
THE ROW
Aust
Villa Farm
Tanhouse Farm

B4461

Elberton Rhine
Redhill Farm
B4461

Red Hill
REDHILL LA

ELBERTON RD

3

Hephills Rhine

Priestpool
Harnhill Quarry (dis)

Old Splott Rhine

AUST RD
Priestpool Farm

88

Ingst Manor Farm
Valley Farm
Old Manor Farm
Ingst Farm
Ingst

INGST HILL

Box Bush Farm

INGST RD

New Leaze

2

BILSHAM LA

Willow Gout

Ingst Rhine

Olveston Common

LEY LA 1
CHURCH HILL 2
Church Farm
Olveston Court (remains of)
DENYS CT

87

Holm Farm
HOLM LA

Mead Lane

Mead Farm

Mead Lane

Catherine Hill
Port Farm

Road under construction

CATHERINE HILL

1

Greenditch Farm
GREENDITCH ST

AWKLEY LA
M4

Walning Farm
REDHAM LA

86

7
D
58
E
59
F

13
7

A   B   C

FIELD LA
Sacks Hill
Cole's Brake
Beech Farm
MUMBLEYS LA

Stonage Field
4
Hay Wood
Bond Lane
Sch
Kington Grove

Water Works
Henley Hill
Jubilee Way
MUMBLEYS HILL
Resr
Marlwood Farm

89
Court Farm
Fierypits Brake
Mumbleys Farm
Gate Farm

Haywood Farm
MUMBLEYS LA

B4461
Camp Farm
VATTINGSTONE LA
Sch

Elberton
QUARRY RD

3
Old Manor
Vineyards Brake
Alveston Down
B4461
DOWN

ELBERTON RD
STRODE GDNS
STRODE COMM

88
Hazel Farm
Stroud Common
WEST VIEW

Oldown
FOXHOLES LA
BRIDLEW
HAZE GDN

The Down House
ALVESTON RD
Upper Hazel
GREENHILL LA

2
VICARAGE LA
Sch
THE CRESCENT
PUMP LA
Lower Hazel

AUST RD
Fernhill Cottage
Old Down
THE DOWN
THE INNER DOWN
HAZEL LA

Olveston
Little Down
DOWN HILL
Fox Inn (PH)
A38

CHURCH HILL
THE STREET
HAW LA
Tockington Hill
Sheepcombe Brake

87
Eastcombe Hill
CATHERINE HILL
NEW RD
OLDOWN HILL
Sch
Sheepcombe House
CHURCH RD B4421

THE GREEN
UPPER TOCKINGTON RD
Home Farm
WASHINGPOOL HILL RD
Rudgeway
GLOUCESTER RD

1
LOWER TOCKINGTON RD
PH
MANOR CL
Willis Brake
RUDGEWAY PARK

HARDY LA
MILL LA
Tockington
Silverhill Brake
Sch

Port Farm
Tockington Mill Rhine
Gorse Covert
Oakleaze
A38

86
60   A   61   B   62   C

13
24

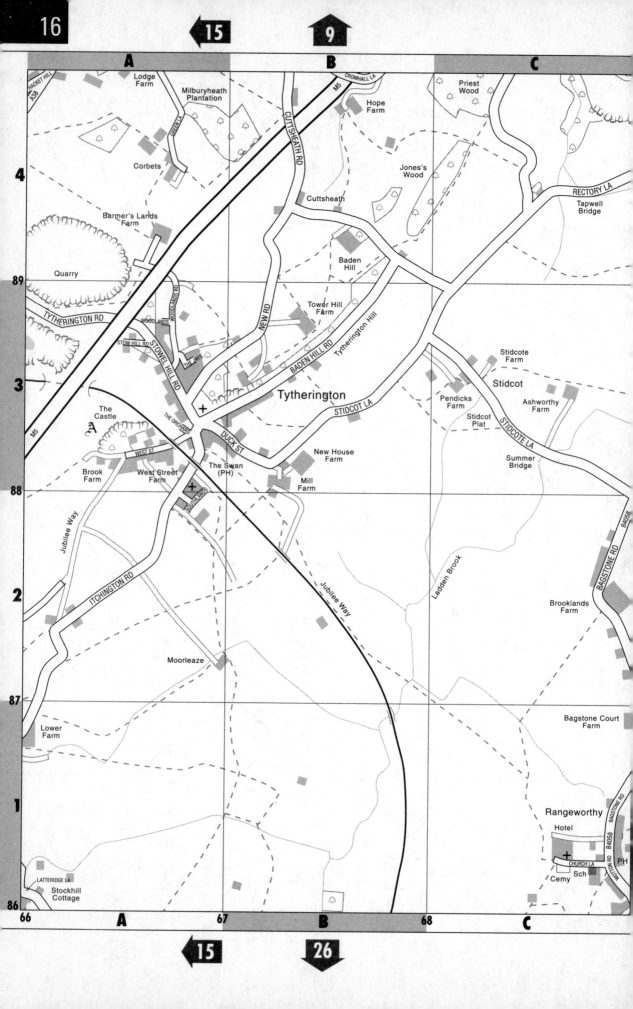

A B C

Haroldfield
Farm

Bunsall
Bridge

B4060

Southwood
Farm

Cherryrock
Farm

4

Cherryrock
Brake

Mounteney's
Farm

STATION RD

Station
House

Chase House
Farm

Kites
Farm

Trading
Est

MOUNTENEY'S LA

89

CHURCH LA

CHASE LA

Chaselane
Farm

Inglestone
Farm

B4509

THE DOWNS

WESTEND
RD

B4509

Saltmoors Ditch

TURNPIKE GATE

AVON CRES

PH

COTSWOLD VIEW

South Moon
Ridings

NORTH ST

HONEYBORNE WAY

3

TH

Trading
Est

HIGH ST

BACK LA

Wickwar

The Walk

HIGHSTREET RD

Sturt
Farm

Little Stanley
Wood

Lower Woods
Lodge

Sturt
Bridge

88

AUBERLEY WAY

OLD HIGH ST

South
Farm

CANTERS LA

POPLAR LA

Little Avon River

Harwood
Farm

Wetmoor
Nature Reserve

SODBURY RD

Poplar
Farm

HORWOOD LA

Lower Wetmoor
Wood

Littley
Wood

2

Bishop's Hill
Wood

Upper
Wetmoor

Hill View
Farm

Bishop's Hill Brook

FRITH LA

PINCOTS LA

Pulling's
Trench

Pincots
Farm

87

Burnt
Wood

Sturgeon
Wood

Bedford's
Wood

WICKWAR RD

1

Bays
Wood

Stonybridge
Wood

Shortwood
Farm

Little Shortwood
Farm

Haskin's
Farm

WOOD LA

Birdsbush
Farm

B4060

86

72 A 73 B 74 C

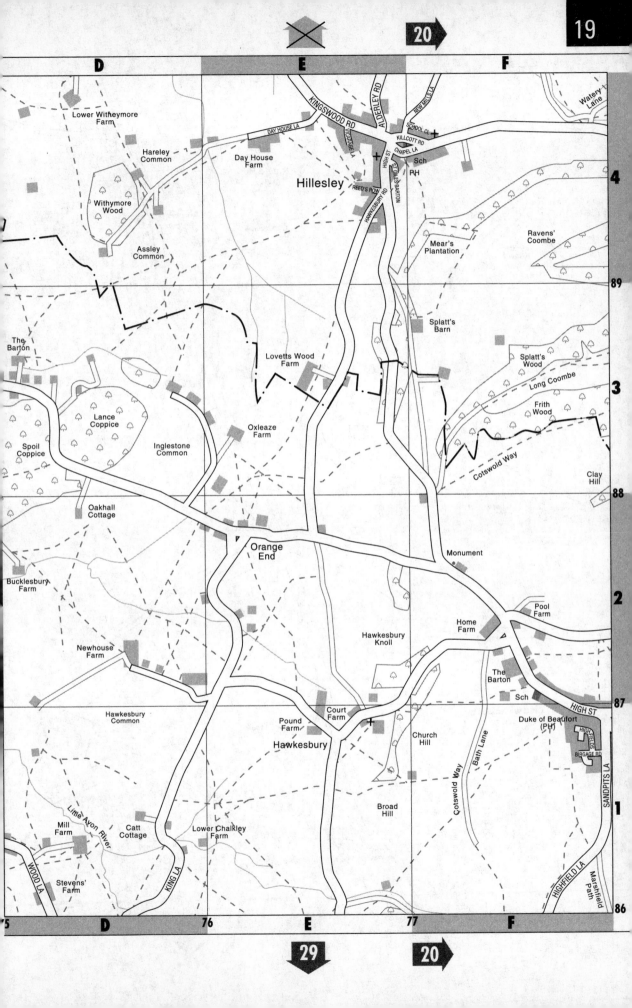

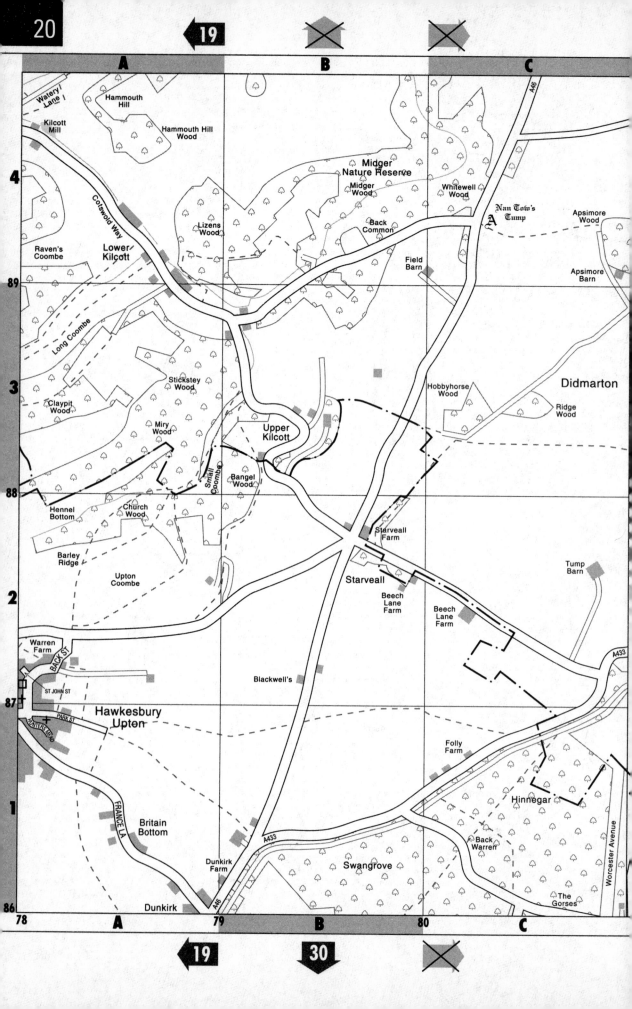

English Stones

English Lake

Salmon Pool

Bridge under construction

The Binn Wall

BEACH RD

BEACH AVE

New Pill Gout

Chittening Warth

SEVERN RD

A403

Red Rhine

Works

Works

Tanks

Crook's Marsh

A403

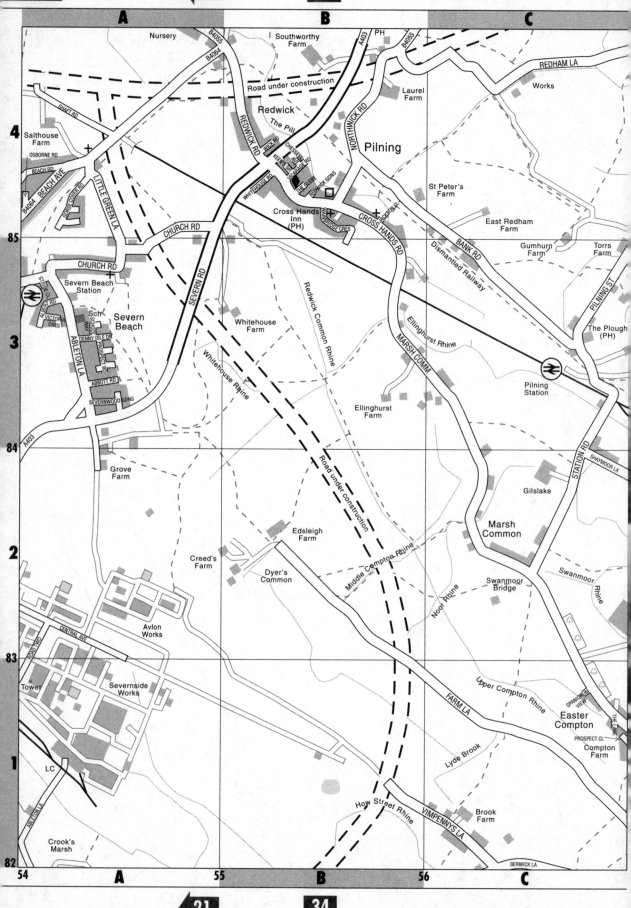

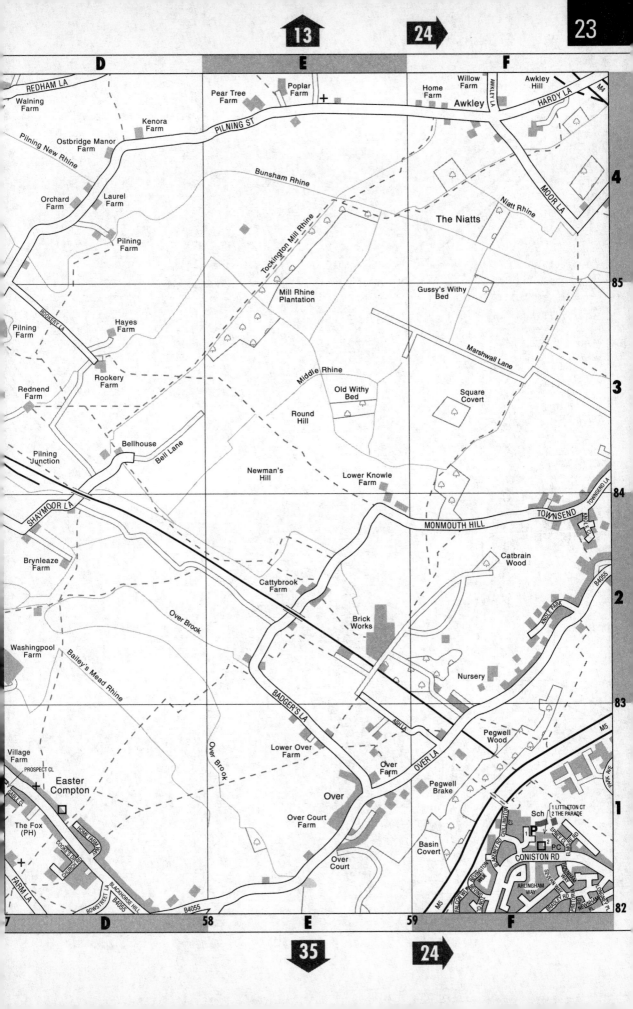

REDHAM LA
Walning Farm
Pilning New Rhine
Ostbridge Manor Farm
Kenora Farm
Pear Tree Farm
Poplar Farm
PILNING ST
Home Farm
Willow Farm
Awkley Hill
HARDY LA
AWKLEY LA
MOOR LA
M4
Awkley
Orchard Farm
Laurel Farm
Pilning Farm
Bunsham Rhine
The Niatts
Niatt Rhine
Tockington Mill Rhine
ROOKERY LA
Pilning Farm
Hayes Farm
Mill Rhine Plantation
Gussy's Withy Bed
Marshwall Lane
Rednend Farm
Rookery Farm
Middle Rhine
Old Withy Bed
Square Covert
Round Hill
Bellhouse
Bell Lane
Newman's Hill
Lower Knowle Farm
Pilning Junction
TOWNSEND LA
TOWNSEND
SHAYMOOR LA
MONMOUTH HILL
Catbrain Wood
Brynleaze Farm
Cattybrook Farm
KNOLE PARK
B4055
Over Brook
Brick Works
Nursery
Washingpool Farm
Bailey's Mead Rhine
BADGER'S LA
ASH LA
Pegwell Wood
M5
Village Farm
PROSPECT CL
Over Brook
Lower Over Farm
OVER LA
Over Farm
Pegwell Brake
Easter Compton
PARK AVE
The Fox (PH)
HOME FARM CL
COOK'S LA
CHURCH LA
Over
Over Court Farm
Over Court
Basin Covert
Sch
1 LITTLETON CT
2 THE PARADE
CHILLINGTON CT
P
PC
CONISTON RD
ARLINGHAM WAY
BASIL CL
FARM LA
BOWSTREET LA
BLACKHORSE HILL
B4055
B4055

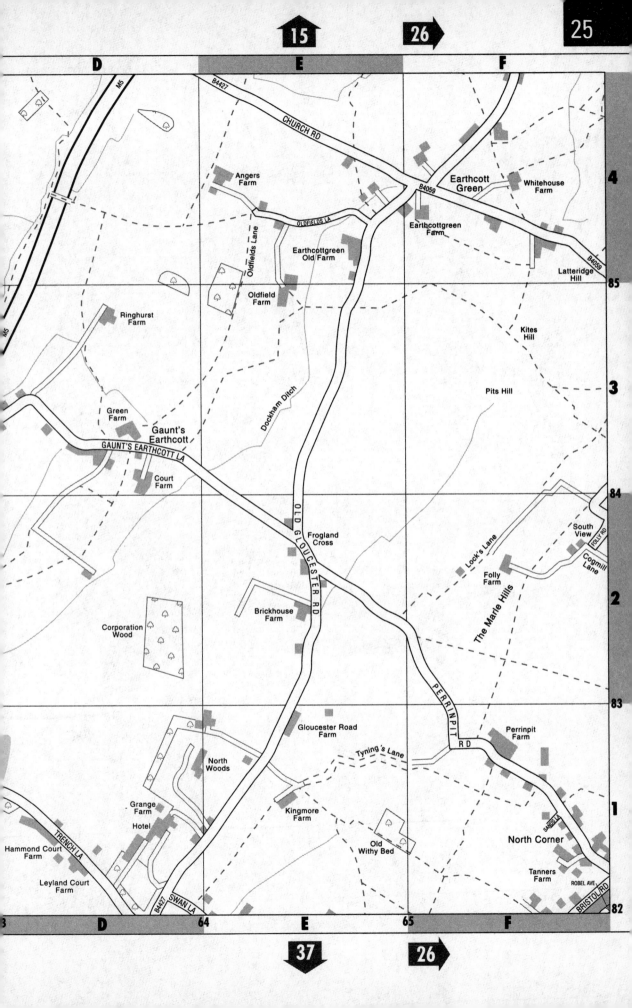

Lower Lark's Farm

El Sub Sta

LATTERIDGE LA

LARK'S LA

4

Pool Farm

PATCH ELM LA

Dowells Farm

Latteridge Hill

85

B4059

Mudgedown Farm

Ladden Bows Bridge

Chaingate House

CHAINGATE LA

Latteridge

FOLLY RD

Wotton Rd

Two Pools Farm

3

NORTHMEAD LA

LC

Sheephouse Farm

Ladden Brook

Acton Court

Acton Lodge

84

B4059

Hill House

LC

White Hart Inn (PH)

LATTERIDGE RD

PARK ST

Iron Acton

B4059

B4059

Sch

Laddenside Farm

Elm Farm

HIGH ST

WOTTON RD

Isle of Rhee

YATE RD

2

Cogmill Lane

Rose & Crown Inn (PH)

HOLLY LA

Holly Hill

B405

STATION RD

BRISTOL RD

LC

Ford

River Frome

Algars Manor

CHILWOOD

ALGARS OR

Lavenham Farm

Brake Farm

Robins Wood

NIBLEY LA

83

BRISTOL RD

Frome Valley Walkway

Cog Mill Farm

Hover's Lane

FRAMPTON END RD

1

Tubb's Bottom

B4058

PH

Frampton Cotterell

ROBEL AVE

WESTERN AVE

CONIFER CL

MILL LA

SCHOOL RD

CHURCH RD

Chestnut Farm

BADMINTON RD

A43

Cemy

Mayshill

A432

82

66

A

67

B

68

C

YATE

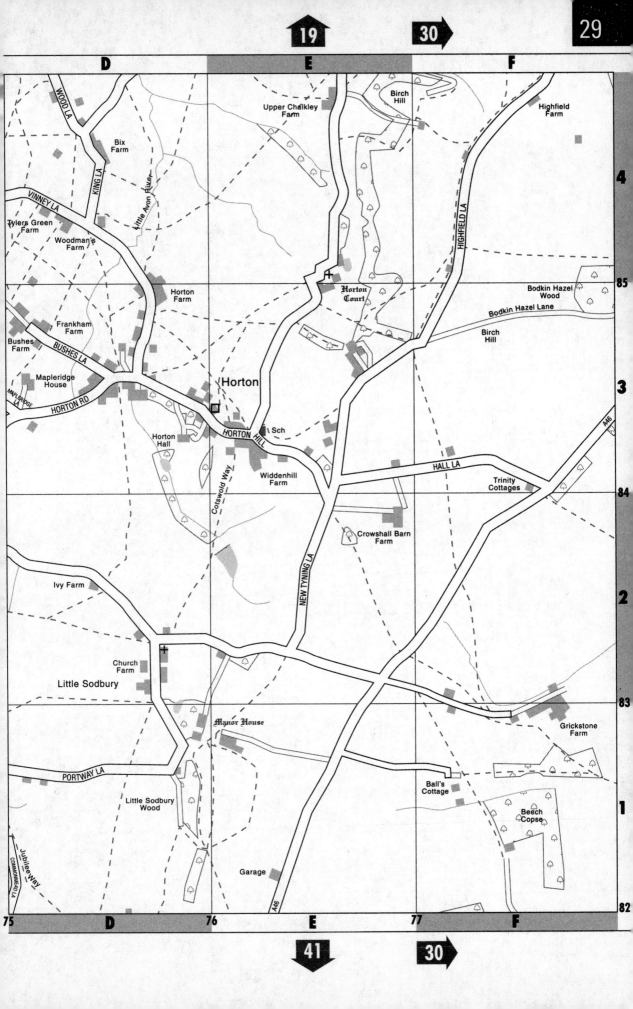

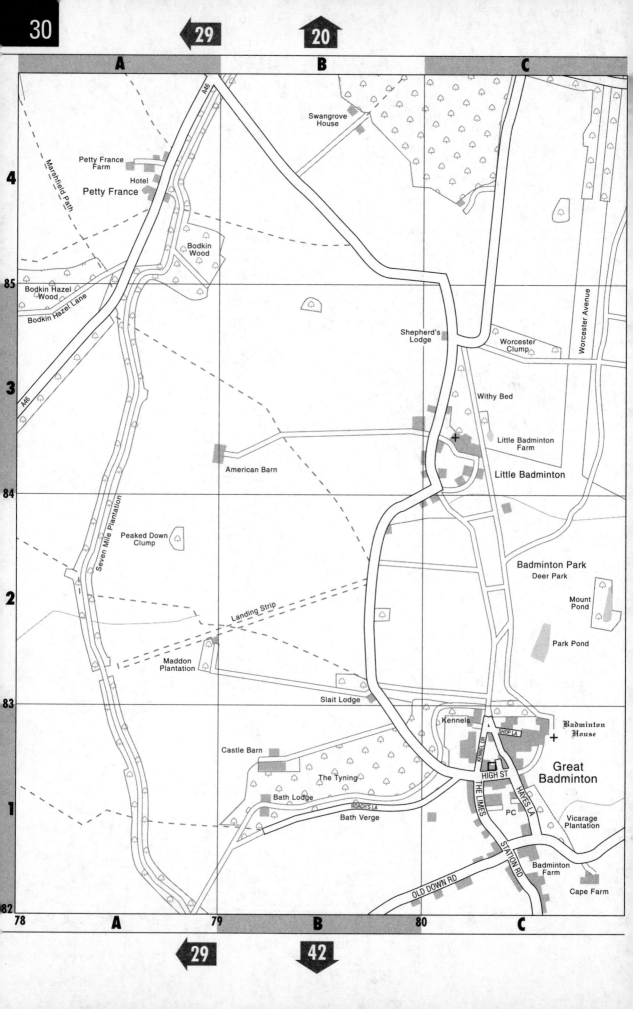

A B C

4

Marshfield Path

Petty France Farm

Hotel

Petty France

A46

Swangrove House

Bodkin Wood

85

Bodkin Hazel Wood

Bodkin Hazel Lane

A46

3

Shepherd's Lodge

Worcester Clump

Worcester Avenue

Withy Bed

Little Badminton Farm

American Barn

Little Badminton

84

Seven Mile Plantation

Peaked Down Clump

Badminton Park
Deer Park

Mount Pond

2

Landing Strip

Park Pond

Maddon Plantation

83

Slait Lodge

Kennels

Badminton House

SHOP LA

Castle Barn

The Tyning

Great Badminton

KENNEL DR

HIGH ST

THE LIMES

HAYES LA

1

Bath Lodge

ROACH'S LA

Bath Verge

PC

Vicarage Plantation

STATION RD

Badminton Farm

OLD DOWN RD

Cape Farm

82

78 A 79 B 80 C

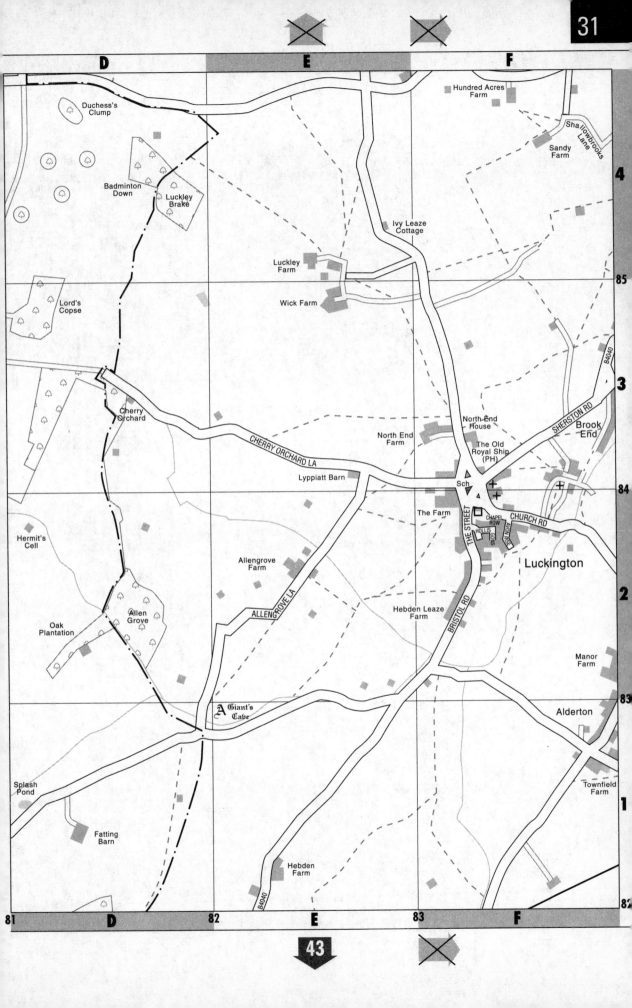

D   E   F

4

85

3

84

2

83

1

82

81   D   82   E   83   F

Duchess's
Clump

Badminton
Down

Luckley
Brake

Lord's
Copse

Cherry
Orchard

CHERRY ORCHARD LA

Lyppiatt Barn

Hermit's
Cell

Allengrove
Farm

ALLENGROVE LA

Allen
Grove

Oak
Plantation

Giant's
Cave

Splash
Pond

Fatting
Barn

B4040

Hebden
Farm

Hundred Acres
Farm

Shallowbrooks
Lane

Sandy
Farm

Ivy Leaze
Cottage

Luckley
Farm

Wick Farm

B4040

SHERSTON RD

Brook
End

North End
House

North End
Farm

The Old
Royal Ship
(PH)

Sch

The Farm

CHURCH RD

CHAPEL
ROW

HOLLIS

THE STREET

AVON RISE

GDNS

Luckington

BRISTOL RD

Hebden Leaze
Farm

Manor
Farm

Alderton

Townfield
Farm

43

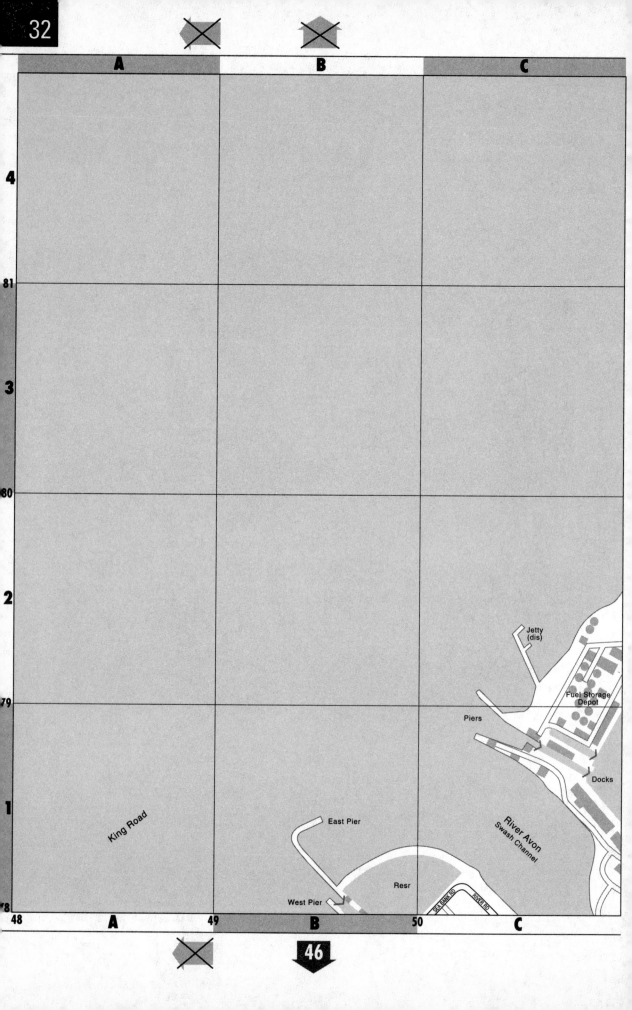

A B C

4

81

3

80

2

79

1

78

48 A 49 B 50 C

Jetty
(dis)

Fuel Storage
Depot

Piers

Docks

King Road

East Pier

River Avon
Swash Channel

Resr

West Pier

SEA BANK RD

RIVER RD

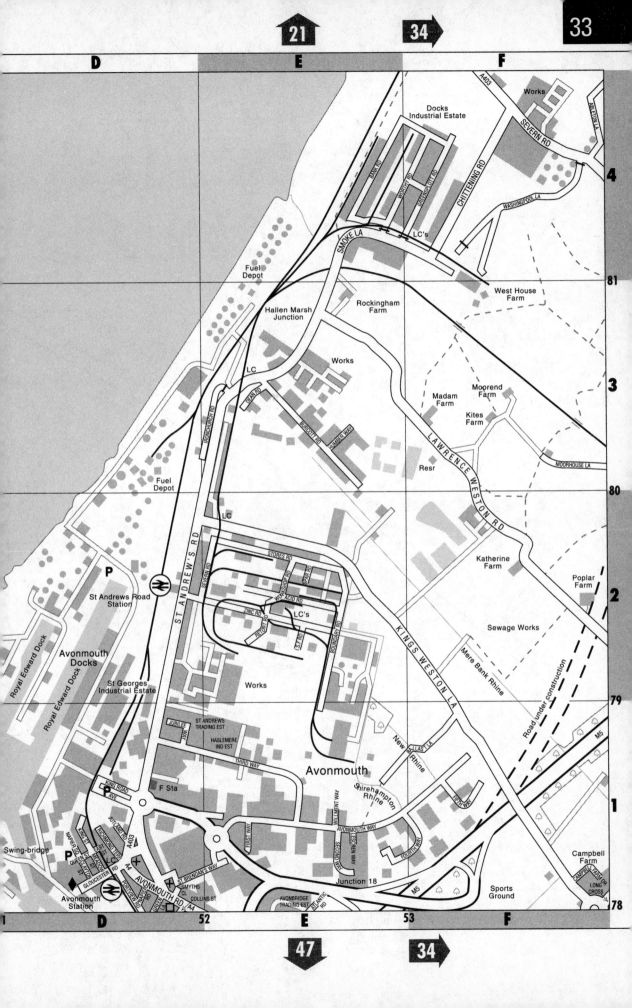

A   B   C

ABLETON LA
BERWICK LA
Bishop Farm
Compton Greenfield
Minor's Farm
Red Rhine
Spaniorum Farm
BOWSTREET LA 1
HOLLYWOOD LA 2
Works
Elmington Manor Farm
Manor Farm
4
Spaniorum Hill
Industrial Estate
Hakes Hill Wood
Sampson House
BERWICK LA
81
Berwick Wood
Camp
Stowick Farm
Sampson Farm
Berwick Lodge
SEVERN RD
Berwick Farm
Berwick
Hallen Marsh
3
Berwick Lodge Farm
Hallen Farm
Road under construction
M5
Hallen
Norton Farm
A4018
CRIBBS CSWY
THE CLOSE
80
King William the IVth (PH)
Haw Wood
B4055
A4018
MOORHOUSE LA
Moor House
Wellinghouse Farm
Mount Skitham
OAKHILL
WINDSOR CRES
HALLEN RD
STATION RD
TREVERDOWE WLK
NETTLESTONE CL
MEADOWLAND RD
GREENACRES RD
TORMARTON CRES
LOVERIDGE CL
BRANDEL
2
Severn House
MARISSAL RD
SILVERHILL
BOWSWELL
COTRITH GR
BRINDLE CL
LANGFIELD
MODECOMBE GR
BICKERTON CL
FITCHETTS WLK
ISON HILL RD 1
SEVERN GRANGE 2
DARLEY CL 3
COUSINS CL 4
GREENSIDE CL 5
GLENEAGLES DR 6
DOLMAN CL
TRATMAN WLK
LOWLIS CL
PEVERELL
VAUGHAN CL
HARMER CL
COLEMAN WLK
STIMPANY CL
Sch
HENBURY CT
Sch
WINDMILL
GREEN DELL CL
COTTLE CL
CONIFER WAY
LAWRENCE WESTON RD
Nature Reserve
AVONMOUTH WAY
Sch
B4057
79
M5
Sch
ATWOOD DR
Moorgrove Wood
BLAISE HAMLET
WOODGROVE RD
BATTERSBY WAY
GRAY'S CL
Sch
CHUR
HENBURY RD
CROW LA
Sch
LORAIN WLK
AYLMINTON WLK
CORBET CL
MOSSGROVE
Cemy
CASTLE LA
PC
Mus
Hazel Brook
RICHESON WLK
SATCHFIELD
Sch
Long Cross
JASMINE CL
GORHAM CL
VINCENT CL
KINGS WESTON RD
PC
HENBURY GDNS
CHALLENGE
1
Lawrence Weston
Sch
MANSEL CL
CALDICOT CL
REDWICK
DE CLIFFORD RD
P
PC
Henbury
LORAIN
SALTMARSH DR
STILE ACRES
COMMONFIELD RD
DEEBURG RD
STONICA CRES
Blaise Castle
HENBURY HILL
ARNALL DR
CHOKESWOOD WLK
RIDINGLEAZE
BROADLANDS DR
Greenhill Plantation
Nature Reserve
College Park
BLETCHLEY CL
ASTER CL
Off
LITTLE MEAD
BROCKLEY
Blaise Castle Estate
COOMBE WAY
NORTHOVER RD
78
Sch
GOODRING HILL
B4057
Limekiln Wood
Coombe Hill
Golf Course
CH
WESTOVER RD 1
WESTOVER CL 2
WESTOVER GDNS 3

54   A   55   B   56   C

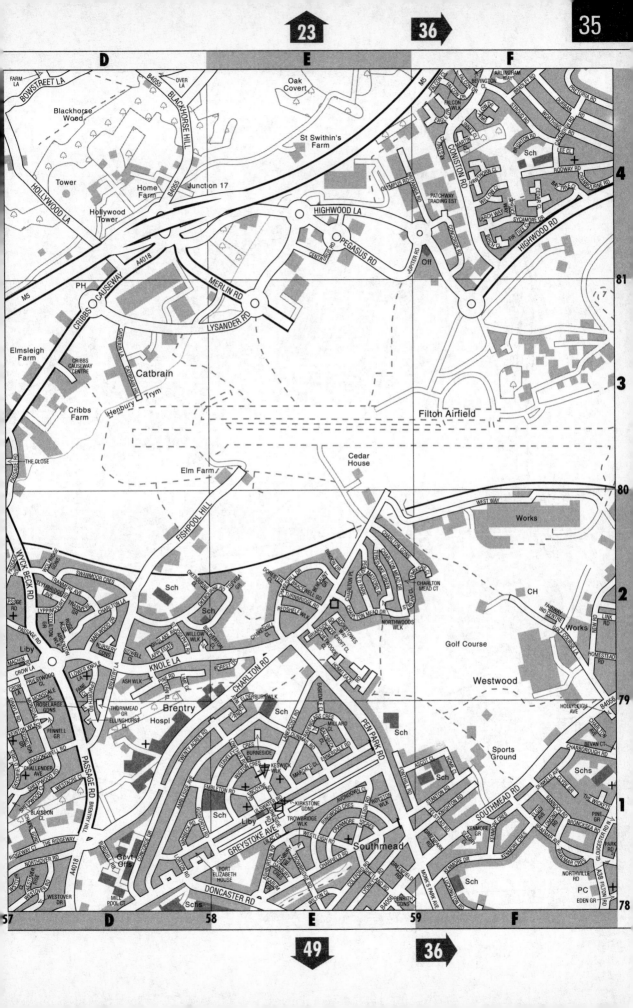

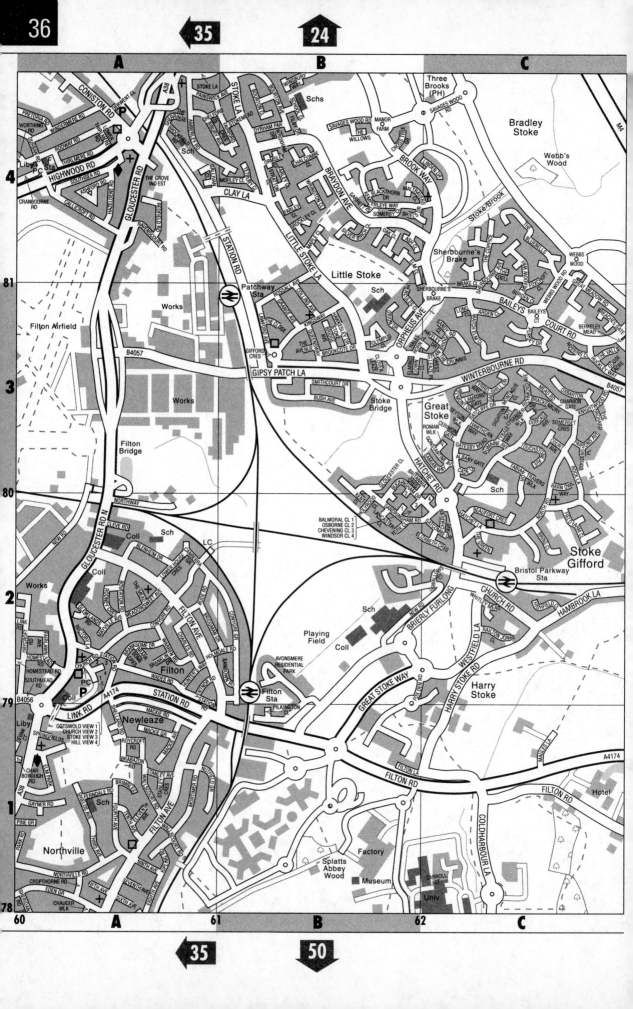

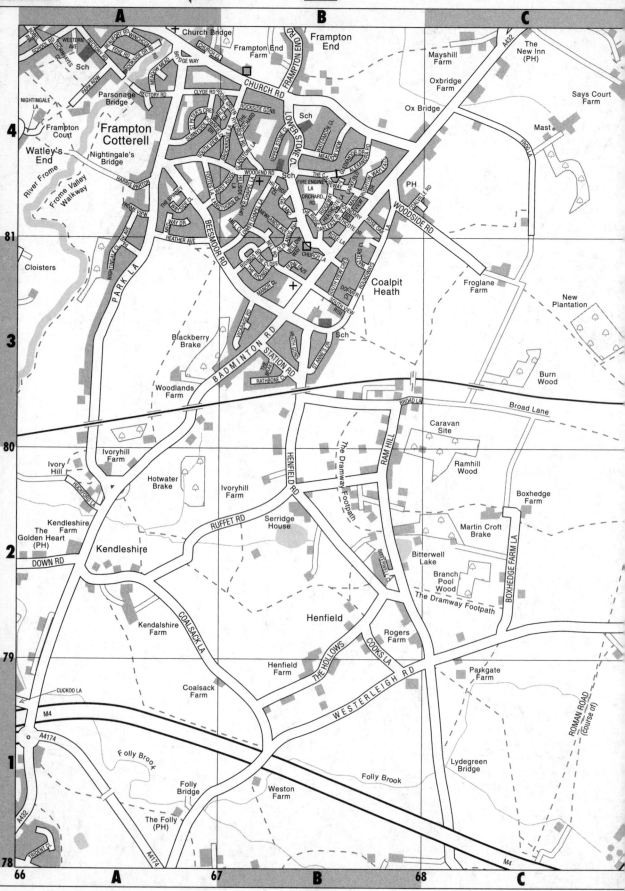

A **B** **C**

Church Bridge
Frampton End
Frampton End Farm
Frampton End
Mayshill Farm
The New Inn (PH)
A432
School Rd
Western Ave
Rectory Rd
Bridgeside Dr Jr
Foxe Rd
Winchcombe
Sch
Church Cl
Oxbridge Farm
Says Court Farm
Park Row
Bridge Way
Meadow Mead
Rectory Rd
Church Rd
Clyde Rd
Rockside Gdns
Ox Bridge
Parsonage Bridge
Nightingale La
Stephens Cres
Gladstone St
Brockridge La
Lower Stone Cl
Sch
Mast

4 Frampton Court
Frampton Cotterell
Sunnyside
South View
West Ridge
Upper Stone Cl
Watermore Cl
Meadow View
Woodend Rd
Sch
PH
Saulville Rd
Woodside Rd

Watley's End
Nightingale's Bridge
Harris Barton
Frome View
The Spinney
Wayside Cl
Way Dr
Lower Chapel La
Upper Chapel La
Hillside
Newlands Ave
The Rinds
Ridgeway
Heathcote Dr
Rose La
Fire Engine La
Orchard Rd
Darlington Rd
Russ Oak
Main Rd

River Frome
Frome Valley Walkway
81 Heather Ave
Beesmoor Rd
Mill La
The Close
The Rinds
Willow Way
Church La
Old Gloucester Rd
Rose Cl
Sisters Cl

Cloisters
Park La
Ringwood
Vicarage Rd
Manor Cl
South View Rise
Dorner Cl
Coalpit Heath
Froglane Farm
New Plantation

3
Blackberry Brake
Badminton Rd
Station Rd
Heath Gdns
St Annes Dr
The Brake
Rathbone Cl
Sch
Burn Wood

Woodlands Farm
Broad La
Broad Lane
Caravan Site

80
Ivoryhill Farm
Henfield Rd
The Dramway Footpath
Ram Hill
Ramhill Wood
Boxhedge Farm

Ivory Hill
Huckerhole
Hotwater Brake
Ivoryhill Farm
Martin Croft Brake

The Golden Heart (PH)
Kendleshire Farm
Ruffet Rd
Serridge House
Bitterwell Lake
Boxhedge Farm La

2 Kendleshire
Down Rd
Butterwell La
Branch Pool Wood
The Dramway Footpath

Coalsack La
Henfield
Rogers Farm

Kendalshire Farm
The Hollows
Cooks La
Westerleigh Rd
Parkgate Farm

79
Henfield Farm
Coalsack Farm

Cuckoo La
Roman Road (course of)
M4
A4174
Lydegreen Bridge

1
Folly Brook
Folly Bridge
Weston Farm
Folly Brook

A432
The Folly (PH)
Trident Cl
A4174
78 M4

66 **A** **67** **B** **68** **C**

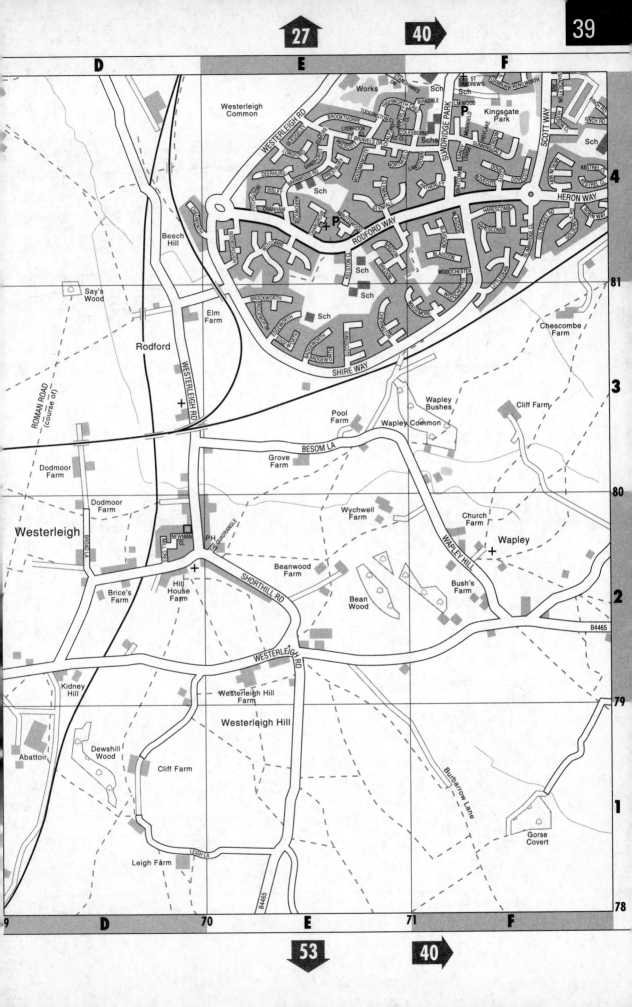

39
28

A **B** **C**

VIRGINIA CL
A432 KENNEDY WAY
MALLARD CL
LOVE LA
DOWNLEAZE
CULVERHILL RD
HOUNDS RD
WOODMANS RD
KINGROVE CRESCENT
GORLANDS RD
HORSE ST
ST JOHNS WAY
B4060
JENNER CL
COLTS GREEN
River Frome
Frome Valley Walkway
COMMONMEAD LA
ZINCH WAY
GRASSINGTON DR
BURCAGE
WOODMANS MEAD RD
TWO STONES
CODMANS VALE
Sch
COTSWOLD RD
Blanchards Farm
BADMINTON RD
A43
HERON WAY
BOWLING RD
LILAC CL
Sch
GAUNTS RD
GREEN HAYES
SMARTS GREEN
ST WICKHAM
STATION CL
Colt's Green
Frome Bridge
P
ROBIN WAY
PUT AVE
GULLIVERS
Smart's Green

4

DODINGTON RD
CLAYPIT HILL
Homestead Farm
Kingrove Farm
KINGROVE LA
BLANCHARDS LA

81
Kingrove Common
Lower Kingrove Farm
Fatting House Farm
MILL LA
Bungalow Farm

Mouswell Farm
Hamwood Farm
Branchley Farm
DODINGTON LA

3
Ham Wood
Dodington Manor

80
The Grove

Lydes Farm
The Link

2
Downs Farm
Lean Tom Plantation
Shepherds Close Farm
B4465

Codrington
Long Sands

79
WAPLEY RD
Codrington Arms (PH)
Barleyclose Cottages
Fat Jack Plantation
Sands Court

Ostlands Farm

1
Tyning Farm
Codrington Court
Barley Close Farm
River Boyd
Springs Farm
M4
Quarry (dis)
B4465

78

72 **A** **73** **B** **74** **C**

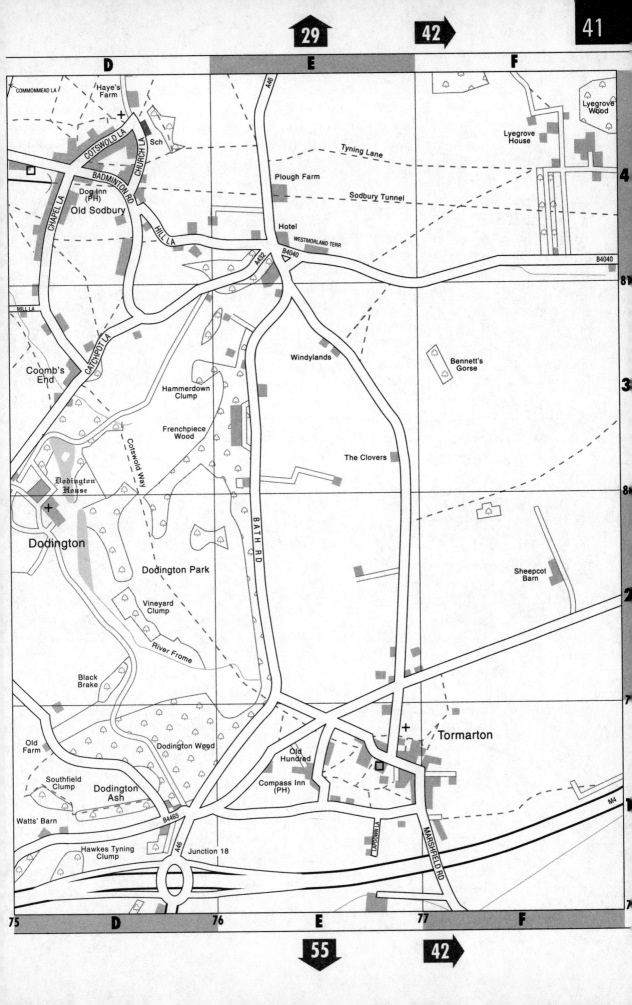

COMMONMEAD LA
Haye's Farm
COTSWOLD LA
CHURCH LA
Sch

D

BADMINTON RD
CHAPEL LA
Dog Inn (PH)
Old Sodbury

A46

Tyning Lane
Plough Farm
Sodbury Tunnel

Lyegrove Wood
Lyegrove House

4

MILL LA
Hotel
WESTMORLAND TERR
B4040

CATCHPOT LA
Coomb's End

A432
B4040

8

Windylands

Bennett's Gorse

3

Hammerdown Clump

Frenchpiece Wood

Cotswold Way

The Clovers

Dodington House

8

Dodington

Dodington Park

BATH RD

Sheepcot Barn

Vineyard Clump

2

River Frome

Black Brake

Old Farm

Tormarton

Southfield Clump
Dodington Ash
Dodington Wood
Old Hundred

7

Watts' Barn
B4465
Compass Inn (PH)

LAPDOWN LA
MARSHFIELD RD
M4

1

A46
Hawkes Tyning Clump
Junction 18

A

B

C

Lyegrove Wood

Lime Avenue

Egg Clump

Withy Moor

4

OLD DOWN RD

Sodbury Tunnel

B4040

81

Newhouse Farm

B4039

B4040

Acton Turville

HUNTERS LA

TORMARTON RD

BURTON RD

Fox & Hounds (PH)

B4039

3

OAKES LA

Vicarage Cottage

Warren Barn

30

Fagot Pile

M4

Pike Cottage

Old Warren

Wall Leaze Wood

2

Parks Farm

Brotton Hill Wood

Warren Gorse

79

Westfield Farm

M4

1

Phyldornick

Little Westfield

Fox Covert

8

78

A

79

B

80

C

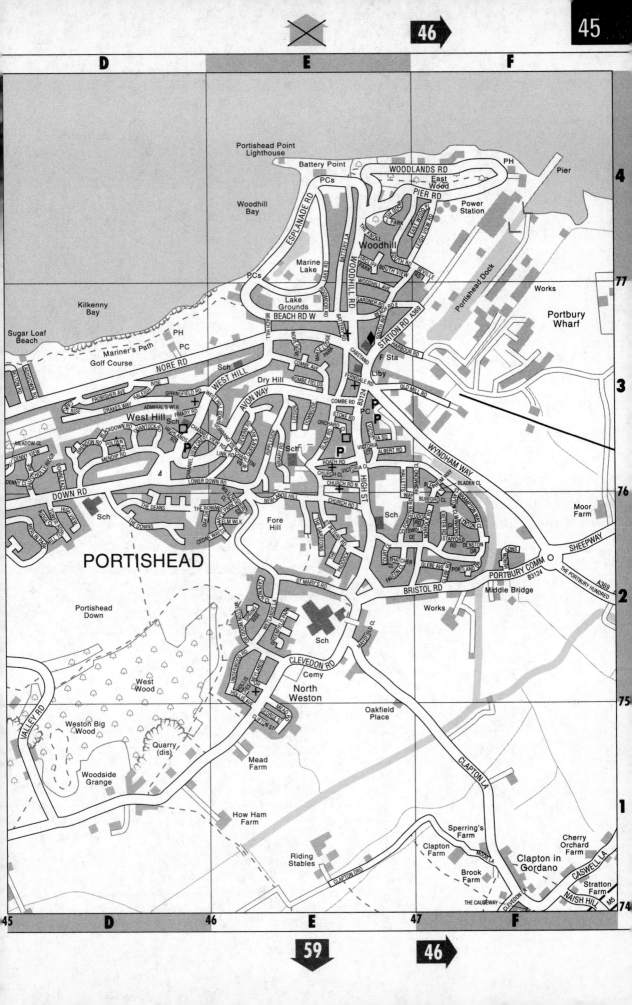

D **E** **F**

4

Portishead Point Lighthouse
Battery Point
PCs
WOODLANDS RD
East Wood
PIER RD
PH
Pier
Woodhill Bay
Woodhill
Power Station
Portishead Dock

77

Kilkenny Bay
Marine Lake
Lake Grounds
Works
Portbury Wharf

Sugar Loaf Beach
Mariner's Path
Golf Course
PH
PC
NORE RD
Sch
BEACH RD W
BEACH RD
STATION RD A369
F Sta
Liby

3

WEST HILL
Dry Hill
COMBE FIELDS
B3124
P
PC
P
OLD MILL RD
Frobisher Ave
Raleigh Rise
Springfield Rd
Admiral's Wlk
West Hill Sch
Friary Rd
AVON WAY
COMBE RD
STOKE RD
ORCHARD
P
Victoria
ALBERT RD
WYNDHAM WAY

West Hill Sch
Sch
Sch
ROATH RD
CHURCH CL
CHURCH RD N
CHURCH RD S
HIGH ST
Sch
Moor Farm

76

DOWN RD
THE DEANS
THE ROWANS
ELM WLK
CEDAR WALK
Fore Hill
NEWLANDS HILL
Sch
BRISTOL RD
PORTBURY COMM
Middle Bridge
B3124
SHEEPWAY
THE PORTBURY HUNDRED
A369

PORTISHEAD
Sch

2

Portishead Down
St Mary's Rd
Sch
CLEVEDON RD
Works

West Wood
Cemy
North Weston
Oakfield Place

75

Weston Big Wood
Quarry (dis)
VALLEY RD
Mead Farm
CLAPTON LA

Woodside Grange

1

How Ham Farm
Sperring's Farm
Cherry Orchard Farm
Clapton Farm
MOOR LA
Clapton in Gordano
CASWELL LA
Riding Stables
Brook Farm
Stratton Farm
CLAPTON DRO
THE CAUSEWAY
CLEVEDON
NAISH HILL
M5

74

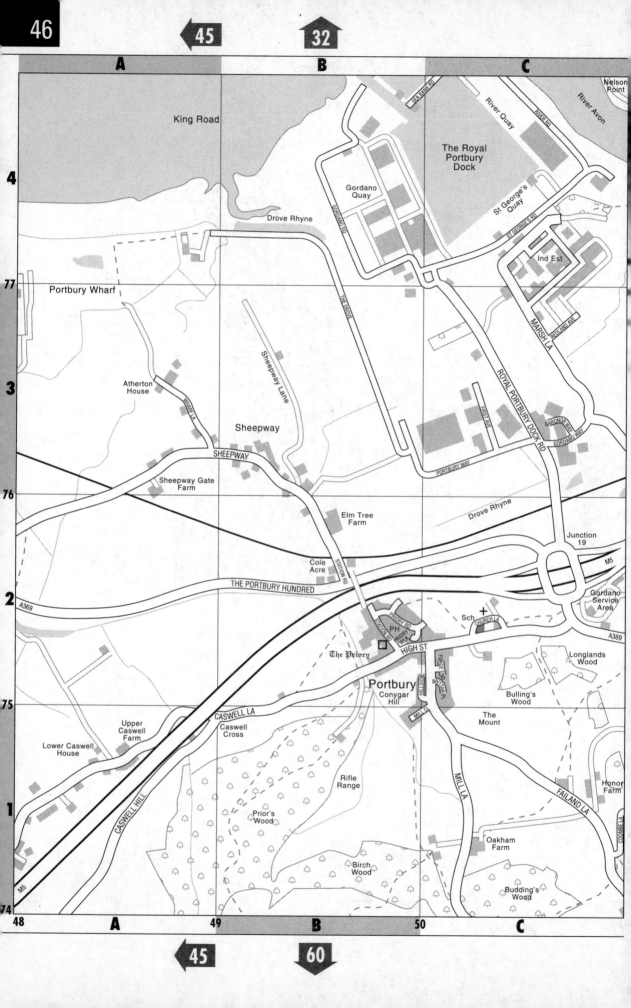

A B C

4

King Road

77

Portbury Wharf

Drove Rhyne

Gordano Quay

The Royal
Portbury
Dock

St George's Quay

Nelson Point

River Avon

River Quay

St George's Rd

Ind Est

Marsh La

3

Atherton House

Sheepway Lane

Sheepway

THE DROVE

GORDANO RD

ROYAL PORTBURY DOCK RD

First Ave

GORDANO WAY

SHEEPWAY

76

Sheepway Gate Farm

Elm Tree Farm

Drove Rhyne

Portbury Way

Junction 19

M5

2

A369

Cole Acre

THE PORTBURY HUNDRED

STATION RD

PRIORY RD
PRIORY WY

PH

The Priory

Sch

CHURCH LA

HIGH ST

Gordano Service Area

A369

Longlands Wood

75

Upper Caswell Farm

Lower Caswell House

CASWELL LA

CASWELL HILL

Caswell Cross

Portbury

Conygar Hill

HILLSIDE

MILL CL

FORGE END RD

BRITTAN PL

Bulling's Wood

The Mount

MILL LA

FAILAND LA

Honor Farm

COOMBE LA

1

Rifle Range

Prior's Wood

Oakham Farm

74

48 A 49 B 50 C

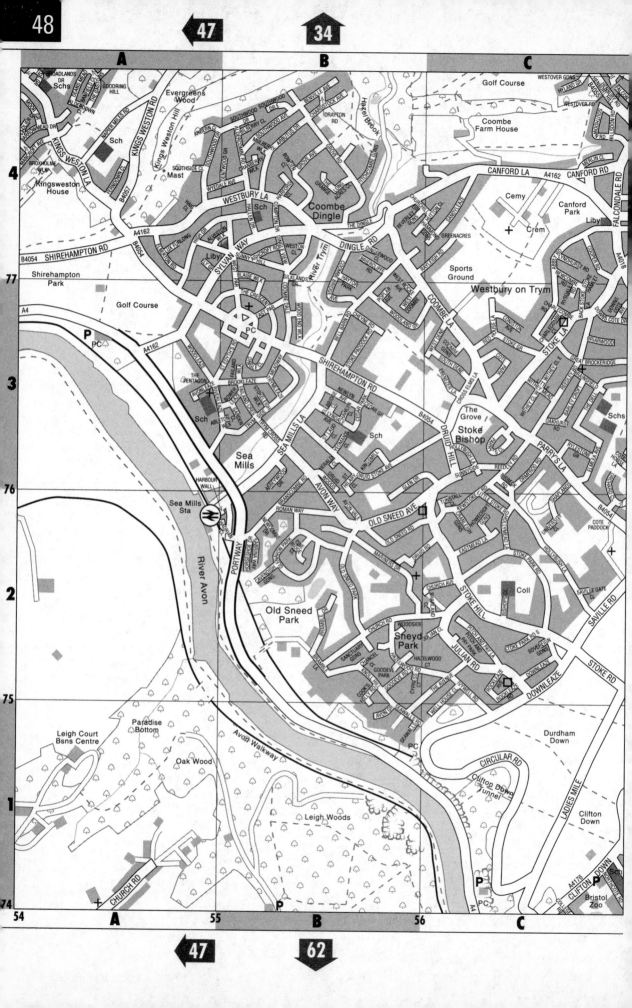

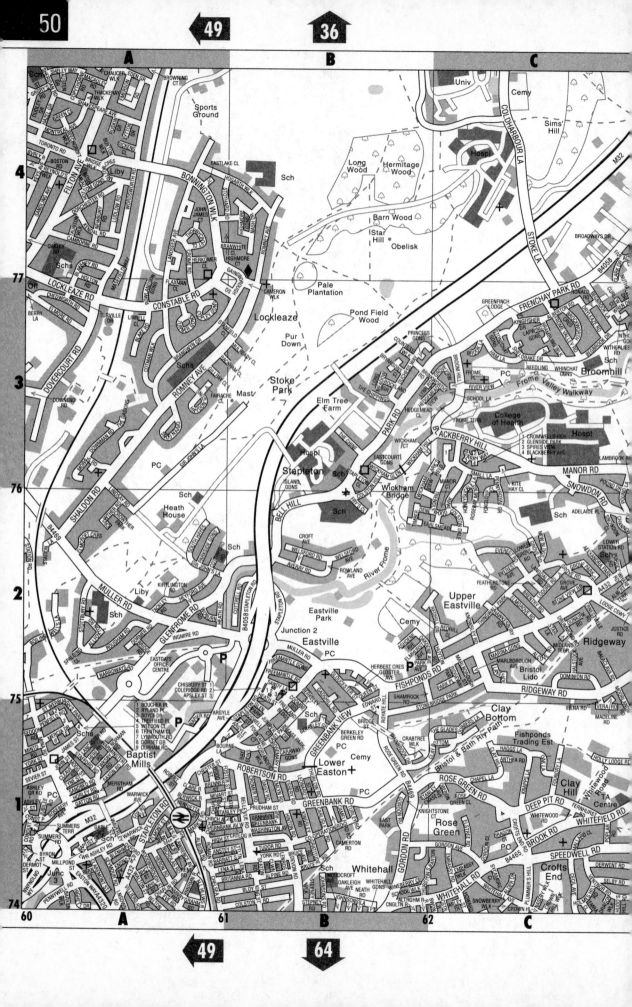

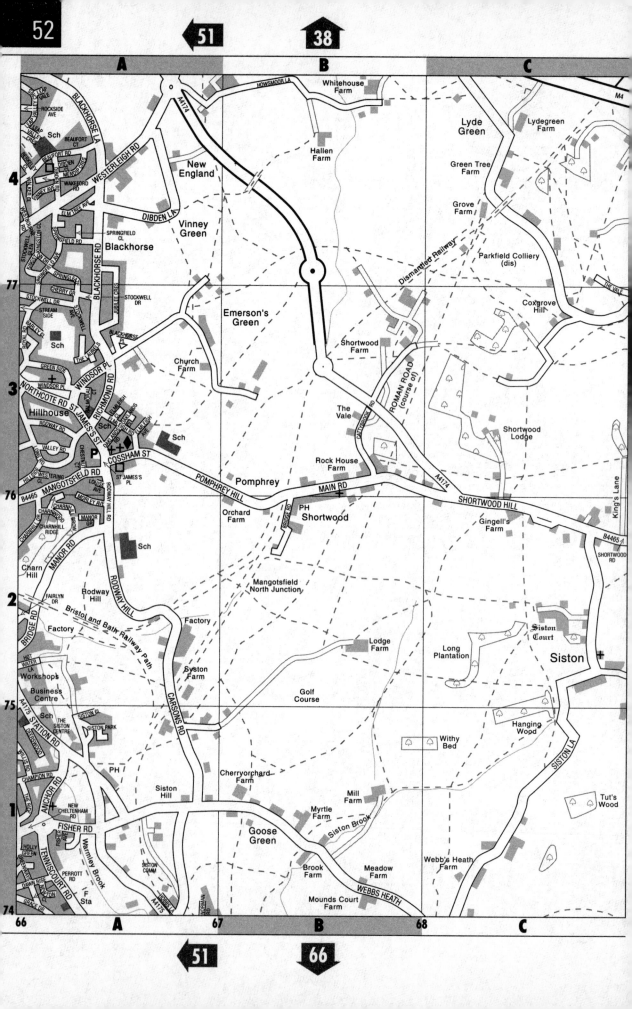

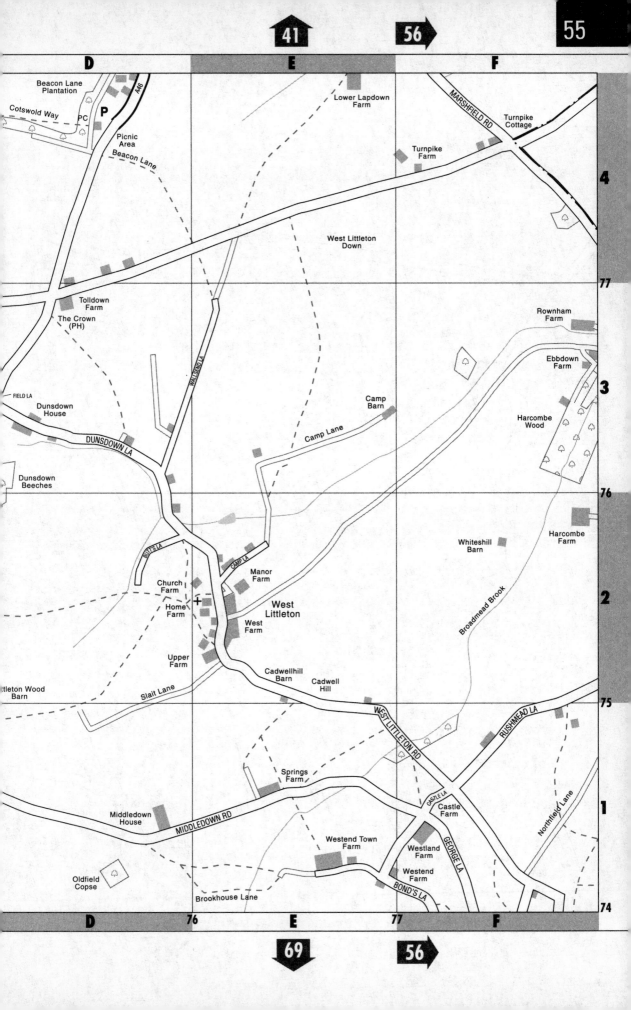

A　　　　　　B　　　　　　C

4

Fox Covert

Kington Down Farm

West Kington

Brook Farm

Down Farm

Mill House

Latim Farm

77

SHIRE HILL

Broadmead Brook

Hazel Grove

3

Lower Shirehill Farm

Gunning's Wood

Shirehill Farm

76

Plough Farm

Hillcrest Farm

Maggs Grave Farm

2

Mountain Bower

New Homeste Farm

Rushmead Farm

TORMARTON RD

RUSHMEAD LA

Downthorns Farm

Highfield Cottages

North Wraxall

75

Northfield Lane

MARTOR IND EST

Culverslade

DOWN RD

Home Farm

Upper Wraxall

1

Hillcrest Farm

The Shoe Inn (PH)

ROMAN R

Upper Farm

Fosse Way

Allot Gdns

Cemy

Th Sh

Northfield House

74

78　　　A　　　79　　　B　　　80　　　C

A420

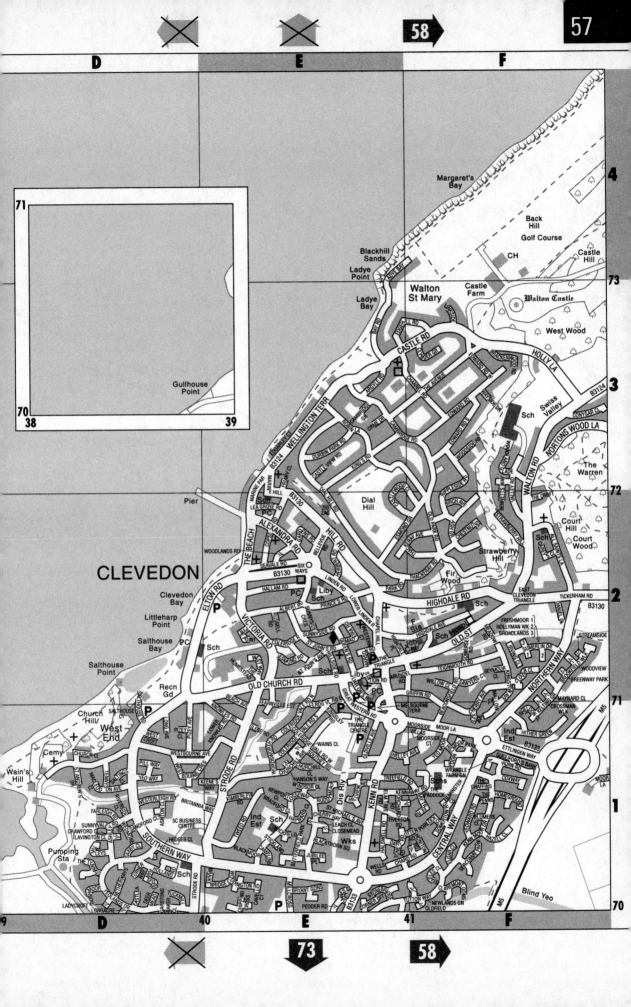

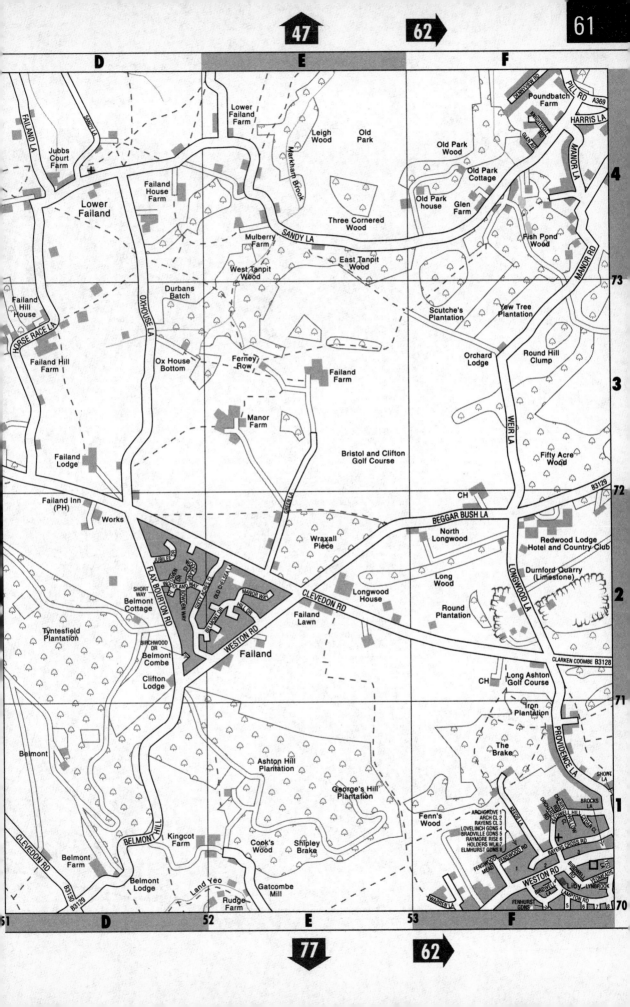

A B C

4

HARRIS LA
PILL RD
CHURCH RD
MANOR RD
THE MANOR CL
A369
PH
Abbots Leigh
Home Farm House
HOME FARM RD
ROSEGROVE AVE
Leigh Warren
ABBOTS LEIGH RD
VALLEY RD
Leigh Woods
Avon Gorge Nature Reserve
Stokeleigh Camp
Nightingale Valley
Suspension Bridge
Toll
New Zig Zag
PORTWAY
BRIDGE VALLEY RD
A4176
A4
The Promenade
CLIFTON DOWN
NORLAND RD
CAMP RD
CLIFTON CL
Observatory
Jack's Hole
Avon Gorge
Coll
Sct
Off
CLIFTON DOWN RD
B3129
GLOUCESTER ST 1
CARTER'S BLDGS 2
JAMES PL 3
WESTFIELD PL 4
WATERLOO ST 5
SION HILL
WEST MALL
CALEDONIA PL
PRINCESS VICTORIA ST
ROYAL YORK CRES
YORK GDNS
CALEDONIA MEWS
BANNERLEIGH RD
BROAD OAKS
CORNWALLIS CRES

73

Warren House Plantation
B3129
NORTH RD
LEIGHWOODS HOUSE
ST MARY'S RD
CHURCH RD
VICARAGE RD
BANNERLEIGH RD
BRIDGE RD
B3129
CYPRESS GDNS
FOYE HOUSE
BURWALLS RD
ROWNHAM HILL
Burgh Walls
River Avon
HOTWELL RD
OXFORD PL
WINDSOR TER
HINTON
FREELAND
JOY HILL
DALE
CORNWALLIS AVE
Leighwoods
CH

3

Upper Farm
Quarry Plantation
Kingcott Farm
BEGGARS BUSH LA
B3129
Golf Course
Rownham Plantation
Rownham House
ROWNHAM HILL
AVON WALKWAY
BENNETT
CABOT
PC
P
VICTORIA TERR 1
WINDSOR CT 2
CUMBERLAND PL 3
ALBERMARLE ROW 4
SOUTH GREEN ST 5
NORTH GREEN ST 6
DOWRY SQ 7
POLYGON RD 8
BRISTOL GATE 10
CORNWALLIS AVE 9
HUMPHRY DAVY WAY 11
LITTLE CAROLINE PL 12
OLDFIELD PL 13
GRENVILLE PL 14
ASHMEAD WAY 15
CUMBERLAND RD 16
BRUNSWICK PL 17
BASIN RD
BRUNEL LOCK RD
MCADAM WAY

72

Summerhouse Plantation
Ashton Court Estate
CLANAGE RD
A3029
CLIFT HOUSE RD
A3029
P

2

Deer Park
Ashton Court
Bower Ashton
Coll
KENNEL LODGE RD
PARKLANDS RD
COURTLANDS LA
ROWNHAM MEAD
BLACKMOORS LA
PORTISHEAD WAY
Sch
BRUNEL WAY
WINTERSTOKE UNDERPASS
A3029
WINTERSTOKE RD
MARSH RD
A3029
Cala Trading Estate
Pill Grove
CLARKEN COOMBE
Church Wood
Lodge
Lodge
The Smyth Arms (PH)
ASHTON RD
B3128
A370
Ashton Gate Trading Estate
ASHTON VALE RD
LC
Colliter's Brook
BROOK GATE

71

Goombe Plantation
Golf Course
Ashton Hill
THE FOLLY
B3128
HOBWELL LA
BEECHFIELD
FOG LANE
LONG ASHTON RD
CHURCH RD
Vic
Parsonage Farm
Ashton Vale
SILBURY RD
Sch
AVEBURY RD
ASHTON DR
DALE RD
TREVANNA RD
TREGARTH LA
SOUTH LIBERTY LA
ANSLEY CRES
SWISS RD

1

SHORT LA
HEATH RIDGE
KEMPE'S CL
ESTUNE WALK
CHESTNUT RD
RIDGEWAY RD
WESTWAY
NORTH VIEW SNUG
WOODSPRING CRES
GLEBE RD
PROVIDENCE LA
WESTON RD
YEOMEADS
LAMPTON RD
WELL CL
BOULTON MEAD
YANLEY LA
A370
Long Ashton
Bridge Farm
Ashton Brook
SCOTT GATE
PARSONAGE RD
HILLSIDE RD

70

54 A 55 B 56 C

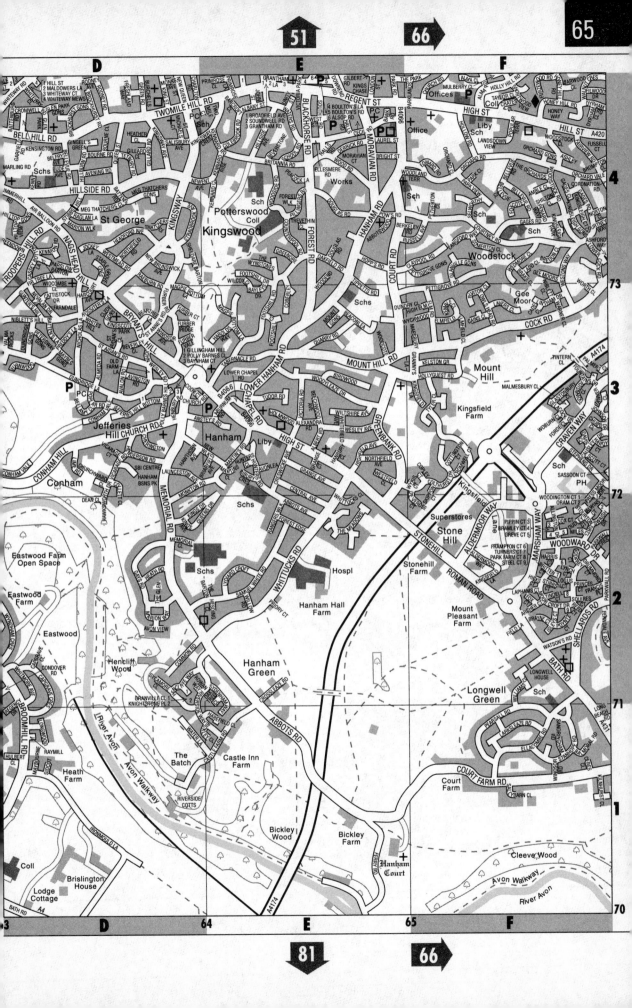

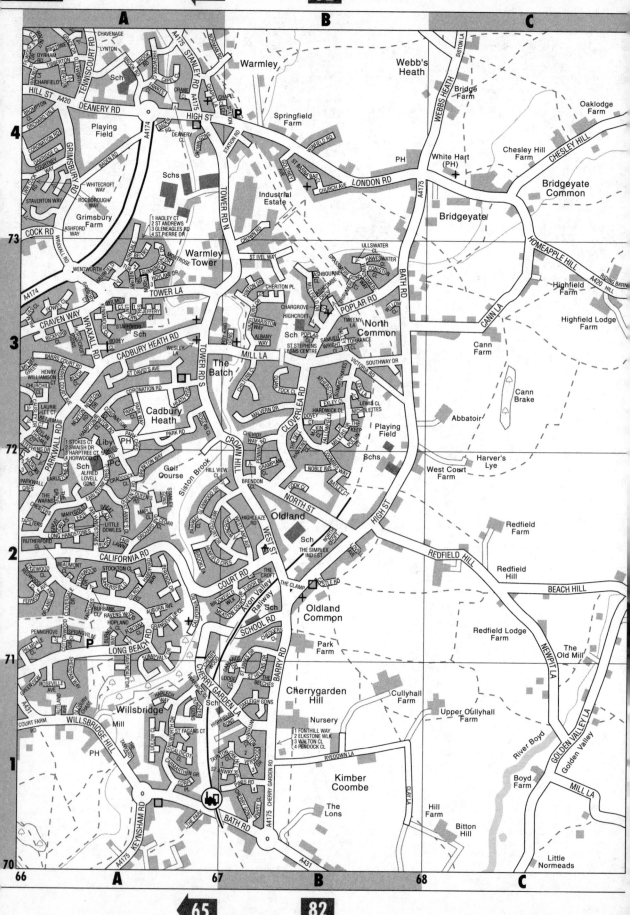

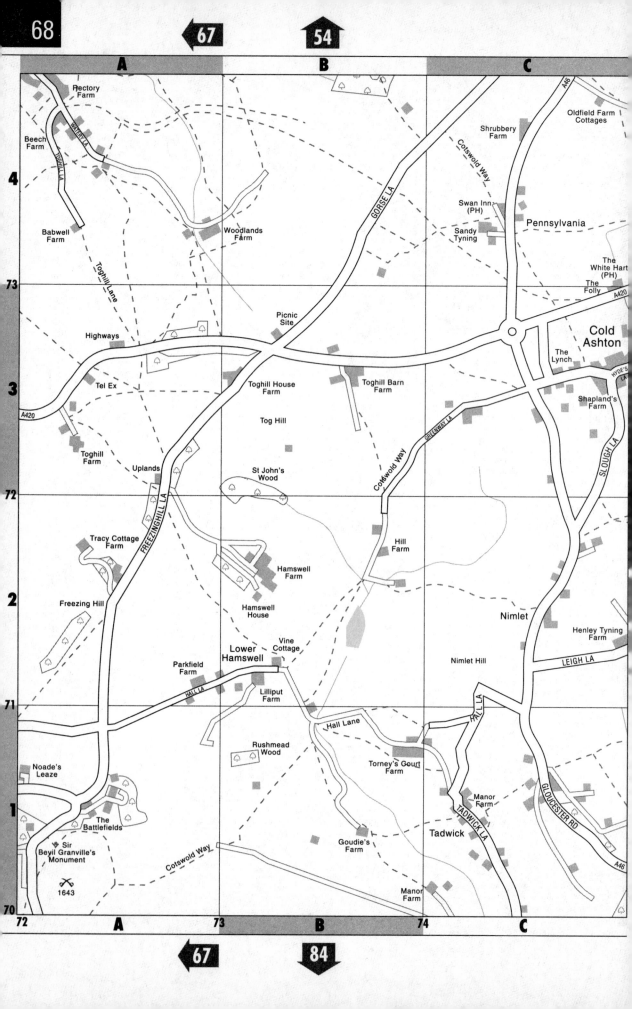

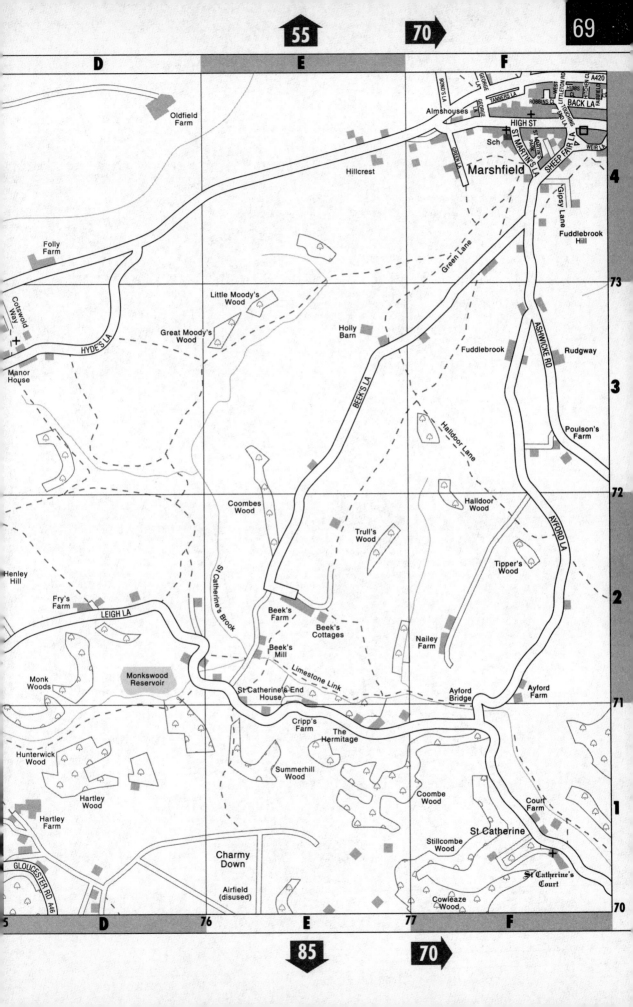

D
E
F

Oldfield Farm

A420
Bond's La
Tanners La
George St
George La
Littleton Rd
Hitchin Rd
West
Back La
Almshouses
HIGH ST
Robbins Cl
Hibbs Cl
Fairfield Cl
Green La
St Martin's Park
Sch
St Martin's La
Sheep Fair La
Weir La
End La

Marshfield

Gipsy Lane

Hillcrest

Fuddlebrook Hill

73

Folly Farm

Green Lane

Cotswold Way

Little Moody's Wood

Holly Barn

Fuddlebrook

Ashwicke Rd

Rudgway

Great Moody's Wood

HYDE'S LA

Manor House

Beek's La

Poulson's Farm

3

Halldoor Lane

Halldoor Wood

72

Coombes Wood

Tipper's Wood

Ayford La

Trull's Wood

Henley Hill

Fry's Farm

LEIGH LA

Nailey Farm

Beek's Farm

2

Beek's Cottages

Monk Woods

Monkswood Reservoir

Beek's Mill

Limestone Link

Ayford Farm

St Catherine's Brook

St Catherine's End House

Ayford Bridge

71

Cripp's Farm

Hunterwick Wood

The Hermitage

Summerhill Wood

Hartley Wood

Coombe Wood

Court Farm

1

Hartley Farm

St Catherine

GLOUCESTER RD A46

Stillcombe Wood

Charmy Down

St Catherine's Court

Airfield (disused)

Cowleaze Wood

70

5
D
76
E
77
F

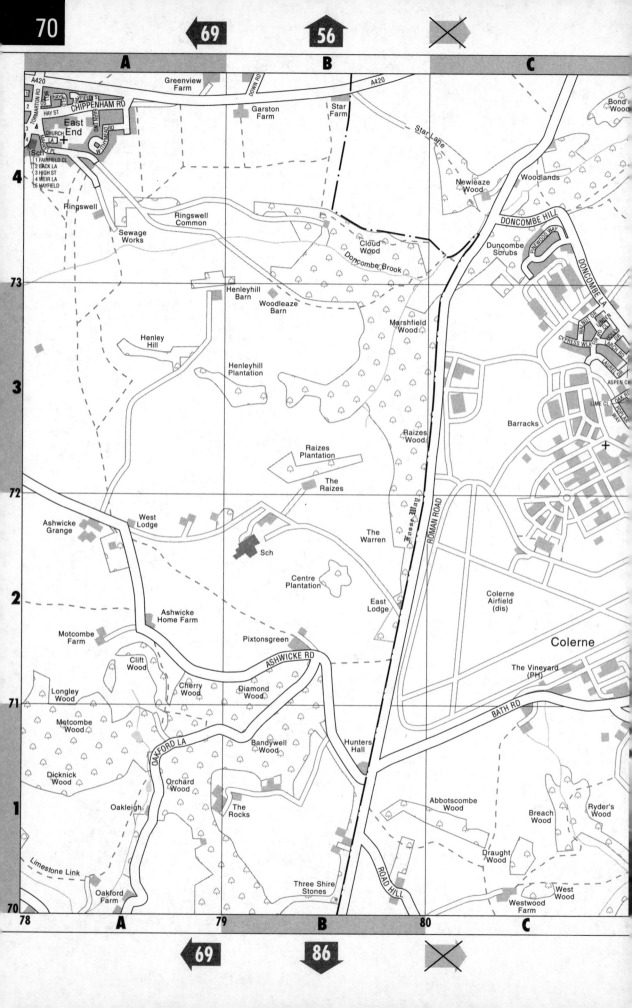

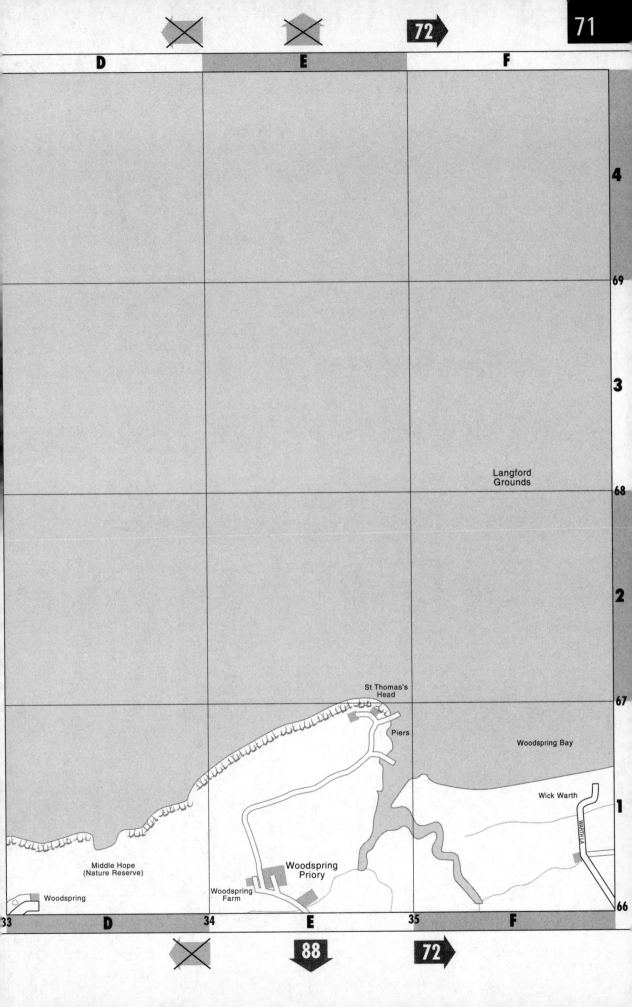

D   E   F

4

69

3

68

Langford
Grounds

2

67

St Thomas's
Head

Piers

Woodspring Bay

Wick Warth

1

WARTH A

Woodspring
Priory

Middle Hope
(Nature Reserve)

Woodspring Farm

Woodspring

66

A B C

4

69

Dowlais Ditch

Kingston Pill

Hook's
Ear

Sea Wall
Farm

3

Treble
House
Farm

68

Channel View
Farm

Broadstone Rhyne

MIDDLE LA

2

Broadstone
Farm

BROADSTONE LA

Wharf
Farm

67

HAM LA

Ham
Farm

HAM LA

Ham Rhyne

Pool
Farm

1

Sewage
Works

Mendip View
Farm

YEO BANK LA

WARTH

Muddy
Lane

Yeo Bank
Farm

Tutshill

66

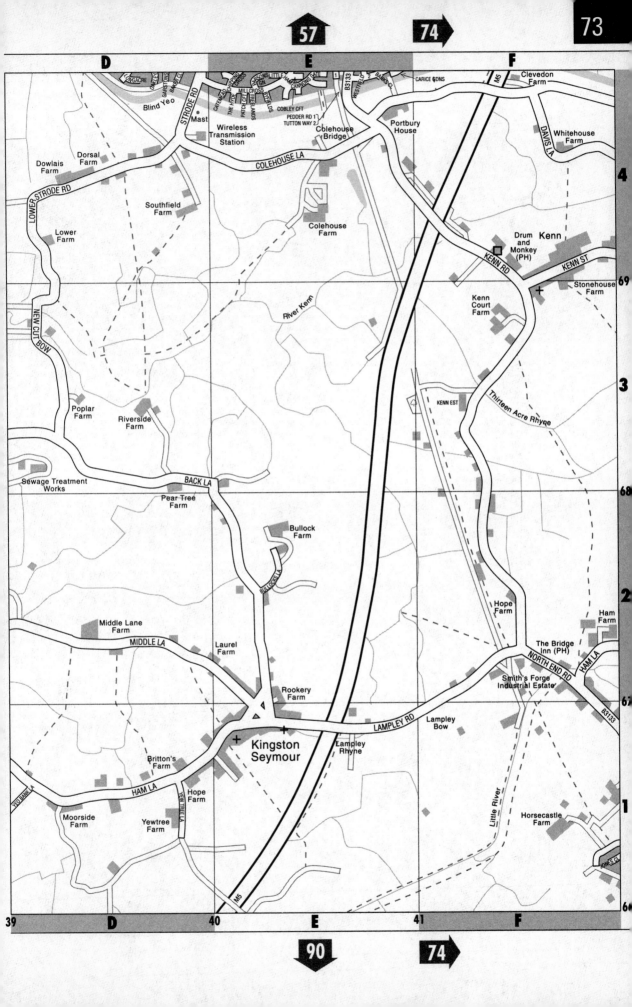

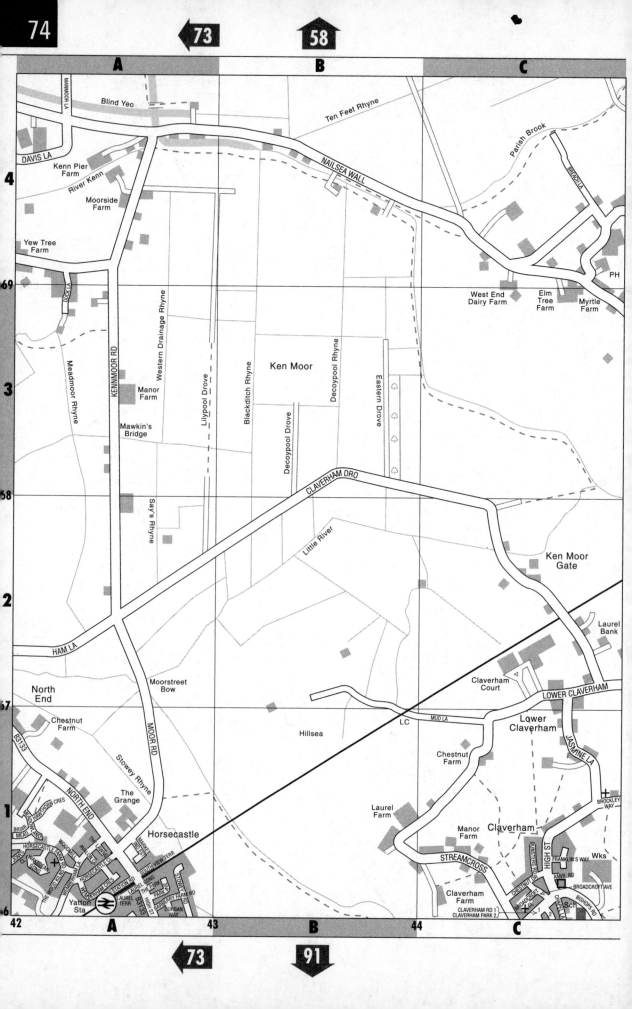

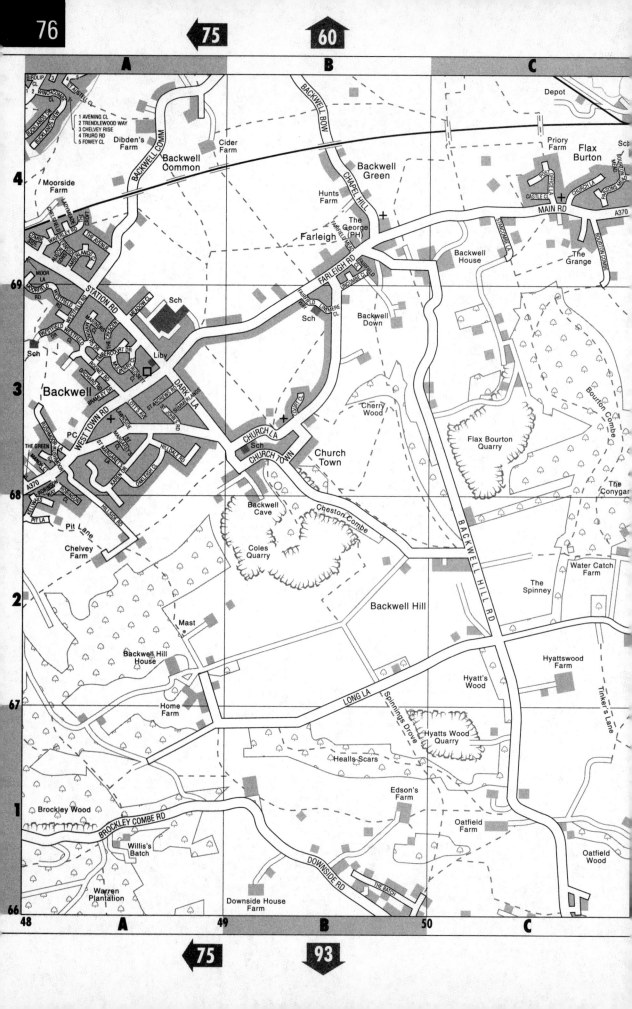

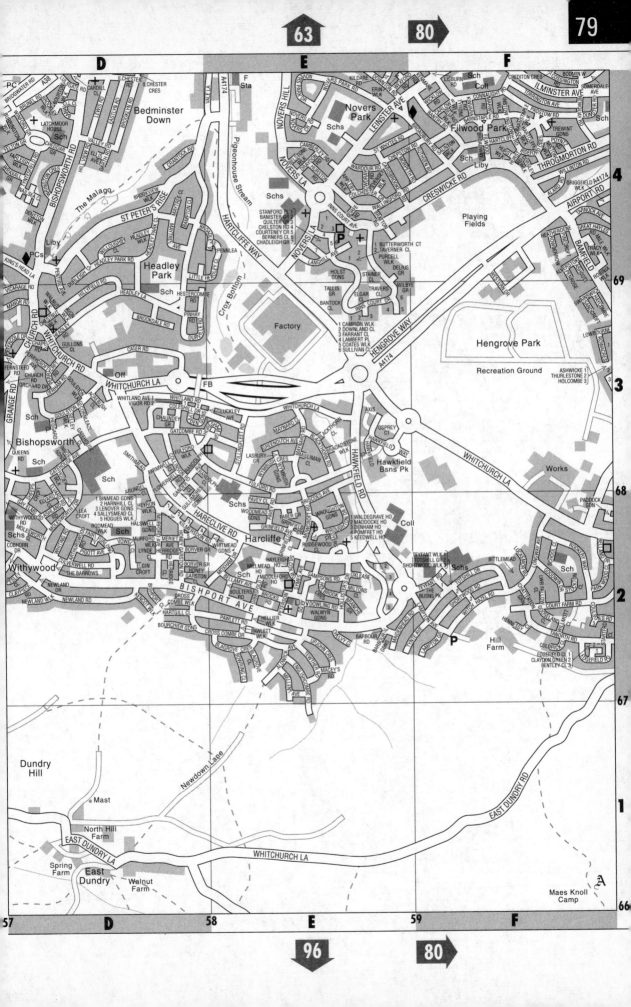

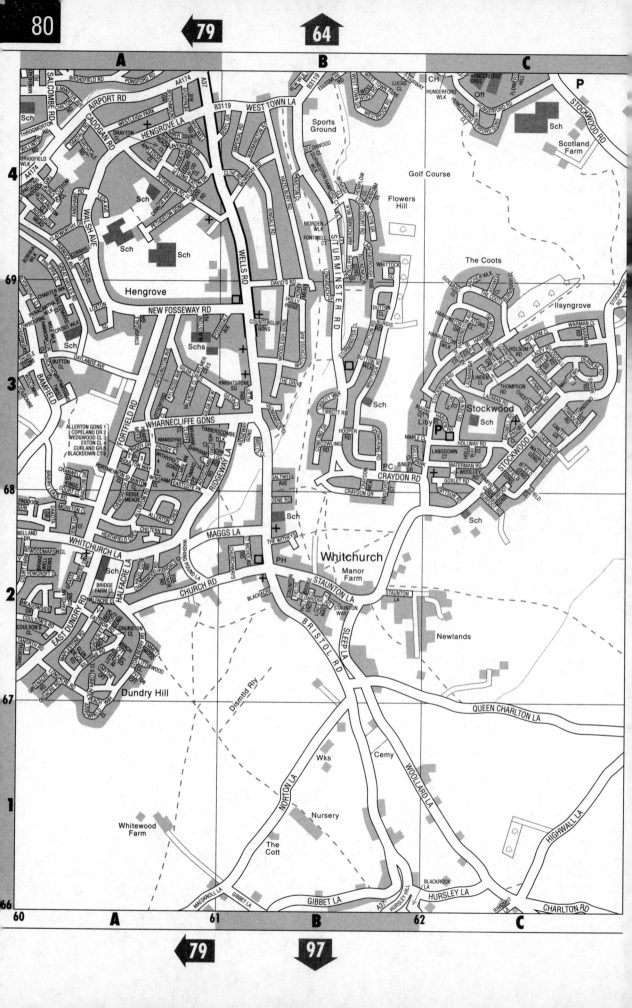

A   **B**   **C**

Londonderry Farm

Nursery

SOMERDALE RD N

KEYNSHAM RD

A4175

4

Field Grove Farm

BATH RD

A431

Clay Lane

CROFT CL

Sch

EDWIN SHORT CL

HIGH ST

CHURCH LA

Works

GOLDEN VALLEY LA

AUBREY MDS

Nursery

Bitton

BREWERY HILL

Barrow Hill

CHURCH RD

ROMAN ROAD

BATH RD

A431

Nursery

Holm-Mead Lane

Mickle Mead

69

Ind Est

Broad Mead

Holm Mead

River Avon

Avon Farm

Mill

Avon Valley Country Park

Sewage Works

1 CHELSEA CL
2 REYNOLDS CL
3 NASH CL
4 RUBENS CL
5 TURNER CL

BROADMEAD LA

Avon Walkway

3

A4

KEYNSHAM BY-PASS

UNITY CT

ASHMEAD RD IND EST

GASTON AVE

LYTTON GR

TA Centre

ASHMEAD RD

PIXASH BSNS CENTRE

PIXASH LA

B3116

BATH RD

DERWEN

SEVERN WAY

Schs

ELLSBRIDGE CL

KING PL

WORLD'S END LA

68

KENNET RD

CHANDAG

SS ACHES

LAMBOURN CL

CHELMER GR

CHERWELL RD

WYE RD

FROME RD

MEDWAY CL

WINDRUSH RD

ORWELL DR

Nursery

Glenavon Farm

Broadway

WEDMORE RD

CHELWOOD

STRATTON CL

CAMERTON CL

QUEENS RD

MEAD LA

AVON LA

River Avon

2

TORRIDGE RD

CALDER CL

WINSMERE CL

1 WANSBECK RD
2 DEVERON GR
3 COLNE GREEN

CONWAY RD

HURN LA

EVENLODE WAY

WAVENEY RD

WITHAM RD

COPSE RD

WICK

BROCKLEY

NORMAN RD

BATH RD

HIGH ST

PH

Playing Field

MARTOCK RD

WAYFORD CL

MANSEL CL 1
LAWSON CL 2

GRANGE RD

HOWARD CL

FRENCHARD RD

WITNEY CL

Liby

BEECH RD

CHESTNUT WALK

HATFIELD RD

THE SHALLOWS

OAKFIELD RD

67

MELLS

HUTTON CL

FES CART RD

MAXWELL

CHERMES

CABOT

KEPPEL CL

CLAVERTON CL

Sch

Saltford

COLLINGWOOD CL

RODNEY RD

COURTENAY RD

Eastover Farm

MANOR RD

Keynsham Manor

MONTAGUE RD

RALEIGH CL 1
MORGAN CL 2

TYNING RD

HARCOURT

GOLF CLUB LA

FAIRWAYS

BERESFORD

UPLANDS RD

THE FOLLY

1

WELLSWAY

B3116

Uplands

Depot

SOMERVILLE CL

THE GLEN

CH

Golf Course

Folly Wood

A4

66

66   **A**   **67**   **B**   **68**   **C**

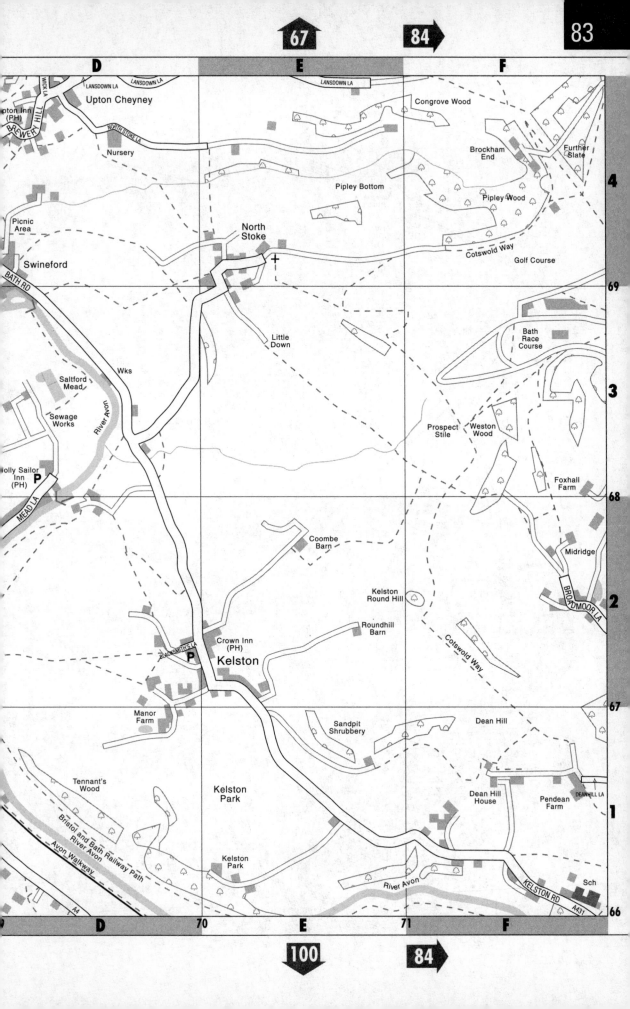

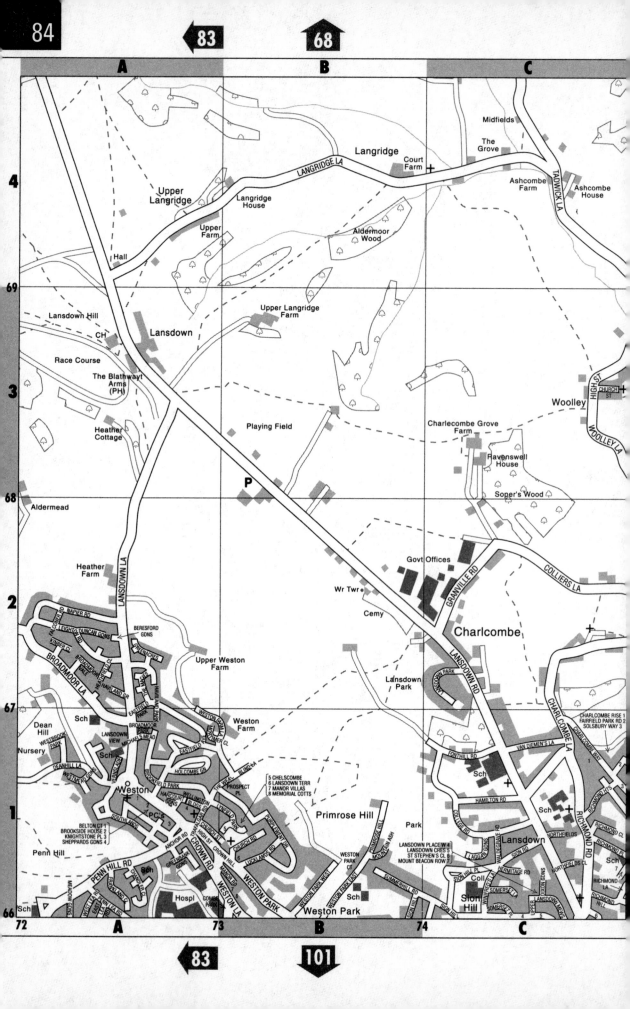

← 85   70   ✕

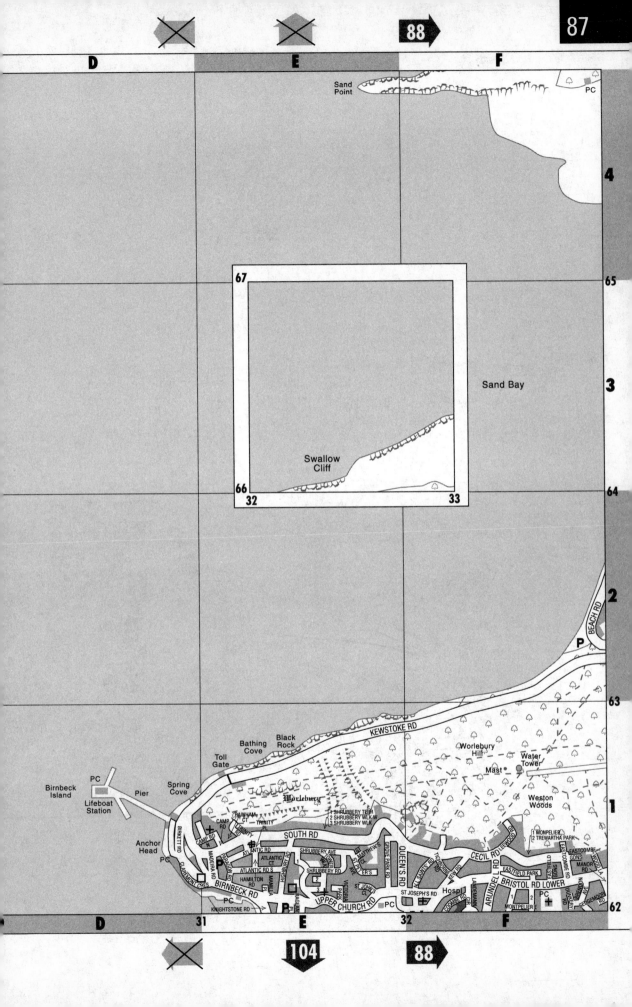

A   B   C

4

M5

Little River

Phipp's
Bridge

Wemberham
House

WEMBERHAM LA

65

M5

Congresbury Yeo

Pilhay
Farm

Pilhay
Bridge

The Elms

Hewish
Farm

East
Hewish

New Rhyne

3

LC

The
Oaks

Pool
Farm

Heathgate
Farm

Works

A370

West
Hewish

Sch

Full Quart
(PH)

Chestnut
Farm

Hewish

The
Grange

Waterman's
Bow

64

The Checketts Arms
(PH)

Palmer's
Elm

Oldbridge River

Willlow
Farm

Goosey Drove

Old
Bridges

2

Balls Yeo Rhyne

Mayfield
Farm

May's
Green

MAYSGREEN RD

MAC'S LA

PUXTON LA

Puxton

Meer Wall Rhyne

A370

Villa
Farm

Grange
Farm

Chestnut
Farm

Meer Wall

63

Puxton Court
Farm

PUXTON RD

Goose Acre
Farm

BALLS BARN LA

Puxton Moor
Farm

Puxton
Moor

1

Rolstone
Court

Hatches Lane

Land
Farm

South
Farm

The
Laurels

WEST ROLSTONE RD

BOX BUSH LA

East
Rolstone

Boxbush
Farm

Blackstone's Rhyne

62

HAVAGE DRO

HAVAGE DRO

39   A   40   B   41   C

A B C

MEETINGHOUSE LA
BISHOPS MEAD
BISHOPS RD
BRATNEY CL
CLEEVE CL
MILLGER RD
WOODVIEW
Cleeve Combe
Cleeve Court
Walnut Tree Farm
Saw Mill
Wrington Warren

4

MAIN RD
Lord Nelson (PH)
P LINDER ST
CHAPEL LA
P
Cleeve Toot
Warren House

L WARNER CL
RHODYATE HILL
RHODYATE LA
A3370
CLEEVE HILL RD
Goblin Combe

Bickley

65

King's Wood
Nature Reserve

Woolmere
Wrington Hill
Wrington Hill Farm

3

Urchin Wood
Corporation Woods
Oatlands

Ball Wood
The Island
Bracken Hill
WRINGTON HILL

The Grove

64

Montreux Farm
Yeowood
Udley
Uplands
Simshill Wood
Littler Plantation
Prestow Wood
Barley Farm

2

WRINGTON RD
Iwood
WEST HAY RD
West Hay
Piercahay
BULTHOUSE LANE
ROPER'S LA
Branches Cross
Barley Wood
LONG LA

Iwood Farm
IWOOD LA
Iwood Manor
CHAPEL HILL
YEOMANS ORCH
HOME CL
ORCHARD CL
OLD HILL
Maines Batch
HIGH ST
Sch
SCHOOL RD

63

Two Rivers Way
ALBURYS
Plough Inn (PH)
BELL WLK
SOUTH MEADOWS
Congresbury Yeo
LADYWELL
PC
BROAD ST
Court House
STATION RD
THE TRIANGLE
F Sta
LAWRENCE RD
PENNAH MORE CL
RICKYARD CL
BAKER'S BLDGS 1
THE COTTS 2
CHURCH WLK
SILVER ST
Wrington
Dismantled Railway
WINTONS
BROOKLYN
MEMORIAL RD
WESTWARD CL
THE ELM
OLD STATION CL
GASTONS
GASTONS ORCH

1

Stoneycroft House
KINGS RD
BUTT'S BATCH
Butt's Batch
COX'S GN
Cox's Green
HANVYAT RD
MILL LA

STOCK LA
B3133
Beam Bridge
HALF YD
Burnett Ind Est
Oakdene Farm
NATES LA

62

45 46 47
A B C

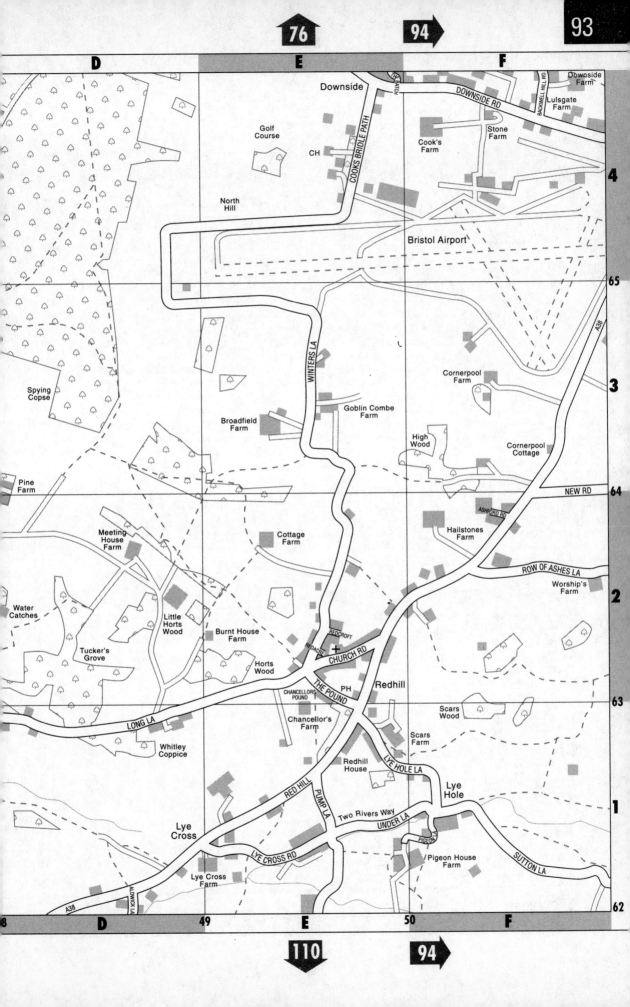

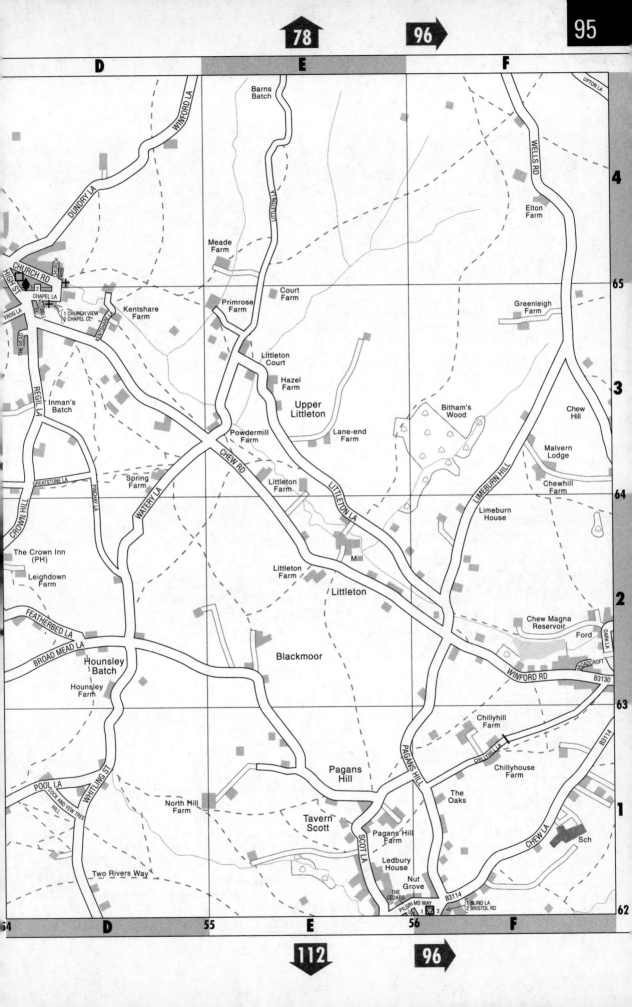

D E F

4

UPTON LA

WELLS RD

WINFORD LA

Barns
Batch

LITTLETON LA

Elton
Farm

Meade
Farm

65

DUNDRY LA

CHURCH RD

CHURCH RISE

HIGH ST

CHAPEL LA

FROG LA

PILLWELL

KENTSHARE LA

Court
Farm

Greenleigh
Farm

Primrose
Farm

1 CHURCH VIEW
2 CHAPEL CL

Kentshare
Farm

THE MEAD

REGIL LA

Inman's
Batch

Littleton
Court

Hazel
Farm

Upper
Littleton

Bitham's
Wood

Chew
Hill

3

Malvern
Lodge

LIMEBURN HILL

Chewhill
Farm

GREATSTONE LA

CROWN HILL

PINCHAY LA

Spring
Farm

WATERY LA

CHEW RD

Powdermill
Farm

Lane-end
Farm

Littleton
Farm

LITTLETON LA

64

Limeburn
House

The Crown Inn
(PH)

Leighdown
Farm

Littleton
Farm

Mill

Littleton

2

Chew Magna
Reservoir

Ford

DARK LA

FEATHERBED LA

BROAD MEAD LA

Hounsley
Batch

Blackmoor

WINFORD RD

BROADCROFT

B3130

Hounsley
Farm

63

Chillyhill
Farm

B3114

WHITLING ST

PAGANS HILL

CHILLYHILL LA

Chillyhouse
Farm

POOL LA

COCK AND YEW TREE HILL

North Hill
Farm

Pagans
Hill

The
Oaks

CHEW LA

Sch

1

Tavern
Scott

SCOT LA

Pagans Hill
Farm

Two Rivers Way

Ledbury
House

Nut
Grove

B3114

THE CEDARS

PILGRIMS WAY

1 BLIND LA
2 BRISTOL RD

62

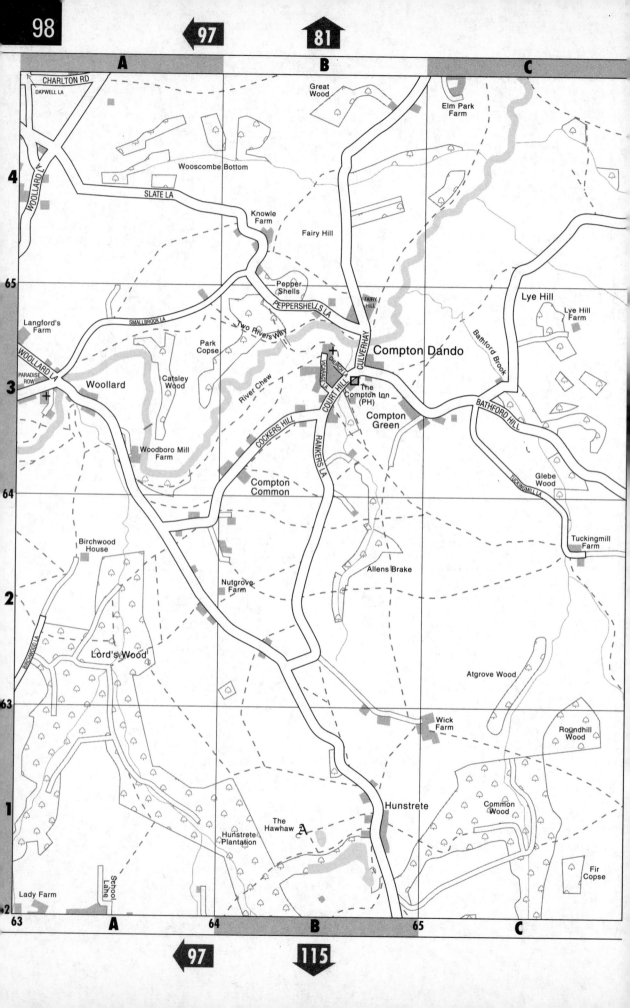

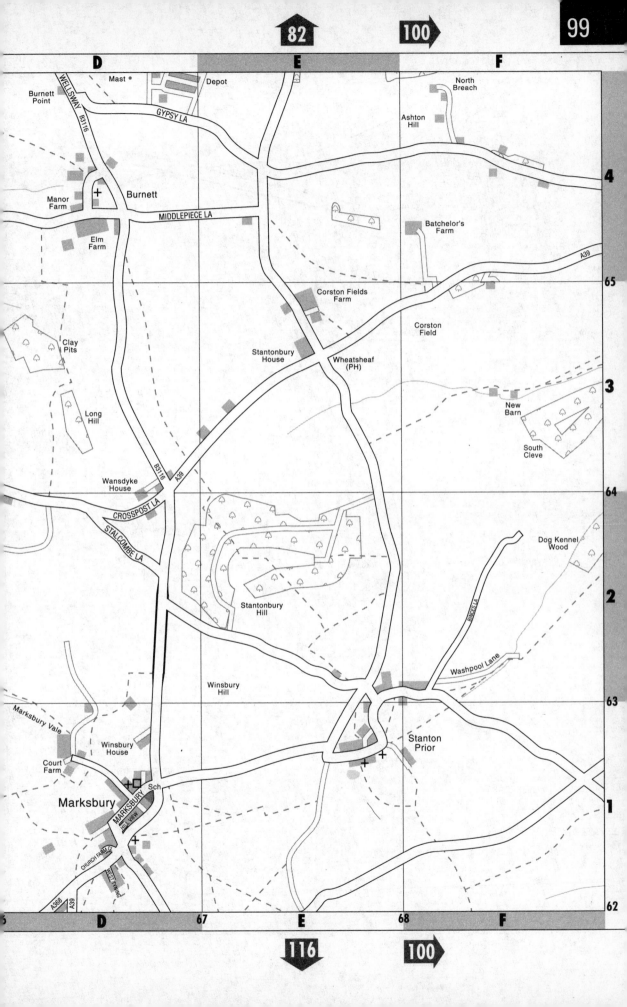

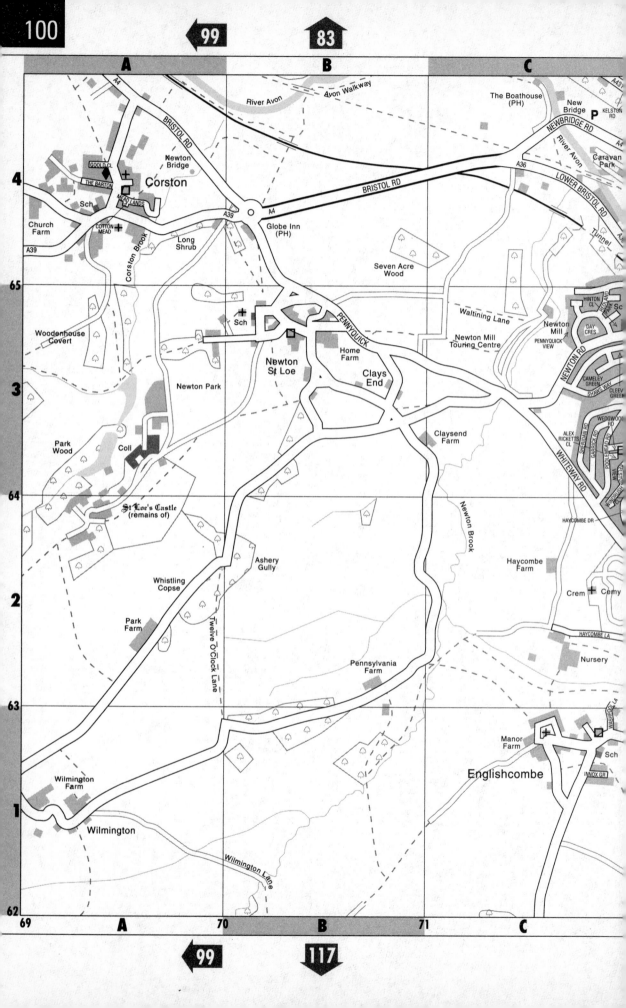

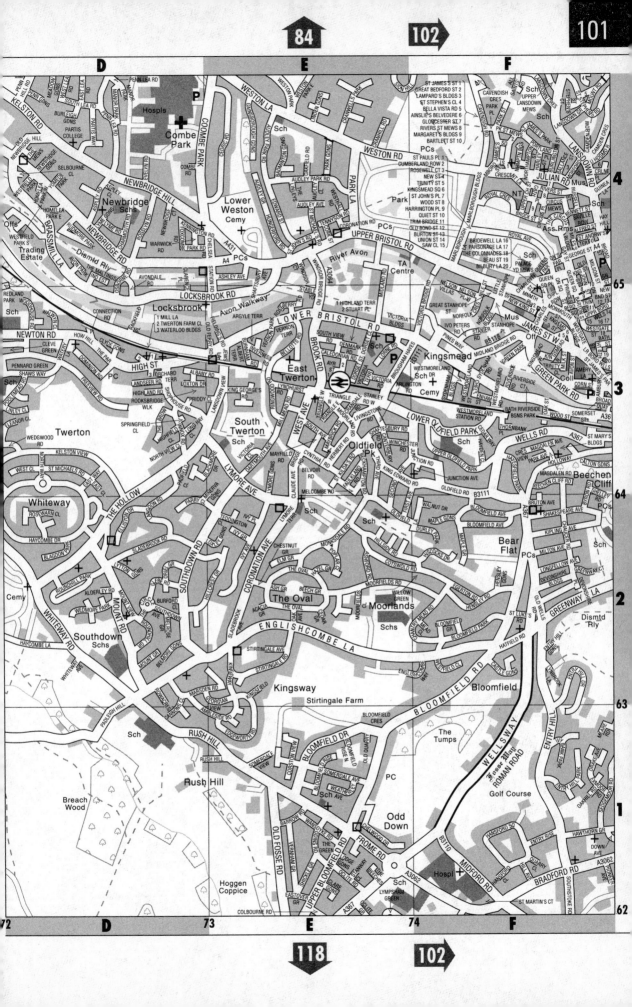

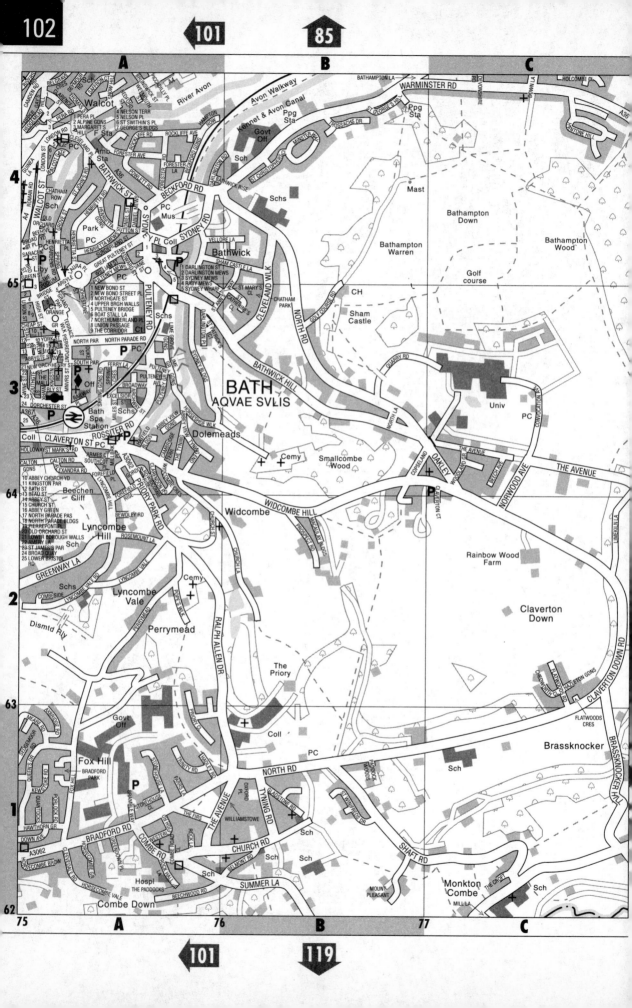

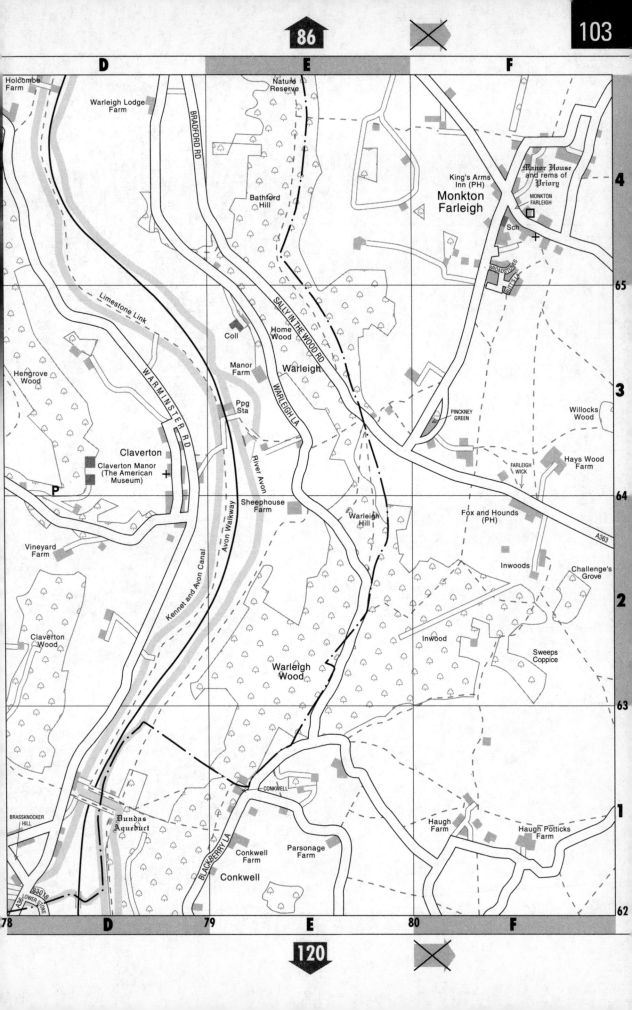

D · E · F

Holcombe Farm

Warleigh Lodge Farm

BRADFORD RD

Nature Reserve

Bathford Hill

Manor House and rems of Priory

King's Arms Inn (PH)

MONKTON FARLEIGH

Monkton Farleigh

Sch

BROADSTONE

MILL LA

4

65

Limestone Link

SALLY IN THE WOOD RD

Coll

Home Wood

Warleigh

Hengrove Wood

WARMINSTER RD

Manor Farm

WARLEIGH LA

Ppg Sta

PINCKNEY GREEN

Willocks Wood

3

Claverton

Claverton Manor (The American Museum)

River Avon

FARLEIGH WICK

Hays Wood Farm

P

Sheephouse Farm

Warleigh Hill

Fox and Hounds (PH)

A363

64

Vineyard Farm

Avon Walkway

Kennet and Avon Canal

Inwoods

Challenge's Grove

Claverton Wood

Warleigh Wood

Inwood

Sweeps Coppice

2

63

BRASSKNOCKER HILL

Dundas Aqueduct

CONKWELL

BLACKBERRY LA

Haugh Farm

Haugh Potticks Farm

1

B3108

A36

LOWER STONE

Conkwell Farm

Parsonage Farm

Conkwell

62

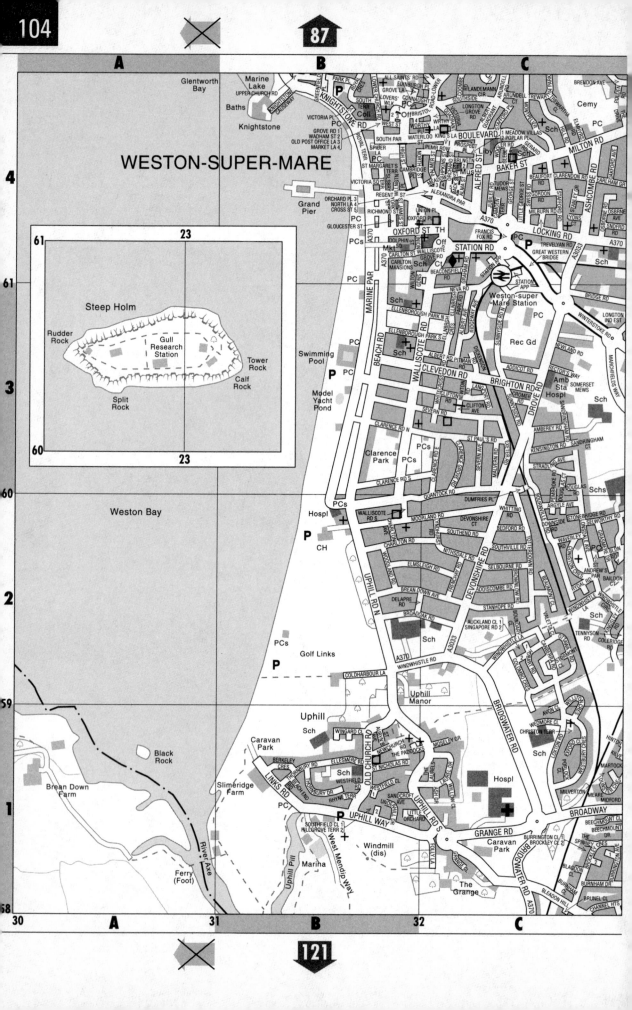

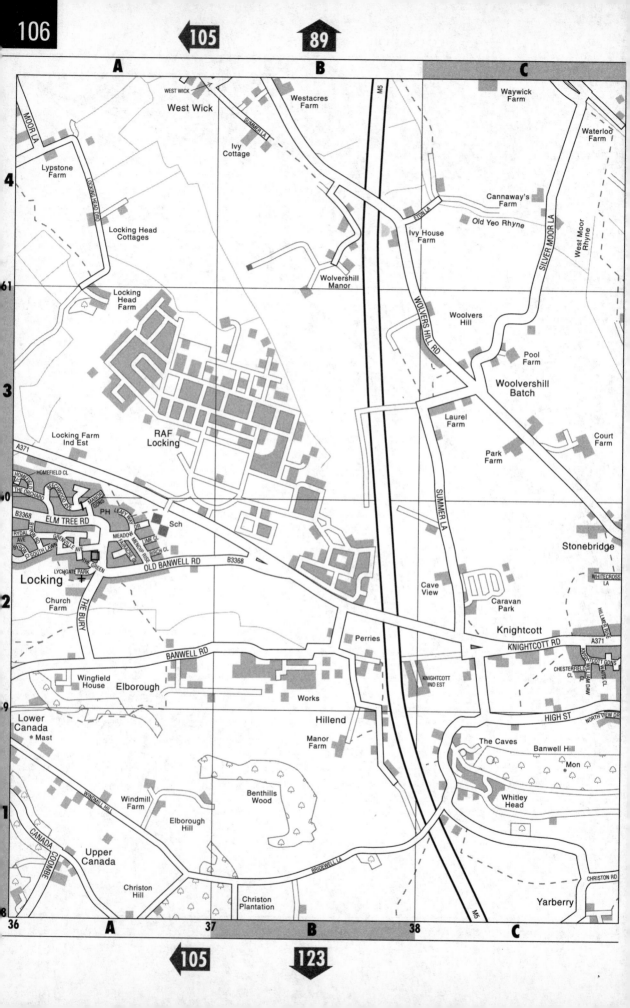

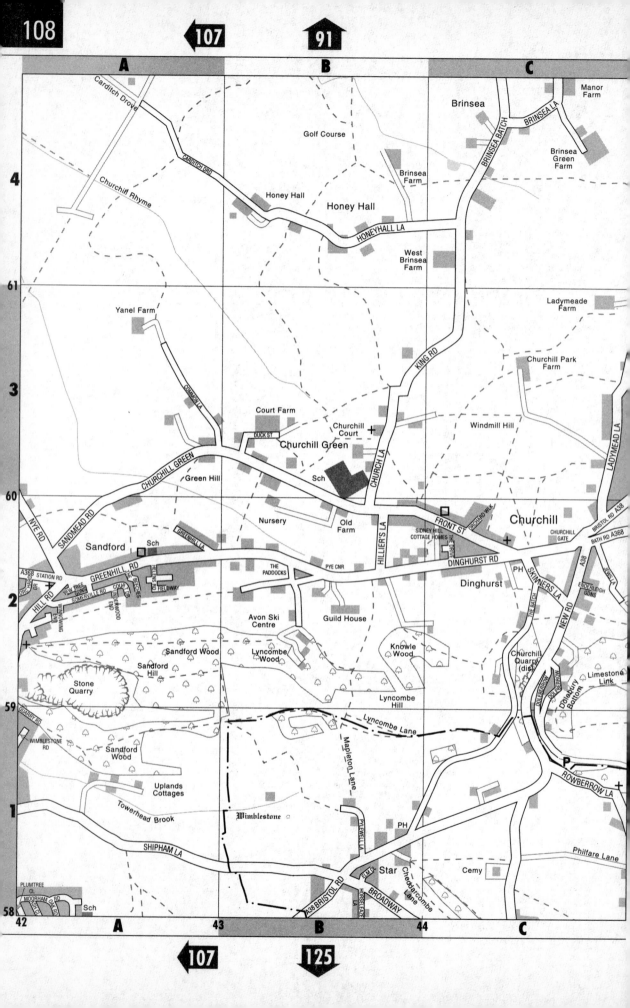

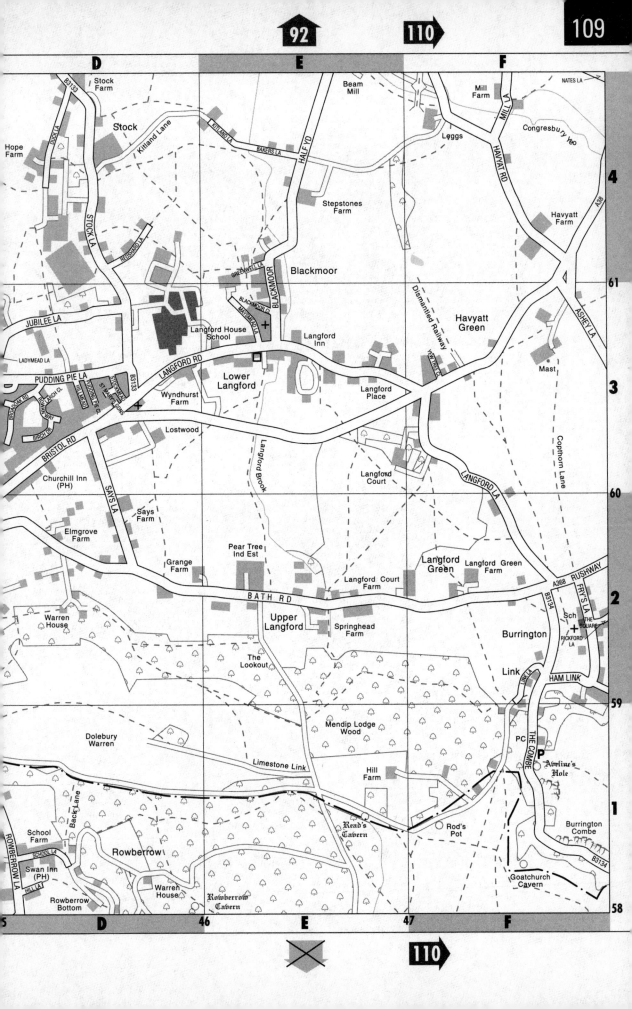

A B C

Caravan and
Camping Site

Cowslip
Green

Cribb's
Farm

Sutton
Farm

Paradise
Farm

4

Perry
Bridge

A38

Aldwick
Court

Aldwick
Wood

Woodlands

Hanging
Wood

Long
Wood

Round
Wood

Aldwick

ALDWICK LA

61

Aldwick
Court Farm

Butcombe
Farm

EMLEY LA

BLAGDON LA

3

ASHLEY LA

Congresbury Yeo

Uxford
Bridge

Dismantled Railway

Bourne

Emley
Farm

60

Wadley
Farm

Sewage
Works

BOURNE LA

HOOKS BATCH

Coombe Lodge
Farm

Home Bay
Point

A368 RUSHWAY

Ridge
Farm

BOURNE LA

Ford

Coombe Lodge
(Coll)

STATION RD

DARK LA

PARK LA

THE BATCH

2

RICKFORD LA

Rickford

PH

LEG LA

Wks

Ridgeon
Wood

Blagdon
Coombe

Home
Farm

MENLEA

LAWS LA

CLANDERS

BATCH

GASTON LA

Fire
Sta

West
End

Burrington Lane

RICKFORD RISE

THE COMBE

HIGH ST

P

BELL SQ

The
Park

POST OFFICE

The New
Inn (PH)

HAM
LINK

Rickford
Rising

Street
End Inn

MEAD LA

GRUB LA

PC

59

The Hill
Gardens

Fuller's
Hay

STREET END

STREET END LA

LIBERTY
LA

THE OLD WATER

CHURCH ST

School

Cemy

East
End

BATH RD

Lower
Hill Farm

Coll

RHODYATE

The Grove

SLADACRE LA

PH

SWANCOMBE

DIPLAND
GR

1

Burrington
Ham

STREET END LA

WESTCROFT

EASTCROFT
CL

A368

THE SCORE

Blagdon

Burrington Coombe

LUVERS LA

Swancombe
Wood

Toad's
Hole

B3134

Lower Ellick
Farm

ELLICK RD

TWO TREES

Lower Ellick
Wood

THE COMBE

B3134

NEWFIELDS

Rhodyate Hill
Farm

58

48 A 49 B 50 C

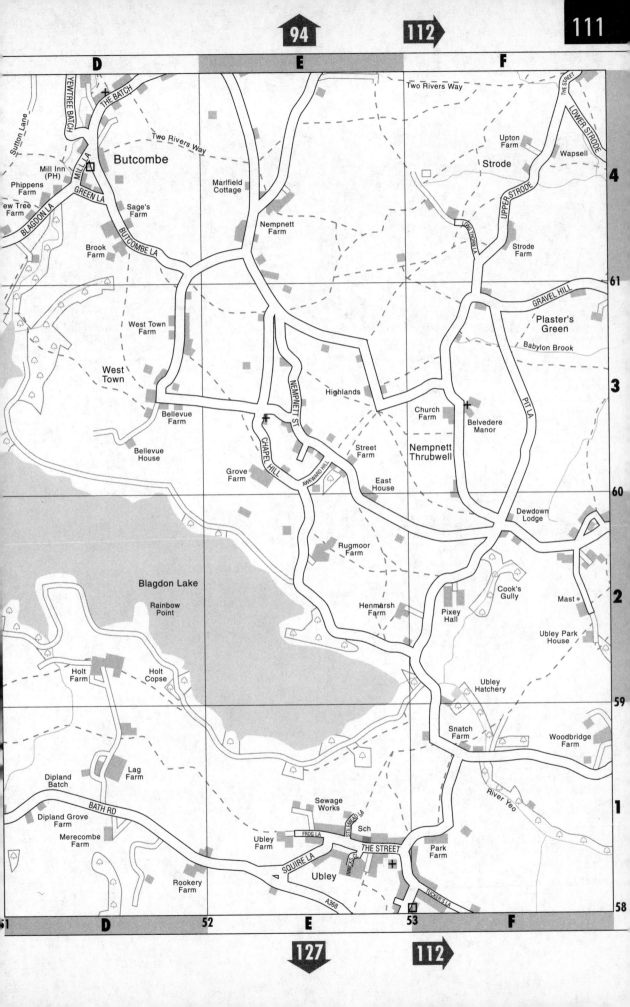

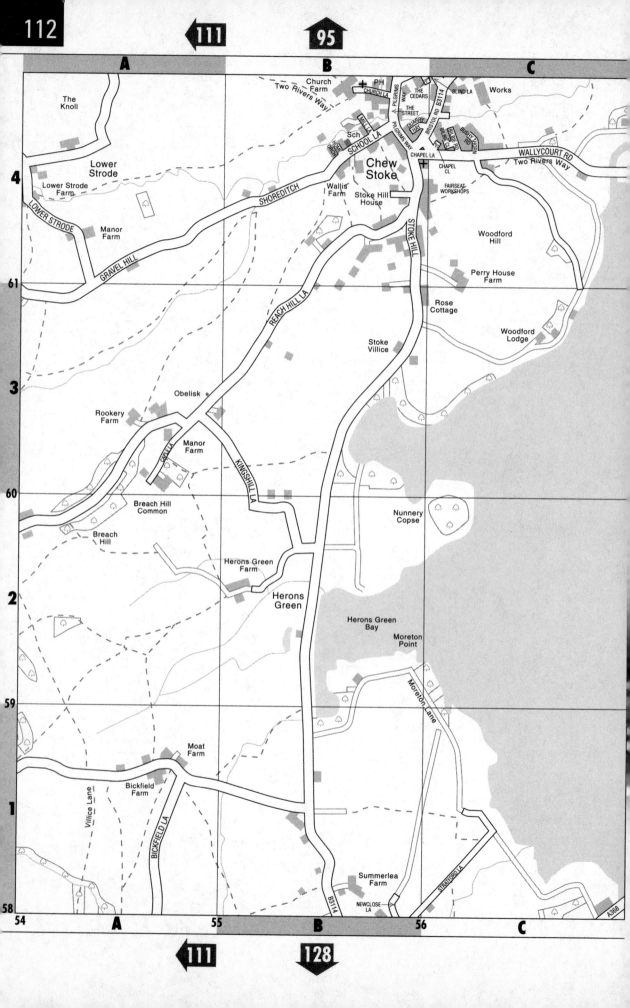

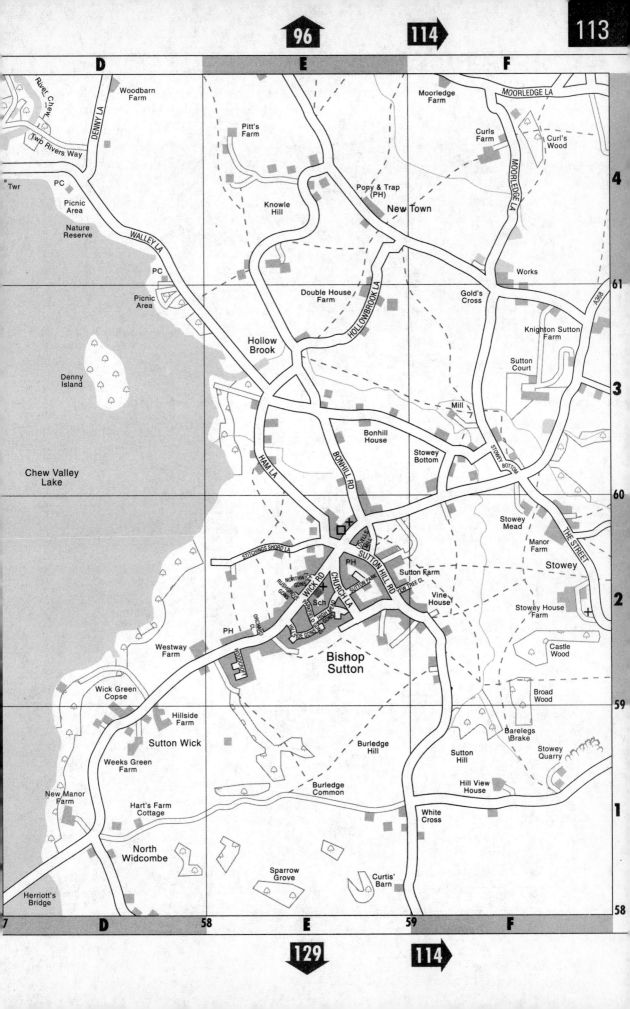

A   B   C

4

Bromley Farm

Curl's Farm

Utcombe Farm

STANTON WICK LA

Stanton Wick

Chelwood Bridge

A37

A368

Chelwood House Hotel

Park Farm

Stanton Wick Farm

61

A368

Round Hill

Resr

Salter's Brook

Fry's Bottom

FEATHERBED LA

Folly Wood

Honey Gaston

Red Hill

Breach

3

Folly Farm

Resr

North End Farm

Dowling's Wood

THE FLAT

North End

60

Taylor's Farm

KING LA

Hill Farm

LOWER BRISTOL RD

Cinderlands Brake

Tynemoor Wood

2

UPPER BRISTOL RD

Clutton

GREENRIDGE

CLUTTON HILL

Warwick Arms (PH)

TWINES WAY
WARWICK GDNS
ROGERS CL
THE MEAD
BROADMILL LA
FURZE LANE
MAYROSE CL
MORSFIELD

Sch

MAYNARD TERR

Tynemore Farm

Station Rd

VENUS LA

STATION RD

59

Church Farm

CHURCH LA

KINGS OAK
MEADOW
CHURCH SQ
VALLEY VIEW
CARLTON CT

Dismantled Railway

Sleight Farm

Cholwell Farm

Bendalls Bridge

Willow Farm

Cholwell House (Off)

Cholwell

MARSH LA

1

Cholwell Farm

Temple Cloud

Limestone Link

THE SQUARE

PH

Paul Wood

PAULWOOD RD
PAULMONT RISE

OAKLANDS
THE DOWN
GOLDNEY
GROSFIELD
FIELDGARDENS RD
GOLD LA
ASHWOOD
CRABTREE
MEADWAY
BARN CL
HAM CL

A37

Sch

Sch

D
E
F

4

Chelwood
Church Farm
Hunstrete House Hotel
Hungerford Bottom
A368
Marksbury Plain

BARN LA

Daniel's Brake
Whidcombe Brake

Purnell's Gully
Cockroad Wood

61

Humstrete Rd

Hartley Barm

Mountain's Lane
POOR HILL
CONYGRE RISE
A39
THE STREET

Hartley Wood

Conygre Brook
LOVE'S LA
Sch
BROOKSIDE DR
MANOR GDNS

3

ING LA
Poacher's Pocket

Blackberry Hill
Barrow Vale
Farmborough

BATH RD
TILLEY LA

Hunters' Rest (PH)

Barrow Hill
Hobb's Wall

60

Nap Hill

Ashdene

SUNNYSIDE
Clutton Hill
Hazeldene Farm
CLUTTON HILL

Cross Ways
B3115

Riding's Farm
The Sleight

2

CUCKOO LA

Dismantled Railway

Kingwell Hall
HAYESWOOD RD
Hayeswood Farm

MAYNARD TERR

Zion Place
Greyfield Farm
Heighgrove Farm

NEW RD

Mearns
B3115

59

THE GUG

Greyfield
SCUMBRUM LA

Mearns Hill
Amesbury Hill
Tyning

Greyfields

SCOBELL RISE
WESTWOOD AVE
EASTWOOD CL

SINEFENCE
PARKLANDS
KINGWELL VALE
MAGGS FOLLY

Amesbury

GREYFIELD RD
Rotcombe
ROTCOMBE LA
ROTCOMBE VALE

PROCTORS HILL

1

MARSH LA

Greyfield Wood Farm
Greyfield Wood
FIELD COMM
LANSDOWN PL
High Littleton
HIGH ST
PH
SOUTHOVER RD
ASTON RD

Rugbourne Farm
Timsbury Bottom Farm
Timsbury Bottom

Long Lands
Limestone Link

BUTTASS RD
Sch
A39
TIMSBURY RD
GOOSARD LA
LANGFORD'S LA
BUNGAY'S HILL
BROOM HILL LA

58

D
64
E
65
F

115
99

A   B   C

The Brendons

Heathercroft

Pendown Hill

Priston New Farm

Pottern Brake

Pottern

4

Mollifrend House

Conygre Brook

The Farmborough (PH)

Old Inn Farmhouse

61

A39   BATH RD   OLD LA

Sewage Works

Castle Farm

Priest Barrow

THE STREET

BRIDGE GDNS   BELLIFANTS

MEADWAY   FERENBERGE CL

THE MEAD

THE BATCH   CHURCH RD

MANOR GDNS

TILLEY CL   TIMSBURY RD   LITTLE LA

Farmborough

Long Wood

3

Tilley Farm

TILLEY LA

Farmborough Common

60

Wallmead House Farm

Lammas Field Farm

Priston Wood

Wallmead Farm

Wall Mead

THE WOODLANDS

PRISTON

Bloomfield

NORTHFIELD

2

BLOOMFIELD RD

Sleight Farm

BLOOMFIELD CL

BLOOMFIELD AVE

LIPPIATT LA

CROCOMBE LA

Tunley Farm

The Sleight

THE GLEBE

Bloomfield Park RD

LIPPIATT LA

CROCOMBE LA

THE MEAD

Sch

OVERDALE

B3115

59

HAYESWOOD RD

NORTH RD

LANSDOWN VIEW

LANSDOWN CRES

LANSDOWN PARK

PARKWAY LA

TUNLEY HILL

Tyning

THE AVENUE

NEWMANS LA

SOMERSET FOLLY

ST MARY'S CL

THE SQUARE

RECTORY

Camerton Inn (PH)

PRIORS HILL

Timsbury

HIGH ST   HARD HILL

BAKERS BAR

CHURCH LANE

SOUTH RD

Hook

PARKWAY

Meadgate West

Meadgate East

Bengrove Wood

1

BO SCHO

SOUTH   HILLVIEW

PH

SOUTH VIEW

CAMERTON RD

PRIORS HILL

LOVES HILL

GREENVALE

GREENVALE DR

ST JOHNS RD

MILL LA

RADFORD HILL

The Folly

Sheep House Farm

Wicklane

Timsbury Bottom

Meadgate Farm

WEEKSLEY LA

Limestone Link

Lynch House

RED HILL

BRIDGE PLACE RD

WICK LA

WHITEBROOK LA

58

66   A   67   B   68   C

115
132

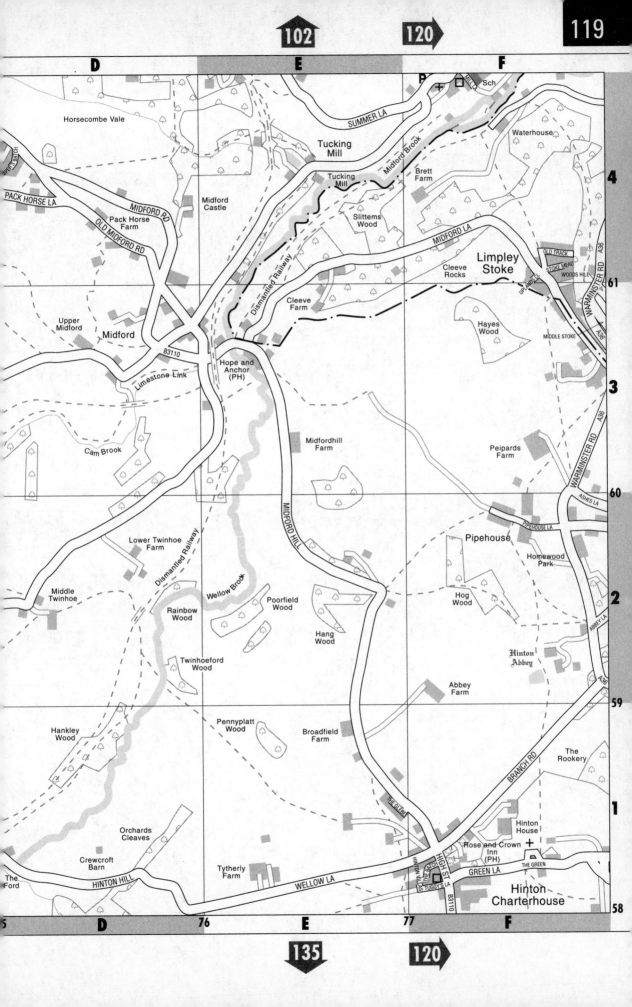

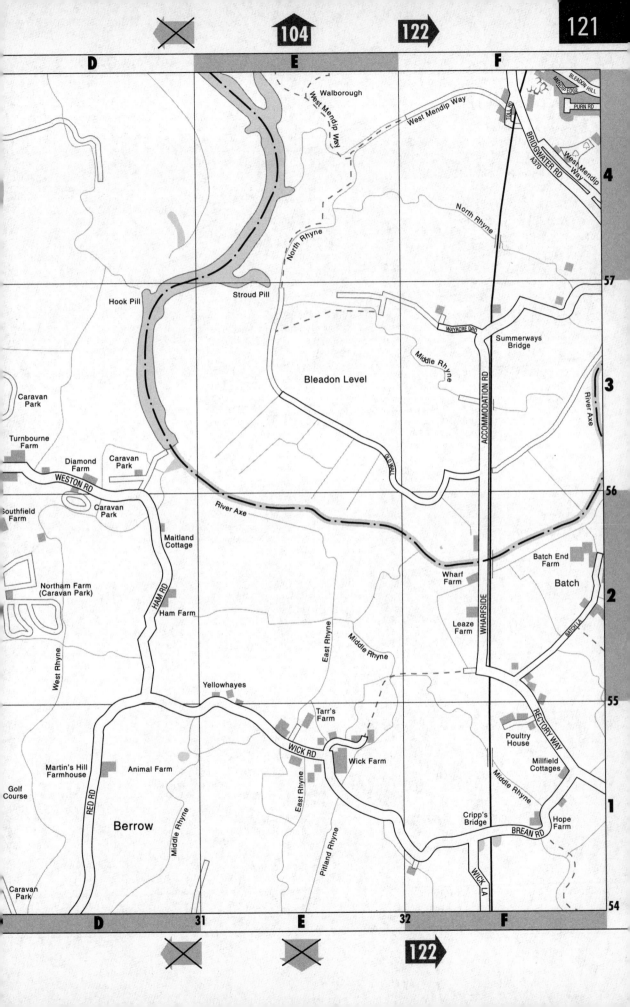

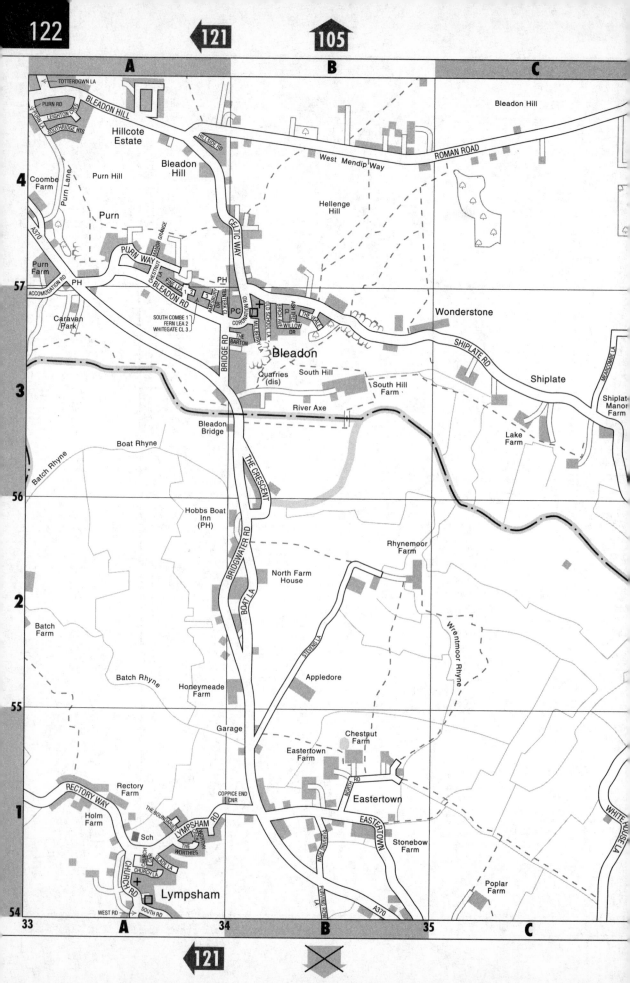

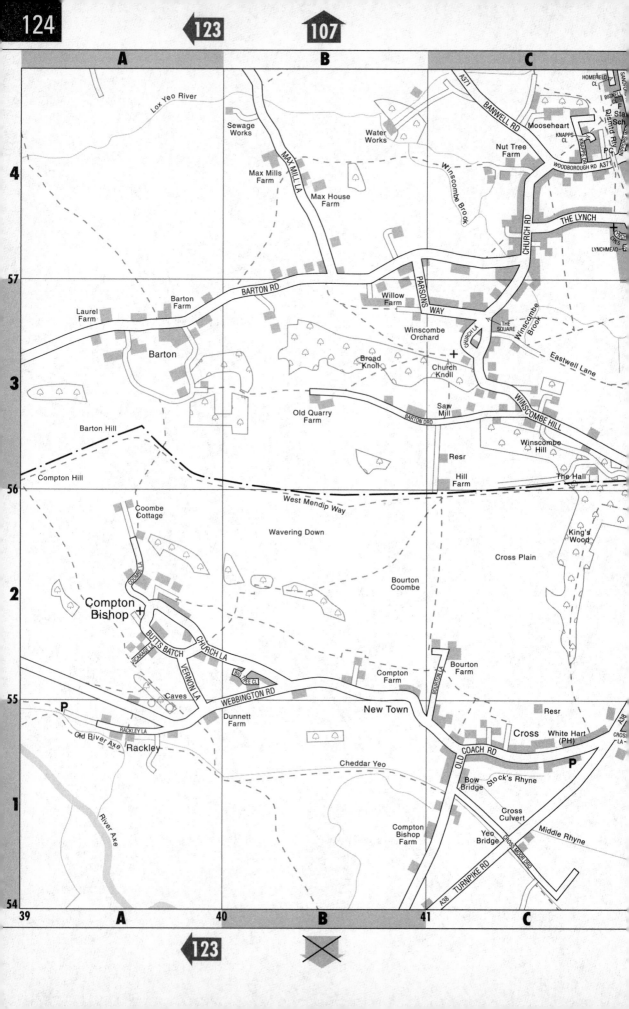

123
107

A   B   C

4

57

Lox Yeo River

Sewage Works

Max Mills Farm

MAX MILL LA

Max House Farm

Water Works

BANWELL RD

A371

HOMEFIELD CL
BIGNELL CL

F Sta
Jd
Sch

Mooseheart

KNAPPS CL

PC

WOODBOROUGH RD A371

KNAPPS RD

Nut Tree Farm

CHURCH RD

Winscombe Brook

THE LYNCH

LYNCHMEAD

LAD CRES

Barton Farm

BARTON RD

Laurel Farm

Barton

Willow Farm

PARSONS
WAY

Winscombe Orchard

CHURCH LA

THE SQUARE

Winscombe Brook

Eastwell Lane

Broad Knoll

Church Knoll

3

Old Quarry Farm

BARTON DRO

Saw Mill

WINSCOMBE HILL

Winscombe Hill

Barton Hill

Resr

Hill Farm

The Hall

Compton Hill

56

West Mendip Way

Coombe Cottage

Wavering Down

King's Wood

Cross Plain

COOMBE LA

Bourton Coombe

2

Compton Bishop

BUTTS BATCH

VICARAGE LA

CHURCH LA

VERNON LA

BIG
TREE CL

Compton Farm

Bourton Farm

BOURTON LA

Caves

WEBBINGTON RD

55

P

RACKLEY LA

Dunnett Farm

New Town

Resr

Cross

White Hart
(PH)

A38

CROSS
LA

Old River Axe   Rackley

Cheddar Yeo

OLD COACH RD

P

1

River Axe

Compton Bishop Farm

Bow Bridge

Stock's Rhyne

Cross Culvert

Yeo Bridge

Middle Rhyne

CROSS MOOR DRO

TURNPIKE RD

A38

54

39   A   40   B   41   C

D E F

Winscombe
Woodborough
Paddingham House
Queensmead Court
Wintrath
BROADWAY
NEW RD
BEECH RD
BEECH LN
NORTH DOWN LA
ROWBERROW LA
LIPPIATT LA
Sch
BRAE RISE
BRAE RD
HILLYFIELDS WAY
HILLYFIELDS
BRIDGEWATER RD
DUNSTER CL
APPLE TREE DR
SOUTHLEAZE RD
THE CHESTNUTS
THE LYNCH
WOODBOROUGH CRES
Lib
ASH PL
HOMESTEAD CL
PLUMTREE CL
NYFORD DR
BRISTOL RD
A38
THE AVENUE
HORSELEAZE LN
MEAD KENMEADE
SYCAMORE RD
COMRADE AVE
THE DRIVE
TURNPIKE RD
THE SQUARE
HOLLOW RD
PH
Sch
GLOVERS RD
TOP LN
CUCK HILL
1 NORTH DOWN LA
2 BARN POOL
3 ALLENS LA
4 COURT LA
5 HIND PITTS
6 THE DRUMHEAD WAY
Shipham
4

Winterhead

SIDCOT LA A371
FOUNTAIN LA
OAKRIDGE LA
Sidcot
1 LYNCH CRES
2 LYNCHMEAD
3 YADLEY CL
Oakridge Farm
Winterhead Farm
Hotel
57

Sidcot Hill Farm
Winterhead Hill Farm
Winterhead Hill
Cuck Hill

FULLERS LA
SOUTHLEAZE
YADLEY LA
Caravan Park
Hotel
Gatcombe
West Mendip Way
WINSCOMBE DRO
Lillypool Farm
LONGBOTTOM
SHIPHAM RD
3

BRIDGWATER RD
Hale Combe
Yadley Lane
Dismid Rhy
Hale Coppice
Shute Shelve Farm
Callow Drove
Callow Hill
56

WINSCOMBE HILL
A371
Rose Wood
Shute Shelve Hill
Mast
Fry's Hill
Callow Rock Quarry
Cheddar
2

Axbridge Hill
Cheddar Wood
55

Manor Farm
CROSS LA
P
HORN'S LA
FERNEL LA
CHURCH LA
Hillside
Cemy
St Michael's Cheshire Home
PARSONAGE
Mushroom Farm
Caravan Site
SHIPHAM RD

Townsend Farm
PROWSES LA
HOLLY GATE WAY
STARRS CL
WEST ST
HIGH ST
BACK LA
THE SQUARE
ST MARY'S ST
CHESTNUT AVE
STATION RD
MEDDOW ST
JUBILEE RD
MENDIP
PADLEY DR
CHEDDAR RD
AXBRIDGE RD
A371
UPPER NEW RD
Bloomfield Farm
Yacht Club
1

P
Hospl
WALNUT CL
OLD CHURCH RD
MOOR RD
CROSS MANOR DR
CROSS MOOR DR
BARNES WALL
WALL GREEN
BAILIFFS CL
AXBRIDGE MOOR DRO
PORTMEADE DRO
Sch
MEADOW ST
MOORLAND ST
PENN WAY
KNIGHT
ORCHARD RD
PARKFIELD RD
Axbridge
Sewage Wks
Cheddar Reservoir
54

42 D 43 E 44 F

A B C

4

Black Down

Ellick House

B3134

THE COMBE

NEWFIELDS

ELLICK RD

Limestone Link

LEAZE LA

Leaze Farm

Limestone Link

Leaze Lane

TWO TREES

Hill Farm

Middle Ellick Farm

BROAD RD

Beacon Batch

Swymmer's Farm

57

Paywell Farm

B3134

Mast

Wireless Station

3

BANKS BATCH

Mendip Farm

Factory

Blackmoor

Nether Wood

56

FIR LA

Collier's Lane

Lower Farm

Gorsey Bigbury Henge

Mendip Farm

Manor Farm

Mendip Farm

+

Outdoor Activities Centre

Nature Reserve

Charterhouse

2

Long Wood

West Mendip Way

Mendip Adventure Base

Velvet Bottom

55

Piney Sleight

Charterhouse Warren Farm

Black Rock

Cheddar Gorge

B3135

1

Blackrock Gate

CLIFF RD

King Down Farm

B3371

B3135

54

48 A 49 B 50 C

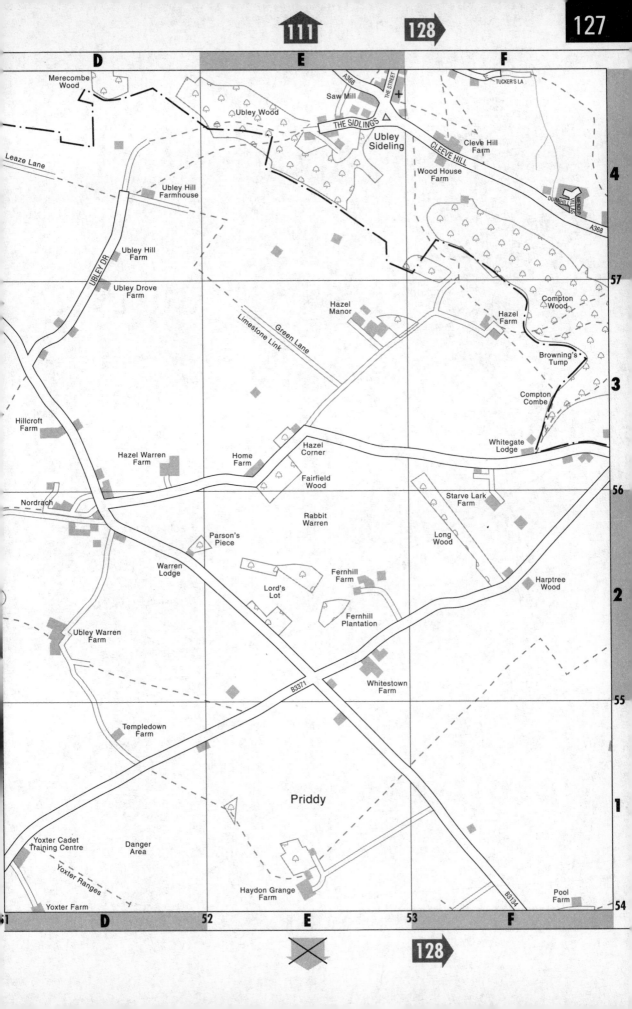

D   E   F

↑ Merecombe Wood

Leaze Lane

Ubley Wood

Saw Mill

THE STREET

A368

THE SIDLINGS

Ubley Sideling

CLEVE HILL

Cleve Hill Farm

TUCKER'S LA

Wood House Farm

DURNHILL VILLAS

MENDIP

A368

4

Ubley Hill Farmhouse

UBLEY DR

Ubley Hill Farm

57

Ubley Drove Farm

Limestone Link

Green Lane

Hazel Manor

Hazel Farm

Compton Wood

Browning's Tump

Compton Combe

3

Hillcroft Farm

Hazel Warren Farm

Home Farm

Hazel Corner

Fairfield Wood

Whitegate Lodge

Nordrach

Rabbit Warren

Starve Lark Farm

56

Parson's Piece

Warren Lodge

Lord's Lot

Fernhill Farm

Long Wood

Harptree Wood

2

Ubley Warren Farm

Fernhill Plantation

Whitestown Farm

B3371

55

Templedown Farm

Priddy

1

Yoxter Cadet Training Centre

Danger Area

Yoxter Ranges

Yoxter Farm

Haydon Grange Farm

B3134

Pool Farm

54

D   52   E   53   F

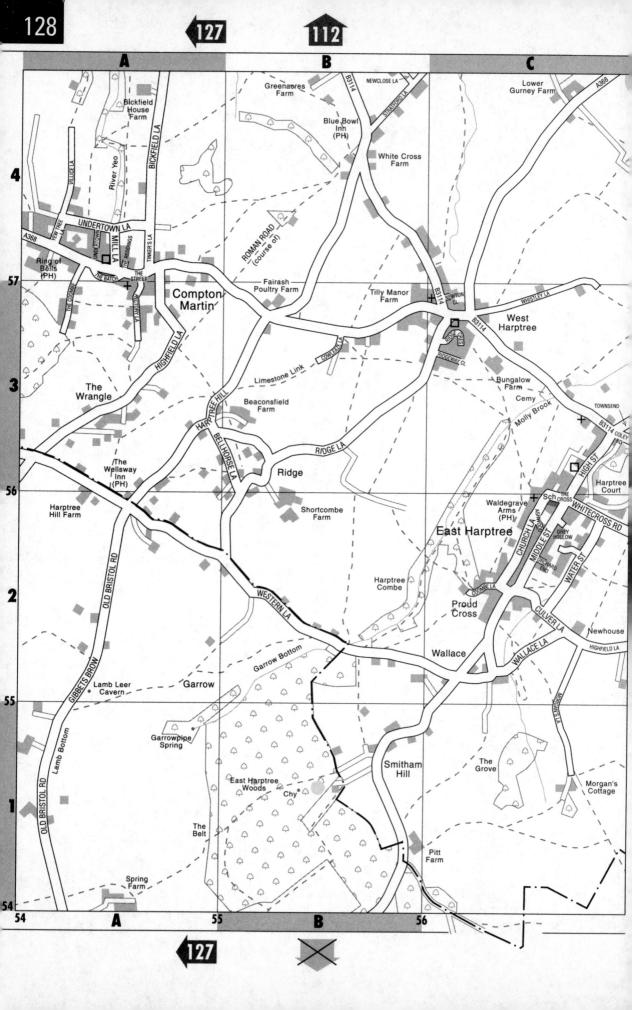

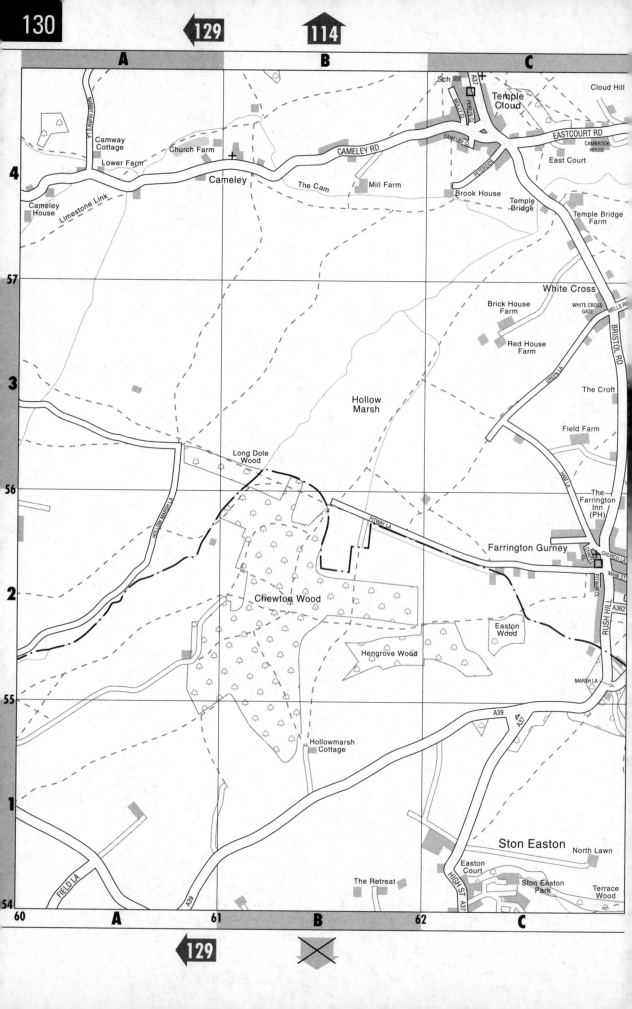

D E F

115 132

Cloud Hill

Highbury Hill

Stephen's Hill

EASTCOURT RD

Cloud Hill Farm

Factory

MARSH LA

Rosewell Farm

A39

LANGFORDS LA

GOOSARD LA

BROOM HILL

Withy Mills Farm

Goosard Bridge

BRISTOL RD

Sewage Works

Hanham House

HANHAM LA

4

Southside House

HIGHBURY RD

The Court

Hallatrow Bridge

HART'S LA

PAULTON RD

Limestone Link

Allard's Farm

57

Hallatrow

CLAREMONT GDNS

B3355

HALLATROW ROAD

Works

Plummer's Hill

VICTORIA TERR

BATH RD

JUBILEE TERR

BRITTEN'S HILL

Brittens

Old Station Inn (PH)

WELLS RD

COMB LA

Butt's Lane

SPRINGHILL CL

PCs CHURCH LA

CHURCH ST

HIGH ST

Cemy

LITTLEBROOK

GREGORY'S TYNING

WALLMEAD

HILLSIDE CL

PAULTO' HILL

3

White Cross Farm

New Town

ROMAN WAY

CAM VIEW

HIGH PARK

ORCHARD

SOMERSET WAY

BROOKSIDE

CHESTNUT

Alexandra TERR

HAM LA

Paulton

BRIMMER WAY

DOWNS WAY

WOODVIEW

WESTVIEW

FARRINGTON RD

CARTER RD

VICTORIA PL

PARK VIEW

F Sta

LAUREL DR

ASHMANS GATES

Liby HIGH ST

PARK RD

LILIAN TERR

Schs

Alexandra Park

BLOOMFIELD

HIGH MERE

Ham

PAULTON RD

RUETT LANE

SPECKLEMEAD

BRITTS FARM CL

TENNIS COURT RD

PLUMPTRE CL

GREENVALE RD

PLUMPTRE RD

LLOYDELLS

SERUM RD

SPRING GROUND RD

RUDGEWAY RD

WINTERFIELD RD

ALPINE RD

OAK VIEW

Dismantled Railway

56

Towns End

Sch

CHURCH LA

FARRINGTON WAY

MAIN LA

Manor House

MANOR GDNS

OLD MILLS LA

ALPINE CL

FIR TREE AVE

CLANDOWN RD

SALISBURY RD

Salisbury

Amb Sta

Hospl

A362

SPRINGFIELD

THE CRESCENT

HILL VIEW

Farrington Gurney

MARSH LA

FARRINGTON FIELDS

Superstore

MONGER LA

MONGER LA

HARTS PADDOCK

2

BOXBURY HILL

PHILLIS HILL

WEST RD

A362

55

Old Mills

SPRINGFIELD BLDGS

OLD MILLS IND EST

Thicketmead Bridge

Thicket Mead

NORTHMEAD RD

SUNSMEAD

Farrington Golf Club

Langley Down Lane

Hillier's Down Wood

Hillier's Down

LANGLEY'S LA

NORTHMEAD CL

SOMER AVE

NORTHMEAD AVE

UNDERHILL LA

Underhill Wood

Underhill Farm

ORCHARD AVE

HIGH MEADOWS

HAYES RD

NORTH RD

B3355

DYMBORO

1

Wellow Brook

White Bridge

CLAPTON RD

Bull's Wood

WOODSIDE

PINEWOOD

GREENACRES

PINEWOOD RD

Providence Place

Sch

MANDY MEADOWS

PAULTON RD

DYMBORO AVE

54

3 64 E 65 F

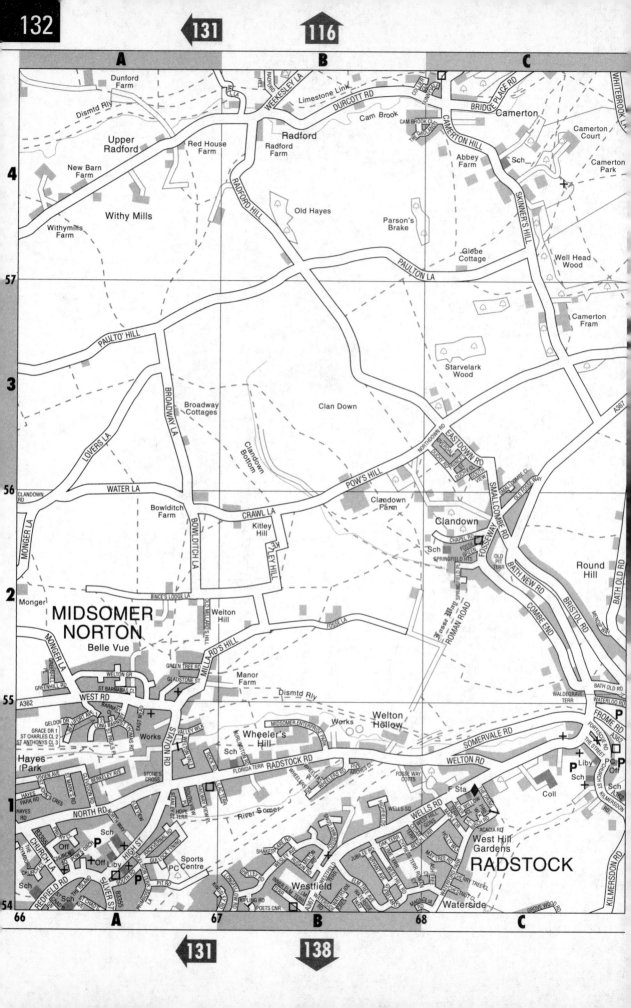

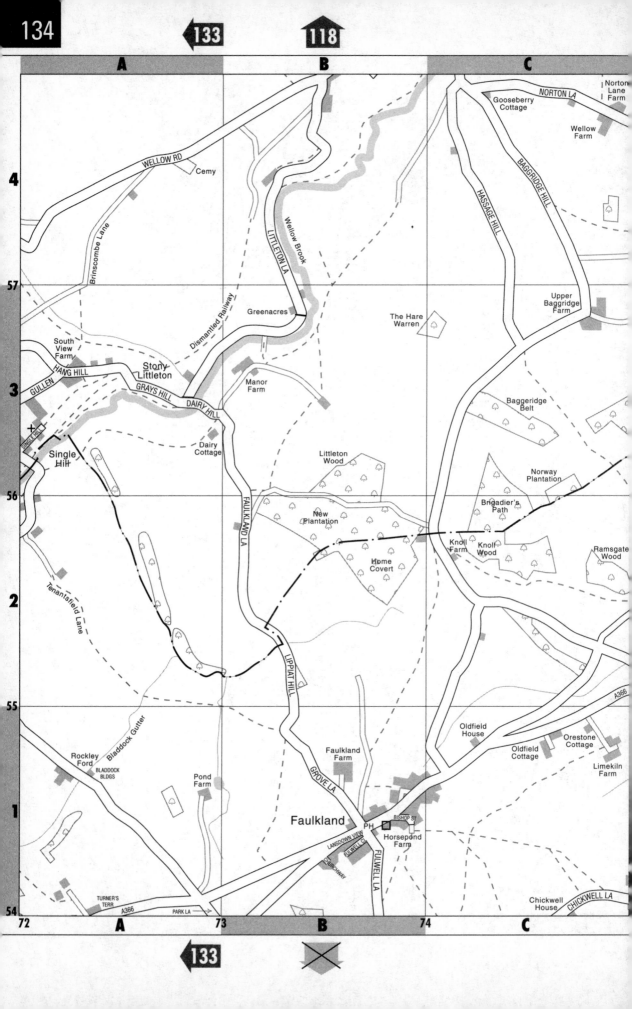

D E F

New Town

Cleaves Wood

Prestick Wood

Norton Barn

Norwood Wood

B3110

4

Tuckson Wood

Tait Wood

NORTON LA

Norwood Farm

Lower Baggridge Farm

57

Breach Brake

Kingfield Brake

Hinton Field

Ring Wood

Norton Brook

Broadlands

BATH RD

Mast

Water Tower

A366

3

New Plantation

Rainbow Brake

Norton House

Foxholes Lane

FARLEIGH RD

Hassage Wood

WELLOW LA

Rainbow Cottage

Sewage Works

CHEVER'S LA

NORTH ST

MILL PADDOCK

56

Hassage House

RINGWELL LA

THE BARTON

BELL HILL

UPPER FARM CL

TOWN BARTON

Norton St Philip

SPRINGFIELD

RINGWELL

HIGH ST

THE PLAIN

Mount Pleasant Farm

CHURCH ST

FAIR CL

George Inn (PH)

Sch

VICARAGE LA

TOWN END

SOUTHFIELD

TELLISFORD LA

2

Tucker's Grave Bottom

Watery Lane

FROME RD

B3110

Tucker's Grave Inn (PH)

Southfield Farm

Bingwell Farm

WELLS RD

MACHLEY LA

55

Chickwell New Farm

1

Peart Farm

CHICKWELL LA

Marrow Pole Lane

Chickwell Farm

ROW LA

Charlton Farm

HAMMER LANE

54

D 76 E 77 F

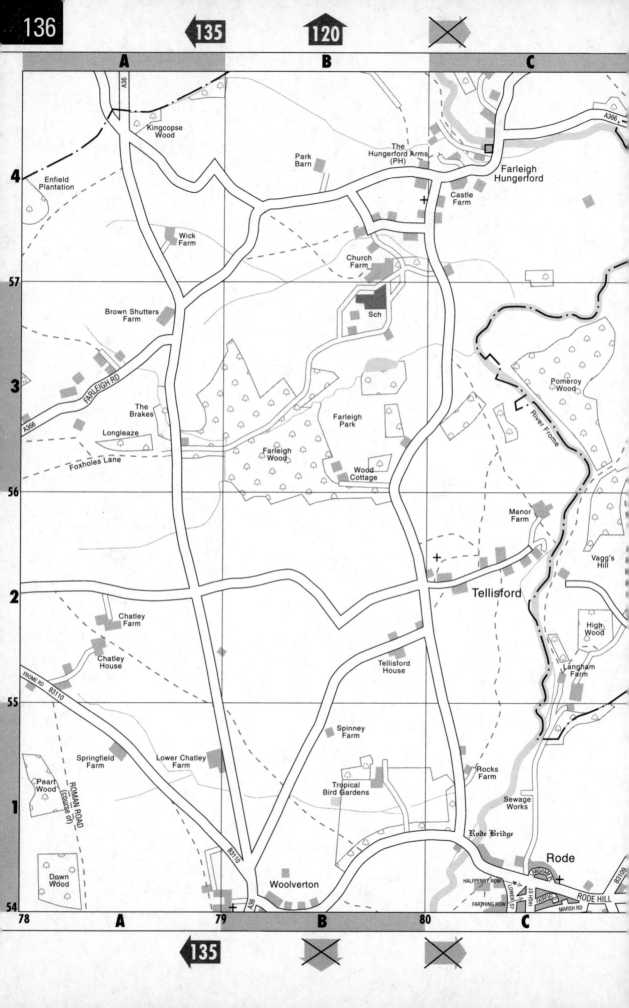

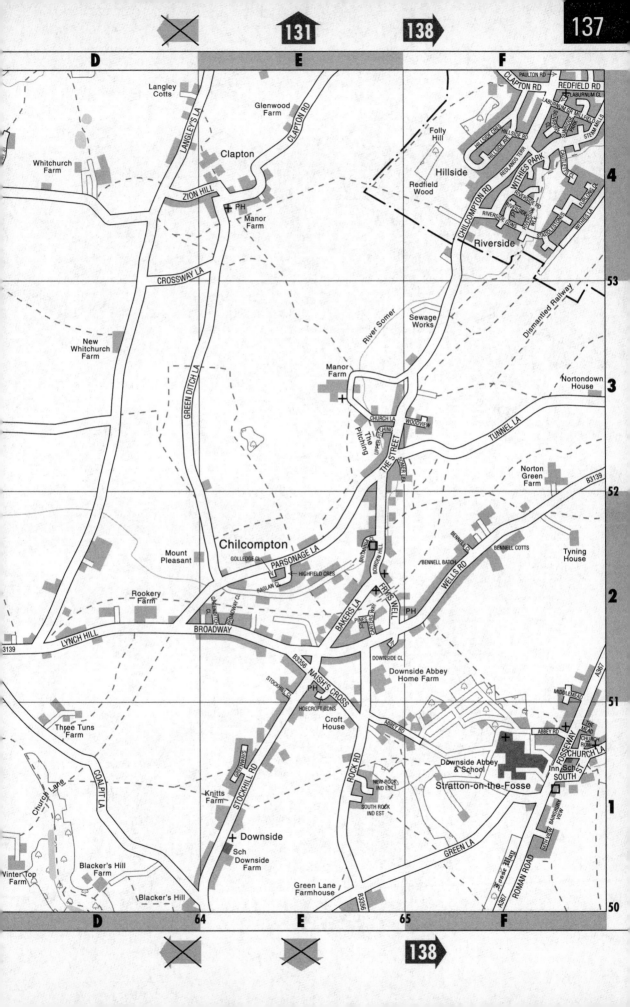

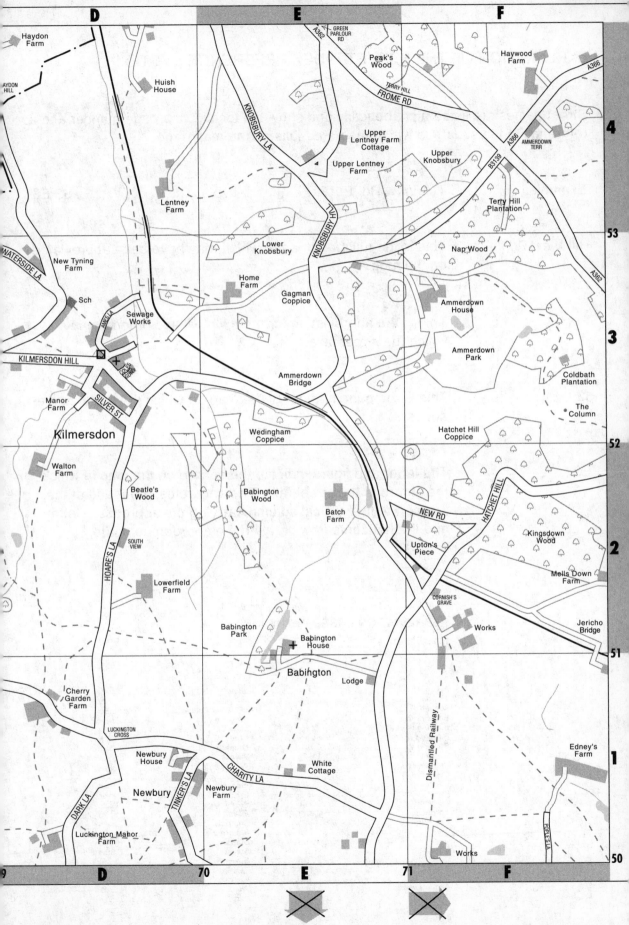

EXPLANATION OF THE STREET INDEX REFERENCE SYSTEM

Street names are listed alphabetically and show the locality, the page number and a reference to the square in which the name falls on the map page.

Example: Hill View Rd. Puck...53 E3

Hill View Rd   This is the full street name, which may have been abbreviated on the map.

Puck   This is the abbreviation for the town, village or locality in which the street falls.

53   This is the page number of the map on which the street name appears.

E3   The letter and figure indicate the square on the map in which the centre of the street falls. The square can be found at the junction of the vertical column carrying the appropriate letter and the horizontal row carrying the appropriate figure.

ABBREVIATIONS USED IN THE INDEX
Road Names

Approach	App	Grove	Gr
Arcade	Arc	Heights	Hts
Avenue	Ave	Industrial Estate	Ind Est
Boulevard	Bvd	Junction	Junc
Buildings	Bldgs	Lane	La
Business Park	Bsns Pk	North	N
Broadway	Bwy	Orchard	Orch
By-Pass	By-Ps	Parade	Par
Causeway	Cswy	Passage	Pas
Circle	Circ	Place	Pl
Circus	Cir	Pleasant	Plea
Close	Cl	Precinct	Prec
Common	Comm	Promenade	Prom
Corner	Cnr	Road	Rd
Cottages	Cotts	South	S
Court	Ct	Square	Sq
Courtyard	Ctyd	Stairs	Strs
Crescent	Cres	Steps	Stps
Drive	Dri	Street, Saint	St
Drove	Dro	Terrace	Terr
East	E	Walk	Wlk
Embankment	Emb	West	W
Esplanade	Espl	Yard	Yd
Gardens	Gdns		

Key to abbreviations of Town, Village and Rural locality names used in the index of street names.

Name	Abbr	Page	Grid
Abbots Leigh	Ab Lei	62	A4
Acton Turville	A Tur	42	C3
Almondsbury	Alm	24	A3
Alveston	Alve	15	D2
Aust	Aust	13	D3
Avonmouth	Avon	33	E1
Axbridge	Axb	125	D1
Backwell	Back	76	A3
Badgworth	Badg	123	F1
Banwell	Ban	107	D1
Barrow Gurney	Ba Gu	77	F3
Bath	Bath	102	B3
Batheaston	Bathe	85	F2
Bathford	Bathf	86	B1
Berrow	Berr	121	D1
Bishop Sutton	Bi Sut	113	E2
Bitton	Bitt	82	C4
Blagdon	Blag	110	C1
Bleadon	Blea	122	B3
Box	Box	86	C2
Bristol	Bris	63	E3
Brockley	Brock	75	E1
Burton	Burt	43	D2
Butcombe	But	111	D4
Charfield	Char	11	D3
Charlcombe	Charl	84	C2
Cheddar	Ched	125	F2
Chew Magna	Ch Mag	96	B2
Chew Stoke	Ch St	112	B4
Chilcompton	Chil	137	D1
Chipping Sodbury	Ch Sod	28	B1
Churchill	Chur	108	C2
Clevedon	Cleve	57	D2
Clutton	Clut	114	C2
Cold Ashton	Co Ash	68	C3
Colerne	Col	70	C2
Compton Bishop	Co Bi	124	A2
Compton Dando	Co Dan	98	B3
Compton Martin	Co Mar	128	A3
Congresbury	Cong	91	F2
Corston	Cor	100	A4
Cromhall	Crom	10	A1
Didmarton	Did	20	C3
Dodington	Dod	41	D2
Doynton	Doyn	54	A1
Dundry	Dun	78	B1
Dyrham	Dyrh	54	B2
East Harptree	E Harp	128	C2
Easton in Gordano	E in G	47	D2
Englishcombe	Engl	100	C1
Falfield	Falf	9	F4
Farmborough	Farm	116	A3
Faulkland	Faulk	134	B1
Frampton Cotterell	Fr Cot	38	A4
Great Badminton	Gr Bad	30	C1
Grittleton	Grit	43	F3
Hawkesbury Upton	H Up	20	A1
Hillesley	Hill	19	E4
Hinton Blewett	Hin Ble	129	F3
Hinton Charterhouse	Hin Cha	119	F1
Holcombe	Hol	138	B1
Horton	Hort	29	E3
Iron Acton	Ir Act	26	B2
Kelston	Kel	83	E2
Keynsham	Keyn	81	F2
Kilmersdon	Kilm	139	D3
Kingston Seymour	K Sey	73	E1
Kingswood	Kings	11	F2
Kingswood	Kingsw	65	E4
Limpley Stoke	Li St	119	F4
Litton	Litt	129	F1
Locking	Lock	106	A2
Long Ashton	Lo Ash	62	A1
Luckington	Luck	31	F2
Lympsham	Lymp	122	A1
Mangotsfield	Mang	51	F4
Marksbury	Marks	99	D1
Marshfield	Marsh	69	F4
Midsomer Norton	Mid No	132	A2
Monkton Farleigh	Mon Far	103	F4
Nailsea	Nail	59	E2
Newport	Newp	4	A4
North Nibley	N Nib	5	E2
North Wraxall	N Wrax	56	C2
Norton St Philip	N St P	135	F2
Oldbury-on-Severn	O-on-S	7	E3
Olveston	Olve	14	A2
Paulton	Paul	131	D3
Peasedown St John	P St J	133	E4
Pensford	Pens	97	F2
Pilning	Piln	22	B4
Portbury	Portb	46	B2
Portishead	Portis	45	D2
Priddy	Priddy	127	E1
Priston	Pris	117	D3
Pucklechurch	Puck	53	D3
Puxton	Pux	90	B2
Radstock	Rad	132	C1
Rockhampton	Rock	8	C4
Rode	Rode	136	C1
Shipham	Ship	125	F4
Siston	Sist	52	C2
Southstoke	Sosto	118	C4
Stinchcombe	Stin	5	D4
Stoke Gifford	St Gif	36	C2
Ston Easton	Ston E	130	C1
Stone	Stone	3	F2
Tellisford	Tell	136	C2
Thornbury	Thorn	8	C1
Timsbury	Tims	116	A1
Tormarton	Tor	41	F1
Tytherington	Tyth	16	B3
Wellow	Well	118	B1
Westerleigh	West	39	D2
Weston in Gordano	W in G	44	C1
Weston-Super-Mare	W-S-M	104	B4
Westwood	Westw	120	C2
Whitchurch	Whit	80	B2
Wick	Wick	67	E3
Wick St Lawrence	W St L	89	D4
Wickwar	Wickw	18	A3
Winford	Win	94	C4
Winscombe	Winsc	125	D4
Winsley	Winsl	120	C2
Winterbourne	Wint	37	F3
Wotton-under-Edge	W-u-E	11	F4
Wraxall	Wrax	60	B2
Wrington	Wring	92	C1
Yate	Yate	27	E1
Yatton	Yatt	91	E4

5c Bsns Centre. Cleve 57 D1
Abbey Church Yd. Bath 102 A3
Abbey Cl. Keyn 81 F3
Abbey Green. Bath 102 A3
Abbey La. Hi Cha 120 A2
Abbey Park. Keyn 81 F3
Abbey Rd. Bris 48 C4
Abbey Rd. Chil 137 E1
Abbey Rd. Chil 137 F1
Abbey St. Bath 102 A3
Abbey St. Kings 11 F3
Abbey View Gdns. Bath 102 A3
Abbey View. Bath 102 A3
Abbey View. Mid No 133 D2
Abbeydale. Wint 37 F3
Abbeygate St. Bath 102 A3
Abbeywood Dr. Bris 48 B3
Abbot's Cl. W-S-M 89 D2
Abbots Ave. Kingsw 65 E2
Abbots Cl. Bris 80 A2
Abbots Horn. Nail 59 E1
Abbots Leigh Rd. Ab Lei ... 62 B4
Abbots Leigh Rd. Lo Ash ... 62 B4
Abbots Rd. Kingsw 65 E1
Abbots Way. Bris 49 F3
Abbotsbury Rd. Nail 59 E1
Abbotsford Rd. Bris 49 D1
Abbotswood. Kingsw 65 E4
Abbotswood. Yate 39 E4
Abbott Rd. Piln 22 A3
Abbotts Farm Cl. Paul 131 E3
Aberdeen Rd. Bris 63 D4
Abingdon Gdns. Bath 118 B4
Abingdon Rd. Bris 51 D2
Ableton La. Avon 33 F4
Ableton La. Piln 22 A3
Ableton Wlk. Bris 48 B3
Abraham Cl. Bris 64 A4
Abson Rd. Wick 53 E2
Acacia Ave. Kingsw 51 E2
Acacia Ave. W-S-M 105 D4
Acacia Cl. Kingsw 51 E2
Acacia Ct. Keyn 81 E2
Acacia Gr. Bath 101 E2
Acacia Rd. Kingsw 51 E2
Acacia Rd. Rad 132 C1
Accommodation Rd. Blea ... 121 F3
Acid Rd. Avon 33 E2
Acorn Gr. Bris 78 C3
Acraman's Rd. Bris 63 E2
Acrebush Cl. Bris 79 D3
Acton Rd. Bris 51 D2
Adams Cl. P St J 133 E4
Addicot Rd. W-S-M 104 C3
Addiscombe Rd. Bris 80 A3
Addiscombe Rd. W-S-M 104 C2
Addison Rd. Bris 63 F2
Adelaide Pl. Bris 50 C2
Adelaide Pl. Bris 64 A4
Admiral's Wlk. Portis 45 D3
Agate St. Bris 63 D2
Aiken St. Bris 64 A3
Ainslie's Belvedere. Bath .. 101 F4
Aintree Dr. Mang 37 F1
Air Balloon Rd. Bris 65 D4
Airport Rd. Bris 80 A4
Aisecombe Way. W-S-M 105 E3
Akeman Way. Avon 47 E4
Alard Rd. Bris 79 F4
Albany Gate. St Gif 36 C4
Albany Rd. Bath 101 E3
Albany Rd. Bris 49 F1
Albany St. Bris 65 E4
Albany Way. Kingsw 66 B3
Albermarle Row. Bris 62 C3
Albert Ave. P St J 133 E4
Albert Ave. W-S-M 104 C3
Albert Cres. Bris 64 A3
Albert Gr. Bris 64 C4
Albert Par. Bris 64 B4
Albert Park Pl. Bris 49 F1
Albert Park. Bris 49 F1
Albert Pl. Bris 49 D4
Albert Pl. Bris 63 E2
Albert Quadrant. W-S-M 104 C4
Albert Rd. Bris 64 A2
Albert Rd. Cleve 57 E2
Albert Rd. Keyn 81 F3
Albert Rd. Kingsw 65 E3
Albert Rd. Mang 51 E2
Albert Rd. Piln 22 A3
Albert Rd. Portis 45 E3
Albert Rd. W-S-M 104 C3
Albert St. Bris 64 A4
Albert Terr. Bath 101 E3
Albert Terr. Bris 50 C2
Alberton Rd. Bris 50 C3
Albion Cl. Mang 51 F3
Albion Pl. Bris 50 A1
Albion St. Bris 64 B4
Alburys. Wring 92 B2
Alcove Rd. Bris 50 C2
Alder Dr. Bris 50 C1
Alder Terr. Rad 132 C1
Aldercombe Rd. Bris 48 B4
Alderdown Cl. Bris 48 A4
Alderley Rd. Bath 101 D2

Alderley Rd. Hill 19 E4
Aldermoor Way. Kingsw 65 F2
Aldernay Ave. Bris 64 C2
Alders The. Bris 37 D1
Alderton Rd. Grit 43 E3
Alderton Rd. Bris 49 F4
Aldwick Ave. Bris 79 E2
Aldwick La. Blag 110 B4
Aldwick La. But 110 B4
Aldwick La. Wring 110 B4
Alex Ricketts Cl. Bath 100 C3
Alexander Way. Yatt 91 D4
Alexandra Cl. Kingsw 51 E2
Alexandra Gdns. Kingsw 51 E2
Alexandra Par. W-S-M 104 C4
Alexandra Park. Bris 49 E1
Alexandra Park. Bris 50 C2
Alexandra Park. Paul 131 F3
Alexandra Pl. Kingsw 51 E2
Alexandra Rd. Bath 102 A3
Alexandra Rd. Bris 49 E4
Alexandra Rd. Bris 63 D4
Alexandra Rd. Bris 78 C4
Alexandra Rd. Cleve 57 E2
Alexandra Rd. Fr Cot 38 B4
Alexandra Rd. Kingsw 65 E3
Alexandra Terr. Paul 131 F4
Alexandra Way. Thorn 8 A2
Alford Rd. Bris 64 B1
Alfred Hill. Bris 63 E4
Alfred Lovell Gdns. Kingsw . 66 A2
Alfred Par. Bris 63 E4
Alfred Pl. Bris 63 E4
Alfred Rd. Bris 49 D2
Alfred Rd. Bris 63 E2
Alfred St. Bath 101 F4
Alfred St. Bris 64 A3
Alfred St. Bris 64 B4
Alfred St. W-S-M 104 C4
Algars Dr. Ir Act 26 C2
Algiers St. Bris 63 E2
Alison Gdns. Back 76 A4
All Hallows Rd. Bris 64 A4
All Saints La. Cleve 57 F2
All Saints' La. Bris 63 E3
All Saints' Rd. Bath 101 F4
All Saints' Rd. Bris 49 D1
All Saints' Rd. W-S-M 87 F1
All Saints' St. Bris 63 E4
Allanmead Rd. Bris 80 A4
Allengrove La. Luck 31 E2
Allens La. Wins 125 E4
Aller Par. W-S-M 105 D1
Aller. W-S-M 105 D1
Allerton Cres. Bris 80 A2
Allerton Gdns. Bris 80 A3
Allerton Rd. Bris 80 A2
Allfoxton Rd. Bris 50 A2
Allington Dr. Kingsw 65 F2
Allington Gdns. Nail 75 E4
Allington Rd. Bris 63 E3
Allison Ave. Bris 64 C2
Allison Rd. Bris 64 C2
Alma Cl. Kingsw 65 F4
Alma Pl. Well 118 B1
Alma Rd. Bris 63 D4
Alma Rd. Kingsw 51 F1
Alma Road Ave. Bris 63 D4
Alma St. Bris 49 D1
Alma St. W-S-M 104 C4
Alma Vale Rd. Bris 63 D4
Almeda Rd. Bris 65 D3
Almond Cl. W-S-M 89 D1
Almond Way. Mang 51 F3
Almondsbury Bsns Centre.
  St Gif 24 B2
Almorah Rd. Bris 63 F2
Alpha Centre The. Yate 27 E2
Alpha Rd. Bris 63 E2
Alpine Cl. Paul 131 F2
Alpine Gdns. Bath 102 A4
Alpine Rd. Bris 50 B1
Alpine Rd. Paul 131 F2
Alsop Rd. Kingsw 51 E1
Alton Rd. Bris 49 F3
Altringham Rd. Bris 64 B4
Alverstoke. Bris 79 F4
Alveston Hill. Thorn 15 D3
Alveston Rd. Olve 14 B2
Alveston Wlk. Bris 48 A4
Alwins Ct. Kingsw 65 F2
Amberey Rd. W-S-M 104 C3
Amberlands Cl. Back 76 A4
Amberley Cl. Keyn 81 F2
Amberley Cl. Mang 51 E4
Amberley Gdns. Nail 59 E1
Amberley Rd. Mang 51 E4
Amberley Rd. St Gif 36 A4
Amberley Way. Wickw 18 A2
Amble Cl. Kingsw 65 F4
Ambleside Ave. Bris 35 D1
Ambleside Rd. Bath 101 E1
Ambra Vale E. Bris 63 D3
Ambra Vale S. Bris 63 D3
Ambra Vale W. Bris 63 D3
Ambra Vale. Bris 63 D3
Ambrose Rd. Bris 63 D3
Ambury. Bath 101 F3

Amercombe Wlk. Bris 80 B4
Amery La. Bath 102 A3
Ames La. Kilm 139 D3
Amesbury Dr. Blea 122 A3
Ammerdown Terr. Faulk 139 F4
Anchor La. Bris 63 E3
Anchor Rd. Bath 84 A1
Anchor Rd. Bris 63 E3
Anchor Rd. Kingsw 52 A1
Anchor Way. E in G 47 E2
Andereach Cl. Bris 80 A4
Andover Rd. Bris 63 F1
Andruss Dr. Dun 78 B1
Angers Rd. Bris 64 A2
Anglesea Pl. Bris 49 D1
Annandale Ave. W-S-M 88 C1
Anson Ct. Keyn 82 B1
Anstey St. Bris 50 B1
Anstey's Rd. Kingsw 65 E3
Antona Ct. Bris 47 E4
Antona Dr. Bris 47 E4
Antrim Rd. Bris 49 D3
Anvil Rd. Yatt 74 C1
Anvil St. Bris 63 F3
Apex Ct. St Gif 24 B2
Apperley Cl. Yate 39 E4
Apple Tree Dr. Wins 125 D4
Appleby Wlk. Bris 79 E4
Applecroft. Well 133 F3
Appledore Cl. Bris 80 A4
Applegate. Bris 35 D2
Appletree Ct. W-S-M 89 D1
Apseleys Mead. St Gif 24 B1
Apsley Cl. W-S-M 88 B1
Apsley Rd. Bris 49 D1
Apsley St. Bris 50 B2
Arbutus Dr. Bris 48 B4
Arcade The. Bris 63 F4
Arch Cl. Lo Ash 61 F1
Archer Cl. Kingsw 65 F2
Archer Wlk. Bris 80 C3
Archfield Rd. Bris 49 E1
Archgrove. Lo Ash 61 F1
Archway St. Bath 102 A3
Arden Cl. St Gif 36 C3
Arden Cl. W-S-M 88 C2
Ardenton Wlk. Bris 35 D2
Ardern Cl. Bris 48 A4
Argus Rd. Bris 63 E2
Argyle Ave. Bris 50 B1
Argyle Ave. W-S-M 104 C2
Argyle Dr. Yate 27 F2
Argyle Pl. Bris 63 D3
Argyle Rd. Bris 51 D1
Argyle Rd. Bris 63 F4
Argyle Rd. Cleve 57 E3
Argyle St. Bath 102 A3
Argyle St. Bris 50 B1
Argyle St. Bris 63 E2
Argyle Terr. Bath 101 E3
Arley Cotts. Bris 49 E1
Arley Hill. Bris 49 E1
Arley Park. Bris 49 E1
Arley Terr. Bris 50 C1
Arlingham Way. Bris 23 F1
Arlington Rd. Bath 101 E3
Arlington Rd. Bris 64 B3
Arlington Villas. Bris 63 D4
Armada Pl. Bris 49 F1
Armes Ct. Bath 102 A3
Armidale Ave. Bris 49 F1
Armoury Sq. Bris 64 A4
Armstrong Ct. Yate 27 E2
Armstrong Way. Yate 27 D2
Arnall Dr. Bris 34 C1
Arneside Rd. Bris 35 E1
Arno's St. Bris 64 A2
Arnold Ct. Ch Sod 28 A1
Arnor Cl. W-S-M 89 D2
Arrowfield Cl. Bris 80 A1
Arthur Skemp Cl. Bris 64 A4
Arthur St. Bris 64 A3
Arthur St. Bris 64 B4
Arthurswood Rd. Bris 79 D2
Arundel Cl. Bris 79 D3
Arundel Rd. Bath 85 D1
Arundel Rd. Bris 49 E2
Arundel Rd. Cleve 57 E2
Arundel Wlk. Keyn 81 E3
Arundell Ct. W-S-M 104 C4
Arundell Rd. W-S-M 87 F1
Ascot Cl. Bris 35 F1
Ascot Cl. Mang 37 F1
Ash Cl. St Gif 36 B4
Ash Cl. Wins 108 A1
Ash Cl. Yate 27 E2
Ash Gr. Bath 101 E2
Ash Gr. Bris 51 E2
Ash Gr. Cleve 57 F2
Ash Gr. W-S-M 104 C1
Ash Hayes Dr. Nail 59 F1
Ash Hayes Rd. Nail 59 F1
Ash La. Alm 23 E1
Ash Rd. Bris 49 F3
Ash Ridge Rd. St Gif 24 A2
Ash Tree Cl. Blea 122 B3
Ash Tree Ct. Rad 132 C1

Ash Wlk. Bris 35 D2
Ashbourne Cl. Kingsw 66 B3
Ashburton Rd. Bris 35 E1
Ashbury Dr. W-S-M 88 A1
Ashcombe Cres. Kingsw 66 B3
Ashcombe Gdns. W-S-M .. 105 D4
Ashcombe Park Rd. W-S-M . 88 A1
Ashcombe Rd. W-S-M 104 C4
Ashcott. Bris 79 F4
Ashcroft Ave. Keyn 81 E3
Ashcroft Rd. Bris 48 B4
Ashcroft. W-S-M 105 D1
Ashdene Ave. Bris 50 B2
Ashdene Rd. W-S-M 105 D4
Ashdown Rd. Portis 45 D3
Ashel's Batch. Litt 129 E1
Asher La. Bris 63 F4
Ashes La. Hi Cha 120 A2
Ashfield Pl. Bris 49 F1
Ashfield Rd. Bris 63 D2
Ashford Dr. W-S-M 105 D1
Ashford Rd. Bath 101 E2
Ashford Rd. Bris 36 A4
Ashford Rd. Wring 93 F2
Ashford Way. Kingsw 66 A4
Ashgrove Ave. Ab Lei 62 A4
Ashgrove Ave. Bris 49 F2
Ashgrove Rd. Bris 49 D1
Ashgrove Rd. Bris 49 F2
Ashgrove Rd. Bris 63 D2
Ashgrove. P St J 133 E4
Ashgrove. Thorn 8 B1
Ashland Rd. Bris 79 D2
Ashleigh Cl. Paul 131 F3
Ashleigh Cl. W-S-M 105 D4
Ashleigh Cres. Yatt 91 D4
Ashleigh Rd. W-S-M 105 D4
Ashleigh Rd. Yatt 91 D4
Ashley Ave. Bath 101 E4
Ashley Cl. Bris 49 F2
Ashley Court Rd. Bris 49 F1
Ashley Down Rd. Bris 49 F1
Ashley Grove Rd. Bris 49 F1
Ashley Grove Rd. Bris 50 A1
Ashley Hill. Bris 49 F1
Ashley La. Blag 110 A3
Ashley La. Winsl 120 C4
Ashley La. Wring 110 A3
Ashley Par. Bris 49 F1
Ashley Park. Bris 49 F2
Ashley Rd. Bathf 86 B1
Ashley Rd. Bris 49 F1
Ashley Rd. Cleve 57 D1
Ashley St. Bris 50 A1
Ashley Trading Est. Bris .. 49 F1
Ashley. Kingsw 65 F4
Ashman Cl. Bris 64 A4
Ashmans Gate. Paul 131 F3
Ashmead Rd Ind Est. Keyn . 82 A3
Ashmead Rd. Keyn 82 A3
Ashmead Way. Bris 62 C3
Ashmead. Clut 114 C1
Ashton Ave. Bris 63 D3
Ashton Cl. Cleve 57 D1
Ashton Cres. Nail 59 E1
Ashton Dr. Bris 62 C1
Ashton Gate Rd. Bris 63 D2
Ashton Gate Terr. Bris 63 D2
Ashton Rd. Bris 62 C2
Ashton Rd. Lo Ash 62 C2
Ashton Vale Rd. Bris 62 C2
Ashton Way. Keyn 81 F3
Ashton. Bris 37 E1
Ashvale Cl. Nail 60 A1
Ashville Rd. Bris 63 D2
Ashwell Cl. Bris 80 C3
Ashwicke Rd. Marsh 70 A2
Ashwicke. Bris 80 A3
Ashwood. E Harp 128 C2
Aspen Cl. Col 70 C3
Aspley Cl. Bath 101 D4
Aspley Rd. Bath 101 D4
Assembly Rooms La. Bris ... 63 E3
Aston Gate Underpass. Bris 62 C2
Astry Cl. Bris 34 A1
Atchley St. Bris 64 A4
Atherston. Kingsw 66 B3
Athlone Wlk. Bris 63 F1
Atholl Cl. W-S-M 88 C2
Atkins Cl. Bris 80 C3
Atlantic Ct. W-S-M 87 E1
Atlantic Rd S. W-S-M 87 E1
Atlantic Rd. Avon 47 E4
Atlantic Rd. W-S-M 87 E1
Atlas Cl. Bris 51 D1
Atlas Rd. Bris 63 F2
Atlas St. Bris 64 A3
Atwell Dr. St Gif 24 A1
Atwood Dr. Bris 34 A1
Aubrey Meads. Bitt 82 C4
Aubrey Rd. Bris 63 D2
Auburn Ave. Kingsw 66 A2
Auburn Rd. Bris 49 D1
Auckland Cl. W-S-M 104 C2
Audley Ave. Bath 101 E4
Audley Cl. Bath 101 E4
Audley Gr. Bath 101 E4
Audley Park Rd. Bath 101 E4

Audrey Wlk. Bris 49 E4
Aust Rd. Aust 13 F3
Aust Rd. Olve 13 F3
Aust Rd. Piln 12 B2
Austen Dr. W-S-M 89 D2
Austen Gr. Bris 50 A4
Avalon Cl. Yatt 74 A1
Avalon House. Nail 59 E1
Avalon Rd. Bris 65 D3
Avebury Rd. Bris 62 C1
Avening Cl. Nail 75 F4
Avening Rd. Bris 65 D4
Avenue The. Back 76 A4
Avenue The. Bath 102 B3
Avenue The. Bath 102 C3
Avenue The. Bris 48 C2
Avenue The. Bris 49 D1
Avenue The. Bris 49 F2
Avenue The. Bris 64 C4
Avenue The. Cleve 57 F3
Avenue The. Keyn 81 F3
Avenue The. St Gif 24 A1
Avenue The. St Gif 36 B3
Avenue The. Tims 116 A1
Avenue The. Wins 125 E4
Avenue The. Yate 27 E1
Avenue The. Yatt 91 D4
Averay Rd. Bris 50 B2
Avon Bsns Pk. Bris 51 D2
Avon Cl. Keyn 81 F3
Avon Cl. W-S-M 104 C1
Avon Cres. Bris 63 D3
Avon Cres. Wickw 18 A3
Avon Ct. Bathe 86 A2
Avon Gorge Ind Est. Avon . 47 E4
Avon Gr. Bris 48 B1
Avon La. Keyn 82 C2
Avon Mill La. Keyn 81 F3
Avon Park. Bath 101 D4
Avon Park. Bris 64 B4
Avon Rd. Char 11 D2
Avon Rd. E in G 47 E3
Avon Rd. Keyn 81 F3
Avon Rise. Luck 31 F2
Avon Riverside Est. Avon .. 47 E4
Avon St. Bath 101 F3
Avon St. Bris 63 F3
Avon Trading Est. Bris ... 64 A3
Avon Vale. Bris 48 B2
Avon Valley Bsns Pk. Bris . 64 C3
Avon View. Kingsw 65 D3
Avon Way. Bris 48 B2
Avon Way. Portis 45 E3
Avon Way. Thorn 15 E4
Avon Wlk. Bris 79 D3
Avonbank Ind Centre. Avon . 47 E4
Avonbridge Trading Est.
  Avon 33 E1
Avondale Bldgs. Bath 85 D1
Avondale Pl. Bathe 85 F2
Avondale Rd. Bath 101 D3
Avondale Rd. Bris 64 B4
Avondown Cl. Bris 35 E1
Avondown Ct. Bris 63 E1
Avonlea. Kingsw 65 E3
Avonleaze. Bris 48 A3
Avonleigh Ct. Bris 63 D1
Avonleigh Rd. Bris 63 D1
Avonmouth Rd. Avon 47 E4
Avonmouth Way. Avon 33 E1
Avonmouth Way. Bris 34 C2
Avonside Rd. Bris 64 B3
Avonside Way. Bris 64 C3
Avonsmere Residential Pk.
  Bris 36 B2
Avonwood Cl. Bris 47 F3
Awdelett Cl. Bris 34 A1
Awkley La. Olve 13 F1
Awkward Hill. But 111 E3
Axbridge Cl. Nail 75 F4
Axbridge Moor Dro. Axb .. 125 E1
Axbridge Rd. Bath 102 A1
Axbridge Rd. Bris 63 F1
Axbridge Rd. Ched 125 F1
Axe Cl. W-S-M 105 D3
Axford Way. P St J 133 E4
Axis. Bris 79 E3
Aycote Cl. W-S-M 88 B1
Ayford La. Marsh 69 F2
Aylesbury Cres. Bris 63 D1
Aylesbury Rd. Bris 63 D1
Aylmer Cres. Bris 80 A3
Aylminton Wlk. Bris 34 A1
Ayr St. Bath 101 E3
Aztec Centre The. St Gif . 24 A1
Aztec West. St Gif 24 A1

Back La. Axb 125 E1
Back La. E in G 47 E3
Back La. K Sey 73 D2
Back La. Litt 129 D1
Back La. Litt 129 F1
Back La. Marsh 69 F4
Back La. Wickw 18 A3
Back Of Kingsdown Par. Bris 63 E4
Back Rd. Bris 63 D2
Back St. H Up 20 A2

Back St. W-S-M 104 C4
Back Stoke La. Bris 48 C3
Backfields La. Bris 63 F4
Backfields. Bris 63 F4
Backwell Bow. Back 60 B1
Backwell Comm. Back 76 A4
Backwell Hill Rd. Back 76 C2
Backwell Wlk. Bris 78 C4
Baden Hill Rd. Tyth 16 B3
Baden Rd. Bris 64 B4
Baden Rd. Kingsw 66 A4
Badenham Gr. Bris 47 F4
Bader Cl. Yate 27 E2
Badger's La. Alm 23 E1
Badgers Cl. St Gif 24 B2
Badgers Rise. Portis 44 C2
Badgers Wlk. Bris 64 B1
Badgeworth. Yate 39 E3
Badminton Centre The. Yate 27 E1
Badminton Ct. Yate 27 E1
Badminton Gdns. Bath 101 E4
Badminton Rd. Bris 49 F1
Badminton Rd. Ch Sod 40 C4
Badminton Rd. Fr Cot 38 B3
Badminton Rd. Mang 51 F4
Badminton Rd. West 38 B3
Badminton Rd. Yate 27 E1
Badminton Trading Est. Yate 27 D1
Badminton Wlk. Mang 51 F4
Badminton. Bris 37 E1
Baggridge Hill. Well 134 C4
Baglyn Ave. Kingsw 51 F2
Bagnell Cl. Bris 80 C3
Bagnell Rd. Bris 80 C3
Bagstone Rd. Wickw 16 C2
Bailbrook Gr. Bath 85 E2
Bailbrook La. Bath 85 E2
Baildon Cres. W-S-M 105 D2
Baildon Ct. W-S-M 104 C2
Baildon Rd. W-S-M 105 D2
Baileys Court Rd. St Gif 36 C4
Baileys Ct Rd. St Gif 37 D3
Baileys Ct. St Gif 36 C3
Bailiffs Cl. Axb 125 E1
Bailiffs' Wall. Axb 125 E1
Bainsbury View. 137 F1
Baker Cl. Cleve 73 D4
Baker St. W-S-M 104 C4
Baker's Bldgs. Wring 92 B1
Bakers Par. Tims 116 A1
Bakers La. Chil 137 E2
Bakers La. Wring 109 E4
Bakersfield. Kingsw 66 A2
Balaclava Rd. Bris 50 C2
Baldwin St. Bris 63 E3
Balfour Rd. Bris 63 D2
Ballance St. Bath 101 F4
Ballast La. Avon 33 F1
Balls Barn La. Ban 90 A1
Balmain St. Bris 64 A4
Balmoral Cl. St Gif 36 B2
Balmoral Ct. Mang 52 A3
Balmoral Rd. Bris 49 F1
Balmoral Rd. Keyn 81 F2
Balmoral Rd. Kingsw 65 F1
Balmoral Rd. W-S-M 88 B3
Baltic Pl. E in G 47 E2
Bamfield. Bris 80 A3
Bampton Cl. Bris 79 D4
Bampton. W-S-M 88 C1
Banfield Cl. Bris 48 A4
Bangor Gr. Bris 64 C3
Bangrove Wlk. Bris 47 F4
Banister Gr. Bris 79 E4
Bank Pl. E in G 47 E2
Bank Rd. Avon 33 E4
Bank Rd. Kingsw 65 E4
Bank Rd. Piln 22 C3
Banks Cl. Cleve 73 E4
Bankside Rd. Bris 64 B2
Bankside. Mang 51 F2
Banner Rd. Bris 49 F1
Bannerdown Cl. Bathe 86 A2
Bannerdown Dr. Bathe 86 A2
Bannerdown Rd. Bathe 86 B3
Bannerleigh La. Lo Ash 62 C3
Bannerleigh Rd. Lo Ash 62 C3
Bannerman Rd. Bris 64 A4
Bannetts Tree Cres. Alve ... 15 D3
Bantock Cl. Bris 79 E3
Bantry Rd. Bris 79 F4
Banwell Cl. Bris 79 D4
Banwell Cl. Keyn 82 A1
Banwell Rd. Ban 123 F4
Banwell Rd. Bath 118 B4
Banwell Rd. Bris 63 D2
Banwell Rd. Lock 106 A2
Banwell Rd. Wins 123 F4
Banwell Rd. Wins 124 C4
Baptist St. Bris 50 A1
Barberry Farm Rd. Yatt 74 A1
Barbour Gdns. Bris 79 E2
Barbour Rd. Bris 79 E2
Barcroft Cl. Bris 65 E4
Barker Wlk. Bris 50 A1
Barley Cl. Mang 52 A3
Barley Croft. Bris 48 C3

Barn End. Marsh 70 A4
Barn Hill. Well 133 F3
Barn La. Pens 115 D4
Barn Owl Way. St Gif 36 C3
Barn Pool. Ship 125 F4
Barnabas St. Bris 49 F1
Barnaby Cl. Mid No 132 A1
Barnack Trading Est. Bris ... 63 E1
Barnard Wlk. Keyn 81 E2
Barnard's Cl. Yatt 91 E4
Barnes St. Bris 64 B4
Barnfield Way. Bathe 86 A2
Barnhill Rd. Ch Sod 28 A1
Barns Cl. Ba Gu 77 F2
Barns Cl. Nail 59 F1
Barnstable House. Bris 63 F4
Barnstaple Rd. Bris 79 F4
Barnstaple Wlk. Bris 79 F4
Barnwood Rd. Yate 39 E4
Barossa Pl. Bris 63 E3
Barrack's La. Bris 47 E4
Barratt St. Bris 50 B1
Barrington Cl. Kingsw 51 F1
Barrington Ct. Bris 63 F2
Barrington Ct. Kingsw 51 F1
Barrow Court La. Ba Gu 77 D3
Barrow Court La. Back 77 D3
Barrow Hill Cres. Bris 47 E4
Barrow Hill Rd. Bris 47 E3
Barrow Hill. Wick 67 D3
Barrow La. Ba Gu 77 F1
Barrow La. Win 94 C4
Barrow Rd. Bath 101 E1
Barrow Rd. Bris 64 A4
Barrow Rd. Lock 105 F1
Barrow St. Ba Gu 77 E3
Barrow St. Lo Ash 77 E3
Barrowmead Dr. Bris 47 F4
Barrows The. Bris 79 D2
Barrows The. W-S-M 105 E4
Barrs Court Ave. Kingsw 66 A3
Barrs Court Rd. Kingsw 66 A3
Barrs Court Rd. Kingsw 66 A3
Barrs La. N Nib 5 F2
Barry Cl. Kingsw 66 B1
Barry Cl. W-S-M 105 D1
Bartlett St. Bath 101 F4
Bartlett's Rd. Bris 63 E1
Bartley St. Bris 63 E2
Barton Cl. Alve 15 D3
Barton Cl. Bris 64 C3
Barton Cl. Wint 37 F3
Barton Dro. Wins 124 B3
Barton Green. Bris 64 A4
Barton Hill Rd. Bris 64 A4
Barton Manor. Bris 64 A3
Barton Rd. .... 124 ""
Barton Rd. Bris 63 F3
Barton Rd. Co Bi 123 F3
Barton Rd. Bath 101 F3
Barton Rd. Bris 63 E4
Barton The. Blea 122 B3
Barton The. Cor 100 A4
Barton The. Kingsw 65 E2
Barton The. N St P 135 F2
Barton Vale. Bris 63 F3
Bartonia Gr. Bris 64 B1
Barwood Cl. Kingsw 65 F4
Batch La. Lymp 121 F2
Batch The. Blag 110 A2
Batch The. But 111 D4
Batch The. Ch Mag 96 A2
Batch The. Chur 108 C2
Batch The. Co Mar 128 A4
Batch The. Farm 116 A3
Batch The. Hin Cha 119 F1
Batch The. Wring 93 E4
Batch The. Yatt 91 D4
Batches The. Bris 63 D1
Batchfield La. West 53 E4
Bates Cl. Bris 64 A4
Bath Bldgs. Bris 49 F1
Bath Hill. Keyn 81 F3
Bath Hill. Well 118 B3
Bath New Rd. Mid No 132 C2
Bath Old Rd. Mid No 132 C2
Bath Rd. Bitt 82 B4
Bath Rd. Bitt 82 C4
Bath Rd. Blag 109 E2
Bath Rd. Blag 110 C1
Bath Rd. Box 86 C3
Bath Rd. Bris 64 B2
Bath Rd. Ch Sod 41 D2
Bath Rd. Chur 109 E2
Bath Rd. Col 70 C1
Bath Rd. Doyn 67 F2
Bath Rd. Farm 117 F3
Bath Rd. Keyn 82 B2
Bath Rd. Kingsw 65 F2
Bath Rd. Kingsw 66 B3
Bath Rd. N St P 135 F3
Bath Rd. P St J 133 E4
Bath Rd. Paul 131 F3
Bath Rd. Sist 66 B3
Bath Rd. Thorn 15 D4
Bath Rd. Tor 41 E2
Bath Rd. Wick 67 F2
Bath Riverside Bsns Park.

Bath 101 F3
Bath St. Bath 101 F3
Bath St. Bris 63 D2
Bath St. Bris 63 F3
Bath St. Kingsw 51 F2
Bath View. Chil 137 F1
Bathampton La. Bath 85 F1
Bathford Hill. Bathf 86 A1
Bathford Hill. Co Dan 98 C3
Bathurst Par. Bris 63 E3
Bathurst Rd. W-S-M 105 E4
Bathwell Rd. Bris 64 A2
Bathwick Hill. Bath 102 B3
Bathwick Rise. Bath 102 A4
Bathwick St. Bath 102 A4
Batley Ct. Kingsw 66 B2
Batstone Cl. Bath 85 D1
Batten Ct. Ch Sod 28 A1
Batten's La. Bris 65 D4
Battens Rd. Bris 65 D4
Battersby Way. Bris 34 C1
Battersea Rd. Bris 64 B4
Battery La. Portis 45 D4
Battery Rd. Portis 45 E3
Battle La. Ch Mag 96 A2
Battson Rd. Bris 80 C2
Baugh Gdns. Mang 37 F1
Baugh Rd. Mang 37 F1
Bay Gdns. Bris 50 B1
Bay Rd. Cleve 57 E3
Bay Tree Cl. Bris 35 F4
Bay Tree Rd. Bath 85 D1
Bay Tree Rd. Cleve 57 F1
Bayleys Dr. Kingsw 65 E3
Baynham Ct. Kingsw 65 D3
Baynton Rd. Bris 63 D2
Bayswater Ave. Bris 49 D2
Bayswater Rd. Bris 49 F4
Baytree Rd. W-S-M 88 B1
Baytree View. W-S-M 88 B1
Beach Ave. Cleve 57 E1
Beach Ave. Piln 22 A4
Beach End Rd. W-S-M 104 B1
Beach Hill. Bitt 66 C2
Beach Hill. Portis 45 E3
Beach La. Bitt 67 E1
Beach Rd E. Portis 45 E3
Beach Rd W. Portis 45 E3
Beach Rd. Piln 21 F4
Beach Rd. W St L 88 A3
Beach Rd. W-S-M 88 A2
Beach The. Cleve 57 E2
Beachgrove Gdns. Bris 51 E1
Beachgrove Rd. Bris 51 D2
Beachley Wlk. Bris 47 E4
Beacon La. Wint 37 E3
Beacon Rd. Bath 85 D1
Beaconlea. Kingsw 65 E3
Beaconsfield Rd. Bris 49 D1
Beaconsfield Rd. Bris 64 A2
Beaconsfield Rd. Bris 64 C4
Beaconsfield Rd. Cleve 57 F2
Beaconsfield Rd. W-S-M 104 C4
Beaconsfield St. Bris 64 A3
Beale Cl. Bris 80 C3
Beam St. Bris 64 B4
Bean Acre The. Bris 47 E4
Bean St. Bris 50 A1
Beanhill Cres. Alve 15 D3
Bearbridge Rd. Bris 78 C2
Beau St. Bath 101 F3
Beauchamp Rd. Bris 49 E2
Beauchamps Dr. Chil 138 A3
Beauford Sq. Bath 101 F3
Beaufort Ave. Mid No 132 A1
Beaufort Ave. Yate 27 E1
Beaufort Cl. Bris 64 B4
Beaufort Cres. St Gif 36 C2
Beaufort Ct. Mang 52 A4
Beaufort East. Bath 85 E1
Beaufort Gdns. Nail 59 E1
Beaufort Hts. Bris 64 C4
Beaufort Park. St Gif 24 B2
Beaufort Pl. Bath 85 E1
Beaufort Pl. Bris 37 D1
Beaufort Pl. Bris 64 A4
Beaufort Rd. Bris 49 D1
Beaufort Rd. Bris 49 F3
Beaufort Rd. Bris 64 C4
Beaufort Rd. Fr Cot 38 A4
Beaufort Rd. Mang 51 F3
Beaufort Rd. Mang 52 A4
Beaufort Rd. W-S-M 104 C4
Beaufort Rd. Yate 27 E1
Beaufort St. Bris 64 A4
Beaufort St. Bris 64 A4
Beaufort. Bris 37 E1
Beauley Rd. Bris 63 D3
Beaumont Cl. Kingsw 66 A2
Beaumont Cl. W-S-M 104 C2
Beaumont St. Bris 64 A4
Beaumont Terr. Bris 64 A4
Beaver Cl. Wint 37 F4
Beazer Cl. Kingsw 51 E2
Becket Ct. Puck 53 D3
Becket Dr. W-S-M 89 D2

Becket Rd. W-S-M 89 D2
Becket's La. Nail 75 F4
Beckford Gdns. Bath 102 A4
Beckford Gdns. Bris 80 A2
Beckford Rd. Bath 102 A4
Beckhampton Rd. Bath 101 E3
Beckington Rd. Bris 63 F1
Beckington Wlk. Bris 63 F1
Beckington. W-S-M 105 D1
Beckspool Rd. Bris 51 E4
Bedford Cres. Bris 49 F3
Bedford Rd. W-S-M 104 C2
Bedford St. Bath 102 A4
Bedminster Down Rd. Bris . 63 D1
Bedminster Par. Bris 63 E2
Bedminster Pl. Bris 63 E2
Bedminster Rd. Bris 63 E1
Bedwin Cl. Portis 44 C2
Beech Ave. Bath 102 C3
Beech Cl. Alve 15 D3
Beech Cl. Kingsw 66 A3
Beech Cl. Ship 125 F4
Beech Dr. Nail 60 A2
Beech Dr. Ship 125 F4
Beech Gr. Bath 101 E2
Beech Leaze. Alve 15 D3
Beech Rd. Bris 49 F3
Beech Rd. Keyn 82 C2
Beech Rd. Ship 125 F4
Beech Rd. Yatt 91 E4
Beech Terr. Rad 132 B1
Beechcroft Wlk. Bris 50 A4
Beechcroft. Dun 78 B1
Beechen Cliff Rd. Bath 101 F3
Beechen Dr. Bris 51 D2
Beeches Gr. Bris 64 B1
Beeches Ind Est. Ir Act 27 D1
Beeches The. Bath 101 E1
Beeches The. Kingsw 66 B1
Beeches The. Wins 108 A2
Beechfield Cl. Lo Ash 62 B1
Beechmont Cl. W-S-M 105 D1
Beechmont Dr. W-S-M 105 D1
Beechmount Gr. Bris 80 A4
Beechwood Ave. Kingsw 65 E3
Beechwood Ave. Lock 106 A2
Beechwood Dr. Bris 80 B4
Beechwood Dr. Portis 44 C3
Beechwood Rd. Bath 102 A1
Beechwood Rd. Bris 51 D2
Beechwood Rd. E in G 47 D2
Beechwood Rd. Nail 59 E1
Beechwood Rd. Portis 44 C3
Beehive Yd. Bath 102 A4
Beek's La. Marsh 69 E3
Beesmoor Rd. Fr Cot 38 A3
Begbrook Dr. Bris 50 C3
Begbrook La. Bris 50 C3
Begbrook Park. Bris 51 D4
Beggar Bush La. Lo Ash 61 F2
Beggar Bush La. Wrax 61 F2
Beggars Bush La. Ab Lei ... 62 A3
Beggarswell Cl. Bris 63 F4
Belfast Wlk. Bris 79 F4
Belfry Ave. Bris 65 D4
Belfry. Kingsw 66 A3
Belgrave Cres. Bath 85 D1
Belgrave Hill. Bris 49 D1
Belgrave Pl. Bris 63 D4
Belgrave Rd. Bath 85 D1
Belgrave Rd. Bris 63 D4
Belgrave Rd. W-S-M 105 D4
Bell Barn Rd. Bris 48 B3
Bell Cl. Farm 115 F3
Bell Hill Rd. Bris 65 D4
Bell Hill. Bris 50 B2
Bell Hill. N St P 135 F2
Bell La. Bris 63 E4
Bell Rd. Fr Cot 38 B3
Bell Sq. Blag 110 C2
Bell Sq. Marsh 70 A4
Bell Wlk. Wring 92 C1
Bella Vista Rd. Bath 101 F4
Bellamy Ave. Bris 79 E2
Bellamy Cl. Bris 65 D3
Belland Dr. Bris 79 F2
Belle Vue Rd. Bris 50 B1
Bellevue Cl. Kingsw 65 F4
Bellevue Cotts. Bris 63 D3
Bellevue Cres. Bris 63 D3
Bellevue Pk. Bris 64 B1
Bellevue Rd. Bris 63 D3
Bellevue Rd. Bris 65 D4
Bellevue Rd. Cleve 57 E2
Bellevue Rd. Kingsw 65 F4
Bellevue Terr. Bris 63 D3
Bellevue Terr. Bris 64 B1
Bellevue. Bris 63 D3
Bellhorse La. E Harp 128 B3
Bellhouse Wlk. Bris 34 A1
Bellifants. Farm 116 A3
Bellotts Rd. Bath 101 E3
Belluton La. Pens 97 E3
Belluton Rd. Bris 64 A2
Belmont Dr. St Gif 36 C2
Belmont Dr. Wrax 61 D2
Belmont Hill. Wrax 61 D1

Belmont Rd. Bath 102 B1
Belmont Rd. Bris 49 F2
Belmont Rd. Bris 64 B2
Belmont Rd. Wins 125 D4
Belmont St. Bris 50 A1
Belmore Gdns. Bath 101 D2
Beloe Rd. Bris 49 F3
Belroyal Ave. Bris 64 C2
Belstone Wlk. Bris 79 E4
Belton Ct. Bath 84 A1
Belton Rd. Bris 64 A4
Belton Rd. Portis 45 D3
Belvedere Cres. W-S-M 88 B1
Belvedere Rd. Bris 49 D2
Belvoir Rd. Bath 101 E3
Belvoir Rd. Bris 49 F1
Benches La. But 94 B2
Benford Cl. Bris 51 E3
Bennell Batch. Chil 137 F2
Bennell Cl. Chil 137 F2
Bennell Cotts. Chil 137 F2
Bennett La. Bath 85 D1
Bennett Rd. Bris 64 C4
Bennett St. Bath 101 F4
Bennett Way. Bris 62 C3
Bennett's Ct. Yate 28 A1
Bennett's Rd. Bath 85 E2
Bennetts Way. Cleve 57 F3
Bensaunt Gr. Bris 35 E2
Bentley Cl. Bris 79 E2
Bentley Rd. W-S-M 89 D2
Benville Ave. Bris 48 B4
Berenda Dr. Bris 66 A2
Beresford Cl. Keyn 82 C1
Beresford Gdns. Bath 84 A2
Berkeley Ave. Bris 49 E2
Berkeley Ave. Mid No 132 A1
Berkeley Ave. Bris 63 E4
Berkeley Cl. Mang 52 A4
Berkeley Cres. W-S-M 104 B1
Berkeley Gdns. Keyn 81 F2
Berkeley Gr. Bris 50 B1
Berkeley Green Rd. Bris 50 B1
Berkeley Green. Bris 37 D1
Berkeley Mead. St Gif 37 D3
Berkeley Pl. Bris 63 D4
Berkeley Rd. Bris 49 D2
Berkeley Rd. Bris 49 E3
Berkeley Rd. Bris 51 D1
Berkeley Rd. Kingsw 65 E4
Berkeley Rd. Mang 51 E3
Berkeley Sq. Bris 63 E4
Berkeley St. Bris 50 B2
Berkshire Rd. Bris 49 E2
Berlington Ct. Bris 63 F3
Berners Cl. Bris 79 E4
Berrow Wlk. Bris 63 F1
Berrows Mead. Wickw 27 D4
Berry La. Bris 49 F3
Berwick La. Alm 34 B4
Berwick Rd. Bris 50 A1
Beryl Gr. Bris 80 B4
Beryl Rd. Bris 63 D2
Besom La. West 39 E3
Bethel Rd. Bris 64 C4
Betjeman Ct. Kingsw 66 A3
Bevan Ct. Bris 35 F1
Beverley Ave. Mang 37 F1
Beverley Cl. Bris 65 D3
Beverley Gdns. Bris 48 B4
Beverley Rd. Bris 49 F4
Beverston Gdns. Bris 34 A1
Beverstone. Kingsw 65 E4
Bevington Cl. Bris 23 F1
Bevington La. Stone 2 C4
Bevington Wlk. Bris 23 F1
Bewdley Rd. Bath 102 A2
Bexley Rd. Bris 51 D2
Bibstone. Kingsw 66 A4
Bibury Ave. St Gif 36 A4
Bibury Cl. Bris 49 E4
Bibury Cl. Nail 60 A1
Bibury Cres. Bris 49 E4
Bibury Cres. Kingsw 65 E3
Bickerton Cl. Bris 34 C2
Bickfield La. Co Mar 128 A4
Bickford Cl. Kingsw 66 A3
Bickley Cl. Kingsw 65 E1
Biddeston Rd. Bris 49 F4
Biddisham Cl. Nail 59 E4
Biddisham La. Badg 123 F1
Biddle St. Yatt 91 D4
Bideford Cres. Bris 79 F4
Bideford Rd. W-S-M 88 C1
Bidwell Cl. Bris 35 D2
Bifield Cl. Bris 80 C3
Bifield Gdns. Bris 80 C3
Bifield Rd. Bris 80 C3
Big Tree Cl. Co Bi 124 B2
Bignell Cl. Wins 124 C4
Bigwood La. Bris 63 E3
Bilberry Cl. Bris 48 B4
Bilbie Cl. Ch St 112 C4
Bilbie Rd. Ch St 112 C4
Bilbie Rd. W-S-M 89 D2
Bilbury La. Bath 101 F3

Billand Cl. Bris 78 C2
Bilsham La. Piln 12 C1
Bince's Lodge La. Mid No . 132 A2
Binces La. Marks 99 F2
Bindon Dr. Bris 35 E2
Binhay Rd. Yatt 91 E4
Binley Gr. Bris 80 B2
Binmead Gdns. Bris 79 D2
Birbeck Rd. Bris 48 C3
Birch Ave. Blea 122 B4
Birch Ave. Cleve 57 F2
Birch Cl. Bris 35 F4
Birch Cl. Lock 106 A2
Birch Croft. Bris 80 A2
Birch Ct. Keyn 81 E2
Birch Dr. Alve 14 C2
Birch Dr. Chur 109 D3
Birch Dr. Puck 53 D3
Birch Gr. Portis 45 E2
Birch Rd. Bris 63 D2
Birch Rd. Kingsw 51 F2
Birch Rd. Rad 132 C1
Birch Rd. Yate 27 E1
Birchall Rd. Bris 49 E2
Birchdale Rd. Bris 80 A4
Birchdene. Nail 60 A1
Birches The. Nail 60 A1
Birchwood Ave. W-S-M 105 D4
Birchwood Dr. Wrax 61 D2
Birchwood La. Pens 97 F1
Birchwood Rd. Bris 64 C2
Birdale Cl. Bris 34 C2
Birdcombe Cl. Nail 59 F2
Birdlip Cl. Nail 76 A4
Birdwell La. Lo Ash 61 F1
Birdwell Rd. Lo Ash 61 F1
Birdwood. Kingsw 65 E3
Birgage Rd. H Up 19 F1
Birkdale. Kingsw 66 A3
Birkdale. Yate 39 F4
Birkett Rd. W-S-M 87 D1
Birkin St. Bris 64 A3
Birnbeck Rd. W-S-M 87 E1
Bisdee Rd. Lock 105 E1
Bishop Ave. W-S-M 89 D2
Bishop Manor Rd. Bris 49 E4
Bishop Rd. Bris 49 E2
Bishop St. Bris 63 F4
Bishop St. Faulk 134 B1
Bishop's Wood. Alm 24 B3
Bishops Cl. Bris 48 C3
Bishops Cove. Bris 78 C3
Bishops Mead. Brock 92 A4
Bishops Rd. Brock 92 A4
Bishopsworth Rd. Bris 79 D4
Bishopthorpe Rd. Bris 49 F4
Bishport Ave. Bris 79 E2
Bishport Cl. Bris 79 D2
Bisley. Yate 39 E4
Bittern Cl. W-S-M 88 C1
Bitterwell Cl. West 38 B2
Bittlemead. Bris 79 F2
Black Boy Hill. Bris 49 D1
Blackacre. Whit 80 B2
Blackberry Ave. Bris 50 C3
Blackberry Dr. W-S-M 89 D1
Blackberry Hill. Bris 50 C3
Blackberry La. Winsl 120 B4
Blackbird Cl. Rod 138 A4
Blackdown Ct. Bris 80 A3
Blackdown Rd. Portis 45 D3
Blackfriars Rd. Nail 59 D1
Blackfriars. Bris 63 E4
Blackhorse Hill. Alm 35 D4
Blackhorse La. Mang 52 A4
Blackhorse Pl. Mang 52 A3
Blackhorse Rd. Kingsw 65 E4
Blackhorse Rd. Mang 52 A4
Blackmoor Cl. Chur 109 E3
Blackmoor Rd. Ab Lei 47 F1
Blackmoor. Chur 109 E3
Blackmoor. Cleve 57 E1
Blackmoor. W-S-M 88 C1
Blackmoors La. Bris 62 C2
Blackmore Dr. Bath 101 E3
Blackrock La. Pens 97 F4
Blacksmith La. Bathe 85 D3
Blacksmith's La. Kel 83 D2
Blackswarth Rd. Bris 64 B4
Blackthorn Cl. Bris 79 E3
Blackthorn Dr. St Gif 36 B4
Blackthorn Gdns. W-S-M 89 D1
Blackthorn Rd. Bris 79 E3
Blackthorn Sq. Cleve 57 E1
Blackthorn Terr. W-S-M 89 D1
Blackthorn Way. Nail 60 A1
Blackthorn Wlk. Kingsw 51 F1
Bladdock Bldgs. Faulk 134 A1
Bladen Cl. Portis 45 F2
Blagdon Cl. Bris 63 F1
Blagdon Cl. W-S-M 104 C1
Blagdon La. Blag 110 C3
Blagdon La. But 110 C3
Blagdon Park. Bath 101 D2
Blagrove Cl. Bris 79 E2
Blagrove Cres. Bris 79 E2
Blaisdon Cl. Bris 34 C1
Blaisdon. Yate 39 F4

Blaise Hamlet. Bris 34 B1
Blaise Wlk. Bris 48 B4
Blake End. W-S-M 88 C2
Blake Rd. Bris 50 A3
Blakeney Gr. Nail 75 E4
Blakeney Mills. Yate 27 E1
Blakeney Rd. Bris 23 F1
Blakeney Rd. Bris 50 A4
Blakes Rd. Thorn 8 A1
Blanchards. Ch Sod 40 B4
Blandford Cl. Bris 49 D3
Blandford Cl. Nail 59 F1
Bleadon Hill. W-S-M 122 A4
Bleadon Rd. Blea 122 A3
Blenheim Cl. P St J 133 E4
Blenheim Dr. Bris 36 A2
Blenheim Dr. Yate 27 E2
Blenheim Gdns. Bath 85 D1
Blenheim St. Bris 50 A1
Blenheim Way. Portis 45 F3
Blenman Cl. Bris 49 D2
Blenman Cl. Bris 51 D4
Blind La. Bath 84 B1
Blind La. Ch St 112 C4
Blind La. Cong 91 F3
Blind La. Pris 117 D2
Bloomfield Ave. Bath 101 F2
Bloomfield Ave. Tims 116 A2
Bloomfield Cl. Tims 116 A2
Bloomfield Cres. Bath 101 E1
Bloomfield Dr. Bath 101 E1
Bloomfield Gr. Bath 101 F2
Bloomfield La. Paul 131 F3
Bloomfield Park Rd. Tims 116 A2
Bloomfield Park. Bath 101 F2
Bloomfield Rd. Bath 101 F2
Bloomfield Rd. Bris 64 B2
Bloomfield Rd. Tims 116 A2
Bloomfield Rise N. Bath 101 E1
Bloomfield Rise. Bath 101 E1
Bloomfield Terr. P St J 133 E4
Bloomfield. W-S-M 105 D1
Bloy St. Bris 50 B1
Bluebell Cl. Thorn 8 B1
Bluebells The. St Gif 36 C4
Blueberry Way. W-S-M 88 C1
Blythe Gdns. W-S-M 89 D2
Boat La. Lymp 122 B2
Boat Stall La. Bath 102 A3
Bobbin La. Westw 120 C2
Bobbin Parr. Westw 120 C2
Bockenem Cl. Thorn 15 E4
Bodey Cl. Kingsw 66 A3
Bodmin Wlk. Bris 79 F4
Bodyce Rd. Alve 15 D3
Boiling Wells La. Bris 50 A2
Bolton Rd. Bris 49 F2
Bond St. Bris 63 F4
Bond's La. Marsh 55 F1
Bonhill Rd. Bi Sut 113 E3
Bonnington Wlk. Bris 50 A4
Boot La. Bris 63 D2
Booth Rd. Bris 63 E2
Bordesley Rd. Bris 80 A2
Borgie Pl. W-S-M 88 C2
Borleyton Wlk. Bris 78 C2
Borver Gr. Bris 79 D2
Boscombe Cres. Mang 51 F4
Boston Rd. Bris 49 F4
Boswell Rd. Westw 120 C2
Boswell St. Bris 50 B1
Botham Cl. W-S-M 89 D2
Botham Dr. Bris 64 B1
Boucher Pl. Bris 50 A1
Boulevard. W-S-M 104 C4
Boulters Rd. Bris 79 E2
Boulton's La. Bris 65 E4
Boulton's Rd. Kingsw 65 E4
Boundaries The. Lymp 122 A1
Boundary Cl. Rod 138 A4
Boundary Cl. W-S-M 104 C2
Boundary Rd. Avon 33 E2
Boundary Rd. Fr Cot 38 B4
Bourchier Gdns. Bris 79 D2
Bourne Cl. Bris 65 D4
Bourne Cl. Wint 37 F4
Bourne La. Blag 110 A2
Bourne La. Bris 50 A1
Bourne Rd. Bris 65 D4
Bourneville Bsns Centre.
  Bris 64 C1
Bournville Rd. Bris 64 C1
Bournville Rd. Bris 64 C1
Bournville Rd. W-S-M 104 C2
Boursland Cl. St Gif 24 B1
Bourton Ave. St Gif 36 B4
Bourton Cl. St Gif 36 B4
Bourton Combe. Back 76 C4
Bourton La. Co Bi 124 C2
Bourton La. Lock 89 E2
Bourton Mead. Back 76 C4
Bourton Mead. Lo Ash 62 A1
Bourton Wlk. Bris 79 D4
Bouverie St. Bris 64 A4
Boverton Rd. Bris 36 A2
Bowden Cl. Bris 48 B4
Bowden Hill. Chil 137 E2

Bowden Pl. Mang 51 F4
Bowden Rd. Bris 64 C4
Bowden Way. Wrax 61 D2
Bower Rd. Bris 63 D2
Bower Wlk. Bris 63 F2
Bowerleaze. Bris 48 B3
Bowditch La. Mid No 132 A2
Bowling Hill Bsns Pk.
  Ch Sod 28 A1
Bowling Hill. Ch Sod 28 A1
Bowling Rd. Ch Sod 40 A4
Bowood. Bris 37 E1
Bowring Cl. Bris 79 E2
Bowsland Way. St Gif 24 B1
Bowstreet La. Alm 35 D4
Box Bush La. Ban 90 B1
Box Rd. Bathe 86 B2
Box Rd. Bathf 86 B2
Box Wlk. Keyn 81 E2
Boxbury Hill. Paul 131 F2
Boxhedge Farm La. West 38 C2
Boyce Dr. Bris 50 A1
Boyce's Ave. Bris 63 D4
Boyd Cl. Wick 67 D4
Boyd Rd. Keyn 82 B2
Brabazon Rd. Bris 36 A1
Bracewell Gdns. Bris 35 E2
Bracey Dr. Bris 51 E3
Brackenbury Dr. St Gif 36 C3
Brackendean. St Gif 24 B1
Brackenwood Rd. Cleve 57 F3
Bracton Dr. Bris 80 A3
Bradford Cl. Cleve 57 E1
Bradford Park. Bath 102 A1
Bradford Rd. Bath 102 A1
Bradford Rd. Bathf 86 A1
Bradford Rd. Winsl 120 C4
Bradhurst St. Bris 64 A3
Bradley Ave. Wint 37 F3
Bradley Cres. Bris 47 F3
Bradley Rd. Bris 23 F1
Bradley Stoke Way. St Gif 24 B1
Bradley Stoke Way. St Gif 37 D3
Bradstone Rd. Wint 37 E3
Bradville Gdns. Lo Ash 77 F4
Bradwell Gr. Bris 49 E4
Brae Rd. Wins 125 D4
Brae Rise. Wins 125 D4
Braemar Ave. Bris 35 F1
Braemar Cres. Bris 35 F1
Bragg's La. Bris 63 F4
Braikenridge Cl. Cleve 57 E1
Braikenridge Rd. Bris 64 B2
Brainsfield. Bris 48 C3
Brake Cl. Kingsw 65 F4
Brake Cl. St Gif 36 C3
Brake The. Fr Cot 38 B3
Brake The. Yate 27 F3
Brakewell Gdns. Bris 80 A2
Bramble Dr. Bris 48 B2
Bramble La. Bris 48 B2
Bramble Rd. W-S-M 88 C2
Bramble Way. Bath 102 A1
Brambles The. Keyn 81 E2
Brambling Wlk. Bris 50 C3
Bramley Cl. E in G 47 E2
Bramley Cl. Kings 11 F2
Bramley Cl. Olve 14 A2
Bramley Cl. P St J 133 E4
Bramley Cl. Yatt 91 D4
Bramley Ct. Kingsw 65 F2
Bramley Dr. Back 76 A3
Bramley Sq. Cong 91 F2
Bramleys The. Nail 75 D4
Brampton Way. Portis 45 F2
Bramshill Dr. W-S-M 88 C2
Branch Rd. Hin Cha 119 F1
Branche St. Bris 79 E2
Brandash Rd. Ch Sod 28 A1
Brandon St. Bris 63 E3
Brandon Steep. Bris 63 E3
Brangwyn Gr. Bris 50 A3
Brangwyn Sq. W-S-M 88 C1
Branksome Cres. Bris 36 A2
Branksome Dr. Bris 36 A2
Branksome Dr. Wint 37 F3
Branksome Rd. Bris 49 D2
Branscombe Rd. Bris 48 B2
Branscombe Way. Portis 44 C2
Branscombe Wlk. Portis 44 C2
Branwhite Cl. Bris 50 A4
Brassknocker Hill. Bath 102 C1
Brassmill La. Bath 101 D4
Bratton Rd. Bris 79 E4
Braunton Rd. Bris 63 E2
Braydon Ave. St Gif 36 B4
Brayne Ct. Kingsw 65 F2
Braysdown Cl. P St J 133 D3
Braysdown La. P St J 133 E3
Braysdown La. P St J 133 E4
Breach La. Nail 74 C4
Breach Rd. Bris 63 D2
Breaches Gate. St Gif 36 C3
Breaches La. Keyn 82 A2
Breaches The. E in G 47 D3
Brean Down Ave. Bris 49 D3
Brean Down Ave. Bris 49 D3

Brean Down Ave. W-S-M .. 104 B2
Brean Rd. Lymp 121 F1
Brecknock Rd. Bris 64 A2
Brecon Cl. Bris 49 D3
Brecon View. W-S-M 105 D1
Bredon Cl. Kingsw 65 F4
Bredon Nook Rd. Bris 49 E4
Bredon. Yate 39 E4
Bree Cl. W-S-M 89 D2
Brendon Ave. W-S-M 104 C4
Brendon Cl. Kingsw 66 B2
Brendon Gdns. Nail 59 F1
Brendon Rd. Bris 63 E2
Brendon Rd. Portis 45 D3
Brenner St. Bris 50 A1
Brent Cl. W-S-M 105 D1
Brent Rd. Bris 49 F3
Brentry Ave. Bris 64 A4
Brentry Hill. Bris 35 D1
Brentry La. Bris 35 D2
Brentry Rd. Bris 50 C2
Brereton Way. Kingsw 66 A2
Brewerton Cl. Bris 35 E2
Brewery Hill. Bitt 82 C4
Brewery La. Hol 138 B1
Briar Cl. Nail 60 A1
Briar Cl. Rod 138 B4
Briar Mead. Yatt 74 A1
Briar Rd. Lock 105 F2
Briar Way. Bris 51 E2
Briar Wlk. Bris 51 E2
Briarfield Ave. Kingsw 65 E3
Briarleaze. Alve 14 C1
Briars The. Back 75 F4
Briarside Rd. Bris 35 E2
Briarwood. Bris 48 C3
Briary Rd. Portis 45 E3
Briavels Gr. Bris 49 F1
Brick St. Bris 63 F4
Bridewell La. Bath 101 F3
Bridewell La. Lock 106 A1
Bridewell St. Bris 63 E4
Bridge Cl. Whit 80 B2
Bridge Farm Cl. Bris 80 A2
Bridge Farm Sq. Cong 91 E2
Bridge Gdns. Farm 116 A3
Bridge Place Rd. Tims 132 C4
Bridge Rd. Bath 101 E3
Bridge Rd. Blea 122 A3
Bridge Rd. Bris 50 A2
Bridge Rd. Ir Act 27 D1
Bridge Rd. Kingsw 52 B2
Bridge Rd. Lo Ash 62 C3
Bridge Rd. Sist 52 B2
Bridge St. Bath 102 A3
Bridge St. Bris 50 B1
Bridge St. Bris 63 E3
Bridge Valley Rd. Bris 62 C4
Bridge Way. Fr Cot 38 A4
Bridge Wlk. Bris 50 A4
Bridgeleap Rd. Mang 51 F4
Bridges Dr. Bris 51 E3
Bridgman Gr. Bris 36 A2
Bridgwater Ct. W-S-M 105 D2
Bridgwater Rd. Ba Gu 77 F1
Bridgwater Rd. Blea 122 B2
Bridgwater Rd. Bris 78 B3
Bridgwater Rd. Dun 78 B3
Bridgwater Rd. Lymp 122 B2
Bridgwater Rd. W-S-M 104 C1
Bridgwater Rd. Wins 125 D3
Bridle Way. Alve 14 C2
Briercliffe Rd. Bris 48 B4
Brierly Furlong. St Gif 36 C2
Briery Leaze Rd. Bris 80 A3
Bright St. Bris 64 A4
Bright St. Kingsw 65 E4
Brighton Cres. Bris 63 E1
Brighton Mews. Bris 63 D4
Brighton Pl. Kingsw 51 E1
Brighton Rd. Bris 35 F4
Brighton Rd. Bris 49 E1
Brighton Rd. W-S-M 104 C3
Brighton St. Bris 63 F4
Brighton Terr. Bris 63 D1
Brigstocke Rd. Bris 63 F4
Brimbles. Bris 36 A1
Brimbleworth La. W-S-M 89 E2
Brimridge Rd. Wins 125 D4
Brinkmarsh La. Falf 9 E1
Brinkworthy Rd. Bris 50 C3
Brinmead Wlk. Bris 78 C2
Brins Cl. St Gif 36 C2
Brinsea Batch. Cong 108 C3
Brinsea La. Cong 108 C4
Brinsea Rd. Cong 91 F1
Brinsham La. Yate 28 A3
Briscoes Ave. Bris 79 E2
Brislington Est. Bris 79 E2
Brislington Trading Est. Bris 64 C1
Bristol And Exeter Mews.
  Bris 63 F3
Bristol Gate. Bris 62 C3
Bristol Hill. Bris 64 B1
Bristol Phoenix. Bris 63 D1
Bristol Rd Lower. W-S-M 87 F1
Bristol Rd. Bris 37 D1
Bristol Rd. Ch St 112 C4

Bristol Rd. Chur 109 D3
Bristol Rd. Co Dan 81 F3
Bristol Rd. Cong 91 E3
Bristol Rd. Cor 100 B4
Bristol Rd. Crom 17 D4
Bristol Rd. Fr Cot 26 A2
Bristol Rd. Ir Act 26 A2
Bristol Rd. Lock 89 E1
Bristol Rd. Luck 31 F2
Bristol Rd. Mid No 132 C2
Bristol Rd. Paul 130 C3
Bristol Rd. Paul 131 F4
Bristol Rd. Pens 97 E4
Bristol Rd. Portis 45 F2
Bristol Rd. Ship 108 B1
Bristol Rd. Thorn 15 D4
Bristol Rd. Whit 80 B2
Bristol Rd. Wins 125 E4
Bristol Rd. Wint 37 E2
Bristol Rd. Wint 37 F4
Bristol Vale Centre For Industry.
  Bris 63 D1
Bristol View. Bath 118 B4
Bristowe House. Bris 51 D3
Britannia Cl. Chil 137 E2
Britannia Cres. St Gif 36 B3
Britannia Rd. Bris 35 F4
Britannia Rd. Bris 50 B1
Britannia Rd. Bris 65 E4
Britannia Rd. Kingsw 65 E4
Britannia Way. Cleve 57 E1
British Rd. Bris 63 E2
Brittan Pl. Portb 46 C2
Britten Ct. Kingsw 65 F2
Britten's Cl. Paul 131 F3
Britten's Hill. Paul 131 F3
Brixham Rd. Bris 63 E1
Brixton Rd. Bris 64 A4
Broad Croft. St Gif 24 B1
Broad La. West 38 B3
Broad La. West 39 D2
Broad La. Yate 27 F3
Broad Mead La. Win 95 D2
Broad Oak Rd. Bris 78 C2
Broad Oaks. Lo Ash 62 C3
Broad Plain. Bris 63 F3
Broad Quay. Bath 101 F3
Broad Quay. Bris 63 E3
Broad Rd. Bris 51 E1
Broad Rd. Priddy 126 C4
Broad St. Bath 102 A4
Broad St. Bris 63 E4
Broad St. Cong 91 E2
Broad St. Kingsw 51 F2
Broad St. Mang 51 F2
Broad St. Wring 92 B1
Broad Street Pl. Bath 102 A4
Broad Weir. Bris 63 F4
Broad Wlk. Bris 64 A1
Broadbury Rd. Bris 79 F4
Broadcroft Ave. Yatt 74 C1
Broadcroft. Ch Yatt 74 C1
Broadcroft. Ch Mag 95 F2
Broadfield Ave. Bris 51 E1
Broadfield Rd. Bris 64 A1
Broadlands Ave. Keyn 81 E3
Broadlands Dr. Bris 34 A1
Broadlands. Cleve 57 F2
Broadleas. Bris 79 E4
Broadleaze Way. Winsc 107 F4
Broadleys Ave. Bris 49 E4
Broadmead La. Keyn 82 A3
Broadmead. Bris 63 F4
Broadmoor La. Bath 84 A2
Broadmoor La. Charl 83 F2
Broadmoor Park. Bath 84 A1
Broadmoor Vale. Bath 84 A2
Broadoak Hill. Bris 78 C2
Broadoak Rd. Chur 109 D3
Broadoak Rd. W-S-M 104 B2
Broadoak Wlk. Bris 51 D2
Broadstone La. K Sey 72 C2
Broadstone Wlk. Bris 79 E3
Broadstones. Mon Far 103 F4
Broadway Ave. Bris 49 E3
Broadway Cl. Chil 137 E2
Broadway La. Paul 132 A3
Broadway Rd. Bris 49 E2
Broadway Rd. Bris 78 C3
Broadway. Bath 102 A3
Broadway. Chil 137 E2
Broadway. Keyn 82 B2
Broadway. Ship 125 F4
Broadway. W-S-M 105 D1
Broadway. Yate 27 F1
Broadways Dr. Bris 50 C4
Brock End. Portis 44 C2
Brock St. Bath 101 F4
Brockhurst Gdns. Bris 65 D4
Brockhurst Rd. Bris 65 D4
Brockley Cl. Nail 59 E1
Brockley Cl. W-S-M 104 C1
Brockley Cl. W-S-M 104 C1
Brockley Combe Rd. Brock .. 76 A1
Brockley Combe Rd. Wring .. 76 A1
Brockley Cres. W-S-M 104 C1
Brockley La. Brock 75 E2
Brockley Rd. Keyn 82 B2

145

Brockley Way. Brock   Chapel Row. Bathf

Brockley Way. Brock 75 D2
Brockley Way. Yatt 75 D2
Brockley Wlk. Bris 79 D4
Brockridge La. Fr Cot 38 B4
Brocks La. Lo Ash 61 F1
Brocks Rd. Bris 79 E2
Brockway. Nail 59 F1
Brockwood. Winsl 120 C4
Brockworth Cres. Bris 50 C3
Brockworth. Yate 39 E3
Bromley Dr. Mang 51 E4
Bromley Heath Ave. Mang 51 E4
Bromley Heath Rd. Mang 37 E1
Bromley Heath Rd. Mang 51 E4
Bromley Rd. Bris 49 F3
Bromley Rd. Pens 96 C1
Brompton Cl. Kingsw 66 A4
Brompton Rd. W-S-M 105 D1
Broncksea Rd. Bris 35 F1
Brook Cl. Lo Ash 62 A1
Brook Gate. Bris 62 C1
Brook Hill. Bris 49 F1
Brook La. Bris 49 F1
Brook La. Bris 50 C3
Brook Lintons. Bris 64 B2
Brook Rd. Bath 101 E3
Brook Rd. Bris 49 F1
Brook Rd. Bris 50 C1
Brook Rd. Bris 51 D2
Brook Rd. Bris 63 E2
Brook Rd. Kingsw 66 A4
Brook Rd. Mang 51 F3
Brook St. Bris 64 B4
Brook St. Ch Sod 28 A1
Brook Way. St Gif 36 B4
Brookcote Dr. St Gif 36 B3
Brookdale Rd. Bris 79 D3
Brookfield Ave. Bris 49 E2
Brookfield Cl. Ch Sod 28 A1
Brookfield La. Bris 49 E1
Brookfield Park. Bath 84 A1
Brookfield Rd. Bris 49 E1
Brookfield Rd. St Gif 36 A4
Brookfield Wlk. Cleve 57 F2
Brookfield Wlk. Kingsw 66 B2
Brookland Rd. Bris 49 E3
Brookland Rd. W-S-M 105 D4
Brooklands. Pris 117 E2
Brooklea. Kingsw 66 A2
Brookleaze Bldgs. Bath 85 D1
Brookleaze. Bris 48 B3
Brooklyn Rd. Bath 85 E1
Brooklyn Rd. Bris 79 D4
Brooklyn. Wring 92 B1
Brookmead. Thorn 15 E4
Brookside Cl. Bathe 85 F3
Brookside Cl. Paul 131 F3
Brookside Dr. Farm 115 F3
Brookside Dr. Fr Cot 38 A4
Brookside House. Bath 84 A1
Brookside Rd. Bris 64 C1
Brookside. E in G 47 E2
Brookside. Paul 131 F3
Brookside. Win 94 C4
Brookthorpe Ave. Bris 34 A1
Brookthorpe. Yate 39 E4
Brookview Wlk. Bris 79 D4
Broom Farm Cl. Nail 75 F4
Broom Hill La. Paul 131 F4
Broom Hill. Bris 50 C3
Broomground. Winsl 120 C4
Broomhill La. Clut 114 C2
Brotherswood Ct. St Gif 24 B2
Brougham Hayes. Bath 101 E3
Brow Hill. Bathe 85 F2
Brow The. Bath 101 D3
Browning Ct. Bris 50 A4
Brownlow Rd. W-S-M 104 C2
Bruce Ave. Bris 50 B1
Bruce Rd. Bris 50 B1
Brummel Way. Paul 131 E3
Brunel Cl. W-S-M 104 C1
Brunel Ct. Yate 27 E1
Brunel Lock Rd. Bris 62 C3
Brunel Rd. Bris 79 D4
Brunel Rd. Nail 59 D1
Brunel Way. Bris 62 C2
Brunel Way. Thorn 15 D4
Brunswick Pl. Bris 62 C3
Brunswick Sq. Bris 63 F4
Brunswick St. Bath 102 A4
Brunswick St. Bris 63 F4
Brunswick St. Bris 64 B4
Bruton Ave. Bath 101 F2
Bruton Ave. Portis 45 D3
Bruton Cl. Nail 75 F4
Bruton. W-S-M 105 D1
Bryansons Cl. Bris 50 B3
Bryant Ave. Rad 132 B1
Bryant Gdns. Cleve 57 E1
Bryant's Hill. Bris 65 D3
Bryants Cl. Bris 37 E1
Brynland Ave. Bris 49 F2
Bsns Pk The. Bris 79 F2
Buckingham Dr. St Gif 36 B3
Buckingham Gdns. Mang 51 F3
Buckingham Pl. Bris 63 D4
Buckingham Pl. Mang 51 F3
Buckingham Rd. Bris 64 B3
Buckingham Rd. W-S-M 105 D1
Buckingham St. Bris 63 E1
Buckingham Vale. Bris 63 D4
Buckland Green. W-S-M 89 D3
Bucklands Batch. Nail 75 F4
Bucklands Dr. Nail 76 A4
Bucklands End. Nail 75 F4
Bucklands Gr. Nail 75 F4
Bucklands La. Nail 75 F4
Bucklands View. Nail 76 A4
Bude Ave. Bris 65 D4
Bude Cl. Nail 60 A1
Bude Rd. Bris 36 A2
Bull La. Bris 64 C3
Bull La. E in G 47 E2
Bull's Hill. Well 118 C1
Bullens Cl. St Gif 24 B1
Buller Rd. Bris 64 B1
Bullocks La. K Sey 73 E2
Bully La. Yate 17 E1
Bumper's Batch. Sosto 119 D4
Bungay's Hill. Paul 115 F1
Bunting Ct. W-S-M 88 C1
Burbank Cl. Kingsw 66 A2
Burchells Ave. Bris 51 D1
Burchells Green Cl. Bris 51 D1
Burchells Green Rd. Bris 51 D1
Burcott Rd. Avon 33 E3
Burden Cl. St Gif 36 C3
Burfoot Gdns. Bris 80 C2
Burfoot Rd. Bris 80 C2
Burford Cl. Bath 101 D2
Burford Cl. Portis 45 F2
Burford Gr. Bris 47 F3
Burgage Cl. Ch Sod 40 A4
Burgess Green Cl. Bris 64 C4
Burghill Rd. Bris 35 D1
Burghley Rd. Bris 49 F1
Burgis Rd. Bris 80 B3
Burleigh Gdns. Bath 101 D4
Burleigh Way. Wickw 18 A3
Burley Ave. Mang 51 F3
Burley Crest. Mang 51 F3
Burley Gr. Mang 51 F2
Burlington Rd. Bris 49 D1
Burlington Rd. Mid No 132 B1
Burlington St. Bath 101 F4
Burlington St. W-S-M 104 C4
Burnbush Cl. Bris 80 C3
Burnell Dr. Bris 63 F4
Burneside Cl. Bris 35 E1
Burney Way. Kingsw 66 A2
Burnham Cl. Kingsw 51 F1
Burnham Cl. W-S-M 104 C1
Burnham Dr. Kingsw 51 F1
Burnham Dr. W-S-M 104 C1
Burnham Rd. Bath 101 E3
Burnham Rd. Bris 47 E3
Burrington Ave. W-S-M 104 C1
Burrington Cl. Nail 59 F1
Burrington Cl. W-S-M 104 C1
Burrington Wlk. Bris 79 D4
Burrough Way. Wint 37 F3
Burrows La. Hol 138 A1
Burton Cl. Bris 63 F3
Burton Cl. Bris 64 C4
Burton Ct. Bris 63 D4
Burton Rd. A Tur 42 C3
Burton St. Bath 101 F3
Burwalls Rd. Lo Ash 62 C3
Bury Hill La. Yate 28 A4
Bury Hill. Wint 37 F2
Bury La. Doyn 67 F4
Bury The. Lock 106 A2
Burycourt Cl. Bris 34 A1
Bush Ave. St Gif 36 B3
Bushes La. Hort 29 D3
Bushy Park. Bris 63 F2
Bushy Thorn Rd. Ch St 112 C4
Butcombe La. But 111 D4
Butcombe Wlk. Bris 80 A3
Butcombe. W-S-M 105 D1
Butham La. Ch Mag 96 A2
Butlass Cl. Paul 115 E1
Butt's Batch. Wring 92 B1
Butt's La. Mon Far 103 F4
Butt's La. Tor 55 D2
Butterfield Cl. Bris 49 F4
Butterfield Park. Cleve 57 E1
Butterfield Rd. Bris 49 F4
Buttermere Rd. W-S-M 105 D3
Butterworth Ct. Bris 79 E4
Button Cl. Bris 80 A3
Buttris Batch. Co Bi 124 A2
Buxton Wlk. Bris 50 A4
Byfields. Cleve 73 E4
Byron Pl. Bris 63 D4
Byron Pl. Kingsw 51 F2
Byron Rd. Bath 101 F2
Byron Rd. Lock 106 A2
Byron Rd. W-S-M 105 D2
Byron St. Bris 50 A1
Byron St. Bris 64 B4

Cabot Cl. Keyn 82 B1
Cabot Cl. Yate 27 F1
Cabot Green. Bris 64 A4
Cabot Rise. Portis 45 D3
Cabot Way. Bris 62 C3
Cabot Way. E in G 47 E2
Cabot Way. W-S-M 89 D2
Cabstand. Portis 45 E3
Cadbury Camp La W. Nail 58 B3
Cadbury Camp La. Nail 59 E3
Cadbury Farm Rd. Yatt 91 E4
Cadbury Halt. W in G 44 C1
Cadbury Heath Rd. Kingsw 66 A3
Cadbury La. W in G 44 C1
Cadbury Rd. Keyn 82 A1
Cadbury Rd. Portis 45 F2
Cadbury Sq. Cong 91 E2
Caddick Cl. Kingsw 51 F1
Cade Cl. Kingsw 65 F3
Cade Cl. St Gif 36 C3
Cadogan Rd. Bris 80 A4
Caen Rd. Bris 63 E2
Caernarvon Rd. Keyn 81 E2
Caine Rd. Bris 49 F4
Cains Cl. Kingsw 65 F3
Cairn Cl. Nail 60 A1
Cairns Rd. Bris 49 E2
Cairns' Cres. Bris 49 F1
Cakenhill Rd. Bris 64 C1
Calcott Rd. Bris 64 A2
Caldbeck Cl. Bris 35 E1
Calder Cl. Keyn 82 A2
Caldicot Cl. Bris 34 B1
Caldicot Cl. Kingsw 66 A1
Caledonia Mews. Bris 62 C3
Caledonia Pl. Bris 62 C4
Caledonian Rd. Bath 101 E3
California Rd. Kingsw 66 A2
Callicroft Rd. Bris 36 A4
Callington Rd. Bris 64 B1
Callowhill Ct. Bris 63 F4
Calton Gdns. Bath 101 F3
Calton Rd. Bath 102 A3
Cam Brook Cl. Tims 132 C4
Camberley Dr. Fr Cot 37 F4
Camberley Rd. Bris 79 E4
Camborne Rd. Bris 50 A4
Cambrian Dr. Yate 27 F2
Cambridge Cres. Bris 49 D4
Cambridge Gr. Cleve 57 E3
Cambridge Park. Bris 49 D2
Cambridge Rd. Bris 49 F2
Cambridge Rd. Cleve 57 F3
Cambridge St. Bris 63 F2
Cambridge st. Bris 64 B4
Cambridge Terr. Bath 102 A3
Cambrook House. Clut 130 C4
Camden Rd. Bath 85 D1
Camden Rd. Bris 63 D3
Camden Row. Bath 101 F4
Camden Terr. Bris 63 D3
Camden Terr. W-S-M 104 C4
Cameley Cl. Clut 130 C4
Cameley Green. Bath 100 C3
Cameley Rd. Clut 130 B4
Camelford Rd. Bris 50 B1
Cameron Wlk. Bris 50 B3
Camerons Cl. Keyn 81 F2
Camerton Cl. Keyn 82 C2
Camerton Hill. Tims 132 C4
Camerton Rd. Bris 50 B1
Camerton Rd. Tims 116 C1
Camp La. Tor 55 E2
Camp Rd N. W-S-M 87 D1
Camp Rd. Bris 62 C4
Camp Rd. O-on-S 7 D3
Camp Rd. W-S-M 87 E1
Camp View. Nail 59 E1
Campbell Farm Dr. Bris 33 F1
Campbell St. Bris 49 F1
Campion Cl. Thorn 8 B1
Campion Cl. W-S-M 105 E4
Campion Dr. St Gif 24 B1
Campion Wlk. Bris 79 E3
Camplins. Cleve 57 E1
Camvale. P St J 133 D4
Camview. Paul 131 E3
Camwal Rd. Bris 64 A3
Canada Coombe. Blea 106 A1
Canada Coombe. Lock 106 A1
Canada Way. Bris 63 D3
Canberra Gr. Bris 36 A2
Canberra Rd. W-S-M 104 C2
Canford La. Bris 48 C4
Canford La. Bris 49 D4
Canford Rd. Bris 48 C4
Cann La. Bitt 66 C3
Cann La. Sist 66 C3
Cannans Cl. Wint 37 F4
Cannon St. Bris 63 E2
Cannon St. Bris 63 E4
Cannon St. Bris 64 B4
Cannons Gate. Cleve 73 E4
Canon's Rd. Bris 63 E3
Canon's Wlk. Kingsw 51 F1
Canons Wlk. W-S-M 88 B1
Canowie Rd. Bris 49 D2
Cantell Gr. Bris 80 C3
Canterbury Cl. W-S-M 89 D2
Canterbury Cl. Yate 27 F2
Canterbury Rd. Bath 101 E3
Canterbury St. Bris 64 A3
Canters Leaze. Wickw 18 A2
Cantock's Cl. Bris 63 E4
Canvey Cl. Bris 49 F4
Canynge Rd. Bris 62 C4
Canynge Sq. Bris 62 C4
Canynge St. Bris 63 F3
Capel Cl. Kingsw 66 A4
Capel Rd. Bris 34 A1
Capenor Cl. Portis 45 E2
Capgrave Cl. Bris 65 D2
Capgrave Cres. Bris 65 D2
Caple La. Ch St 112 A3
Caraway Gdns. Bris 50 B1
Cardigan Cres. W-S-M 105 E4
Cardigan Rd. Bris 49 D3
Cardill Cl. Bris 79 D4
Carditch Dro. Cong 108 A4
Carey's Cl. Cleve 57 F2
Carice Gdns. Cleve 73 E4
Carisbrooke Rd. Bris 79 E4
Carlingford Terr Rd. Rad 133 D1
Carlingford Terr. Rad 133 D1
Carlisle Rd. Bris 50 B1
Carlow Rd. Bris 79 F4
Carlton Cl. Clut 114 C2
Carlton Ct. Bris 49 D4
Carlton Mansions. W-S-M 104 B4
Carlton Pk. Bris 64 B4
Carlton St. W-S-M 104 B4
Carmarthen Cl. Yate 27 F2
Carmarthen Gr. Kingsw 66 A1
Carmarthen Rd. Bris 49 D3
Carnarvon Rd. Bris 49 E1
Caroline Cl. Keyn 81 E2
Caroline Pl. Bath 101 F4
Carpenters La. Keyn 81 F3
Carre Gdns. W-S-M 88 C2
Carrington Rd. Bris 63 D2
Carroll Ct. Bris 36 C1
Carsons Rd. Sist 52 A1
Carter Rd. Paul 131 E3
Carter's Bldgs. Bris 62 C4
Carters Way. Chil 137 E2
Cartledge Rd. Bris 50 B1
Cashmore Ho. Bris 64 A4
Cassell Rd. Bris 51 E3
Cassey Bottom La. Bris 65 D4
Castle Cl. Back 76 C4
Castle Cl. Bris 34 C1
Castle Ct. Thorn 8 A1
Castle Farm La. Dun 78 A1
Castle Farm Rd. Kingsw 65 E1
Castle Gdns. Bath 101 F2
Castle Hill. Ban 107 E1
Castle La. Marsh 55 F1
Castle Rd. Cleve 57 F3
Castle Rd. Kingsw 51 E1
Castle Rd. Kingsw 66 B2
Castle Rd. Puck 53 E3
Castle Rd. W-S-M 88 C2
Castle St. Bris 63 F4
Castle St. Thorn 8 A1
Castle View Rd. Cleve 57 E3
Castlewood Cl. Cleve 57 E3
Caswell Hill. Portb 46 A1
Caswell La. Portb 46 B1
Catbrain Hill. Bris 35 D3
Catbrain La. Bris 35 D3
Catchpot La. Ch Sod 41 D3
Catemead. Cleve 73 E4
Cater Rd. Bris 79 D3
Catherine Hill. Olve 13 F1
Catherine Mead St. Bris 63 E2
Catherine Pl. Bath 101 F4
Catherine St. Avon 47 E4
Catherine Way. Bathe 86 A3
Catley Gr. Lo Ash 62 A1
Cato St. Bris 50 A1
Catsley Pl. Bath 85 E1
Cattistock Dr. Bris 65 D3
Cattle Market Rd. Bris 63 F3
Cattybrook Rd. Puck 52 B3
Cattybrook St. Bris 64 A4
Caulfield Rd. W-S-M 89 D2
Causeway The. Cong 91 E2
Causeway The. Fr Cot 38 B4
Causeway The. W in G 45 F1
Causeway The. Yatt 91 E4
Causeway View. Nail 59 E1
Causeway. Nail 59 D2
Causley Dr. Kingsw 66 A3
Cautletts Cl. Mid No 137 F4
Cavan Wlk. Bris 63 E1
Cave Ct. Bris 63 F4
Cave Dr. Bris 51 E3
Cave St. Bris 63 F4
Cavell Ct. Cleve 57 E1
Cavendish Cl. Keyn 82 B1
Cavendish Cres. Bath 101 F4
Cavendish Gdns. Bris 48 B2
Cavendish Rd. Bath 101 F4
Cavendish Rd. Bris 35 F4
Cavendish Rd. Bris 49 D3
Caveners Ct. W-S-M 88 A1
Caversham Dr. Nail 60 A1
Cecil Ave. Bris 50 C1
Cecil Rd. Bris 62 C4
Cecil Rd. Kingsw 65 E4
Cecil Rd. W-S-M 87 F1
Cedar Ave. W-S-M 88 B1
Cedar Cl. Bris 35 F4
Cedar Cl. Kingsw 66 A2
Cedar Cl. Lo Ash 61 F1
Cedar Dr. Keyn 81 E2
Cedar Gr. Bath 101 E2
Cedar Gr. Bris 48 B3
Cedar Hall. Bris 51 E4
Cedar Park. Bris 48 B3
Cedar Row. Bris 47 F3
Cedar Terr. Rad 132 B1
Cedar Way. Bath 101 F3
Cedar Way. Nail 60 A1
Cedar Way. Portis 45 E2
Cedar Way. Puck 53 E3
Cedar Way. Wint 37 E3
Cedarhurst Rd. Portis 44 C2
Cedars The. Ch St 95 E1
Cedric Rd. Bath 101 E4
Celandine Cl. Thorn 8 B1
Celestine Rd. Yate 27 E2
Celtic Way. Blea 122 B4
Cemetery Rd. Bris 64 A2
Cennick Ave. Kingsw 51 F1
Centaurus Rd. Bris 35 E4
Central Ave. Avon 22 A2
Central Ave. Kingsw 65 E3
Central Way. Cleve 57 F1
Ceres Cl. Kingsw 65 F1
Cerimon Gate. St Gif 36 C3
Cerney Gdns. Nail 60 A1
Cerney La. Bris 47 F3
Cesson Cl. Ch Sod 40 B4
Chadleigh Gr. Bris 79 E4
Chaffinch Dr. Rod 138 A4
Chaffins The. Cleve 57 F1
Chaingate La. Ir Act 27 D3
Chakeshill Cl. Bris 35 E2
Chakeshill Dr. Bris 35 E2
Chalcombe Cl. St Gif 36 B4
Chalcroft Wlk. Bris 78 C2
Chalfont Rd. W-S-M 105 E4
Chalford Cl. Yate 39 E4
Chalks Rd. Bris 64 B4
Chalks The. Ch Mag 96 A2
Challender Ave. Bris 34 C1
Challoner Ct. Bris 63 E3
Challow Dr. W-S-M 88 A1
Champion Rd. Kingsw 52 A1
Champneys Ave. Bris 34 C2
Chancel Cl. Nail 59 E1
Chancellors Pound. Wring 93 E2
Chancery St. Bris 64 A4
Chandag Rd. Keyn 82 A2
Chandler Cl. Bath 84 A1
Chandos Rd. Bris 49 E1
Chandos Rd. Keyn 81 F4
Chandos Trading Est. Bris 64 A3
Channel Hts. W-S-M 104 C1
Channel Rd. Cleve 57 F3
Channel View Cres. Portis 45 D3
Channel View Rd. Portis 45 D3
Channel's Hill. Bris 49 D4
Channon's Hill. Bris 50 C2
Chantry Cl. Nail 59 E1
Chantry Dr. W-S-M 89 D2
Chantry Gr. Bris 34 B1
Chantry La. Mang 37 F1
Chantry Mead Rd. Bath 101 F2
Chantry Rd. Bris 49 D1
Chantry Rd. Thorn 8 A1
Chapel Barton. Bris 63 D1
Chapel Barton. Nail 59 E1
Chapel Cl. Ch St 112 C4
Chapel Cl. Kingsw 66 A4
Chapel Cl. Nail 59 F1
Chapel Cl. Paul 130 C2
Chapel Cl. Win 95 D3
Chapel Gdns. Bris 35 D1
Chapel Green La. Bris 49 D1
Chapel Hill. Back 76 B4
Chapel Hill. But 111 E3
Chapel Hill. Cleve 57 E2
Chapel Hill. Newp 4 A4
Chapel Hill. Wring 92 B2
Chapel La. A Tur 43 D3
Chapel La. Bris 34 B1
Chapel La. Bris 50 C1
Chapel La. Bris 51 D2
Chapel La. Bris 51 E4
Chapel La. Brock 92 A4
Chapel La. Ch Sod 41 D4
Chapel La. Ch St 112 B4
Chapel La. Dyrh 54 B3
Chapel La. Hill 19 E4
Chapel La. Kingsw 66 A4
Chapel La. Thorn 9 D1
Chapel La. Win 95 D3
Chapel La. Yatt 91 F4
Chapel Rd. Bris 50 A1
Chapel Rd. Bris 79 D3
Chapel Rd. Kingsw 65 E3
Chapel Rd. Mid No 132 C2
Chapel Rd. O-on-S 7 E3
Chapel Row. Bath 101 F3
Chapel Row. Bathf 86 B1

Chapel Row. E in G 47 E2
Chapel Row. Luck 31 F2
Chapel St. Bris 64 A3
Chapel St. Thorn 15 D4
Chaplin Rd. Bris 50 A1
Chapter St. Bris 63 F4
Charbon Gate. St Gif 36 C3
Charborough Rd. Bris 35 F1
Charbury Wlk. Bris 47 F3
Chard Cl. Nail 75 F4
Chard Rd. Cleve 57 E1
Chardstock Ave. Bris 48 B4
Chardyke Dr. Clut 114 C1
Charfield Rd. Bris 35 E1
Charfield Rd. Kings 11 F3
Charfield. Kingsw 66 A4
Chargrove. Kingsw 66 B3
Chargrove. Yate 39 E4
Charis Ave. Bris 49 E4
Charity La. Hol 139 E1
Charity La. Kilm 139 E1
Charlcombe La. Bath 84 C2
Charlcombe La. Charl 84 C2
Charlcombe Rise. Bath 84 C1
Charlcombe View Rd. Bath . 85 D1
Charlcombe Way. Bath 84 C1
Charlecombe Ct. Bris 48 C3
Charlecombe Rd. Bris 48 C3
Charles Ave. St Gif 36 C2
Charles Cl. Thorn 8 B2
Charles Pl. Bris 63 D3
Charles Rd. Bris 36 A2
Charles St. Bath 101 F3
Charles St. Bris 63 E4
Charlotte St S. Bris 63 E3
Charlotte St. Bath 101 F3
Charlotte St. Bris 63 E4
Charlotte St. Bris 63 F4
Charlton Ave. Bris 35 F1
Charlton Ave. W-S-M 104 B2
Charlton Dr. Wrax 60 B4
Charlton Gdns. Bris 35 E2
Charlton La. Bris 35 D2
Charlton La. Kilm 84 B4
Charlton Mead Ct. Bris 35 E2
Charlton Mead Dr. Bris 35 E2
Charlton Park. Keyn 81 E3
Charlton Park. Rod 138 A4
Charlton Pl. Bris 35 E2
Charlton Rd. Bris 35 E2
Charlton Rd. Bris 51 D1
Charlton Rd. Co Dan 81 E2
Charlton Rd. Hol 138 B2
Charlton Rd. Keyn 81 E2
Charlton Rd. Kilm 138 B2
Charlton Rd. Rod 138 A4
Charlton Rd. W-S-M 104 B2
Charlton St. Bris 64 A4
Charlton View. Portis 45 E3
Charminster Rd. Bris 51 D2
Charmouth Rd. Bath 101 D4
Charnell Rd. Kingsw 51 F2
Charnhill Brow. Kingsw 52 A2
Charnhill Cres. Kingsw 51 F2
Charnhill Dr. Kingsw 51 F2
Charnhill Ridge. Kingsw 52 A2
Charnhill Vale. Kingsw 51 F2
Charnwood. Kingsw 52 A2
Charter Rd. W-S-M 105 D4
Charter Wlk. Bris 80 A3
Charterhouse Cl. Nail 59 F1
Charterhouse Rd. Bris 64 B4
Chase La. Kings 18 B3
Chase La. Wickw 18 B3
Chase Rd. Kingsw 51 E1
Chase The. Bris 51 E2
Chatcombe. Yate 39 F4
Chatham Park. Bath 102 A3
Chatham Row. Bath 102 A4
Chatsworth Pk. Thorn 8 B1
Chatsworth Rd. Bris 51 D2
Chatsworth Rd. Bris 64 B2
Chatterton Green. Bris 79 F2
Chatterton Rd. Yate 27 E1
Chatterton Sq. Bris 63 F3
Chatterton St. Bris 63 F3
Chaucer Rd. Bath 101 F2
Chaucer Rd. Rod 138 A4
Chaucer Rd. W-S-M 105 D2
Chaucer Wlk. Bris 50 A4
Chaundey Gr. Bris 79 D3
Chavenage. Kingsw 66 A4
Cheap St. Bath 102 A3
Cheapside St. Bris 63 F2
Cheapside. Bris 63 F4
Cheddar Cl. Nail 75 F4
Cheddar Gr. Bris 79 D4
Cheddar Rd. Axb 125 E1
Chedworth Rd. Bath 102 C2
Chedworth Rd. Bris 50 A3
Chedworth. Kingsw 51 F2
Chedworth. Yate 39 F4
Cheese La. Bris 63 F3
Chelford St Gif 36 A4
Chelmer Gr. Keyn 81 F2
Chelmsford Wlk. Bris 64 C3
Chelscombe. Bath 84 B1
Chelsea Cl. Keyn 82 A3

Chelsea Rd. Bath 101 E4
Chelsea Rd. Bris 50 A1
Chelsea Rd. Bris 64 A4
Chelsfield. Back 76 A4
Chelston Rd. Bris 79 E4
Chelswood Ave. W-S-M 105 E4
Chelswood Gdns. W-S-M .. 105 E4
Cheltenham La. Bris 49 F1
Cheltenham Rd. Bris 49 F1
Cheltenham St. Bath 101 F3
Chelvey Batch. Brock 75 F2
Chelvey La. Brock 75 F2
Chelvey Rd. Nail 75 E2
Chelvey Rise. Nail 60 A1
Chelvy Cl. Bris 79 E2
Chelwood Dr. Bath 101 E1
Chelwood Rd. Bris 47 E4
Chelwood Rd. Keyn 82 C2
Chepstow Park. Mang 37 F1
Chepstow Rd. Bris 79 E4
Chepstow Wlk. Keyn 81 E3
Chequers Cl. Kingsw 66 B2
Cherington Rd. Bris 49 E4
Cherington Rd. Nail 60 A1
Cherington. Kingsw 65 D3
Cherington. Yate 39 E3
Cheriton Pl. Bris 49 D4
Cheriton Pl. Kingsw 66 B3
Cherry Ave. Cleve 57 F1
Cherry Cl. Yatt 91 D4
Cherry Garden La. Kingsw .. 66 A1
Cherry Garden Rd. Kingsw . 66 B1
Cherry Gdns. Kingsw 66 B1
Cherry Gr. Mang 52 A3
Cherry Gr. Yatt 91 D4
Cherry Hay. Cleve 57 E1
Cherry La. Bris 63 F4
Cherry Orchard La. Bris 64 C4
Cherry Orchard La. Luck 31 E3
Cherry Rd. Ch Sod 28 A1
Cherry Rd. Lo Ash 61 F1
Cherry Rd. Nail 59 E4
Cherry Tree Cl. Bris 51 E1
Cherry Tree Cl. Keyn 81 E2
Cherry Tree Cl. Rad 132 C1
Cherry Tree Cres. Bris 51 E1
Cherry Wood. Kingsw 66 A1
Cherrytree Rd. Bris 51 E1
Cherrywood Rd. W-S-M 88 C1
Cherrywood Rise. W-S-M .. 88 C1
Chertsey Rd. Bris 49 D1
Cherwell Cl. Thorn 15 E4
Cherwell Rd. Keyn 82 A2
Chescombe Rd. Yatt 91 D4
Chesham Road N. W-S-M .. 105 D4
Chesham Road S. W-S-M .. 105 D4
Chesham Way. Kingsw 51 E1
Cheshire Cl. Yate 27 F2
Chesle Cl. Portis 44 C2
Chesle Way. Portis 44 C2
Cheslefield. Portis 44 C2
Chesley Hill. Wick 66 C4
Chessel Cl. St Gif 24 B1
Chessel St. Bris 63 D2
Chessell Ave. Piln 22 B4
Chessington Ave. Bris 80 A3
Chester Park Rd. Bris 51 D1
Chester Rd. Bris 64 C4
Chester St. Bris 50 A1
Chesterfield Ave. Bris 49 F1
Chesterfield Cl. Ban 106 C2
Chesterfield Rd. Bris 49 F1
Chesterfield Rd. Mang 51 F3
Chestermaster Cl. Alm 24 A3
Chesters. Kingsw 66 A2
Chesterton Dr. Nail 60 A1
Chestnut Ave. Axb 125 E1
Chestnut Ave. W-S-M 89 D1
Chestnut Cl. Ban 107 D2
Chestnut Cl. Bris 80 C3
Chestnut Cl. Cong 91 E2
Chestnut Cl. Paul 131 F3
Chestnut Cl. Rad 132 C1
Chestnut Ct. Mang 52 A3
Chestnut Dr. Ch Sod 28 A1
Chestnut Dr. Thorn 8 B1
Chestnut Dr. Yatt 74 C1
Chestnut Gr. Bath 101 E2
Chestnut Gr. Cleve 57 F2
Chestnut Gr. Westw 120 C2
Chestnut La. Blea 122 A4
Chestnut Park Est. Kings .. 11 F2
Chestnut Rd. Kingsw 51 F2
Chestnut Rd. Lo Ash 62 A1
Chestnut Rd. Mang 51 E3
Chestnut Way. Kingsw 51 F2
Chestnut Wlk. Bris 79 D3
Chestnut Wlk. Keyn 82 C2
Chestnuts The. Wins 125 D4
Chetwoode Cl. Bris 35 E2
Chevening Cl. St Gif 36 B2
Chever's La. N St P 135 F3
Cheviot Dr. Thorn 15 F4
Cheviot Way. Kingsw 66 B3
Chew Hill. Ch Mag 96 A2
Chew La. Ch Mag 95 F1
Chew La. Ch St 95 F1
Chew Rd. Ch Mag 95 E3

Chew Rd. Win 95 E3
Chew St. Ch Mag 96 A2
Chewton Cl. Bris 51 D2
Chewton Rd. Co Dan 81 F1
Chewton Rd. Keyn 81 F1
Cheyne Rd. Bris 48 B3
Che Ivey Rd. Brock 75 E3
Chichester Pl. Rad 133 D1
Chichester Way. Yate 27 E2
Chickwell La. Faulk 135 D1
Chilcompton Rd. Chil 137 F4
Chilcompton Rd. Mid No ... 137 F4
Chillington Ct. Bris 23 F1
Chillyhill La. Ch Mag 95 F1
Chillyhill La. Ch St 95 F1
Chiltern Cl. Bris 80 A2
Chiltern Cl. Kingsw 66 B3
Chiltern Park. Thorn 15 F4
Chilton Rd. Bath 85 D1
Chilton Rd. Bris 80 A4
Chilwood Cl. Ir Act 26 C2
Chimes The. Nail 75 E4
Chine The. Bris 50 B3
Chine View. Mang 51 F4
Chiphouse Rd. Kingsw 51 F2
Chippenham Rd. Marsh 70 A4
Chipperfield Dr. Kingsw 51 F1
Chipping Cross. Cleve 73 E4
Chipping The. Kings 11 F2
Chippings The. Bris 50 B3
Chisbury St. Bris 50 B2
Chittening Rd. Avon 33 F4
Chock La. Bris 49 D4
Christchurch Ave. Mang 51 E3
Christchurch Cl. Nail 59 F1
Christchurch La. Mang 51 E3
Christchurch Rd. Bris 63 D4
Christian Cl. W-S-M 89 D2
Christmas St. Bris 63 E4
Christmas Steps. Bris 63 E4
Christon Rd. Ban 107 D1
Christon Rd. Blea 123 E3
Christon Terr. W-S-M 104 C1
Chubb Cl. Kingsw 65 F3
Church Ave. Bris 48 C2
Church Ave. Bris 50 A1
Church Ave. Falf 9 F4
Church Ave. Sist 66 B4
Church Cl. Bathf 86 A1
Church Cl. Bris 34 C1
Church Cl. Cleve 57 D1
Church Cl. Fr Cot 38 A4
Church Cl. Portis 45 E3
Church Cl. Yatt 91 E4
Church Cnr. Lymp 122 A1
Church Ct. Mid No 132 A1
Church Dr. Bris 64 C4
Church Dr. Cong 91 E2
Church Farm Cl. Marks 99 D1
Church Hayes Cl. Nail 75 F4
Church Hayes Dr. Nail 75 F4
Church Hill. Bris 64 C1
Church Hill. Hi Cha 120 A3
Church Hill. Kilm 133 E2
Church Hill. O-on-S 7 D3
Church Hill. Olve 14 A2
Church Hill. Tims 116 A1
Church La. Axb 125 E1
Church La. Back 76 B3
Church La. Back 76 C4
Church La. Bath 102 B2
Church La. Bathe 85 F2
Church La. Bi Sut 113 E2
Church La. Bitt 82 C4
Church La. Blea 123 E2
Church La. Bris 34 C1
Church La. Bris 63 D3
Church La. Bris 63 E2
Church La. Bris 63 F3
Church La. Ch Sod 41 D4
Church La. Ch St 112 B4
Church La. Chil 137 E3
Church La. Chil 137 F1
Church La. Chur 108 B3
Church La. Clut 114 C2
Church La. Co Bi 124 A2
Church La. Co Dan 98 B3
Church La. Crom 10 A1
Church La. E Harp 128 C2
Church La. Farm 116 A3
Church La. Fr Cot 38 B3
Church La. Li St 120 A3
Church La. Lo Ash 62 B1
Church La. Lock 105 F1
Church La. Lymp 122 A1
Church La. Mang 37 F1
Church La. Marsh 70 A4
Church La. Mid No 132 A1
Church La. Nail 59 E1
Church La. Nail 59 E2
Church La. Paul 131 D2
Church La. Paul 131 F3
Church La. Portb 46 C2
Church La. Tims 116 A1
Church La. Wickw 16 C1
Church La. Wickw 18 A3
Church La. Wins 124 C3
Church La. Wint 37 E3

Church La. Yatt 91 E4
Church Leaze. Bris 47 E3
Church Par. Bris 64 C1
Church Pl. E in G 47 E2
Church Rd N. Portis 45 E3
Church Rd S. Portis 45 E2
Church Rd. Ab Lei 62 A4
Church Rd. Alm 23 D1
Church Rd. Alm 24 A3
Church Rd. Alve 15 D1
Church Rd. Bath 84 B1
Church Rd. Bath 102 B1
Church Rd. Bitt 82 C4
Church Rd. Bris 36 A2
Church Rd. Bris 48 B2
Church Rd. Bris 49 D4
Church Rd. Bris 49 F3
Church Rd. Bris 51 D4
Church Rd. Bris 63 E2
Church Rd. Bris 64 B4
Church Rd. Bris 79 D3
Church Rd. Bris 80 A2
Church Rd. Doyn 54 A1
Church Rd. Dun 78 B1
Church Rd. E in G 47 D2
Church Rd. Fr Cot 38 B4
Church Rd. Kingsw 51 F1
Church Rd. Kingsw 51 F2
Church Rd. Lo Ash 62 B3
Church Rd. Luck 31 F2
Church Rd. Lymp 122 A1
Church Rd. O-on-S 7 D2
Church Rd. O-on-S 7 D3
Church Rd. P St J 133 D4
Church Rd. Piln 22 A3
Church Rd. St Gif 36 C2
Church Rd. Thorn 8 A1
Church Rd. W-S-M 88 C1
Church Rd. Whit 80 A2
Church Rd. Whit 97 D4
Church Rd. Wick 67 D3
Church Rd. Win 95 D4
Church Rd. Wins 124 C4
Church Rd. Wint 37 F2
Church Rd. Yate 27 F1
Church Rd. Yatt 91 E4
Church Rise. Win 95 D4
Church Row. Chil 137 F1
Church Sq. Clut 114 C1
Church Sq. Mid No 132 A1
Church St. Ban 107 D2
Church St. Bath 84 A1
Church St. Bath 102 A2
Church St. Bath 102 A3
Church St. Bathf 86 A1
Church St. Blag 110 C1
Church St. Bris 50 A1
Church St. Bris 63 F3
Church St. Bris 64 A3
Church St. Charl 84 C3
Church St. N St P 135 F2
Church St. Paul 131 E3
Church St. Pens 97 E3
Church St. Rad 132 C1
Church Town. Back 76 B3
Church View. Bris 36 A2
Church View. Mang 51 E3
Church View. Newp 4 B4
Church View. Win 95 D3
Church Wlk. E in G 47 E2
Church Wlk. Wring 92 B1
Churchdown Wlk. Bris 47 F3
Churchend La. Char 10 C2
Churchfarm Cl. Yate 27 F2
Churchhill Rd. Bris 64 B2
Churchill Ave. Cleve 57 E1
Churchill Cl. Cleve 57 E1
Churchill Cl. Kingsw 66 A3
Churchill Dr. Bris 48 B4
Churchill Gate. Chur 108 C2
Churchill Green. Chur 108 A3
Churchill Rd. W-S-M 105 D4
Churchlands Rd. Bris 63 D1
Churchpath Rd. E in G 47 E2
Churchward Cl. Kingsw 65 D3
Churchward Rd. W-S-M 89 D2
Churchward Rd. Yate 27 D2
Churchway. Faulk 134 B1
Churchways Ave. Bris 49 F3
Churchways Cres. Bris 49 F3
Churchways. Whit 80 B2
Churston Cl. Bris 80 A2
Circle The. Bath 101 D2
Circular Rd. Bris 48 C1
Circus Mews. Bath 101 F4
Circus Pl. Bath 101 F4
Circus The. Bath 101 F4
City Bsns Pk. Bris 64 A4
City Rd. Bris 49 F1
Clamp The. Kingsw 66 B2
Clanage Rd. Bris 62 C2
Clanders Batch. Blag 110 B2
Clandown Rd. Paul 131 F2
Clapton Dro. W in G 45 E1
Clapton La. W in G 45 F1
Clapton Rd. Mid No 131 E1
Clapton Rd. Ston E 131 E1

Clare Ave. Bris 49 E1
Clare Gdns. Bath 101 E1
Clare Rd. Bris 49 E1
Clare Rd. Bris 50 A1
Clare Rd. Bris 51 E1
Clare St. Bris 63 E3
Clare St. Bris 64 B4
Clare Wlk. Thorn 8 A1
Claremont Ave. Bris 49 E2
Claremont Bldgs. Bath 85 D1
Claremont Cres. W-S-M 87 D1
Claremont Gdns. Cleve 57 F1
Claremont Gdns. Nail 59 E1
Claremont Rd. Bath 85 D1
Claremont Rd. Bris 49 E2
Claremont St. Bris 50 A1
Claremont Terr. Bris 64 B4
Claremont Wlk. Bath 85 D1
Clarence Ave. Mang 51 F3
Clarence Gdns. Mang 51 F3
Clarence Grove Rd. W-S-M 104 C3
Clarence Pl. Bath 101 D1
Clarence Pl. Bris 63 E4
Clarence Rd E. W-S-M 104 C3
Clarence Rd N. W-S-M 104 B3
Clarence Rd S. W-S-M 104 B3
Clarence Rd. Bris 51 D1
Clarence Rd. Bris 63 F3
Clarence Rd. Bris 64 A4
Clarence Rd. Mang 51 F3
Clarence St. Bath 102 A4
Clarendon Rd. Bath 102 A3
Clarendon Rd. Bris 49 E1
Clarendon Rd. W-S-M 104 C4
Clark Dr. Bris 50 C4
Clark St. Bris 64 A4
Clarke St. Bris 63 E2
Clarken Cl. Nail 59 F1
Clarken Coombe. Lo Ash 62 A2
Clarkson Ave. W-S-M 88 B1
Clatworthy Dr. Bris 80 A4
Claude Ave. Bath 101 E3
Clavell Rd. Bris 34 C1
Claverham Cl. Yatt 91 E4
Claverham Dro. Yatt 74 B3
Claverham Park. Yatt 91 F4
Claverham Rd. Bris 51 D3
Claverham Rd. Yatt 91 F4
Claverton Ct. Bath 102 C2
Claverton Down Rd. Bath .. 102 C2
Claverton Rd W. Keyn 82 B2
Claverton Rd. Keyn 82 B2
Claverton St. Bath 102 A3
Clay Bottom. Bris 50 C1
Clay Hill. Bris 50 C1
Clay La. Bitt 66 B1
Clay La. St Gif 36 B4
Clay La. Thorn 8 C1
Clay Pit Rd. Bris 49 D2
Claydon Green. Bris 79 F2
Clayfield Rd. Bris 64 C2
Clayfield. Yate 27 F3
Claymore Cres. Bris 51 D1
Claypiece Rd. Bris 79 D2
Claypit Hill. Ch Sod 40 A4
Claypool Rd. Kingsw 65 F4
Clayton Cl. Portis 45 E2
Clayton St. Avon 33 D1
Clayton St. Bris 64 A4
Cleave St. Bris 50 A1
Cleeve Ave. Mang 51 F4
Cleeve Dr. Brock 92 A4
Cleeve Gdns. Mang 51 E4
Cleeve Gr. Keyn 81 E3
Cleeve Green. Bath 101 E2
Cleeve Hill Extension. Mang 51 F4
Cleeve Hill Rd. Brock 92 B4
Cleeve Hill. Co Mar 127 F4
Cleeve Hill. Mang 51 E4
Cleeve La. Wick 53 E1
Cleeve Lawns. Mang 51 F4
Cleeve Lodge Cl. Mang 51 F3
Cleeve Lodge Rd. Mang 51 F3
Cleeve Park Rd. Mang 51 F4
Cleeve Pl. Nail 60 A1
Cleeve Rd. Bris 51 E1
Cleeve Rd. Bris 64 A2
Cleeve Rd. Mang 51 F4
Cleeve Rd. Yate 27 F1
Cleeve Wood Rd. Mang 51 E4
Cleevedale Rd. Bath 102 A1
Clement St. Bris 63 F4
Cleve Rd. Bris 36 A2
Clevedale. Mang 51 E4
Clevedon La. W in G 59 E4
Clevedon Rd. Bris 49 E2
Clevedon Rd. Lo Ash 61 E2
Clevedon Rd. Lo Ash 77 D4
Clevedon Rd. Mid No 132 A1
Clevedon Rd. Nail 59 E2
Clevedon Rd. Portis 45 E3
Clevedon Rd. W-S-M 104 C3
Clevedon Rd. Wrax 60 B2
Clevedon Rd. Wrax 60 B3
Clevedon Terr. Bris 63 E4
Cleveland Cl. Thorn 15 F4
Cleveland Pl. Bath 102 A4

Cleveland Wlk. Bath

Cleveland Wlk. Bath 102 B3
Cliff Court Dr. Bris 51 D4
Cliff Rd. Priddy 126 A1
Cliff Rd. W-S-M 88 A1
Cliffe Dr. Li St 120 A3
Clifford Gdns. Bris 47 F3
Clifford Rd. Bris 51 E2
Clift House Rd. Bris 63 D2
Clift House Spur. Bris 62 C2
Clift Pl. Bris 63 E3
Clift Rd. Bris 63 D2
Clifton Ave. W-S-M 104 C3
Clifton Cl. Bris 62 C4
Clifton Down Rd. Bris 63 D4
Clifton Down. Bris 62 C4
Clifton Hill. Bris 63 D3
Clifton Park Rd. Bris 62 C4
Clifton Park. Bris 63 D4
Clifton Pl. Bris 64 A4
Clifton Rd. Bris 63 D4
Clifton Rd. W-S-M 104 C3
Clifton St. Bris 63 E2
Clifton St. Bris 64 A4
Clifton St. Portis 45 E1
Clifton Vale Cl. Bris 63 D3
Clifton Vale. Bris 63 D3
Clifton View. Bris 63 F2
Clifton Wood Rd. Bris 63 D3
Cliftonwood Cres. Bris 63 D3
Cliftonwood Terr. Bris 63 D3
Clinton Rd. Bris 63 E1
Clive Rd. Bris 80 B4
Cloisters Rd. Wint 37 F3
Clonmel Rd. Bris 63 E1
Close The. Bris 35 D3
Close The. Fr Cot 38 B3
Close The. Kingsw 51 E2
Close The. St Gif 24 B1
Close The. St Gif 36 B3
Close The. W in G 44 C1
Closemead. Cleve 57 E1
Clothier Rd. Bris 64 C1
Clouds Hill Ave. Bris 64 C4
Clouds Hill Rd. Bris 64 C4
Clovelly Cl. Bris 64 C4
Clovelly Rd. Bris 64 C4
Clovelly Rd. W-S-M 89 D1
Clover Cl. Cleve 57 F2
Clover Ground. Bris 49 D4
Clover Leaze. St Gif 36 B3
Cloverdale Dr. Kingsw 66 A2
Cloverlea Rd. Kingsw 66 B3
Clutton Hill. Clut 115 D2
Clyde Ave. Keyn 81 F2
Clyde Gdns. Bath 101 D3
Clyde Gdns. Bris 65 D3
Clyde Gr. Bris 35 F1
Clyde La. Bris 49 E1
Clyde Park. Bris 49 D1
Clyde Rd. Bris 49 D1
Clyde Rd. Bris 64 A2
Clyde Rd. Fr Cot 38 A4
Clyde Terr. Bris 63 E2
Clyde Terr. Bris 64 A2
Clydesdale Cl. Bris 80 A3
Clynder Gr. Cleve 57 F3
Co-operation Rd. Bris 50 B1
Coalbridge Cl. W-S-M 88 C1
Coaley Rd. Bris 47 E3
Coalpit La. Chil 137 D1
Coalpit Rd. Bathe 86 A2
Coalsack La. West 38 A2
Coalville Rd. Fr Cot 38 B4
Coape Rd. Bris 80 C3
Coates Gr. Nail 60 A1
Coates Wlk. Bris 79 E3
Cobblestone Mews. Bris 63 D4
Cobhorn Dr. Bris 78 C2
Cobley Croft. Cleve 73 E4
Cobourg Rd. Bris 49 F1
Cobthorn Way. Cong 91 F3
Cock And Yew Tree Hill. Win 95 D1
Cock La. Dyrh 54 B3
Cock Rd. Kingsw 65 F3
Cockers Hill. Co Dan 98 B3
Codben St. Bris 64 B4
Codrington Rd. Bris 49 E2
Cody Ct. Kingsw 65 D3
Cogan Rd. Kingsw 51 F2
Cogsall Rd. Bris 80 C3
Coker Rd. W-S-M 89 D1
Colbourne Rd. Bath 101 E1
Colchester Cres. Bris 79 E4
Coldharbour La. Bris 36 C1
Coldharbour La. W-S-M 104 B2
Coldharbour Rd. Bris 49 D2
Coldpark Gdns. Bris 78 C3
Coldpark Rd. Bris 78 C3
Coldrick Cl. Bris 79 F2
Cole Rd. Bris 64 A3
Colebrook Rd. Bris 65 E4
Coleford Rd. Bris 35 E1
Colehouse La. Cleve 73 E4
Coleridge Rd. Bris 50 B2
Coleridge Rd. Cleve 57 E2
Coleridge Rd. W-S-M 105 D2
Coleridge Vale Rd E. Cleve 57 E1
Coleridge Vale Rd N. Cleve 57 E1

Coleridge Vale Rd S. Cleve 57 E1
Coleridge Vale Rd W. Cleve 57 E1
Coles Gdns. Kilm 139 D3
Colesborne Cl. Yate 39 E4
Coleshill Dr. Bris 79 D3
Coley Rd. E Harp 129 D2
Colin Rd. Thorn 8 B1
College Ave. Bris 51 D3
College Ct. Bris 51 D3
College Fields. Bris 62 C4
College Green. Bris 63 E3
College Park Dr. Bris 34 C1
College Rd. Bath 84 C1
College Rd. Bris 49 D4
College Rd. Bris 51 D3
College Rd. Bris 62 C4
College Sq. Bris 63 E3
College St. Bris 63 E3
Collet Cl Lock 89 E2
Collett Cl. Kingsw 65 D3
Collier Cl. Tims 132 B4
Colliers La. Charl 84 C2
Collin Rd. Bris 64 B2
Collingwood Ave. Kingsw 51 F1
Collingwood Cl. Keyn 82 C1
Collingwood Cl. W-S-M 88 C2
Collingwood Rd. Bris 49 D1
Collins Ave. St Gif 36 B3
Collins St. Avon 47 D4
Collinson Rd. Bris 79 D3
Colliter Cres. Bris 63 D1
Collum La. W St L 88 C3
Collum La. W-S-M 88 C3
Coln Sq. Thorn 15 E4
Colne Green. Keyn 82 A2
Colombo Cres. W-S-M 104 C2
Colonnades The. Bath 101 F3
Colston Ave. Bris 63 E4
Colston Cl. Kingsw 51 E2
Colston Cl. Wint 37 F2
Colston Cl. Bris 49 E2
Colston Dale. Bris 50 C2
Colston Hill. Bris 50 B3
Colston Par. Bris 63 F3
Colston Rd. Bris 50 B1
Colston St. Bris 63 E4
Colston St. Kingsw 51 E2
Colthurst Dr. Kingsw 65 F2
Colts Green. Ch Sod 40 C4
Colwyn Rd. Bris 50 B1
Colyton. W-S-M 89 D1
Comb Paddock. Bris 49 D4
Combe Ave. Portis 45 E3
Combe End. Mid No 132 C2
Combe Fields. Portis 45 E3
Combe Hay La. Bath 118 A3
Combe Hay La. Sosto 118 A3
Combe La. Paul 131 D3
Combe Rd. Bath 101 D4
Combe Rd. Portis 45 E3
Combe Road Cl. Bath 102 A1
Combe Side. Back 76 A4
Combe The. Blag 109 F1
Combeside. Bath 102 A2
Combfactory La. Bris 64 A4
Commercial Rd. Bris 63 E3
Common (E) The. St Gif 24 B1
Common La. Chur 108 A3
Common La. E in G 47 D1
Common Mead La. Bris 37 D1
Common Rd. Kingsw 65 D2
Common Rd. Wint 37 F4
Common The. Bris 51 D4
Common The. St Gif 24 B1
Commonfield Rd. Bris 34 A1
Commonmead La. Ch Sod 29 D1
Compton Dr. Bris 48 B4
Compton Green. Keyn 81 F2
Compton St. Bris 64 B4
Comrade Ave. Ship 125 F4
Comyn Wlk. Bris 51 D3
Concorde Dr. Bris 35 D1
Concorde Rd. Bris 35 F4
Condor Cl. W-S-M 105 D3
Condover Rd. Bris 65 D2
Conduit Pl. Bris 50 A1
Conduit Rd. Bris 50 A1
Congleton Rd. Bris 64 B4
Conham Hill. Kingsw 65 D3
Conham Rd. Bris 64 C3
Conham Vale. Bris 65 D3
Conham Vale. Kingsw 65 D3
Conifer Cl. Bris 51 E3
Conifer Cl. Fr Cot 26 A1
Conifer Way. Lock 105 F3
Coniston Ave. Bris 48 C3
Coniston Cl. Kingsw 66 B3
Coniston Cres. W-S-M 104 C2
Coniston Rd. Bris 23 F1
Conkwell. Winsl 103 E1
Connaught Rd. Bris 79 F4
Connection Rd. Bath 101 D3
Constable Dr. W-S-M 88 C2
Constable Rd. Bris 50 C1
Constantine Ave. St Gif 36 C3
Constitution Hill. Bris 63 D3

Convent Cl. Bris 34 B2
Convocation Ave. Bath 102 C3
Conway Green. Keyn 82 A2
Conway Rd. Bris 64 B2
Conygar Gr. Bris 36 B2
Conygre Green. Tims 116 A1
Conygre Rd. Bris 36 A2
Conygre Rise. Farm 115 F3
Cook Cl. Kingsw 66 B2
Cook St. Avon 47 E4
Cook's Folly Rd. Bris 48 B2
Cook's La. Ban 107 D2
Cook's La. Cleve 58 A1
Cook's La. Cleve 58 B1
Cooke's Dr. Alm 23 D1
Cooksley Rd. Bris 64 B4
Cooks Bridle Path. Wring 93 E4
Cooks Cl. St Gif 24 B1
Cooks La. West 38 B4
Cookworthy Cl. Bris 64 A3
Coombe Ave. Thorn 8 A1
Coombe Bridge Ave. Bris 48 B3
Coombe Cl. Bris 34 B2
Coombe Dale. Bris 48 B3
Coombe Dale. Wring 94 A4
Coombe Gdns. Bris 48 C3
Coombe La. Bris 48 C3
Coombe La. Co Bi 124 A2
Coombe La. E Harp 128 C2
Coombe La. E n G 47 D1
Coombe Park. Bath 101 E4
Coombe Rd. Bris 50 B1
Coombe Rd. Nail 59 F1
Coombe Rd. W-S-M 104 C4
Coombe The. Blag 110 B2
Coombe The. Co Mar 128 A3
Coombe Way. Bris 34 C1
Coombes Way. Kingsw 66 B2
Cooper Rd. Thorn 15 D4
Cooper Rd. Bris 48 C4
Cooperage La. Bris 63 D3
Cooperage Rd. Bris 64 B4
Coots The. Bris 80 C3
Cope Park. Alm 24 B3
Copeland Dr. Bris 80 A3
Copford La. Lo Ash 62 A1
Copley Ct. Kingsw 65 F3
Copley Gdns. Bris 50 A3
Copley Gdns. W-S-M 88 C1
Copperfield Dr. W-S-M 88 C2
Coppice End Cnr. Lymp 122 B1
Coppice The. Bris 78 C2
Coppice The. St Gif 36 C4
Copse Cl. W-S-M 105 D1
Copse End. Winsc 107 F1
Copse Rd. Bris 64 A2
Copse Rd. Cleve 57 E2
Copse Rd. Keyn 82 B2
Copseland. Bath 102 B3
Copythorne Rd. Bris 50 A4
Coralberry Dr. W-S-M 88 C1
Corbet Cl. Bris 34 B1
Cordington Pl. Bris 63 D4
Cordwell Wlk. Bris 49 E4
Corey Cl. Bris 49 F1
Corfe Cl. Nail 59 E1
Corfe Cres. Keyn 81 F2
Corfe Pl. Kingsw 66 A1
Corfe Rd. Bris 79 E4
Coriander Wlk. Bris 50 B1
Corinthian Ct. Bris 63 F3
Cork St. Bath 101 E4
Corker's Hill. Bris 64 C3
Cormorant Cl. W-S-M 88 C1
Corn St. Bath 101 F3
Corn St. Bris 63 E3
Corner Croft. Cleve 57 E1
Cornhill Dr. Bris 80 A4
Cornish Gr. Bris 80 C3
Cornish Rd. Bris 80 C3
Cornish Wlk. Bris 80 C3
Cornish's Grave. Kilm 139 F2
Cornleaze. Bris 79 D3
Cornwall Cres. Yate 27 F2
Cornwall Rd. Bris 49 E2
Cornwallis Ave. Bris 63 D3
Cornwallis Ave. W-S-M 88 C2
Cornwallis Cres. Bris 62 C3
Cornwallis Gr. Bris 63 D3
Coronation Ave. Bath 101 E2
Coronation Ave. Bris 51 D2
Coronation Ave. Keyn 81 E2
Coronation Cl. Kingsw 66 A3
Coronation Pl. Bris 63 E3
Coronation Rd. Ban 107 D2
Coronation Rd. Bath 101 E4
Coronation Rd. Blea 122 B3
Coronation Rd. Bris 63 E3
Coronation Rd. Kingsw 66 A3
Coronation Rd. Kingsw 66 A4
Coronation Rd. Mang 51 F2
Coronation Rd. W-S-M 88 C1
Corondale Rd. W-S-M 105 D4
Corridor The. Bath 102 A3
Corsley Wlk. Bris 79 F3
Corston View. Bath 101 E1
Corston Wlk. Bris 47 E4

Corston. W-S-M 105 D1
Cossham Cl. Thorn 8 B1
Cossham Rd. Bris 64 B4
Cossham Rd. Puck 53 D2
Cossham St. Mang 52 A3
Cossham Wlk. Bris 51 D1
Cossington Rd. Bris 79 F4
Cossins Rd. Bris 49 D2
Costers Cl. Alve 15 D3
Costiland Dr. Bris 78 C3
Cote Dr. Bris 49 D3
Cote House La. Bris 49 D3
Cote La. Bris 49 D3
Cote Lea Park. Bris 49 D4
Cote Paddock. Bris 48 C2
Cote Rd. Bris 49 D2
Cotham Brow. Bris 49 E1
Cotham Gdns. Bris 49 D1
Cotham Gr. Bris 49 E1
Cotham Hill. Bris 63 E4
Cotham Lawn Rd. Bris 49 E1
Cotham Park N. Bris 49 E1
Cotham Park. Bris 49 E1
Cotham Rd S. Bris 63 E4
Cotham Rd. Bris 63 E4
Cotham Side. Bris 49 E1
Cotham Vale. Bris 49 E1
Cotman Wlk. Bris 50 A3
Cotman Wlk. W-S-M 88 C1
Cotrith Gr. Bris 34 C2
Cotswold Cl. Portis 45 F2
Cotswold La. Ch Sod 41 D4
Cotswold Rd. Bath 101 E2
Cotswold Rd. Bris 63 E2
Cotswold Rd. Ch Sod 40 A4
Cotswold View. Bris 36 A2
Cotswold View. Char 11 D3
Cotswold View. Kingsw 51 E1
Cotswold View. Wickww 18 A3
Cottage Pl. Bris 63 E4
Cottington Ct. Kingsw 65 F3
Cottisford Rd. Bris 50 A2
Cottle Gdns. Bris 80 C3
Cottle Rd. Bris 80 C3
Cottles La. Winsl 120 C3
Cotton Mead. Cor 100 A4
Cottonwood Dr. Kingsw 66 A2
Cottrell Ave. Bris 51 E1
Cottrell Rd. Bris 50 B2
Cotts The. Wring 92 B3
Coulson Dr. W-S-M 89 D2
Coulson Wlk. Bris 51 E1
Coulson's Cl. Bris 80 A2
Coulson's Rd. Bris 80 A2
Counterpool Rd. Kingsw 65 E4
Counterslip Gdns. Bris 80 B3
Counterslip. Bris 63 F3
Countess Wlk. Bris 50 B3
County St. Bris 64 A2
Court Ave. St Gif 36 C3
Court Ave. Yatt 91 E4
Court Cl. Back 76 B3
Court Cl. Bris 49 F4
Court Cl. Portis 45 E2
Court Farm Rd. Bris 79 F2
Court Farm Rd. Kingsw 65 F1
Court Gdns. Bathe 86 A2
Court Hay. E in G 47 D2
Court Hill. Co Dan 98 B3
Court La. Bathf 86 A1
Court La. Cleve 58 A1
Court La. Wick 67 D3
Court La. Wins 125 F4
Court Mead. Stone 3 F2
Court Meadow. Stone 3 F2
Court Pl. W-S-M 88 C1
Court Rd. Bris 49 F3
Court Rd. Fr Cot 37 F4
Court Rd. Kingsw 65 E4
Court Rd. Kingsw 66 B2
Court Rd. W St L 88 A3
Court View Cl. Alm 24 A3
Court View. Wick 67 E3
Courtenay Rd. Keyn 82 A1
Courtenay Wlk. W-S-M 89 D2
Courtenay Cres. Bris 79 E4
Courtfield Gr. Bris 51 D2
Courtlands La. Bris 62 C2
Courtlands. Keyn 81 F3
Courtlands. St Gif 24 B1
Courtmead. Sosto 118 C4
Courtney Rd. Kingsw 65 F4
Courtney Way. Kingsw 66 A4
Courtside Mews. Bris 49 E1
Courtville Cl. Alve 15 D2
Courtyard The. Nail 59 F1
Cousins Cl. Bris 34 B2
Cousins La. Bris 64 C4
Couzens Cl. Yate 28 A1
Couzens Pl. St Gif 36 C3
Coventry Rd. Bris 64 C3
Cowdray Rd. Bris 79 E4
Cowleaze La. E Harp 128 B3
Cowler Wlk. Bris 78 C2
Cowling Dr. Bris 80 B3
Cowling Rd. Bris 80 B3
Cowper Rd. Bris 49 E1

Cowper St. Bris 64 B4
Cowship La. Crom 17 E3
Cowship La. Wickw 17 E3
Cowslip La. Blea 123 E2
Cox Ct. Kingsw 65 F2
Cox's Green. Wring 92 C1
Coxley Dr. Bath 85 D1
Coxway. Cleve 57 F1
Crabtree Cl. Dun 78 B1
Crabtree La. Dun 78 B1
Crabtree Wlk. Bris 50 B1
Craddock Cl. Kingsw 66 A2
Cranberry Wlk. Bris 48 B4
Cranbourne Chase. W-S-M 88 A1
Cranbourne Rd. Bris 35 F4
Cranbrook Rd. Bris 49 E2
Crandale Rd. Bath 101 D3
Crandell Cl. Bris 34 C2
Crane Cl. Kingsw 66 A4
Cranford Cl. W-S-M 88 B1
Cranham Cl. Kingsw 51 F1
Cranham Dr. St Gif 24 B1
Cranham Rd. Bris 49 E4
Cranham. Yate 39 E4
Cranhill Rd. Bath 101 E4
Cranleigh Court Rd. Yate 27 E1
Cranleigh Gdns. Bris 48 C2
Cranleigh Rd. Bris 80 A3
Cranleigh. Sosto 118 C4
Cranmore Ave. Keyn 81 F3
Cranmore Cres. Bris 35 E1
Cranmore Pl. Bath 118 C4
Cranmore. W-S-M 105 D1
Cranside Ave. Bris 49 E2
Cransley Cres. Bris 49 E4
Crantock Ave. Bris 79 D4
Crantock Dr. Alm 24 B3
Crantock Rd. Yate 27 E1
Cranwell Gr. Bris 80 A3
Cranwells Park. Bath 101 E4
Crates Cl. Kingsw 65 F4
Craven Way. Kingsw 65 F3
Crawford Cl. Cleve 57 D1
Crawl La. Mid No 132 B2
Craydon Gr. Bris 80 B2
Craydon Rd. Bris 80 B3
Craydon Wlk. Bris 80 B3
Crediton Cres. Bris 63 F1
Crediton. W-S-M 89 D1
Crescent La. Bath 101 F4
Crescent Rd. Bris 51 E3
Crescent The. Back 76 A3
Crescent The. Bris 48 B3
Crescent The. Bris 49 E3
Crescent The. Kingsw 51 E2
Crescent The. Lymp 122 B3
Crescent The. Olve 14 B2
Crescent The. Paul 131 D2
Crescent The. Pens 96 C1
Crescent The. W-S-M 88 A1
Crescent View. Bath 101 F3
Crescent View. Wick 67 E4
Cresswell Cl. W-S-M 89 D1
Crest The. Bris 64 B1
Creswicke Ave. Kingsw 65 E3
Creswicke Rd. Bris 79 F4
Crew's Hole Rd. Bris 64 C4
Crewkerne Cl. Nail 60 A1
Cribbs Causeway Centre.
Bris 35 E3
Cribbs Causeway. Bris 35 D3
Crickback La. Ch Mag 96 A2
Cricket Field Green. Nail 59 E1
Cricklade Cl. Nail 60 A1
Cricklade Rd. Bris 49 F2
Cripps Rd. Bris 63 E2
Crispin La. Thorn 8 A1
Crispin Way. Kingsw 51 F1
Crockerne Dr. E in G 47 E2
Crocombe La. Tims 116 B2
Crocombe. Tims 116 B2
Croft Ave. Bris 50 B2
Croft Cl. Bitt 82 B4
Croft Rd. Bath 85 D1
Croft The. Back 76 A4
Croft The. Bath 102 C1
Croft The. Cleve 57 F2
Croft The. Kingsw 66 B2
Croft The. Lock 105 F2
Croft The. Mang 51 F3
Croft The. Westw 120 C2
Croft View. Bris 49 E3
Crofton Ave. Bris 49 F3
Crofts End Rd. Bris 50 C1
Crokeswood Wlk. Bris 34 A1
Crome Rd. Bris 50 A4
Cromer Rd. Bris 50 B1
Cromer Rd. W-S-M 104 C3
Cromhall La. Crom 9 F1
Cromwell Ct. Kingsw 65 F3
Cromwell Dr. W-S-M 89 D2
Cromwell Rd. Bris 49 F1
Cromwell Rd. Bris 65 D4
Cromwell St. Bris 63 E2
Cromwells Hide. Bris 50 C3
Crook's La. W-S-M 88 A2
Croomes Hill. Mang 51 E3
Cropthorne Rd. Bris 36 A1

Cropthorne Rd. Bris

Crosby Row. Bris

Crosby Row. Bris ... 63 D3
Cross Combe Dr. Bris ... 79 E2
Cross Combez Wlk. Bris ... 79 D2
Cross Elms La. Bris ... 48 C3
Cross Hands Rd. Piln ... 22 B4
Cross La. Co Bi ... 125 D1
Cross Lanes. E in G ... 47 E2
Cross Manor Rd. Axb ... 125 D1
Cross Moor Dr. Axb ... 125 D1
Cross Moor Dro. Co Bi ... 124 C2
Cross St. Bris ... 51 E1
Cross St. Keyn ... 81 F4
Cross St. W-S-M ... 104 C4
Cross The. E Harp ... 128 C2
Cross Tree Gr. St Gif ... 36 B4
Cross Wlk. Bris ... 80 A3
Crossfield Rd. Kingsw ... 51 F2
Crossleaze Rd. Kingsw ... 65 D2
Crossley Cl. Wint ... 37 F4
Crossman Ave. Wint ... 37 F3
Crossman Wlk. Cleve ... 57 F1
Crosspost La. Co Dan ... 99 D2
Crossway La. Ston E ... 137 D4
Crossways. Bris ... 64 A1
Crossways Rd. Thorn ... 8 A1
Crossways. Newp ... 4 C2
Crow La. Bris ... 34 C1
Crow La. Bris ... 63 E3
Crow Meadow. Kings ... 11 F2
Crowe Hill. Li St ... 120 A3
Crowe La. Hi Cha ... 120 A3
Crown Gdns. Kingsw ... 66 A4
Crown Glass Pl. Nail ... 59 F2
Crown Hill Wlk. Bris ... 50 C1
Crown Hill. Bath ... 84 B1
Crown Hill. Bris ... 64 C4
Crown Hill. Kingsw ... 66 B2
Crown Hill. Win ... 95 D2
Crown House. Nail ... 59 E1
Crown La. Kingsw ... 51 E2
Crown Rd. Bath ... 84 A1
Crown Rd. Kingsw ... 51 E1
Crown Rd. Kingsw ... 66 B3
Crowndale Rd. Bris ... 64 A2
Crownleaze. Kingsw ... 51 E2
Crows Gr. St Gif ... 24 B2
Crowther Park. Bris ... 50 A2
Crowther Rd. Bris ... 50 A2
Crowther St. Bris ... 63 D2
Crowthers Ave. Yate ... 27 F2
Croydon St. Bris ... 64 A4
Crunnis The. St Gif ... 36 C3
Cuck Hill. Ship ... 125 F4
Cuckoo La. Clut ... 115 D2
Cuckoo La. Wint ... 37 F2
Cuckoo La. Wrax ... 60 A3
Cuffington Ave. Bris ... 64 B2
Culleysgate La. Wick ... 67 F3
Culver La. E Harp ... 128 C2
Culver St. Bris ... 63 E3
Culverhay. Co Dan ... 98 B3
Culverhill Rd. Ch Sod ... 28 A1
Culvers Rd. Keyn ... 81 F3
Culverwell Rd. Bris ... 79 D2
Cumberland Basin Rd. Bris . 62 C3
Cumberland Cl. Bris ... 63 D3
Cumberland Gr. Bris ... 49 F1
Cumberland Pl. Bris ... 62 C3
Cumberland Rd. Bris ... 63 D3
Cumberland Row. Bath ... 101 F3
Cumberland St. Bris ... 63 F4
Cumbria Cl. Thorn ... 8 C1
Cunningham Gdns. Bris ... 51 D3
Curland Gr. Bris ... 80 A3
Curlew Cl. Bris ... 50 C3
Curlew Gdns. W-S-M ... 88 C1
Currells La. Win ... 77 D1
Curtis La. St Gif ... 37 D2
Custom Cl. Bris ... 80 A4
Cutler Rd. Bris ... 78 C3
Cutsheath Rd. Tyth ... 16 B4
Cuttsheath Rd. Thorn ... 16 B4
Cygnet Cres. W-S-M ... 88 C1
Cynthia Rd. Bath ... 101 E3
Cypress Ct. Bris ... 48 B2
Cypress Gdns. Lo Ash ... 62 C3
Cypress Gr. Bris ... 49 E3
Cypress Terr. Rad ... 132 B1
Cypress Wlk. Col ... 70 C3

Dafford St. Bath ... 85 E1
Dafford's Bldgs. Bath ... 85 E1
Daglands The. Tims ... 132 C4
Dairy Hill. Well ... 134 A3
Daisy Green La. N Nib ... 5 E1
Daisy Rd. Bris ... 50 B1
Dakota Dr. Bris ... 80 A2
Dalby Ave. Bris ... 63 E2
Daldry Gdns. Olve ... 14 A2
Dale St. Bris ... 63 F4
Dale St. Bris ... 64 C4
Daley Cl. W-S-M ... 89 D2
Dalkeith Ave. Bris ... 51 E1
Dalrymple Rd. Bris ... 49 F1
Dalston Rd. Bris ... 63 D2
Dalton Sq. Bris ... 63 F4
Dalwood. W-S-M ... 89 D1
Dame Court Cl. W-S-M ... 88 C2

Damery La. N Nib ... 4 A1
Damery La. Stone ... 4 A1
Dampier Rd. Bris ... 63 D2
Danbury Cres. Bris ... 35 E1
Danbury Wlk. Bris ... 35 E1
Dancey Mead. Bris ... 78 C4
Dane Cl. Winsl ... 120 C4
Dane Rise. Winsl ... 120 C4
Daneacre Rd. Mid No ... 133 D2
Dangerfield Ave. Bris ... 78 C3
Daniel Cl. Cleve ... 57 F2
Daniel Mews. Bath ... 102 A4
Daniel St. Bath ... 102 A4
Dapps Hill. Keyn ... 81 F3
Dapwell La. Co Dan ... 81 D1
Dark La. Back ... 76 A3
Dark La. Ban ... 107 E1
Dark La. Blag ... 110 C2
Dark La. Ch Mag ... 95 F2
Dark La. Hi Cha ... 120 A3
Dark La. Hol ... 138 B1
Dark La. Hol ... 139 D1
Darley Cl. Bris ... 34 B2
Darlington Mews. Bath ... 102 A4
Darlington Pl. Bath ... 102 A3
Darlington Rd. Bath ... 102 A4
Darlington St. Bath ... 102 A4
Darmead. W-S-M ... 89 D1
Darnley Ave. Bris ... 49 F3
Dart Cl. Thorn ... 15 D4
Dart Rd. Cleve ... 57 E1
Dartmoor St. Bris ... 63 D2
Dartmouth Ave. Bath ... 101 E3
Dartmouth Cl. W-S-M ... 89 D1
Dartmouth Wlk. Keyn ... 81 E4
Daubeny Cl. Bris ... 51 D3
Daventry Rd. Bris ... 63 F1
Davey St. Bris ... 49 F1
David's La. Alve ... 15 D2
David's Rd. Bris ... 80 B3
David's Rd. Thorn ... 8 B1
Davids Cl. Alve ... 15 D2
Davin Cres. E in G ... 47 E2
Davis Cl. Kingsw ... 65 F3
Davis Ct. Thorn ... 8 B1
Davis La. Yatt ... 73 F4
Davis St. Avon ... 47 D4
Dawes Cl. Cleve ... 57 E1
Dawley Cl. Wint ... 37 F4
Dawlish Rd. Bris ... 63 E1
Dawn Rise. Kingsw ... 52 A1
Day Cres. Bath ... 100 C3
Day House La. Hill ... 19 E4
Day's Rd. Bris ... 64 A3
De Clifford Rd. Bris ... 34 B1
De Verose Ct. Kingsw ... 65 F2
Deacon Cl. Wint ... 37 F3
Deacons Cl. W-S-M ... 88 C1
Deadmill La. Bath ... 85 E2
Dean Ave. Thorn ... 8 B1
Dean Cl. Kingsw ... 65 D2
Dean Cl. W-S-M ... 89 D2
Dean Cres. Bris ... 63 E2
Dean La. Bris ... 63 E2
Dean Rd. Avon ... 33 E3
Dean Rd. Yate ... 27 E2
Dean St. Bris ... 63 E2
Dean St. Bris ... 63 F4
Dean's Dr. Bris ... 51 D1
Deanery Cl. Kingsw ... 66 A4
Deanery Rd. Bris ... 63 E3
Deanery Rd. Kingsw ... 66 A4
Deanhill La. Charl ... 84 A1
Deans Mead. Bris ... 48 A4
Deans The. Portis ... 45 D2
Debecca's La. E in G ... 47 D2
Deep Coombe Dr. Bris ... 63 D1
Deep Pit Rd. Bris ... 50 C1
Deer Mead. Cleve ... 57 D1
Deerhurst. Kingsw ... 51 F2
Deerhurst. Yate ... 39 E4
Deering Cl. Bris ... 34 A1
Deerleap. Ship ... 125 F4
Deerswood. Kingsw ... 52 A1
Delabere Ave. Bris ... 51 D3
Delapre Rd. W-S-M ... 104 B2
Delius Gr. Bris ... 79 E4
Dell The. Bris ... 48 C3
Dell The. Kingsw ... 66 B3
Dell The. Nail ... 59 E1
Dell The. St Gif ... 36 C4
Dell The. W-S-M ... 88 C2
Delvin Rd. Bris ... 49 E4
Denbigh St. Bris ... 49 F1
Dene Cl. Keyn ... 81 F2
Dene Rd. Whit ... 80 B2
Denham House. Bris ... 79 E2
Denleigh Cl. Bris ... 80 A2
Denmark Ave. Bris ... 63 E3
Denmark Pl. Bris ... 49 F2
Denmark Rd. Bath ... 101 E3
Denmark St. Bris ... 63 E3
Denning Ct. W-S-M ... 89 D2
Dennisworth. Puck ... 53 D3
Dennor Park. Bris ... 80 A4
Denny Cl. Portis ... 45 D3

Denny Isle Dr. Piln ... 22 A3
Denny La. Ch Mag ... 96 A1
Denny View. Portis ... 45 D3
Dennyview Rd. Ab Lei ... 61 F4
Denston Dr. Portis ... 45 F2
Denston Wlk. Bris ... 79 D4
Dentwood Gr. Bris ... 48 A4
Denys Ct. Olve ... 14 A2
Derby Rd. Bris ... 49 F2
Derby St. Bris ... 64 B4
Derham Cl. Yatt ... 91 D4
Derham Park. Yatt ... 91 D4
Derham Rd. Bris ... 79 D3
Dermot St. Bris ... 50 A1
Derrick Rd. Kingsw ... 65 E4
Derricke Rd. Bris ... 80 C3
Derry Rd. Bris ... 63 D1
Derwent Cl. Bris ... 36 A1
Derwent Ct. Thorn ... 15 E4
Derwent Gr. Keyn ... 82 A3
Derwent Rd. Bris ... 50 C1
Derwent Rd. W-S-M ... 105 D2
Desmond Rd. Lock ... 89 E2
Deveron Gr. Keyn ... 82 A2
Devil's Gr. Char ... 11 D1
Devon Gr. Bris ... 64 B4
Devon Rd. Bris ... 50 B1
Devonshire Bldgs. Bath ... 101 F2
Devonshire Ct. W-S-M ... 104 C2
Devonshire Dr. Portis ... 44 C3
Devonshire Pl. Bath ... 101 F2
Devonshire Rd. Bath ... 85 F1
Devonshire Rd. Bris ... 49 D2
Devonshire Rd. W-S-M ... 104 C2
Dial Hill Rd. Cleve ... 57 E2
Dial La. Ba Gu ... 77 E1
Dial La. Mang ... 51 E3
Dial La. Win ... 77 E1
Diamond St. Bris ... 63 E2
Dibden Cl. Mang ... 52 A4
Dibden La. Mang ... 52 A4
Dibden Rd. Mang ... 52 A4
Dickens Cl. Bris ... 50 A4
Dickenson Rd. W-S-M ... 104 C3
Dickenson's Gr. Cong ... 91 F2
Didsbury Cl. Bris ... 34 C1
Dighton Gate. St Gif ... 36 C3
Dighton St. Bris ... 63 E4
Dillon Ct. Bris ... 64 B4
Dimond Rd. Bris ... 64 C4
Dinder Cl. Nail ... 75 F4
Dinghurst Rd. Chur ... 108 C2
Dingle Cl. Bris ... 48 B3
Dingle Rd. Bris ... 48 B4
Dingle The. Bris ... 48 B4
Dingle The. Wint ... 37 F2
Dingle View. Bris ... 48 B4
Dinglewood Cl. Bris ... 48 B4
Dings Wlk. Bris ... 64 A3
Dipland Gr. Blag ... 110 C1
Dixon Gdns. Bath ... 84 C1
Dixon Rd. Bris ... 64 C1
Dock Gate La. Bris ... 63 D3
Dodington La. Dod ... 40 B3
Dodington Rd. Ch Sod ... 40 A4
Dodisham Wlk. Bris ... 51 D3
Doleberrow. Chur ... 108 C2
Dolemoor La. Cong ... 91 D2
Dolemoor La. Cong ... 91 E2
Dolman Cl. Bris ... 34 C2
Dolphin Sq. W-S-M ... 104 B4
Dominion Rd. Bath ... 101 D3
Dominion Rd. Bris ... 50 C2
Donald Rd. Bris ... 78 C4
Doncaster Rd. Bris ... 49 E4
Doncombe Hill. Col ... 70 C4
Doncombe La. Col ... 70 C4
Donegal Rd. Bris ... 63 E1
Dongola Ave. Bris ... 49 F2
Dongola Rd. Bris ... 49 F2
Donnington Wlk. Keyn ... 81 E2
Doone Rd. Bris ... 49 F4
Dorcas Ave. St Gif ... 36 C3
Dorchester Cl. Nail ... 59 E1
Dorchester Rd. Bris ... 50 A4
Dorchester St. Bath ... 102 A3
Dorester Cl. Bris ... 35 E2
Dorian Cl. Bris ... 49 F4
Dorian Rd. Bris ... 49 F4
Dormer Cl. Fr Cot ... 38 B3
Dormer Rd. Bris ... 50 A2
Dorset Cl. Bath ... 101 E3
Dorset Gr. Bris ... 50 A1
Dorset Rd. Bris ... 49 D2
Dorset Rd. Kingsw ... 51 E1
Dorset St. Bath ... 101 E3
Dorset St. Bris ... 63 D2
Dorset Way. Yate ... 28 A2
Douglas Ct. W-S-M ... 104 C3
Douglas Rd. Bris ... 49 F4
Douglas Rd. Kingsw ... 65 E4
Douglas Rd. W-S-M ... 104 C3
Doulton Way. Bris ... 80 A3
Dove La. Bris ... 63 F4
Dove La. Bris ... 64 A4
Dove St S. Bris ... 63 E4
Dove St. Bris ... 63 E4
Dovecote. Yate ... 39 F4

Dovedale. Thorn ... 15 E4
Dover Pl. Bath ... 85 D1
Dovercourt Rd. Bris ... 50 A3
Dovers La. Bathf ... 86 B1
Dovers Park. Bathf ... 86 B1
Dovey Ct. Kingsw ... 66 B3
Dowdeswell Cl. Bris ... 34 C2
Dowding Rd. Bath ... 85 D1
Dowland. W-S-M ... 89 D1
Dowling Rd. Bris ... 79 E2
Down Ave. Bath ... 102 A1
Down Cl. Portis ... 44 C3
Down Hill. Olve ... 14 B2
Down La. Bath ... 85 F1
Down Leaze. Alve ... 15 D3
Down Rd. Alve ... 15 D3
Down Rd. Marsh ... 56 B1
Down Rd. Portis ... 45 D2
Down Rd. Wint ... 37 F2
Down The. Alve ... 14 C3
Down The. Olve ... 14 B2
Down View. Bris ... 49 F2
Downend Park Rd. Mang ... 51 E3
Downend Park. Bris ... 49 F3
Downend Rd. Bris ... 49 F3
Downend Rd. Bris ... 51 E3
Downend Rd. Kingsw ... 51 E1
Downend Rd. Mang ... 51 E3
Downfield Cl. Alve ... 15 D3
Downfield Dr. Fr Cot ... 38 A4
Downfield Rd. Bris ... 49 D1
Downland Cl. Bris ... 79 E3
Downleaze Dr. Ch Sod ... 40 A4
Downleaze. Bris ... 48 C2
Downleaze. Mang ... 51 E4
Downleaze. Portis ... 45 D3
Downman Rd. Bris ... 50 A3
Downs Cl. Alve ... 15 D3
Downs Cl. W-S-M ... 88 C1
Downs Cote Ave. Bris ... 48 C3
Downs Cote Dr. Bris ... 49 D3
Downs Cote Gdns. Bris ... 49 D3
Downs Cote Park. Bris ... 49 D3
Downs Cote View. Bris ... 49 D3
Downs Park E. Bris ... 49 D2
Downs Park W. Bris ... 49 D2
Downs Rd. Bris ... 49 D3
Downs Rd. Dun ... 78 B1
Downs The. Portis ... 45 D2
Downs The. Wickw ... 17 F4
Downside Cl. Bath ... 85 F1
Downside Cl. Chil ... 137 E2
Downside Cl. Kingsw ... 65 F3
Downside Rd. Bris ... 49 D1
Downside Rd. W-S-M ... 104 C2
Downside Rd. Wring ... 93 F4
Downside. Portis ... 45 E3
Downsway. Paul ... 131 E3
Downton Rd. Bris ... 79 E4
Dowry Rd. Bris ... 63 D3
Dowry Sq. Bris ... 63 D3
Doynton La. Doyn ... 54 A2
Doynton La. Dyrh ... 54 A2
Dr White's Cl. Bris ... 63 F3
Dragon Rd. Wint ... 37 E3
Dragon Wlk. Bris ... 50 C1
Dragons Hill Cl. Keyn ... 81 F3
Dragons Hill Ct. Keyn ... 81 F3
Dragons Hill Gdns. Keyn ... 81 F3
Dragonswell Rd. Bris ... 35 D1
Drake Ave. Bath ... 101 F1
Drake Cl. Keyn ... 82 B1
Drake Cl. W-S-M ... 88 C2
Drake Rd. Bris ... 63 D2
Drakes Way. Portis ... 45 D3
Draycot Pl. Bris ... 63 E3
Draycott Rd. Bris ... 49 E4
Draydon Rd. Bris ... 79 E4
Drayton Cl. Bris ... 80 A4
Drayton Rd. Bris ... 48 B4
Drayton. W-S-M ... 105 D2
Dring The. Rad ... 132 C1
Drive The. Bris ... 49 D3
Drive The. Bris ... 80 B3
Drive The. Chur ... 108 C2
Drive The. Pens ... 96 C1
Drive The. Ship ... 125 F4
Drive The. W-S-M ... 104 C4
Drove Ct. Nail ... 59 F2
Drove Rd. W-S-M ... 104 C3
Drove The. Portb ... 46 B3
Drove Way. Winsc ... 107 F4
Druetts Cl. Bris ... 49 F3
Druid Hill. Bris ... 48 C3
Druid Rd. Bris ... 48 C3
Druid Stoke Ave. Bris ... 48 B3
Druid Woods. Bris ... 48 B3
Drumbead Way The. Ship . 125 F4
Drummond Ct. Kingsw ... 65 F2
Drummond Rd. Bris ... 50 C2
Drumond Rd. Bris ... 49 F1
Dryleaze Rd. Bris ... 51 D4
Dryleaze. Keyn ... 81 F4
Drysdale Cl. W-S-M ... 88 B1
Dubbers La. Bris ... 50 C1
Dublin Cres. Bris ... 49 D3
Duchess Way. Bris ... 50 B3

Duchy Cl. Mid No ... 132 C3
Duchy Rd. Mid No ... 132 C3
Ducie Rd. Bris ... 64 A4
Ducie Rd. Mang ... 51 F3
Duck La. Chur ... 109 D4
Duck La. Yatt ... 74 A3
Duck St. Chur ... 108 B3
Duck St. Tyth ... 16 B3
Duckmoor Rd. Bris ... 63 D2
Dudley Cl. Keyn ... 81 F2
Dudley Ct. Kingsw ... 65 F2
Dudley Gr. Bris ... 50 A4
Dugar Wlk. Bris ... 49 E2
Duke St. Bath ... 102 A3
Dulverton Rd. Bris ... 49 E2
Dumaine Ave. St Gif ... 36 C3
Dumfries Pl. W-S-M ... 104 C3
Dumpers La. Ch Mag ... 96 A1
Duncan Gdns. Bath ... 84 A2
Duncombe La. Bris ... 51 D1
Duncombe Rd. Bris ... 51 D1
Dundas Cl. Bris ... 34 C1
Dundonald Rd. Bris ... 49 D3
Dundridge Gdns. Bris ... 65 D3
Dundridge La. Bris ... 65 D3
Dundry Cl. Kingsw ... 65 E3
Dundry La. Dun ... 78 B2
Dundry La. Win ... 95 D3
Dundry View. Bris ... 64 A1
Dunkeld Ave. Bris ... 35 F1
Dunkerry Rd. Bris ... 63 E2
Dunkerton Hill. P St J ... 117 F1
Dunkerton Hill. Pris ... 117 F1
Dunkery Cl. Nail ... 59 F1
Dunkery Rd. W-S-M ... 87 F1
Dunkirk Rd. Bris ... 50 C2
Dunkite La. W-S-M ... 88 C2
Dunmail Rd. Bris ... 35 E1
Dunmore St. Bris ... 63 F2
Dunsdown La. Tor ... 55 D3
Dunster Cres. W-S-M ... 105 D1
Dunster Gdns. Kingsw ... 66 A1
Dunster Gdns. Nail ... 59 F1
Dunster Rd. Bris ... 79 F4
Dunster Rd. Keyn ... 81 F2
Dunsters Rd. Yatt ... 74 C1
Durban Rd. Bris ... 35 F4
Durban Way. Yatt ... 74 A1
Durbin Park Rd. Cleve ... 57 E3
Durbin Wlk. Bris ... 64 A4
Durcott Rd. Tims ... 132 B4
Durham Gr. Keyn ... 81 E2
Durham Park. Bris ... 49 D2
Durham Rd. Bris ... 50 A1
Durham Rd. Char ... 11 D3
Durleigh Cl. Bris ... 79 D4
Durley Hill. Keyn ... 81 E4
Durley Park. Bath ... 101 F2
Durnford Ave. Bris ... 63 D2
Durnford Rd. Bris ... 63 E2
Durnford St. Bris ... 63 D2
Durnhill. Co Mar ... 127 F4
Dursley Cl. Yate ... 27 F1
Dursley Rd. Bris ... 47 F3
Durston. W-S-M ... 105 D1
Durville Rd. Bris ... 79 D3
Durweston Wlk. Bris ... 80 B4
Dutton Cl. Bris ... 80 B3
Dutton Rd. Bris ... 80 B3
Dutton Wlk. Bris ... 80 B3
Dyer's La. Yate ... 27 E2
Dyers Cl. Bris ... 79 E2
Dylan Thomas Ct. Kingsw ... 66 A3
Dymboro Ave. Mid No ... 131 F1
Dymboro Cl. Mid No ... 131 F1
Dymboro Gdns. Mid No ... 131 F1
Dymboro The. Mid No ... 131 F1
Dyrham Cl. Bris ... 49 E3
Dyrham Cl. Kingsw ... 65 F4
Dyrham Cl. Thorn ... 8 B1
Dyrham Par. St Gif ... 36 B4
Dyrham Rd. Kingsw ... 65 F4
Dyrham. Bris ... 37 E1
Dyson Cl. Yatt ... 91 D4

Eagle Cl. W-S-M ... 105 E4
Eagle Cres. Puck ... 53 E2
Eagle Dr. Bris ... 35 F4
Eagle Park. Bathe ... 85 F3
Eagle Rd. Bathe ... 85 F3
Eagle Rd. Bris ... 64 B1
Eagles The. Yatt ... 91 D4
Eagles Wood Bsns Pk.
   St Gif ... 24 B2
Earl Russell Way. Bris ... 64 A4
Earl St. Bris ... 63 E4
Earlesfield. Nail ... 59 E1
Earlham Gr. W-S-M ... 105 D4
Earlsmead. Bris ... 50 C2
Earlstone Cl. Kingsw ... 66 A2
Earlstone Cres. Kingsw ... 66 A2
Easedale Cl. Bris ... 35 E1
East Cl. Bath ... 101 D3
East Clevedon Triangle.
   Cleve ... 57 F2
East Croft. Bris ... 49 E4
East Dundry La. Dun ... 79 D1

East Dundry La. Dun

East Dundry Rd. Bris 79 F1
East Dundry Rd. Whit 79 F1
East Gr. Bris 49 F1
East Hill. Bris 49 D4
East Lea Rd. Bath 101 D4
East Mead. Mid No 132 A1
East Par. Bris 48 B3
East Park Dr. Bris 50 B1
East Park. Bris 50 B1
East Priory Cl. Bris 49 D4
East Ridge Dr. Bris 78 C3
East Shrubbery. Bris 49 D1
East St. Avon 33 D1
East St. Ban 107 E2
East St. Bris 63 E2
East St. Bris 63 F4
East View. Mang 51 F3
East Way. Bath 101 D3
East Wlk. Yate 27 F1
East Wood Pl. Portis 45 F4
Eastbury Rd. Bris 51 D2
Eastbury Rd. Thorn 8 B1
Eastcombe Gdns. W-S-M 87 F1
Eastcombe Rd. W-S-M 87 F1
Eastcote Pk. Bris 80 A3
Eastcourt Gdns. Bris 50 B3
Eastcourt Rd. Clut 130 C4
Eastcroft Cl. Blag 110 C1
Eastcroft. Blag 110 C1
Eastdown Rd. Mid No 132 C3
Eastertown. Lymp 122 B1
Eastfield Ave. Bath 84 A1
Eastfield Gdns. W-S-M 87 F1
Eastfield Park. Bath 84 A1
Eastfield Park. W-S-M 87 F1
Eastfield Rd. Bris 49 D4
Eastfield Rd. Bris 49 E1
Eastfield Rd. Lock 105 F1
Eastfield Terr. Bris 49 D3
Eastfield. Bris 49 D4
Eastgate Office Centre. Bris 50 A2
Eastlake Cl. Bris 50 A4
Eastland Ave. Thorn 8 B1
Eastland Rd. Thorn 8 B1
Eastlea. Cleve 57 D1
Eastleigh Cl. Kingsw 51 F2
Eastleigh Rd. Bris 35 E1
Eastleigh Rd. Kingsw 51 F2
Eastley Cl. Falf 9 F4
Eastlyn Rd. Bris 79 D4
Eastmead La. Ban 107 E2
Eastmead La. Bris 48 C2
Eastnor Rd. Bris 80 A2
Easton Hill Rd. Thorn 8 B1
Easton Rd. Bris 64 A4
Easton Rd. E in G 47 E2
Easton Way. Bris 64 A4
Eastover Cl. Bris 49 D4
Eastover Gr. Bath 101 E1
Eastover Rd. Paul 115 E1
Eastville. Bath 85 D1
Eastway Cl. Nail 59 E1
Eastway Sq. Nail 59 F2
Eastway. Nail 59 F2
Eastwood Cl. Paul 115 E1
Eastwood Cres. Bris 64 C4
Eastwood Rd. Bris 64 C4
Eastwoods. Bathe 86 A2
Eaton Cl. Bris 51 D2
Eaton Cl. Bris 80 C3
Eaton Cres. Bris 63 D4
Eaton St. Bris 63 E2
Ebdon Rd. W ST L 89 D3
Ebdon Rd. W-S-M 88 C2
Ebenezer La. Bris 48 C3
Ebenezer St. Bris 64 B4
Eckweek La. P St J 133 E4
Eckweek La. P St J 133 F4
Eckweek Rd. P St J 133 E4
Eclipse Office Pk. Kingsw . 51 E2
Eden Cl. Bris 36 A1
Eden Park Cl. Bathe 86 A2
Eden Park Dr. Bathe 86 A2
Edgarley Ct. Cleve 57 E3
Edgecombe Ave. W-S-M 88 B1
Edgecombe Cl. Kingsw 51 F1
Edgecorner La. Burt 43 D2
Edgecumbe Rd. Bris 49 E1
Edgefield Cl. Bris 79 F2
Edgefield Rd. Bris 79 F2
Edgehill Rd. Bris 57 E3
Edgeware Rd. Bris 63 E2
Edgeware Rd. Kingsw 51 F1
Edgewood Cl. Bris 80 A4
Edgewood Cl. Kingsw 66 A2
Edgeworth Rd. Bath 101 E1
Edgeworth. Yate 39 E3
Edgeworth. Yate 39 E3
Edinburgh Pl. W-S-M 104 C1
Edinburgh Rd. Keyn 81 F2
Edington Gr. Bris 35 D1
Edmund Cl. Mang 51 E3
Edmund Ct. Puck 53 D3
Edna Ave. Bris 64 C2
Edward Rd S. Cleve 57 F3
Edward Rd W. Cleve 57 F3
Edward Rd. Bris 64 A2
Edward Rd. Cleve 57 F3

Edward Rd. Kingsw 65 F4
Edward St. Bath 101 E4
Edward St. Bath 102 A4
Edward St. Bris 50 B1
Edward St. Bris 64 B4
Edwin Short Cl. Bitt 82 C4
Effingham Rd. Bris 49 F2
Egerton Brow. Bris 49 E2
Egerton Rd. Bath 101 F2
Egerton Rd. Bris 49 E2
Eggshill La. Yate 27 E1
Eighth Ave. Bris 36 A1
Eirene Terr. E in G 47 E2
Elberton Rd. Aust 14 A2
Elberton Rd. Bris 34 A4
Elberton Rd. Olve 14 A4
Elberton. Kingsw 66 A4
Elbury Ave. Bris 51 E1
Elderberry Wlk. W-S-M 89 D1
Elderbury Wlk. Bris 35 E2
Elderwood Dr. Kingsw 66 A2
Elderwood Rd. Bris 80 A4
Eldon Pl. Bath 85 D1
Eldon Terr. Bris 63 E2
Eldon Way. Bris 64 B3
Eleanor Cl. Bath 101 D3
Eleventh Ave. Bris 36 A1
Elfin Rd. Bris 51 D3
Elgar Cl. Bris 79 E3
Elgar Cl. Cleve 57 F1
Elgin Ave. Bris 35 F1
Elgin Croft. Bris 79 D2
Elgin Park. Bris 49 D1
Elgin Rd. Bris 51 D1
Eliot Cl. W-S-M 105 D2
Elizabeth Cl. Lock 105 E2
Elizabeth Cl. Thorn 15 E4
Elizabeth Cres. St Gif 36 C2
Elizabeth House. E in G 47 E2
Elkstone Wlk. Kingsw 66 B1
Ellacombe Rd. Kingsw 65 F1
Ellan Hay Rd. St Gif 37 D3
Ellbridge Cl. Bris 48 B3
Ellenborough Park N.
  W-S-M 104 B3
Ellenborough Park Rd.
  W-S-M 104 C3
Ellenborough Park S.
  W-S-M 104 B3
Ellerncroft Rd. W-u-E 11 F4
Ellesmere Rd. Bris 64 B1
Ellesmere Rd. Kingsw 65 E4
Ellesmere Rd. W-S-M 104 B1
Ellesmere. Thorn 15 E4
Ellfield Cl. Bris 78 C3
Ellick Rd. Blag 126 B4
Ellicks Cl. St Gif 24 C1
Ellinghurst Cl. Bris 35 D1
Elliot Rd. Bris 49 F3
Elliott Ave. Bris 37 E1
Ellis Ave. Bris 79 D4
Elliston Dr. Bath 101 D2
Elliston La. Bris 49 E1
Elliston Rd. Bris 49 E1
Ellsbridge Cl. Keyn 82 A3
Ellsworth Rd. Bris 34 C2
Elm Cl. Ch Sod 28 A1
Elm Cl. Nail 59 E4
Elm Cl. Ship 108 B1
Elm Cl. St Gif 36 B4
Elm Cl. Yatt 91 D4
Elm Ct. Keyn 81 E2
Elm Gr. Bath 85 E1
Elm Gr. Bath 101 E2
Elm Gr. Lock 105 F2
Elm La. Bris 49 D1
Elm Park. Bris 36 A1
Elm Rd. Bris 49 F3
Elm Rd. Kingsw 65 F3
Elm Rd. Paul 131 D2
Elm Terr. Rad 132 B1
Elm Terr. Rod 138 B4
Elm Tree Ave. Mang 52 A4
Elm Tree Ave. Rad 132 B1
Elm Tree Rd. Cleve 57 E1
Elm Tree Rd. Lock 106 A2
Elm View. Mid No 132 A1
Elm Wlk. Portis 45 E2
Elm Wlk. Yatt 91 D4
Elm Wood. Yate 39 F4
Elmcroft Cres. Bris 50 A2
Elmdale Gdns. Bris 51 D2
Elmdale Rd. Bris 63 D1
Elmdale Rd. Bris 63 D4
Elmfield Cl. Kingsw 65 F3
Elmfield Rd. Bris 49 D4
Elmfield. Kingsw 65 F3
Elmgrove Ave. Bris 64 A4
Elmgrove Dr. Yate 27 F1
Elmgrove Park. Bris 49 E1
Elmgrove Rd. Bris 49 E1
Elmgrove Rd. Bris 50 C2
Elmhurst Ave. Bris 50 B2
Elmhurst Est. Bathe 86 A2
Elmhurst Gdns. Lo Ash 77 A3
Elmhurst Rd. Lock 105 F1

Elmhyrst Rd. W-S-M 104 C4
Elming Down Cl. St Gif 36 B3
Elmlea Ave. Bris 48 C3
Elmleigh Ave. Mang 52 A3
Elmleigh Cl. Mang 52 A3
Elmleigh Rd. Mang 52 A3
Elmore Rd. Bris 23 F1
Elmore Rd. Bris 50 A3
Elmore. Kingsw 51 F1
Elmore. Yate 39 E4
Elms Gr. St Gif 24 A1
Elms The. Bris 37 E1
Elmsleigh Rd. W-S-M 104 B2
Elmsley La. W St L 88 B3
Elmtree Cl. Kingsw 51 E1
Elmtree Dr. Bris 78 C3
Elmtree Way. Kingsw 51 E1
Elmvale Dr. Lock 105 F2
Elsbert Dr. Bris 78 C3
Elstree Rd. Bris 50 C1
Elton La. Bris 49 E1
Elton Rd. Bris 49 E1
Elton Rd. Bris 51 E1
Elton Rd. Bris 63 E4
Elton Rd. Cleve 57 E2
Elton Rd. W-S-M 89 D2
Elton St. Bris 63 F4
Elvard Cl. Bris 79 D2
Elvard Rd. Bris 79 D2
Elvaston Rd. Bris 63 F2
Elwell La. Dun 77 F1
Elwell La. Win 77 F1
Ely Gr. Bris 48 A4
Embassy Rd. Bris 50 C1
Embassy Wlk. Bris 50 C1
Embercourt Dr. Back 76 A3
Embleton Rd. Bris 35 E1
Emerson Sq. Bris 50 A4
Emery Gate. Ban 107 D2
Emery Rd. Bris 64 C1
Emlyn Cl. W-S-M 89 D2
Emlyn Rd. Bris 50 B1
Emmett Wood. Bris 80 A2
Emra Cl. Bris 50 C1
Enderleigh Gdns. Chur 108 C2
Enfield Rd. Bris 51 D2
Engine Common La. Yate .. 27 E3
Engine La. Nail 75 D4
England's Cres. Wint 37 F4
Englishcombe La. Bath 101 E2
Englishcombe Rd. Bris 79 E2
Englishcombe Way. Bath .. 101 F2
Enmore. W-S-M 105 D1
Ennerdale Cl. W-S-M 105 D3
Ennerdale Rd. Bris 35 E1
Entry Hill Dr. Bath 101 F2
Entry Hill Gdns. Bath 101 F2
Entry Hill Park. Bath 101 F1
Entry Hill. Bath 101 F1
Entry Rise. Bath 101 F1
Epney Cl. Bris 23 F1
Epsom Cl. Mang 37 F1
Epworth Rd. Bris 35 D2
Equinox. St Gif 24 B2
Erin Wlk. Bris 79 E4
Ermine Way. Bris 47 E4
Ermleet Rd. Bris 49 E1
Ernestville Rd. Bris 50 C2
Ernist Barker Cl. Bris 64 A4
Ervine Terr. Bris 63 F4
Esgar Rise. W-S-M 88 C2
Eskdale Cl. W-S-M 105 E4
Eskdale. Thorn 15 E4
Esmond Gr. Cleve 57 E2
Esplanade Rd. Portis 45 D4
Essery Rd. Bris 50 B1
Essex St. Bris 63 E2
Esson Rd. Bris 51 D1
Estoril. Yate 27 F1
Estune Wlk. Lo Ash 62 A1
Etloe Rd. Bris 49 D2
Eton La. Ban 106 C4
Eton Rd. Bris 64 B2
Ettlingen Way. Cleve 57 F1
Ettricke Dr. Bris 51 D3
Eugene St. Bris 63 E4
Eugene St. Bris 63 F4
Evans Rd. Bris 49 D1
Eve Rd. Bris 50 A1
Evelyn Rd. Bath 101 D4
Evelyn Rd. Bris 49 E4
Evelyn Terr. Bath 85 D1
Evenlode Gdns. Bris 47 F3
Evenlode Way. Keyn 82 A2
Evercreech Rd. Bris 80 A2
Everest Ave. Bris 50 C2
Everest Rd. Bris 50 C2
Evergreen Cl. Winsc 107 F1
Ewart Rd. W-S-M 105 E4
Exbourne. W-S-M 89 D1
Excelsior St. Bath 102 A3
Excelsior Terr. Mid No 132 A1
Exchange Ave. Bris 63 E3
Exeter Bldgs. Bris 49 D1
Exeter Rd. Bris 63 D2
Exeter Rd. Portis 45 F2
Exeter Rd. W-S-M 104 C3
Exford Cl. W-S-M 104 C1

Exley Cl. Kingsw 66 B3
Exmoor Rd. Bath 101 F1
Exmoor St. Bris 63 D2
Exmouth Rd. Bris 63 F1
Exton Cl. Bris 80 A3
Exton. W-S-M 105 D1
Eyer's La. Bris 63 F4

Faber Gr. Bris 79 E2
Fabian Dr. St Gif 36 C3
Factory Rd. Wint 37 F4
Failand Cres. Bris 48 B3
Failand La. Portb 46 C1
Failand La. Wrax 61 D4
Failand Wlk. Bris 48 B3
Fair Cl. N St P 135 F2
Fair Furlong. Bris 79 D2
Fair Hill. Ship 125 F4
Fair Lawn. Kingsw 66 A2
Fair View Dr. Bris 49 E1
Fairacre Cl. Bris 50 A3
Fairacre Cl. Lock 106 A2
Fairacres Cl. Keyn 81 F3
Fairfax St. Bris 63 E4
Fairfield Ave. Bath 85 D1
Fairfield Cl. Back 76 B4
Fairfield Cl. Marsh 69 F4
Fairfield Cl. W-S-M 88 A1
Fairfield Mead. Back 76 B4
Fairfield Park Rd. Bath 85 D1
Fairfield Pl. Bris 63 D2
Fairfield Rd. Bath 85 D1
Fairfield Rd. Bris 49 F1
Fairfield Rd. Bris 63 E2
Fairfield St. Bris 64 A2
Fairfield Terr. P St J 133 E4
Fairfield Way. Back 76 B3
Fairfield. Rode 136 C1
Fairfoot Rd. Bris 64 A2
Fairford Cl. Kingsw 51 F1
Fairford Cres. St Gif 36 B4
Fairford Rd. Bris 47 E4
Fairhaven Rd. Bris 49 E2
Fairhaven. Yate 27 F1
Fairlawn Ave. Bris 36 A2
Fairlawn Rd. Bris 49 F1
Fairlyn Dr. Kingsw 51 F2
Fairoaks. Kingsw 66 A2
Fairseat Workshops. Ch St 112 C4
Fairview Rd. Kingsw 65 F4
Fairview. W-S-M 88 C2
Fairway Cl. Kingsw 66 A2
Fairway Cl. W-S-M 88 A1
Fairway Ind Centre. Bris .. 35 F2
Fairway. Bris 64 B1
Fairways. Keyn 82 C1
Fairy Hill. Co Dan 98 B3
Falcon Cl. Bris 35 F4
Falcon Cl. Bris 48 C4
Falcon Cl. Portis 45 E2
Falcon Cres. W-S-M 105 E4
Falcon Dr. Bris 35 F4
Falcon Way. Thorn 8 B1
Falcon Wlk. Bris 23 F1
Falcondale Rd. Bris 48 C4
Falcondale Wlk. Bris 49 D4
Falconer Rd. Bath 84 A2
Falfield Rd. Bris 64 B2
Falfield Wlk. Bris 49 E4
Falkland Rd. Bris 49 F1
Fallodon Ct. Bris 49 D3
Fallodon Way. Bris 49 D3
Fallowfield. Kingsw 66 B3
Fallowfield. W-S-M 88 C2
Falmouth Cl. Nail 60 A1
Falmouth Rd. Bris 49 F2
Fane Cl. Bris 35 D2
Fanshawe Rd. Bris 80 A4
Far Handstones. Kingsw .. 66 A2
Faraday Rd. Bris 62 C3
Farington Rd. Bris 49 E4
Farleigh Hospital Cotts.
  Back 77 D4
Farleigh La. Crom 10 B1
Farleigh Rd. Back 76 B4
Farleigh Rd. Cleve 57 D1
Farleigh Rd. Keyn 81 E2
Farleigh Rd. N St P 136 A3
Farleigh Rise. Mon Far 86 C1
Farleigh View. Westw 120 C2
Farleigh Wick. Mon Far 103 F3
Farleigh Wlk. Bris 79 D4
Farler's End. Nail 75 F4
Farley Cl. St Gif 36 B4
Farm Ct. Mang 51 F3
Farm La. Alm 22 C1
Farm La. Piln 22 C1
Farm La. Well 118 C1
Farm Lees. Char 11 D3
Farm Rd. Lock 105 F1
Farm Rd. Mang 51 F4
Farmer Rd. Bris 78 C2
Farmhouse Cl. Nail 59 F1
Farmhouse Ct. Nail 59 F1
Farmwell Cl. Bris 79 D3
Farndale Rd. W-S-M 105 E4
Farndale. Bris 65 D3
Farne Cl. Bris 49 D3

Farr St. Avon 47 D4
Farr's La. Bris 63 E3
Farrant Cl. Bris 79 E3
Farrington Fields. Paul 131 E2
Farrington Rd. Paul 131 E3
Farrington Way. Paul 131 D2
Farrs La. Bath 102 A1
Farthing Row. Rode 136 C1
Faukland View. P St J 133 F4
Faukland La. Well 134 B2
Faukland Rd. Bath 101 E3
Faversham Dr. W-S-M 105 D1
Fawkes Cl. Kingsw 66 A4
Fearnville Est. Cleve 57 E1
Featherbed La. Clut 114 B3
Featherbed La. Pens 114 B3
Featherbed La. Win 95 D2
Featherstone Rd. Bris 50 C2
Fedden Village. Portis 44 C3
Feeder Rd. Bris 64 A3
Felix Rd. Bris 64 A4
Felstead Rd. Bris 35 F1
Feltham Rd. Puck 53 E3
Felton Gr. Bris 79 D4
Felton La. Win 94 C4
Felton St. Win 94 B4
Fenbrook Cl. Bris 37 D1
Feniton. W-S-M 89 D1
Fennel La. Axb 125 D1
Fennel Gr. Bris 35 D1
Fenners. W-S-M 89 D2
Fenshurst Gdns. Lo Ash .. 77 F4
Fenswood Mead. Lo Ash .. 61 F1
Fenswood Rd. Lo Ash 61 F1
Fenton Cl. Keyn 82 B2
Fenton Rd. Bris 49 E2
Ferenberge Cl. Farm 116 A3
Fermaine Ave. Bris 64 C2
Fern Cl. Bris 35 D2
Fern Gr. Nail 75 E4
Fern Lea. Blea 122 A3
Fern Rd. Mang 51 E3
Fernbank Rd. Bris 49 E1
Ferndale Ave. Bris 65 D1
Ferndale Ave. Kingsw 66 A2
Ferndale Rd. Bath 85 E2
Ferndale Rd. Bris 36 A1
Ferndale Rd. Portis 45 E3
Ferndean. St Gif 24 B1
Ferndown Cl. Bris 48 A4
Ferndown. Yate 27 F1
Fernhill La. Bris 34 A1
Fernhill. Alve 24 B4
Fernhill. Olve 24 B4
Fernhurst Rd. Bris 50 C1
Fernlea Gdns. E in G 47 D2
Fernlea Rd. W-S-M 105 E4
Fernleaze. Fr Cot 38 B3
Fernside. Back 76 A4
Fernsteed Rd. Bris 78 C3
Ferry La. Bath 102 A3
Ferry Rd. Kingsw 65 E1
Ferry St. Bris 63 F3
Ferry Steps Ind Est. Bris .. 64 A2
Fiddes Rd. Bris 49 E2
Field La. Aust 14 A4
Field La. Dyrh 54 C3
Field La. Kingsw 65 F2
Field La. Ston E 130 A1
Field La. Tyth 15 F2
Field Rd. Bris 51 E1
Field View Dr. Bris 51 E3
Fielders The. W-S-M 89 D2
Fieldgardens Rd. Clut 114 C1
Fielding's Rd. Bath 101 E3
Fieldings. Winsl 120 C4
Fieldway. Wins 108 A2
Fiennes Cl. Kingsw 51 F2
Fifth Ave. Bris 36 A1
Fifth Way. Avon 33 F1
Filby Dr. St Gif 36 B4
Filer Cl. P St J 133 E4
Filton Ave. Bris 36 A1
Filton Ave. Bris 36 A2
Filton Gr. Bris 49 F3
Filton La. Bris 36 B1
Filton Rd. Bris 36 B1
Filton Rd. Bris 37 D1
Filwood Broadway. Bris .. 79 F4
Filwood Dr. Kingsw 65 F4
Filwood Rd. Bris 51 D2
Finch Cl. Thorn 8 B1
Finch Cl. W-S-M 105 F4
Finch Rd. Ch Sod 40 A4
Finmere Gdns. W-S-M 89 D2
Fir La. Priddy 126 A3
Fir Rd. Col 70 C3
Fir Tree Ave. Lock 105 F2
Fir Tree Ave. Paul 131 F2
Fir Tree Cl. Bris 35 F4
Fir Tree La. Bris 65 D4
Fircliff Park. Portis 45 D4
Fire Engine La. Fr Cot 38 B4
Fireclay Rd. Bris 64 B3
Firework Cl. Kingsw 66 A4
Firgrove Cres. Yate 28 C1

Firgrove La. P St J 117 D1
Firs Ct. Keyn 81 E2
Firs The. Bath 102 A1
Firs The. Li St 120 A3
Firs The. Mang 51 F3
First Ave. Bath 101 E2
First Ave. Bris 64 C3
First Ave. Portb 46 C3
First Ave. Rod 138 B4
First Way. Avon 33 E1
Fisher Ave. Kingsw 52 A1
Fisher Rd. Kingsw 52 A1
Fishponds Rd. Bris 50 C2
Fishpool Hill. Bris 35 D2
Fitchett Wlk. Bris 34 C2
Fitzgerald Rd. Bris 63 F2
Fitzroy Rd. Bris 51 D1
Fitzroy St. Bris 64 A2
Fitzroy Terr. Bris 49 D1
Five Acre Dr. Bris 50 C4
Five Arches Cl. Mid No 132 B1
Flagstaff Rd. Blea 123 E4
Flamingo Cres. W-S-M 105 F4
Flat The. Clut 114 B3
Flatwoods Cres. Bath 102 C2
Flatwoods Rd. Bath 102 C2
Flax Bourton Rd. Wrax 61 D2
Flaxman Cl. Bris 50 A3
Flaxpits La. Wint 37 F3
Florence Gr. W-S-M 105 D4
Florence Park. Alm 24 B3
Florence Park. Bris 49 D2
Florence Rd. Kingsw 51 F2
Florida Terr. Mid No 132 B1
Flowers Hill Cl. Bris 64 C1
Flowers Hill. Bris 64 C1
Flowerwell Rd. Bris 79 D3
Folleigh Cl. Lo Ash 62 A1
Folleigh Dr. Lo Ash 62 A1
Folleigh La. Lo Ash 62 A1
Folliot Cl. Bris 51 D4
Folly Bridge Cl. Yate 27 E1
Folly La. Bris 64 A3
Folly La. Ship 125 F4
Folly La. W-S-M 104 C1
Folly Rd. Ir Act 25 F2
Folly The. Mang 51 F4
Fontana Cl. Kingsw 66 A2
Fonthill Rd. Bath 84 C1
Fonthill Rd. Bris 35 E1
Fonthill Way. Kingsw 66 B1
Fontmell Ct. Bris 80 B4
Fontwell Dr. Mang 37 F1
Footes La. Fr Cot 38 A4
Footshill Cl. Kingsw 65 E3
Footshill Dr. Kingsw 65 E3
Footshill Rd. Kingsw 65 E3
Ford La. P St J 133 E4
Ford La. Litt 129 E1
Ford Rd. Well 118 C1
Ford St. Bris 64 B3
Forde Cl. Kingsw 65 F3
Fordell Pl. Bris 64 A2
Forefield Pl. Bath 102 A4
Forefield Rise. Bath 102 A3
Forest Ave. Bris 51 D2
Forest Dr. Bris 35 E2
Forest Edge. Kingsw 65 E2
Forest Hills. Alm 24 A3
Forest Rd. Bris 51 D1
Forest Rd. Kingsw 65 E4
Forest Wlk. Bris 51 D1
Forest Wlk. Kingsw 65 E4
Forester Ave. Bath 102 A4
Forester La. Bath 102 A4
Forester Rd. Bath 102 A4
Forester Rd. Portis 45 E2
Forge End. Portb 46 C2
Fortescue Rd. Rad 132 C1
Fortfield Rd. Bris 80 A3
Forty Acre La. Alve 15 D2
Foss La. O-on-S 7 F3
Fosse Barton. Nail 59 E1
Fosse Cl. Nail 59 E1
Fosse Gdns. Bath 118 B4
Fosse Green. Mid No 132 C2
Fosse La. Bathe 86 A2
Fosse La. Mid No 132 B2
Fosse La. Nail 59 E1
Fossedale Ave. Bris 80 B3
Fossefield Rd. Kilm 138 A4
Fosseway Gdns. Rad 132 B1
Fosseway S. Kilm 138 A4
Fosseway The. Bris 63 D4
Fosseway. Chil 137 F1
Fosseway. Chil 138 A2
Fosseway. Cleve 57 E1
Fosseway. Mid No 132 C2
Fosseway. Rod 138 B4
Foster St. Bris 50 A1
Foundry La. Bris 50 C1
Fountain Ct. St Gif 24 B2
Fountain La. Wins 125 D4
Fountaine Ct. Bris 50 B1
Fountains Dr. Kingsw 65 F3

Four Acre Ave. Mang 51 F4
Four Acre Cres. Mang 37 F1
Four Acre Rd. Mang 51 F4
Four Acres Cl. Bris 78 C3
Four Acres Cl. Nail 75 F4
Four Acres. Bris 78 C2
Fourth Ave. Bris 36 A1
Fourth Ave. Rod 138 B4
Fourth Way. Avon 33 F1
Fowey Cl. Nail 76 A4
Fowey Rd. W-S-M 89 D2
Fox And Hounds La. Keyn .. 81 F3
Fox Ave. Yate 27 E1
Fox Ct. Kingsw 65 F2
Fox Den Rd. St Gif 36 B2
Fox Hill. Bath 102 A1
Fox House. Bris 64 C2
Fox Rd. Bris 50 A1
Foxborough Gdns. St Gif ... 24 B1
Foxcombe Rd. Bath 101 D4
Foxcombe Rd. Bris 80 A2
Foxcote Rd. Bris 63 D2
Foxcote. Kingsw 65 F4
Foxcroft Cl. St Gif 36 C3
Foxcroft Rd. Bris 64 B4
Foxe Rd. Fr Cot 38 A4
Foxfield Ave. St Gif 24 B2
Foxglove Cl. Bris 50 C2
Foxglove Cl. Thorn 8 E1
Foxholes La. Olve 14 B2
Foye House. Lo Ash 62 B3
Fraley Rd. Bris 49 D4
Frampton Cres. Bris 51 E2
Frampton Ct. Kingsw 65 F2
Frampton End Rd. Fr Cot ... 38 B4
Frampton End Rd. Ir Act 26 B2
France La. H Up 20 A1
Francis Fox Rd. W-S-M 104 C4
Francis Pl. Kingsw 65 F2
Francis Rd. Bris 49 E4
Francis Rd. Bris 63 E1
Francombe Gr. Bris 49 F3
Frankland Cl. Bath 84 A1
Frankley Bldgs. Bath 85 D1
Franklin Ct. Bris 63 F3
Franklin's Way. Yatt 74 C1
Franklyn La. Bris 49 F1
Franklyn St. Bris 49 F1
Fraser Cl. W-S-M 88 C2
Fraser St. Bris 63 E2
Frayne Rd. Bris 63 D2
Frederick Ave. P St J 133 E4
Frederick Pl. Bris 63 D4
Fredrick St. Bris 64 A2
Free Tank. Bris 63 F3
Freeland Bldgs. Bris 50 B1
Freeland Pl. Bris 62 C3
Freelands. Cleve 73 E4
Freemans La. Ba Gu 77 D1
Freemantle Gdns. Bris 50 B2
Freemantle La. Bris 49 E1
Freemantle Rd. Bris 49 E1
Freemantle Rd. Bris 50 B2
Freemantle Sq. Bris 49 E1
Freestone Rd. Bris 64 A3
Freeview Rd. Bath 101 E4
Freezinghill La. Co Ash 68 A2
French Cl. Nail 59 F2
French Ct. P St J 133 E4
Frenchay Hill. Bris 51 E4
Frenchay Park Rd. Bris 50 C3
Frenchay Rd. Bris 51 E3
Frenchay Rd. W-S-M 104 C2
Frenchfield Rd. P St J 133 E4
Freshford La. Hi Cha 120 A3
Freshland Way. Bris 65 D4
Freshmoor. Cleve 57 F2
Friar Ave. W-S-M 88 C2
Friary Cl. Cleve 57 E3
Friary Cl. Westw 120 C2
Friary Grange Park. Wint 37 F3
Friary Rd. Bris 49 E2
Friary Rd. Portis 45 D3
Friendly Row. E in G 47 E3
Friendship Gr. Nail 59 F1
Friendship Rd. Bris 64 A1
Friendship Rd. Nail 59 F2
Friezewood Rd. Bris 63 D2
Fripp Cl. Bris 64 A3
Frith La. Yate 17 F2
Frobisher Ave. Portis 45 D3
Frobisher Cl. W-S-M 88 C2
Frobisher Rd. Bris 63 D2
Frog La. Bris 63 E3
Frog La. Co Mar 111 E1
Frog La. N Nib 5 D3
Frog La. Win 94 B4
Frog La. Win 94 C3
Frog La. Yate 38 C4
Frogmore St. Bris 63 E3
Frome Ct. Thorn 15 E4
Frome Glen. Wint 37 F2
Frome Old Rd. Rad 133 D1
Frome Pl. Bris 50 C3
Frome Rd. Bath 101 E1
Frome Rd. Ch Sod 28 A1
Frome Rd. Kilm 139 D1

Frome Rd. N St P 135 F2
Frome Rd. Rad 133 D1
Frome St. Bris 63 F4
Frome Terr. Bris 50 C3
Frome Valley Rd. Bris 50 C3
Frome View. Fr Cot 38 A4
Frome Way. Wint 37 F3
Fromeside Park. Bris 51 D4
Front St. Chur 108 C2
Froomshaw Rd. Bris 51 D4
Frost Hill. Yatt 91 E4
Fry's Cl. Bris 50 B2
Fry's La. Blag 109 F2
Fry's Well. Chil 137 E2
Frys Hill. Kingsw 51 F1
Fryth House. Wrax 60 B2
Fryth Way. Nail 59 E1
Fulford Rd. Bris 79 E3
Fulford Wlk. Bris 79 D3
Fullens Cl. W-S-M 105 E4
Fuller Rd. Bath 85 E1
Fullers La. Wins 125 D3
Fullers Way. Bath 118 B4
Fulmar Cl. Thorn 8 E1
Fulmar Rd. W-S-M 88 C1
Fulwell Cl. Faulk 134 B1
Fulwell La. Faulk 134 B1
Furber Ct. Bris 65 D3
Furber Rd. Bris 65 D3
Furber Ridge. Bris 65 D3
Furber Vale. Bris 65 D3
Furland Rd. W-S-M 88 B1
Furlong Cl. Mid No 137 F4
Furnleaze. Clut 114 C2
Furnwood. Bris 65 D3
Furze Cl. W-S-M 88 A1
Furze Rd. Bris 51 E2
Furze Rd. W-S-M 88 A2
Furzewood Rd. Kingsw 65 F4
Fussell Ct. Kingsw 65 F4
Fylton Croft. Bris 80 A2

Gable Cl. Alm 23 D1
Gable Rd. Bris 50 A1
Gables Cl. Ban 107 D2
Gadshill Dr. St Gif 36 C3
Gadshill Rd. Bris 50 B1
Gages Cl. Kingsw 65 F4
Gages Rd. Kingsw 65 F4
Gainsborough Dr. W-S-M ... 88 C2
Gainsborough Gdns. Bath . 101 E4
Gainsborough Rd. Keyn 81 F3
Gainsborough Sq. Bris 50 A4
Gallivan Cl. St Gif 36 A4
Galway Rd. Bris 63 F1
Gambril La. Crom 9 F3
Gander Cl. Bris 79 D3
Garden Cl. Bris 48 B3
Gardeners Wlk. La Ash 62 A1
Gardens Rd. Cleve 57 E2
Gardens The. Kingsw 51 E2
Gardner Ave. Bris 78 C4
Gardner Rd. Portis 45 E3
Garfield Rd. Bris 65 D4
Garner Ct. W-S-M 89 D2
Garnet St. Bris 63 D2
Garnett Pl. Bris 51 F4
Garonor Way. E in G 46 C3
Garrett Dr. St Gif 36 B4
Garrick Rd. Bath 100 C3
Garsdale Rd. W-S-M 105 E4
Garston La. Blag 110 C2
Garstons Cl. Wring 92 C1
Garstons Orch. Wring 92 B1
Garstons The. Portis 45 E2
Garstons. Bathf 86 B1
Garstons. Cleve 73 D4
Garstons. Wring 92 C1
Garth Rd. Bris 79 D4
Gas La. Bris 64 A3
Gasferry Rd. Bris 63 D3
Gaskins The. Bris 50 A3
Gaston Ave. Keyn 81 F3
Gastons The. Bris 48 A4
Gatcombe Dr. St Gif 36 C2
Gatcombe Rd. Bris 79 D3
Gatehouse Ave. Bris 79 D3
Gatehouse Cl. Bris 79 D3
Gatesby Mead. St Gif 36 C3
Gathorne Rd. Bris 63 D2
Gatton Rd. Bris 50 A1
Gaunt's Earthcott La. Alve ... 25 D2
Gaunt's La. Bris 63 E3
Gaunts Cl. Portis 44 C2
Gaunts Rd. Ch Sod 40 A4
Gay Elms Rd. Bris 79 D2
Gay St. Bath 101 F4
Gay's Hill. Bath 102 A4
Gayner Rd. Bris 36 A1
Gays Rd. Kingsw 65 D2
Gaythorne Cres. Yate 27 E1
Gazelle Rd. W-S-M 105 D2
Gazzard Cl. Wint 37 F4
Gazzard Rd. Wint 37 F4
Gee Moors. Kingsw 65 F4
Geldof Dr. Mid No 132 A1
Gelfe Rd. Bris 63 D3
Geoffrey Cl. Bris 78 C3

George & Dragon La. Bris ... 64 B4
George La. Marsh 55 F1
George St. Bath 101 F4
George St. Bris 64 B4
George St. Portis 45 E1
George St. W-S-M 104 C4
George Whitefield Ct. Bris .. 63 F4
George's Bldgs. Bath 102 A4
George's Rd. Bath 85 D1
Georgian View. Bath 101 E1
Gerald Rd. Bris 63 D2
Gerard Rd. W-S-M 104 C4
Gerrish Ave. Bris 64 B4
Gerrish Ave. Mang 51 F3
Gibbet La. Whit 80 B1
Gibbets Brow. Priddy 128 A2
Gibbsfold Rd. Bris 79 E2
Gibson Rd. Bris 49 E1
Gifford Cl. Wickw 27 D4
Gifford Cres. St Gif 36 B3
Gifford Rd. Bris 34 C2
Gilbeck Rd. Nail 59 E1
Gilbert Rd. Bris 64 B4
Gilbert Rd. Kingsw 51 E1
Gilberyn Dr. W-S-M 89 D2
Gilda Cl. Bris 80 B3
Gilda Cres. Bris 80 A3
Gilda Par. Bris 80 B3
Gilda Sq W. Bris 80 A3
Gill Ave. Bris 51 D3
Gill Mews. W-S-M 89 D2
Gillard Cl. Bris 65 D4
Gillard Rd. Bris 65 D4
Gillebank Cl. Bris 80 B2
Gillingham Hill. Bris 65 D3
Gillingham Terr. Bath 85 D1
Gillingstool. Thorn 15 E4
Gillmore Cl. W-S-M 88 B1
Gillmore Rd. W-S-M 88 B1
Gillray Cl. Bris 50 A3
Gillson Cl. Lock 105 E1
Gilpin Cl. Kingsw 51 F1
Gilroy Cl. Kingsw 66 A2
Gilslake Ave. Bris 35 D2
Gimblet Rd. W-S-M 89 D2
Gingell's Green. Bris 65 D4
Glades The. Bris 50 C1
Gladstone Dr. Kingsw 51 F2
Gladstone La. Fr Cot 38 B4
Gladstone Rd. Bath 102 B1
Gladstone Rd. Bris 80 A3
Gladstone Rd. Kingsw 51 E1
Gladstone St. Bris 63 D2
Gladstone St. Bris 64 B4
Gladstone St. Kingsw 51 E2
Gladstone St. Mid No 132 A2
Glaisdale Rd. Bris 51 D3
Glanville Dr. Hin Ble 129 F3
Glanville Gdns. Kingsw 65 F4
Glass House La. Bris 64 A3
Glastonbury Cl. Kingsw 65 F3
Glastonbury Cl. Nail 60 A1
Glastonbury Way. W-S-M ... 89 D1
Glebe Ave. Portis 45 E1
Glebe Field. Alm 24 A3
Glebe Rd. Bath 101 D4
Glebe Rd. Bris 64 C4
Glebe Rd. Cleve 57 E1
Glebe Rd. Lo Ash 62 B1
Glebe Rd. Portis 45 F2
Glebe Rd. W-S-M 104 C4
Glebe The. Hi Cha 120 A2
Glebe The. Hin Cha 119 E1
Glebe The. Piln 22 B4
Glebe The. Tims 116 A2
Glebe The. Wring 92 B1
Glebe Wlk. Keyn 81 E2
Glebelands Rd. Bris 36 A2
Glebelands. Rad 132 B1
Gledemoor Dr. Fr Cot 38 B4
Glen Ave. Ab Lei 61 F4
Glen Dr. Bris 48 B3
Glen La. Bris 64 B1
Glen Park Gdns. Bris 65 D4
Glen Park. Bris 50 B1
Glen Park. Bris 65 D4
Glen The. Bris 49 D2
Glen The. Keyn 82 C1
Glen The. Kingsw 65 D2
Glen The. W-S-M 88 A1
Glen The. Yate 27 F1
Glen Yeo Terr. Cong 91 E2
Glena Ave. Bris 64 A1
Glenarm Rd. Bris 64 C1
Glenarm Wlk. Bris 64 C1
Glenavon Park. Bris 48 B2
Glenburn Rd. Bris 51 D1
Glencoyne Sq. Bris 35 E1
Glendale. Bris 51 E2
Glendale. Bris 62 C3
Glendale. Mang 51 F4
Glendare St. Bris 64 B3
Glendevon Rd. Bris 80 A2
Glendinning Ave. Bris 51 D3
Gleneagles Cl. Nail 60 A1
Gleneagles Cl. W-S-M 88 C2
Gleneagles Dr. Bris 34 B2
Gleneagles Rd. Kingsw 66 A3

Gleneagles. Yate 27 F1
Glenfall. Yate 39 E4
Glenfrome Rd. Bris 50 A2
Glenroy Ave. Bris 51 D1
Glenside Cl. Bris 51 E4
Glenside Park. Bris 50 C3
Glentworth Rd. Bris 49 E1
Glentworth Rd. Bris 63 D3
Glenview Rd. Bris 64 B1
Glenwood Dr. Kingsw 66 A3
Glenwood Rd. Bris 49 E4
Glenwood Rise. Portis 44 C3
Glenwood. Bris 51 E2
Gloster Ave. Bris 50 B2
Gloucester Cl. St Gif 36 B3
Gloucester La. Bris 63 F4
Gloucester Rd N. Bris 36 A1
Gloucester Rd. Alve 14 C1
Gloucester Rd. Avon 33 D1
Gloucester Rd. Bath 85 E3
Gloucester Rd. Bathe 85 E3
Gloucester Rd. Bris 36 A4
Gloucester Rd. Bris 49 F2
Gloucester Rd. Kingsw 51 F2
Gloucester Rd. St Gif 24 A2
Gloucester Rd. Thorn 8 B1
Gloucester Row. W-u-E 11 F4
Gloucester St. Bath 101 F4
Gloucester St. Bris 50 B2
Gloucester St. Bris 62 C4
Gloucester St. Bris 63 F4
Gloucester St. W-S-M 104 B4
Glovers Field. Ship 125 F4
Glyn Vale. Bris 63 F1
Goddard Dr. W-S-M 89 D2
Godfrey Ct. Kingsw 65 F2
Goffenton Dr. Bris 51 D3
Goldcrest Rd. Ch Sod 39 F4
Golden La. Kings 11 F2
Golden Valley La. Bitt 66 C1
Goldfinch Way. Puck 53 E2
Goldney Ave. Bris 63 D3
Goldney Ave. Sist 66 B4
Goldney Cl. Clut 114 C1
Goldney Rd. Bris 63 D3
Goldney Way. Clut 114 C1
Goldsbury Wlk. Bris 34 A1
Golf Club La. Keyn 82 C1
Golf Course La. Bris 35 F2
Golf Course Rd. Bath 102 B3
Golledge Cl. Chil 137 E2
Gooch Way. W-S-M 89 D2
Good Shepherd Cl. Bris 49 E1
Goodeve Park. Bris 48 B2
Goodeve Rd. Bris 48 B2
Goodhind St. Bris 64 A4
Goodneston Rd. Bris 51 D2
Goodring Hill. Bris 34 A1
Goodwin Dr. Bris 79 F2
Goodwin Dr. Nail 59 E2
Goodwood Gdns. Mang 37 F1
Goold Cl. Cor 100 A4
Goolden St. Bris 64 A2
Goosard La. Paul 131 F2
Goose Acre. St Gif 36 C3
Goose Green Way. Yate 27 F2
Goose Green. Fr Cot 38 B4
Goose Green. Yate 27 F2
Gooseland Cl. Bris 79 F2
Goosy La. Lock 89 E1
Gordano Gdns. E in G 47 D2
Gordano Rd. E in G 46 B4
Gordano View. Portis 45 E3
Gordano Way. E in G 46 C3
Gordon Ave. Bris 50 C1
Gordon Cl. Bris 51 D1
Gordon Rd. Bath 102 A3
Gordon Rd. Bris 49 F1
Gordon Rd. Bris 50 B1
Gordon Rd. Bris 63 D4
Gordon Rd. P St J 133 E4
Gordon Rd. W-S-M 104 C4
Gore Rd. Bris 63 D2
Gore's Marsh Rd. Bris 63 D1
Gorham Cl. Bris 34 B1
Gorlands Rd. Ch Sod 28 A1
Gorlangton Cl. Bris 80 A4
Gorse Cover Rd. Piln 22 A4
Gorse Hill. Bris 51 E2
Gorse La. Bris 63 D3
Gorse La. Co Ash 68 B4
Gorse La. Marsh 54 C1
Gosforth Rd. Bris 35 D1
Goslet Rd. Bris 80 C3
Goss Barton. Nail 59 E1
Goss Cl. Nail 59 E1
Goss La. Nail 59 E1
Goss View. Nail 59 E1
Gotley Rd. Bris 80 B4
Goulston Rd. Bris 79 D3
Goulston Wlk. Bris 79 D3
Goulter St. Bris 64 A3
Gournay Ct. Paul 131 D2
Gourney Cl. Bris 34 A1
Grace Cl. Ch Sod 28 A1
Grace Cl. Yatt 91 D4

Grace Ct. Mang 51 E3
Grace Dr. Kingsw 66 A4
Grace Dr. Mid No 132 A3
Grace Park Rd. Bris 64 B1
Grace Rd. Mang 51 E3
Grace Rd. W-S-M 89 D2
Gradwell Cl. W-S-M 89 D2
Graeme Cl. Bris 51 D2
Graham Cl. Bris 50 A1
Graham Rd. Bris 63 E2
Graham Rd. Mang 51 F3
Graham Rd. W-S-M 104 C4
Grainger Cl. Bris 47 F4
Graitney Cl. Brock 92 A4
Grampian Cl. Kingsw 66 B2
Granby Hill. Bris 62 C3
Grand Par. Bath 102 A3
Grandmother's Rock La.
　　Bitt 67 E1
Grange Ave. Kingsw 65 E3
Grange Ave. St Gif 36 B3
Grange Cl N. Bris 49 D3
Grange Cl. W-S-M 104 C1
Grange Court Rd. Bris ... 49 D3
Grange Dr. Bris 51 E3
Grange End. Rod 138 A4
Grange Park. Bris 49 D3
Grange Park. Bris 51 E4
Grange Rd. Bris 63 D4
Grange Rd. Bris 79 D3
Grange Rd. Keyn 82 B2
Grange Rd. W-S-M 104 C1
Grange The. Bris 48 B4
Grangeville Cl. Bris 66 A2
Grangewood Cl. Bris 51 E3
Granny's La. Kingsw 65 F3
Grantham Cl. Bris 65 E4
Grantham Rd. Bris 51 E1
Grantson Cl. Bris 64 C1
Granville Cl. Kingsw 65 D2
Granville Rd. Bath 84 C2
Granville St. Bris 64 B3
Grasmere Cl. Bris 49 D4
Grasmere Dr. W-S-M 104 C2
Grass Meers Dr. Bris 80 A2
Grassington Dr. Ch Sod . 40 A4
Grassmere Gdns. Kingsw . 66 B3
Grassmere Rd. Yatt 91 D4
Gratitude Rd. Bris 50 B1
Gravel Hill Rd. Yate 28 A3
Gravel Hill. Ch St 112 A4
Gravel Hill. Win 112 A4
Graveney Cl. Bris 64 B1
Gray's Cl. Bris 34 C1
Grayle Rd. Bris 35 D1
Grays Hill. Well 134 A3
Great Ann St. Bris 63 F4
Great Bedford St. Bath .. 101 F4
Great Brockeridge. Bris . 48 C3
Great Dowles. Kingsw ... 66 A2
Great George Sq. Bris ... 63 E3
Great George St. Bris 63 F4
Great Hayles Rd. Bris 80 A4
Great Leaze. Kingsw 66 A4
Great Meadow Rd. St Gif . 36 C3
Great Meadow. St Gif 37 D3
Great Park Rd. Brad S ... 24 B2
Great Pulteney St. Bath . 102 A4
Great Stanhope St. Bath . 101 F3
Great Stoke Way. St Gif . 36 B2
Great Stoke. St Gif 37 D3
Great Western Bridge.
　　W-S-M 104 C4
Great Western La. Bris ... 64 A3
Great Western Rd. Cleve . 57 E1
Great Western Way. Bris . 63 F3
Greatstone La. Win 94 C3
Green Cl. Bris 50 A4
Green Croft. Bris 51 D1
Green Dell Cl. Bris 34 B2
Green Ditch La. Chil 137 D3
Green Ditch La. Ston E .. 137 D3
Green Dragon Rd. Wint .. 37 E3
Green Hayes. Ch Sod 40 B4
Green La. Avon 33 D1
Green La. But 94 B2
Green La. But 111 D4
Green La. Chil 137 F1
Green La. Hin Cha 119 F1
Green La. Marsh 69 F4
Green La. Paul 130 C3
Green La. Thorn 16 A4
Green La. Win 94 B2
Green La. Wrax 61 E2
Green Park Rd. Bath 101 F3
Green Park. Bath 101 F3
Green Parlour Rd. Kilm ... 133 E1
Green Side. Mang 52 A3
Green St. Bath 102 A4
Green St. Bris 63 F2
Green St. Well 133 F3
Green The. Back 75 F3
Green The. Bath 101 E1
Green The. Crom 17 D4
Green The. E in G 47 E2
Green The. Hin Cha 119 F1

Green The. Kingsw 51 F1
Green The. Lock 106 A2
Green The. Olve 14 A1
Green The. St Gif 36 C2
Green The. Wins 125 D4
Green Tree Rd. Mid No .. 132 A2
Green Wlk. Bris 64 A1
Greenacre Rd. Bris 80 A2
Greenacre. W-S-M 88 A1
Greenacres. Bath 84 A4
Greenacres. Bris 48 C4
Greenbank Ave W. Bris .. 50 B1
Greenbank Ave W. Bris .. 50 B1
Greenbank Gdns. Bath ... 84 A1
Greenbank Rd. Bris 50 B1
Greenbank Rd. Bris 63 D2
Greenbank Rd. Kingsw ... 65 E3
Greenbank View. Bris 50 B1
Greendale Rd. Bris 49 D2
Greendale Rd. Bris 63 F1
Greenditch Ave. Bris 79 E3
Greenditch Cl. Chil 137 E2
Greenditch St. Piln 13 E1
Greendown Pl. Bath 102 A1
Greendown. Bris 65 D4
Greenfield Ave. Bris 49 E4
Greenfield Cres. Nail 59 F2
Greenfield Park. Portis ... 45 E2
Greenfield Pl. W-S-M 104 B4
Greenfield Rd. Bris 35 E1
Greenfields Ave. Ban 107 D2
Greenfinch Lodge. Bris .. 50 C3
Greenhaven. Bris 50 B1
Greenhill Cl. Nail 59 E1
Greenhill Cl. W-S-M 89 D2
Greenhill Down. Alve 15 D2
Greenhill Gdns. Alve 15 D2
Greenhill Gr. Bris 63 D1
Greenhill La. Alve 14 C2
Greenhill La. Bris 34 B1
Greenhill La. Wins 108 A2
Greenhill Par. Alve 15 D3
Greenhill Pl. Mid No 132 A2
Greenhill Rd. Alve 15 D3
Greenhill Rd. Mid No 132 A2
Greenhill Rd. Wins 108 A2
Greenhill. Alve 15 D2
Greenland Rd. W-S-M 88 B1
Greenlands Rd. P St J ... 133 E4
Greenlands Way. Bris 34 C2
Greenleaze Ave. Mang ... 37 F1
Greenleaze Cl. Mang 37 E1
Greenleaze. Bris 64 A1
Greenmore Rd. Bris 64 A1
Greenore. Kingsw 65 E4
Greenpark Rd. Bris 35 F1
Greenridge Cl. Bris 78 C2
Greenridge. Clut 114 C2
Greenside Cl. Bris 34 B2
Greenslade Gdns. Nail ... 59 E2
Greensplott Rd. Avon 33 F4
Greenvale Cl. Tims 116 A1
Greenvale Dr. Tims 116 A1
Greenvale Rd. Paul 131 E3
Greenvale. Tims 116 A1
Greenview. Kingsw 66 A1
Greenway Bush La. Bris . 63 D2
Greenway Ct. Bath 101 F2
Greenway Dr. Bris 49 E4
Greenway La. Bath 102 A2
Greenway La. Co Ash 68 C3
Greenway Park. Bris 49 E4
Greenway Park. Cleve ... 57 F2
Greenway Rd. Bris 49 D1
Greenway The. Bris 51 E2
Greenways Rd. Yate 27 F2
Greenways. Chil 137 E1
Greenways. Kingsw 52 A1
Greenwell La. Chur 109 E4
Greenwood Cl. Bris 49 F4
Greenwood Dr. Alve 14 C2
Greenwood Rd. Bris 64 A1
Greenwood Rd. W-S-M ... 88 C1
Gregory Ct. Kingsw 66 A3
Gregorys Tyning. Paul ... 131 F3
Greinton. W-S-M 105 D1
Grenville Ave. Lock 106 A2
Grenville Cl. Bris 64 C4
Grenville Pl. Bris 62 C3
Grenville Rd. Bris 49 F2
Greve Ct. Kingsw 65 F2
Greville Rd. Bris 63 D2
Greville St. Bris 63 E2
Grey Hollow. E Harp 128 C2
Greyfield Comm. Paul 115 E1
Greyfield Rd. Paul 115 E1
Greyfield View. Clut 114 C1
Greylands Rd. Bris 78 C4
Greystoke Ave. Bris 35 E1
Greystoke Gdns. Bris 49 D4
Greystones. Mang 37 F1
Grib La. Blag 110 C1
Griffin Cl. W-S-M 89 D1
Griffin Rd. Cleve 57 F1
Griggfield Wlk. Bris 80 A4
Grimsbury Rd. Kingsw ... 66 A4
Grindell Rd. Bris 64 B4

Grinfield Ave. Bris 79 E2
Grinfield Cl. Bris 79 E2
Grinfield Ct. Bris 79 E2
Grittleton Rd. Bris 49 F4
Grosvenor Bridge Rd. Bath . 85 E1
Grosvenor Park. Bath 85 E1
Grosvenor Pl. Bath 85 E1
Grosvenor Rd. Bris 49 F1
Grove Ave. Bris 48 B4
Grove Ave. Bris 50 C2
Grove Ave. Bris 63 E3
Grove Bank. Bris 37 E1
Grove Ind Est The. Bris .. 36 A4
Grove La. Dyrh 54 B3
Grove La. Faulk 134 B1
Grove La. W-S-M 104 B4
Grove Leaze. Bris 47 E3
Grove Park Ave. Bris 64 B1
Grove Park Rd. Bris 64 B1
Grove Park Rd. W-S-M ... 87 E1
Grove Park Terr. Bris 50 C2
Grove Park. Bris 49 E1
Grove Pk. Bris 64 B1
Grove Rd. Bris 48 B4
Grove Rd. Bris 49 D1
Grove Rd. Bris 50 C2
Grove Rd. W-S-M 88 B1
Grove Rd. W-S-M 104 B4
Grove St. Bath 102 A4
Grove The. Bris 63 E3
Grove The. Kingsw 66 A2
Grove The. Wickw 27 D4
Grove The. Winsc 107 F1
Grove The. Wrax 60 B2
Grove View. Bris 50 C3
Grove Wood Rd. Rod 138 C4
Grovesend Rd. Thorn 15 E4
Guernsey Ave. Bris 64 C2
Gug The. Paul 115 E1
Guildford Rd. Bris 64 C3
Guinea La. Bath 101 F4
Guinea La. Bris 51 D2
Guinea St. Bris 63 E3
Gullen. Well 134 A3
Gulliford's Bank. Cleve ... 57 F1
Gullimores Gdns. Bris ... 79 D2
Gullivers Pl. Ch Sod 40 A4
Gullon Wlk. Bris 78 C3
Gullons Cl. Bris 79 D3
Gully La. Rock 8 C4
Gully The. Wint 37 F4
Gullybrook La. Bris 64 A3
Gunter's Hill. Bris 65 D3
Guthrie Rd. Bris 63 D4
Gwilliam St. Bris 63 F3
Gwyn St. Bris 49 F1
Gypsy La. Keyn 99 D4
Haberfield Hill. Ab Lei 47 F1
Hacket Hill. Thorn 15 F4
Hacket La. Thorn 15 F4
Hadley Ct. Kingsw 66 A3
Hadley Rd. Bath 102 A1
Hadrian Cl. Bris 48 B2
Hagg Hill. Tims 116 A1
Haggs La. Bris 50 C1
Haig Cl. Bris 48 A4
Halbrow Cres. Bris 51 E3
Haldon Cl. Bris 63 E1
Hales Horn Cl. St Gif 36 B3
Half Yd. Wring 109 E4
Halface Cl. Bris 80 A2
Halface La. Bris 80 A2
Halfpenny Row. Rode 136 C1
Halifax Rd. Yate 27 E2
Hall End La. Yate 17 E1
Hall La. Co Ash 68 A2
Hall La. Co Ash 68 C2
Hall La. Hort 29 F3
Hall St. Bris 63 D1
Hallam Rd. Cleve 57 E2
Hallards Cl. Bris 47 F4
Hallatrow Rd. Paul 131 E3
Hallen Cl. Bris 34 B2
Hallen Dr. Bris 48 B4
Hallen Rd. Bris 34 B2
Halletts Way. Portis 45 E3
Halliwell Rd. Portis 44 B2
Halls Rd. Kingsw 65 E4
Halsbury Rd. Bris 49 D2
Halstock Ave. Bris 50 C2
Halston Dr. Bris 63 F4
Halswell Gdns. Bris 79 D2
Halswell Rd. Cleve 57 E1
Halt End. Whit 80 B2
Ham Cl. Clut 114 C1
Ham Gr. Paul 131 F4
Ham Green. E in G 47 E2
Ham La. Bi Sut 113 E3
Ham La. Bris 50 C3
Ham La. Dun 78 B2
Ham La. K Sey 72 C1
Ham La. O-on-S 7 E3
Ham La. Paul 130 C3
Ham La. Paul 131 F3
Ham La. Wick 53 F1
Ham La. Wrax 60 A2
Ham La. Yatt 74 A2

Ham Link. Blag 109 F2
Ham Rd. Berr 121 D2
Ham Wood Cl. W-S-M 105 D1
Hamble Cl. Thorn 15 E4
Hambledon Rd. Lock 89 E2
Hambrook La. Bris 37 D2
Hambrook La. St Gif 37 D2
Hamersmith Rd. Bris 64 B4
Hamilton Rd. Bath 84 C1
Hamilton Rd. Bris 63 D2
Hamilton Rd. Bris 64 A4
Hamilton Rd. W-S-M 87 E1
Hamlet The. Nail 60 A2
Hammer La. Faulk 135 E1
Hammond Cl. Bris 64 B1
Hammond Gdns. Bris 48 C4
Hampden Cl. Yate 27 E2
Hampden Rd. Bris 64 A2
Hampden Rd. W-S-M 88 C1
Hampshire Way. Yate 27 F2
Hampstead Rd. Bris 64 B2
Hampton Cl. Kingsw 66 A3
Hampton Cnr. Bris 47 F3
Hampton La. Bris 49 D1
Hampton Park. Bris 49 D1
Hampton Rd. Bris 49 D1
Hampton Row. Bath 102 A4
Hampton St. Kingsw 51 E1
Hampton View. Bath 85 D1
Hams La. Badg 123 E1
Hams Rd. Keyn 81 F4
Hanbury Cl. Kingsw 65 E3
Hanbury Rd. Bris 63 D4
Handel Ave. Bris 64 B4
Handel Rd. Keyn 81 F3
Handford Way. Kingsw ... 66 A2
Hanford Ct. Bris 80 B4
Hang Hill. Well 134 A3
Hanham Bsns Pk. Kingsw . 65 D3
Hanham La. Paul 131 F4
Hanham Rd. Kingsw 65 E1
Hanham Way. Nail 59 E1
Hannah More Cl. Wring .. 92 C1
Hannah More Rd. Nail ... 75 E4
Hanny's La. Ch Mag 96 A2
Hanover Cl. W-S-M 89 D2
Hanover Ct. Bris 63 F4
Hanover Ct. Rad 133 E1
Hanover Pl. Bris 63 D3
Hanover St. Bath 85 D1
Hanover St. Bris 63 E3
Hanover St. Bris 64 A3
Hansford Cl. Bath 101 F1
Hansford Sq. Bath 101 F1
Hanson's Way. Cleve 57 E1
Hantone Hill. Bath 102 C4
Happerton La. E in G 47 E1
Hapsburg Cl. W-S-M 89 D2
Harbour Rd. Portis 45 E3
Harbour Wall. Bris 48 B2
Harbour Way. Bris 63 E3
Harbury Rd. Bris 49 E4
Harbutts. Bath 85 F1
Harcombe Hill. Wint 37 F2
Harcombe Rd. Wint 37 E3
Harcourt Ave. Bris 65 D3
Harcourt Cl. Keyn 82 C1
Harcourt Gdns. Bath 84 A1
Harcourt Hill. Bris 49 E2
Harcourt Rd. Bris 49 D2
Harden Rd. Bris 80 C3
Hardenhuish Rd. Bris 64 B3
Harding Pl. Keyn 82 A3
Hardwick Cl. Bris 64 C2
Hardwick Cl. Kingsw 66 B3
Hardwick Rd. E in G 47 E3
Hardwicke. Yate 39 E4
Hardy Ave. Bris 63 D2
Hardy Ct. Kingsw 65 F3
Hardy La. Olve 14 A1
Hardy La. Piln 23 F4
Hardy Rd. Bris 63 D1
Hareclive Rd. Bris 79 E2
Harefield Cl. Kingsw 65 E3
Harescombe. Yate 39 F4
Harewood Rd. Bris 51 D1
Harford Cl. Bris 48 B4
Harford Dr. Bris 37 E1
Harford Sq. Ch Mag 96 A2
Harington Pl. Bath 101 F3
Harlech Way. Kingsw 66 A1
Harleston Rd. Bris 64 A4
Harley La. Cleve 58 B3
Harley St. Bath 101 F4
Harmer Cl. Bris 34 C2
Harmony Dr. Portis 44 C2
Harnhill Cl. Bris 79 D2
Harolds Way. Kingsw 65 E3
Harptree Ct. Kingsw 66 A2
Harptree Gr. Bris 63 D2
Harptree Hill. E Harp 128 A3
Harptree. W-S-M 105 D1
Harrier Path. W-S-M 105 F4
Harrington Ave. Bris 80 C3
Harrington Gr. Bris 80 C3
Harrington Rd. Bris 80 C3
Harrington Wlk. Bris 80 C3
Harris Barton. Fr Cot 38 A4

Harris Ct. Kingsw 65 F2
Harris La. Ab Lei 61 F4
Harrow Rd. Bris 64 B2
Harrowdene Rd. Bris 64 A2
Harry Stoke Rd. St Gif ... 36 C1
Hart's La. Paul 131 D4
Hartcliffe Rd. Bris 79 F4
Hartcliffe Way. Bris 79 E4
Hartcliffe Wlk. Bris 79 F4
Hartcombe Rd. E in G ... 47 D1
Hartfield Ave. Bris 49 E1
Hartgill Cl. Bris 79 D2
Hartington Park. Bris 49 E1
Hartland. W-S-M 89 D1
Hartley Cl. Ch Sod 28 A1
Harts Paddock. Mid No .. 131 F2
Harvey Cl. W-S-M 89 D2
Harveys La. Bris 64 C4
Harwood Gdns. W-S-M .. 88 C2
Haselbury Gr. Keyn 82 C1
Haskins Ct. Kingsw 66 A2
Haslands. Nail 75 E4
Haslemere Ind Est. Avon . 33 E1
Hassage Hill. Well 134 C4
Hassell Dr. Bris 64 A4
Hastings Cl. Bris 63 E1
Hastings Rd. Bris 63 E1
Hatchet Hill. Kilm 139 F2
Hatchet La. St Gif 36 C2
Hatchet Rd. St Gif 36 C3
Hatchmere. Thorn 15 E4
Hatfield Bldgs. Bath 102 A3
Hatfield Rd. Bath 101 F2
Hatfield Rd. W-S-M 105 D4
Hatherley Rd. Bris 49 F2
Hatherley. Yate 39 F4
Hathway Wlk. Bris 64 A4
Hatters' La. Ch Sod 28 A1
Havage Dro. Ban 107 E4
Haven The. Kingsw 51 F1
Haversham Cl. W-S-M ... 88 B1
Haverstock Rd. Bris 64 A2
Haviland Gr. Bath 84 A2
Haviland Park. Bath 84 A1
Havory. Bath 85 E1
Havyat Rd. Wring 109 F4
Haw La. Olve 14 A2
Hawarden Terr. Bath 85 D1
Hawburn Cl. Bris 64 B1
Haweswater Cl. Kingsw .. 66 B3
Hawke Rd. W-S-M 88 C2
Hawkesbury Rd. Bris 50 C2
Hawkesbury Rd. Hill 19 E4
Hawkesley Dr. St Gif 36 B3
Hawlyn Cl. Bris 48 B3
Hawthorn Ave. Kingsw ... 65 D3
Hawthorn Cl. Bris 35 F4
Hawthorn Cl. Char 11 D2
Hawthorn Cl. Portis 44 C3
Hawthorn Coombe. W-S-M . 88 C2
Hawthorn Cres. Thorn ... 8 B1
Hawthorn Cres. Yatt 74 A1
Hawthorn Gdns. W-S-M .. 88 B1
Hawthorn Gr. Bath 101 F1
Hawthorn Hill. W-S-M ... 88 C1
Hawthorn Hts. W-S-M ... 88 B2
Hawthorn Park. W-S-M .. 88 C2
Hawthorn Rd. Rad 133 D1
Hawthorn Way. Nail 60 A1
Hawthorn Way. St Gif ... 36 C3
Hawthorne Cl. Puck 53 E3
Hawthorne Gdns. Kingsw . 51 F2
Hawthorne St. Bris 64 A2
Hawthornes The. Kingsw . 51 F2
Hawthorns La. Keyn 81 F3
Hay Hill. Bath 101 F4
Hay La. Win 94 B3
Hay Leaze. Yate 27 E2
Hay St. Marsh 70 A4
Hay St. Ston E 137 D4
Haycombe Dr. Bath 101 D2
Haycombe La. Engl 100 C2
Haycombe. Bris 79 F3
Haycroft La. Newp 4 B3
Haycroft Rd. Bris 36 A2
Hayden Cl. Bath 101 F3
Haydock Cl. Mang 37 F1
Haydon Gate. Rod 138 C4
Haydon Gdns. Bris 50 A3
Haydon Hill. Rod 138 C4
Haydon Ind Est. Rod 138 C4
Hayeley Dr. St Gif 36 C3
Hayes Cl. Bris 64 A4
Hayes La. Gr Bad 30 C1
Hayes Park Rd. Mid No .. 131 F1
Hayes Rd. Mid No 131 F1
Hayesfield Park. Bath 101 F3
Hayeswood Rd. Farm 115 F2

Hayeswood Rd. Tims 116 A1
Hayfield. Marsh 70 A4
Hayleigh House. Bris 79 E2
Haymarket The. Bris 63 E4
Haymarket Wlk. Bris 63 E4
Haynes La. Mang 51 E3
Haythorn Ct. Mang 51 F3
Haytor Park. Bris 48 B3
Hayward Cl. Cleve 57 E1
Hayward Rd. Bris 64 B4
Hayward Rd. Kingsw 51 E2
Haywood Cl. W-S-M 105 D1
Haywood Gdns. W-S-M 105 D1
Hazel Ave. Bris 49 D1
Hazel Cres. Thorn 8 B1
Hazel Gr. Bath 101 E2
Hazel Gr. Bris 50 A4
Hazel La. Olve 14 C2
Hazel Terr. Rod 138 B4
Hazelbury Dr. Kingsw 66 B3
Hazelbury Rd. Nail 59 E1
Hazelcote Rd. Bris 80 A2
Hazeldene Rd. Bris 36 A4
Hazeldene Rd. W-S-M 105 D4
Hazell Cl. Cleve 57 F1
Hazelton Rd. Bris 49 E2
Hazelwood Ct. Bris 48 B2
Hazelwood Rd. Bris 48 B2
Hazelton Gdns. Bath 102 C2
Headford Ave. Bris 65 D4
Headford Rd. Bris 63 E1
Headley La. Bris 79 D3
Headley Park Ave. Bris 79 D4
Headley Park Rd. Bris 79 D4
Headley Rd. Bris 79 D3
Headley Wlk. Bris 79 D3
Healey Dr. Dyrh 54 B3
Heart Meers. Bris 80 A3
Heath Cl. Wint 37 F3
Heath Ct. Mang 51 E4
Heath Gdns. Fr Cot 38 B3
Heath Gdns. Mang 51 E4
Heath Rd. Bris 50 A2
Heath Rd. Kingsw 65 D2
Heath Rd. Mang 51 E4
Heath Rd. Nail 59 F2
Heath Ridge. Lo Ash 62 A1
Heath Rise. Kingsw 66 A3
Heath St. Bris 50 B2
Heath Wlk. Mang 51 E4
Heathcote Dr. Fr Cot 38 B4
Heathcote La. Fr Cot 38 B4
Heathcote Rd. Bris 51 D1
Heathcote Rd. Mang 51 F3
Heathcote Wlk. Bris 51 E1
Heather Ave. Fr Cot 38 A3
Heather Cl. Bris 65 D4
Heatherdene. Bris 79 F4
Heathfield Cl. Bath 84 A2
Heathfield Cl. Keyn 81 E3
Heathfield Cres. Bris 80 A2
Heathfield Rd. Nail 59 F2
Heathfield Way. Nail 59 F1
Heathgate. Yatt 91 D4
Hebden Rd. Westw 120 C2
Heber St. Bris 64 B4
Hebron Rd. Bris 63 E2
Hedgemead Cl. Bris 50 B3
Hedgemead View. Bris 50 C3
Hedges Cl. Cleve 57 D1
Hedges The. Lock 89 E1
Hedwick Ave. Bris 64 C4
Hedwick St. Bris 64 C4
Heggard Cl. Bris 79 D3
Helens Rd. Wins 108 A2
Hellier Wlk. Bris 79 E2
Helston Rd. Nail 60 A1
Hemming Way. Lock 105 F2
Hemmings Par. Bris 64 A4
Hemplow Cl. Bris 80 B4
Hempton La. St Gif 24 A1
Hen La. Win 94 C2
Henacre Rd. Bris 47 F4
Henbury Gdns. Bris 34 C1
Henbury Hill. Bris 34 C1
Henbury Rd. Bris 34 C1
Henbury Rd. Kingsw 65 D3
Hencliffe Rd. Bris 80 B4
Hencliffe Way. Kingsw 65 D2
Henderson Rd. Kingsw 65 D3
Hendre Rd. Bris 63 D1
Heneage La. Falf 9 F4
Henfield Cres. Kingsw 66 A2
Henfield Rd. Fr Cot 38 B2
Henfield Rd. West 38 B2
Hengaston St. Bris 63 D1
Hengrove Ave. Bris 80 A4
Hengrove La. Bris 80 A4
Hengrove Rd. Bris 64 A1
Hengrove Way. Bris 79 E3
Henleaze Ave. Bris 49 D3
Henleaze Gdns. Bris 49 D3
Henleaze Park Dr. Bris 49 E3
Henleaze Park. Bris 49 E3
Henleaze Rd. Bris 49 D3
Henleaze Terr. Bris 49 D4
Henley Gr. Bris 49 D3

Henley La. Yatt 91 E4
Henley Lodge. Yatt 91 E4
Henley Park. Yatt 91 E4
Henley View. Well 118 B1
Hennessy Cl. Bris 79 F2
Henrietta Gdns. Bath 102 A4
Henrietta Mews. Bath 102 A4
Henrietta Pl. Bath 102 A4
Henrietta Rd. Bath 102 A4
Henrietta St. Bath 102 A4
Henrietta St. Bris 50 A1
Henrietta St. Bris 63 E4
Henry St. Bath 102 A3
Henry St. Bris 63 F2
Henry Williamson Ct.
    Kingsw 66 A3
Henshaw Cl. Bris 51 E1
Henshaw Rd. Bris 51 E1
Henshaw Wlk. Bris 51 E1
Hensley Gdns. Bath 101 F2
Hensley Rd. Bath 101 F2
Hensman's Hill. Bris 63 D3
Hepburn Rd. Bris 49 F1
Herald Cl. Bris 48 B3
Herapath St. Bris 64 B3
Herbert Cres. Bris 50 B2
Herbert Rd. Bath 101 E3
Herbert Rd. Cleve 57 E2
Herbert St. Bris 63 E2
Herbert St. Bris 64 B4
Hercules Cl. St Gif 36 B3
Hereford Rd. Bris 50 A1
Hereford St. Bris 63 E2
Heritage Cl. P St J 133 E4
Herkomer Cl. Bris 50 A4
Herluin Way. W-S-M 105 D3
Hermes Cl. Keyn 82 B1
Hermitage Cl. Bris 47 F4
Hermitage Rd. Bath 84 C1
Hermitage Rd. Mang 51 F3
Hern La. Ba Gu 77 F3
Heron Cl. W-S-M 105 F4
Heron Rd. Bris 50 A1
Heron Way. Ch Sod 40 A4
Herridge Cl. Bris 79 D2
Herridge Rd. Bris 79 D2
Hersey Gdns. Bris 78 C2
Hesding Cl. Kingsw 65 E2
Hestercombe Rd. Bris 79 D3
Heyford Ave. Bris 50 A2
Heyron Wlk. Bris 79 D2
Heywood Rd. E in G 47 E2
Heywood Terr. E in G 47 E2
Hibbs Cl. Marsh 69 F4
Hicks Common Rd. Wint .. 37 F3
Hicks Cl. Kingsw 65 F2
High Acre. Paul 131 F2
High Bannerdown. Bathe .. 86 A2
High Elm. Kingsw 65 F3
High Gr. Bris 48 A4
High Mead Gdns. Bi Sut .. 113 E2
High Meadows. Mid No .. 131 F1
High Park. Bris 64 A1
High Park. Paul 131 E3
High St. Axb 125 D1
High St. Ban 107 D1
High St. Bath 84 A1
High St. Bath 85 F1
High St. Bath 101 D3
High St. Bath 102 A3
High St. Bathe 85 F2
High St. Bathf 86 B1
High St. Bitt 82 C4
High St. Blag 110 B2
High St. Bris 47 E4
High St. Bris 49 D1
High St. Bris 49 D4
High St. Bris 50 A1
High St. Bris 63 E3
High St. Ch Mag 96 A2
High St. Ch Sod 28 A1
High St. Charl 84 C3
High St. Cong 91 E2
High St. Doyn 53 F1
High St. Dyrh 54 B2
High St. E Harp 128 C3
High St. H Up 19 F1
High St. Hi Cha 120 A3
High St. Hill 19 E4
High St. Hin Cha 119 F1
High St. Ir Act 26 B2
High St. Keyn 81 F3
High St. Keyn 82 C2
High St. Kings 11 F2
High St. Kingsw 51 E2
High St. Kingsw 65 E3
High St. Kingsw 65 F4
High St. Kingsw 66 A4
High St. Kingsw 66 B2
High St. Mang 51 E2
High St. Marsh 69 F4
High St. Mid No 132 A1
High St. N St P 135 F2
High St. Nail 59 F1
High St. Paul 115 E1
High St. Paul 131 F3
High St. Pens 97 F2

High St. Portb 46 B2
High St. Portis 45 E3
High St. Rode 136 C1
High St. Ston E 130 C1
High St. Thorn 15 D4
High St. Tims 116 A1
High St. W-S-M 88 C1
High St. W-S-M 104 B4
High St. Well 118 B1
High St. Wick 67 E3
High St. Wickw 18 A3
High St. Win 95 D4
High St. Wint 37 E3
High St. Wring 92 B2
High St. Yatt 74 C1
High St. Yatt 91 D4
High View. Portis 45 D2
Higham St. Bris 63 F2
Highbury Pl. Bath 85 D1
Highbury Rd. Bris 49 F4
Highbury Rd. Bris 63 E1
Highbury Rd. Paul 131 D4
Highbury Rd. W-S-M 87 E1
Highbury Terr. Bath 85 D1
Highbury Villas. Bris 63 E4
Highcroft. Kingsw 66 B3
Highdale Ave. Cleve 57 F2
Highdale Cl. Bris 80 A2
Highdale Pl. Cleve 57 E2
Highdale Rd. Cleve 57 F2
Highett Dr. Bris 50 A1
Highfield Ave. Kingsw 65 E3
Highfield Cl. Bath 101 D3
Highfield Cl. St Gif 36 C2
Highfield Cres. Chil 137 E3
Highfield Dr. Portis 44 C2
Highfield Gdns. Kingsw 66 B1
Highfield Gr. Bris 49 E3
Highfield La. Co Mar 128 A3
Highfield La. E Harp 129 D2
Highfield La. H Up 29 F4
Highfield La. Hort 29 F4
Highfield Rd. Ch Sod 28 A1
Highfield Rd. Keyn 81 F1
Highfield Rd. P St J 133 E4
Highfield Rd. W-S-M 105 D1
Highfields. H Up 19 F1
Highfields. Pens 96 C1
Highfields. Rad 132 B1
Highgrove St. Bris 64 A2
Highland Cl. W-S-M 88 A1
Highland Cres. Bris 49 D3
Highland Rd. Bath 101 D3
Highland Sq. Bris 49 D1
Highland Terr. Bath 101 E3
Highlands Dr. N Nib 5 F2
Highlands Rd. Lo Ash 62 A1
Highlands Rd. Portis 45 D3
Highleaze Rd. Kingsw 66 B2
Highmead Gdns. Bris 78 C2
Highmore Ct. Bris 50 A4
Highmore Gdns. Bris 50 B4
Highnam St Gif 24 A1
Highridge Cres. Bris 78 C3
Highridge Green. Bris 78 C3
Highridge Park. Bris 78 C3
Highridge Rd. Bris 63 D1
Highridge Rd. Bris 78 C2
Highridge Rd. Dun 78 C2
Highridge Wlk. Bris 78 C4
Highview Rd. Kingsw 51 F1
Highwall La. Co Dan 80 C1
Highway. Yate 27 C1
Highwood La. Bris 35 E4
Highwood Rd. Bris 35 F4
Highworth Cres. Yate 39 E4
Highworth Rd. Bris 64 B3
Hill Ave. Bath 101 F1
Hill Ave. Bris 63 F2
Hill Burn. Bris 49 E3
Hill Crest. Bris 64 A1
Hill Dr. Wrax 61 E2
Hill End Dr. Bris 34 B2
Hill Gay Cl. Portis 44 C2
Hill Gr. Bris 49 E3
Hill House Rd. Mang 51 F3
Hill La. Ch Sod 41 D4
Hill La. Nail 58 B2
Hill La. O-on-S 1 C1
Hill La. Rock 2 A2
Hill La. Ship 109 D1
Hill Lawn. Bris 64 B2
Hill Moor. Cleve 57 F1
Hill Park. Cong 91 F3
Hill Rd E. W-S-M 88 C1
Hill Rd. Cleve 57 E2
Hill Rd. Dun 78 B1
Hill Rd. W-S-M 88 C1
Hill Rd. W-S-M 104 C4
Hill Rd. Wins 108 A2
Hill St. Bris 63 E3
Hill St. Bris 63 F2
Hill St. Bris 64 C4
Hill St. Kingsw 65 F4
Hill The. Alm 24 A2
Hill The. Hi Cha 120 B3
Hill Top. Portis 45 D2
Hill View Cl. Kingsw 66 B2

Hill View Ct. W-S-M 105 E4
Hill View Rd. Bath 85 D1
Hill View Rd. Bris 79 D4
Hill View Rd. Puck 53 E3
Hill View Rd. W-S-M 105 D4
Hill View. Bris 36 A2
Hill View. Bris 49 E3
Hill View. Bris 63 D3
Hill View. Kingsw 51 E1
Hill View. Marks 99 D1
Hill View. Paul 131 D2
Hill View. Pris 117 D3
Hillbrook Rd. Thorn 15 E4
Hillburn Rd. Bris 65 D4
Hillcrest Cl. Nail 59 F1
Hillcrest Dr. Bath 101 E2
Hillcrest Rd. Nail 59 F1
Hillcrest Rd. Portis 44 C3
Hillcrest. Pens 97 F2
Hillcrest. Thorn 8 A1
Hillcroft Cl. W-S-M 88 A1
Hilldale Rd. Back 76 A3
Hillesley Rd. Kings 11 F2
Hillfields Ave. Bris 51 E2
Hillgrove St N. Bris 63 E4
Hillgrove Terr. W-S-M 104 B1
Hillier's La. Chur 108 B2
Hillmead. Chur 109 D3
Hillmer Rise. Ban 106 C2
Hillpath. Ban 107 D1
Hills Cl. Keyn 82 A3
Hillsborough Rd. Bris 64 B2
Hillsborough. Bris 63 D3
Hillsdon Rd. Bris 48 C4
Hillside Ave. Bris 65 E4
Hillside Ave. Mid No 137 F4
Hillside Cl. Fr Cot 38 B4
Hillside Cl. Paul 131 F3
Hillside Cres. Mid No 137 F4
Hillside Gdns. Bi Sut 113 E2
Hillside Gdns. W-S-M 88 A1
Hillside La. Fr Cot 38 B4
Hillside Rd. Back 76 A2
Hillside Rd. Bath 101 E2
Hillside Rd. Blea 122 A4
Hillside Rd. Bris 65 D4
Hillside Rd. Cleve 57 E2
Hillside Rd. Lo Ash 62 A1
Hillside Rd. Mid No 137 F4
Hillside Rd. Portis 44 B2
Hillside St. Bris 64 A2
Hillside View. P St J 133 E4
Hillside W. Lock 105 F1
Hillside. Bris 63 E4
Hillside. Mang 52 A3
Hillside. Portb 46 C2
Hilltop Gdns. Bris 50 B4
Hilltop Gdns. Kingsw 51 E1
Hilltop Rd. Kingsw 51 E1
Hilltop View. Bris 65 D4
Hillview Ave. Cleve 57 E1
Hillview Gdns. Win 94 B4
Hillview Rd. Blea 123 E2
Hillview. Tims 116 A1
Hillyfield Rd. Bris 79 D3
Hillyfields Way. Wins 125 D4
Hillyfields. Wins 125 D4
Hilverton Gdns. Bris 49 F1
Hind Pitts. Wins 125 D4
Hinton Cl. Bath 100 C3
Hinton Cl. Keyn 82 C2
Hinton Dr. Kingsw 66 B3
Hinton Hill. Hin Cha 119 D1
Hinton La. Bris 62 C3
Hinton Rd. Bris 50 B1
Hinton Rd. Bris 51 D2
Hinton Villas. Hin Cha 119 F1
Hinton. W-S-M 104 C1
Hippisley Dr. Axb 125 E1
Hiscocks Dr. Bath 101 F2
Hitchen La. Marsh 69 F4
Hither Green. Cleve 57 F1
Hoare's La. Kilm 139 D2
Hobart Rd. W-S-M 104 C2
Hobb's La. Bris 63 E3
Hobbiton Rd. W-S-M 89 D3
Hobbs Ct. Nail 59 F1
Hobbs La. Ba Gu 77 F2
Hobbs La. Sist 52 A1
Hobhouse Cl. Bris 49 E4
Hobwell La. Lo Ash 62 B1
Hockey's La. Bris 51 D2
Hoddon La. Puck 53 E3
Hodshill. Sosto 118 C3
Hoecroft Gdns. Chil 137 E2
Hogarth Mews. W-S-M 89 D2
Hogarth Wlk. Bris 50 B4
Hogarth Wlk. W-S-M 89 D2
Hogues Wlk. Bris 79 D2
Holbeach Way. Bris 80 A2
Holbrook Cres. Bris 79 E2
Holbrook La. Wick 67 D4
Holcombe Cl. Bath 85 F1
Holcombe Gn. Bath 84 A1
Holcombe La. Bath 85 F1
Holcombe Vale. Bath 85 F1

Holcombe. Bris 80 A3
Holdenhurst Rd. Bris 51 E1
Holders Wlk. Lo Ash 61 F1
Holford Cl. Nail 59 F1
Holford Ct. Bris 80 A3
Holland Rd. Bath 85 D1
Holland Rd. Cleve 57 D1
Holland St. Bris 63 F3
Holland St. W-S-M 105 D4
Hollidge Gdns. Bris 63 E2
Hollies La. Bathe 86 A3
Hollis Ave. Portis 45 E2
Hollis Cl. Lo Ash 78 A4
Hollis Cres. Portis 45 E2
Hollis Gdns. Luck 31 F2
Hollister's Dr. Bris 79 E2
Hollow La. W-S-M 88 C3
Hollow Marsh La. Hin Ble .. 130 A2
Hollow Rd. Alm 24 A2
Hollow Rd. Kingsw 65 F4
Hollow Rd. Wins 125 F4
Hollow The. Bath 101 D2
Hollow The. Pris 117 E2
Holloway. Bath 101 F3
Hollowbrook La. Ch Mag .. 113 E3
Hollowmead Cl. Yatt 91 F4
Hollows The. West 38 B2
Hollway Cl. Bris 80 C3
Hollway Rd. Bris 80 C3
Holly Cl. Alve 14 C2
Holly Cl. Bris 51 D1
Holly Cl. Nail 60 A2
Holly Cl. Puck 53 E4
Holly Cl. W-S-M 89 D1
Holly Cres. Kingsw 51 F1
Holly Dr. Col 70 C3
Holly Gr. Bris 51 E2
Holly Green. Kingsw 52 A1
Holly Hill Rd. Kingsw 51 F1
Holly Hill. Ir Act 26 C2
Holly La. Cleve 57 F3
Holly Lodge Rd. Bris 50 C1
Holly Ridge. Portis 45 D3
Holly Wlk. Keyn 81 E2
Holly Wlk. Rad 132 C1
Hollybush Cl. A Tur 43 D3
Hollybush Cl. Winsl 120 C4
Hollybush La. Bris 48 C2
Hollybush La. Bris 48 C3
Hollyguest Rd. Kingsw 65 F3
Hollyleigh Ave. Bris 35 F1
Hollyman Wlk. Cleve 57 F2
Hollymead La. Bris 48 C2
Hollyridge. Bris 80 B3
Hollywood La. Alm 35 D4
Hollywood Rd. Bris 64 B1
Holm La. Piln 13 D1
Holm Rd. Lock 105 F1
Holmdale Rd. Bris 36 B2
Holmes Gr. Bris 49 D3
Holmes Hill Rd. Bris 65 E4
Holmes St. Bris 64 A3
Holmesdale Rd. Bris 63 F2
Holmoak Rd. Keyn 81 E2
Holms Rd. W-S-M 105 D3
Holmwood Cl. Wint 37 E3
Holmwood. Kingsw 65 E3
Holsom Cl. Bris 80 C3
Holsom Rd. Bris 80 C3
Holst Gdns. Bris 79 E4
Holton Rd. Bris 50 A3
Holy Well Cl. Bris 64 C3
Holyrood Cl. St Gif 36 B2
Home Cl. Bris 35 F1
Home Cl. Wring 92 C2
Home Farm Cl. P St J 133 D4
Home Farm Rd. Ab Lei 62 A4
Home Farm Way. Alm 23 D1
Home Ground. Bris 49 D3
Home Orch. Ch St 112 B4
Home Orch. Yate 27 E1
Homeapple Hill. Sist 66 C3
Homefield Cl. Keyn 82 C2
Homefield Cl. Lock 106 A3
Homefield Cl. Winsc 107 F1
Homefield Dr. Bris 51 D3
Homefield Rd. Keyn 82 C2
Homefield Rd. Puck 53 D3
Homefield. Cong 91 F2
Homefield. Lock 106 A3
Homefield. Thorn 15 D4
Homefield. Yate 27 F2
Homeground. Cleve 57 F1
Homelea Park E. Bath 101 D4
Homelea Park W. Bath 101 D4
Homeleaze Rd. Bris 35 C2
Homemead Dr. Bris 64 B1
Homestead Gdns. Bris 35 F2
Homestead Rd. Bris 35 F2
Homestead The. Cleve 57 E2
Homestead The. Keyn 81 F1
Homestead Way. Wins 125 D4
Homestead. Portis 44 C2
Honey Garston Cl. Bris 79 D2
Honey Garston Rd. Bris 79 D2
Honey Hill Rd. Kingsw 65 F4
Honey Way. Bris 65 F4
Honeyborne Way. Wickw 18 A3

Honeyhall La. Cong 108 B4
Honeylands. Portis 45 E2
Honeymead. Bris 80 B3
Honeysuckle Cl. St Gif 24 C1
Honeysuckle La. Bris 50 C2
Honiton Rd. Bris 51 D2
Honiton Rd. Cleve 57 F1
Honiton. W-S-M 89 D1
Hook La. Hin Ble 129 F2
Hooks Batch. Blag 110 B2
Hooper Rd. Bris 80 B3
Hope Ct. Bris 63 D3
Hope Rd. Bris 63 E2
Hope Rd. Ir Act 27 D1
Hope Sq. Bris 62 C3
Hope Terr. Mid No 132 A1
Hopechapel Hill. Bris 62 C3
Hopetoun Rd. Bris 49 F2
Hopewell Gdns. Bris 47 F4
Hopkins Ct. Bris 49 D1
Hopkins St. W-S-M 104 C4
Hopland Cl. Kingsw 66 A2
Hopp's Rd. Kingsw 65 E4
Horesham Gr. Bris 79 E3
Horfield Rd. Bris 63 E4
Horley Rd. Bris 50 A1
Horn's La. Axb 125 D1
Hornbeam Wlk. Keyn 81 E2
Hornbeams The. Bris 37 D1
Horse La. Thorn 8 B3
Horse Race La. Wrax 61 D3
Horse St. Ch Sod 28 A1
Horsecastle Cl. Yatt 74 A1
Horsecastle Farm Rd. Yatt .. 74 A1
Horsecombe Brow. Bath 102 A1
Horsecombe Gr. Bath 102 A1
Horsecombe Vale. Bath 102 A1
Horsecroft Gdns. Kingsw .. 66 A3
Horsefair The. Bris 63 F4
Horsefield Rd. Char 11 D3
Horseleaze La. Ship 108 B3
Horsepool La. Doyn 67 F4
Horsepool Rd. Bris 78 C2
Horseshoe Dr. Bris 48 B2
Horseshoe La. Ch Sod 28 A1
Horseshoe La. Thorn 15 D4
Horseshoe Wlk. Bath 102 A3
Hortham La. Alve 24 C3
Horton Hill. Hort 29 E3
Horton Rd. Ch Sod 28 B2
Horton St. Bris 63 F4
Horwood Ct. Kingsw 66 A2
Horwood La. Wickw 18 A2
Horwood Rd. Nail 59 F1
Hosey Wlk. Bris 79 D3
Host St. Bris 63 E4
Hot Bath St. Bath 101 F3
Hot Water La. Kingsw 52 A2
Hottom Gdns. Bris 50 A4
Hotwell Rd. Bris 62 C3
Houlgate Way. Axb 125 D1
Houlton St. Bris 63 F4
Hounds Cl. Ch Sod 28 A1
Hounds Rd. Ch Sod 28 A1
Hover's La. Fr Cot 26 A2
How Hill. Bath 101 D3
Howard Ave. Bris 64 C4
Howard Cl. Keyn 82 B2
Howard Rd. Bris 49 D2
Howard Rd. Bris 63 E2
Howard Rd. Kingsw 51 E2
Howard Rd. Thorn 8 B1
Howard St. Bris 50 C1
Howecroft Gdns. Bris 48 C2
Howes Cl. Kingsw 66 A3
Howett Rd. Bris 64 B4
Howsmoor La. Mang 52 B4
Hoylake Dr. Kingsw 66 A3
Hoylake. Yate 39 F4
Huckford La. West 38 A2
Huckford Rd. Wint 37 F3
Huckley Way. St Gif 36 C3
Hudd's Hill Gdns. Bris 64 C4
Hudd's Hill Rd. Bris 64 C4
Hudd's Vale Rd. Bris 64 C4
Hudson Cl. Ch Sod 39 F4
Hughenden Rd. Bris 49 D1
Hughenden Rd. Bris 49 F3
Hughenden Rd. W-S-M 105 D4
Huish Ct. Rad 133 D1
Hulbert Cl. Bris 65 D1
Hulse Rd. Bris 64 B1
Humber Way. Avon 33 E3
Humberstan Wlk. Bris 79 D3
Humphry Davy Way. Bris .. 62 C3
Hung Rd. Bris 47 F3
Hungerford Cl. Bris 80 C4
Hungerford Cres. Bris 64 C1
Hungerford Gdns. Bris 80 C4
Hungerford Rd. Bath 101 D4
Hungerford Rd. Bris 80 C4
Hungerford Terr. Well 118 B1
Hungerford Wlk. Bris 64 C1
Hunstrete Rd. Farm 115 F3
Hunt's La. Yatt 91 F4
Hunter's La. A Tur 42 C3
Hunter's Way. Bris 36 A2
Hunters Cl. Kingsw 65 E3

Hunters Dr. Kingsw 51 F1
Hunters Mead. H Up 20 A1
Hunters Rd. Kingsw 65 E3
Huntingham Rd. Bris 78 C2
Huntley Gr. Nail 60 A1
Hunts La. Bris 49 F3
Hurle Cres. Bris 49 D1
Hurle Rd. Bris 49 D1
Hurlingham Rd. Bris 49 F1
Hurn La. Keyn 82 A2
Hurn Rd. Cleve 57 F1
Hursley Hill. Pens 97 E4
Hursley La. Pens 80 C1
Hurst Rd. Bris 79 F4
Hurst Rd. W-S-M 105 D3
Hurst Wlk. Bris 79 F4
Hurston Rd. Bris 79 E4
Hurstwood Rd. Mang 51 E3
Hutton Cl. Bris 48 C4
Hutton Cl. Keyn 82 A1
Hutton Hill. Lock 105 F1
Hutton Moor Rd. W-S-M 105 E4
Huyton Rd. Bris 50 C2
Hyde Ave. Thorn 8 A2
Hyde The. Cleve 73 E4
Hyde's La. Co Ash 69 D3
Hyland Gr. Bris 48 C1

I.S.F Rd. Avon 33 E2
Ida Rd. Bris 64 B4
Iddesleigh Rd. Bris 49 D2
Idstone Rd. Bris 51 D2
Idwal Cl. P St J 133 E4
Iford Cl. Keyn 82 C2
Iford Hill. Westw 120 C1
Iford Rd. Hi Cha 120 B2
Ilchester Cres. Bris 63 D1
Ilchester Rd. Bris 79 D4
Ilex Ave. Cleve 57 F1
Ilex Cl. Bris 78 C3
Ilex La. Winsc 107 F1
Ilminster Ave. Bris 79 F4
Ilminster Cl. Cleve 57 F1
Ilminster Cl. Nail 75 E4
Ilminster. W-S-M 105 D1
Ilsyn Gr. Bris 80 B4
Imber Court Cl. Bris 80 A4
Imperial Rd. Bris 49 D1
Imperial Rd. Bris 80 B4
Imperial Wlk. Bris 64 A1
Ingleside Rd. Bris 51 E1
Inglestone Rd. Wickw 18 A3
Ingleton Dr. W-S-M 89 D2
Ingmire Rd. Bris 50 A2
Ingst Hill. Aust 13 E2
Ingst Rd. Aust 13 F2
Inkerman Cl. Bris 49 F4
Inner Down The. Olve 14 B2
Inner Elm Terr. Rad 132 B1
Innicks Cl. Co Mar 111 E1
Innox Gdns. Bris 79 D3
Innox Gr. Engl 100 C1
Innox La. Bathe 85 D3
Innox Rd. Bath 101 D3
Inns Court Ave. Bris 79 E4
Inns Court Dr. Bris 79 E3
Instow Rd. Bris 79 F4
Instow Wlk. Bris 79 F4
Instow. W-S-M 89 D1
Inverness Rd. Bath 101 E3
Ipswich Dr. Bris 64 C3
Irby Rd. Bris 63 D2
Irena Rd. Bris 50 C1
Ireton Rd. Bris 63 D2
Iron Hogg La. Falf 9 E2
Ironchurch Rd. Avon 33 E3
Ironmould La. Bris 65 D1
Irving Cl. Cleve 57 F2
Irving Cl. Kingsw 51 F2
Island Gdns. Bris 50 B2
Island The. Mid No 132 A1
Isleys Ct. Kingsw 65 F2
Islington Rd. Bris 63 D2
Ison Hill Rd. Bris 34 B2
Itchington Rd. Alve 15 F2
Itchington Rd. Tyth 15 F2
Itchington Rd. Tyth 16 A2
Ivo Peters Rd. Bath 101 F3
Ivor Rd. Bris 64 B4
Ivy Ave. Bath 101 E2
Ivy Bank Park. Bath 101 F1
Ivy Ct. Portis 44 C3
Ivy Gr. Bath 101 E2
Ivy La. Bris 51 D2
Ivy Pl. Bath 101 E2
Ivybridge. W-S-M 89 D1
Ivywell Rd. Bris 48 C2
Iwood La. Cong 92 A1

Jackson Cl. Piln 22 B4
Jacob St. Bris 63 F4
Jacob's Wells Rd. Bris 63 D3
Jamaica St. Bris 63 F4
James Cl. Kingsw 51 F2
James Pl. Bris 62 C4
James Rd. Kingsw 51 F2
James St W. Bath 101 F3

James St. Bris 50 A1
James St. Bris 63 F4
Jane St. Bris 64 A4
Jarvis St. Bris 64 A3
Jasmine Cl. W-S-M 89 D1
Jasmine Gr. Bris 34 B1
Jasmine La. Yatt 74 C1
Jasper St. Bris 63 D2
Jays The. Tyth 16 A3
Jean Rd. Bris 64 C1
Jefferies Hill Bottom. Bris .. 65 D3
Jeffery Ct. Kingsw 66 A3
Jellicoe Ct. W-S-M 88 C2
Jena Ct. Keyn 82 B2
Jenner Cl. Ch Sod 40 B4
Jersey Ave. Bris 64 C2
Jesmond Rd. Cleve 57 E2
Jesse Hughes Ct. Bath 85 E1
Jessop Underpass. Bris 62 C2
Jews La. Bath 101 D3
Jews La. Chur 108 C2
Jocelin Dr. W-S-M 88 C2
Jocelyn Rd. Bris 49 F4
Jockey La. Bris 65 D4
John Cabot Ct. Bris 63 D3
John Carr's Terr. Bris 63 D3
John James Ct. Bris 50 A4
John St. Bath 101 F4
John St. Bris 50 A1
John St. Bris 63 E4
John St. Bris 65 E4
John Wesley Rd. Bris 65 D3
Johnson Dr. Kingsw 65 F3
Johnsons La. Bris 50 B1
Johnsons Rd. Bris 50 B1
Johnstone St. Bath 102 A3
Jones Cl. Yatt 73 F1
Joy Hill. Bris 62 C3
Jubilee Cres. Mang 52 A3
Jubilee Dr. Thorn 8 B1
Jubilee Dr. Wrax 61 D2
Jubilee La. Chur 109 D3
Jubilee La. Crom 17 D4
Jubilee Pl. Bris 63 E3
Jubilee Pl. Cleve 57 E1
Jubilee Rd. Axb 125 D1
Jubilee Rd. Bris 50 A1
Jubilee Rd. Bris 63 E3
Jubilee Rd. Bris 64 C4
Jubilee Rd. Kingsw 51 F2
Jubilee Rd. Rad 132 B1
Jubilee Rd. W-S-M 104 C4
Jubilee St. Bris 63 F3
Jubilee Terr. Paul 131 F3
Jubilee Way. Avon 33 D1
Julian Cl. Bris 48 C2
Julian Rd. Bath 101 F4
Julian Rd. Bris 48 C2
Julius Rd. Bris 49 E2
Junction Ave. Bath 101 F3
Junction Rd. Bath 101 F3
Junction Rd. Bris 64 B2
Juniper Ct. Bris 50 B1
Jupiter Rd. Bris 35 F4
Justice Ave. Keyn 82 C2
Justice Rd. Bris 51 D2
Jutland Rd. Avon 33 D1

Karen Dr. Back 76 A3
Kathdene Gdns. Bris 49 F2
Kathrine Dr. Char 11 D3
Keats Rd. Rod 138 B4
Keble Ave. Bris 78 C3
Keeds La. Lo Ash 61 F1
Keedwell Hill. Lo Ash 61 F1
Keedwell House. Bris 79 E2
Keel's Hill. P St J 133 E4
Keen's Gr. Piln 22 B4
Keene's Way. Cleve 57 E1
Keep The. Kingsw 66 B3
Keep The. W-S-M 89 D2
Keinton Wlk. Bris 35 D1
Kellaway Ave. Bris 49 E3
Kellaway Cres. Bris 49 E3
Kellways. Back 76 A2
Kelston Cl. Keyn 82 B2
Kelston Cl. Yate 39 E4
Kelston Gdns. Bris 49 E4
Kelston Gdns. W-S-M 89 D3
Kelston Gr. Kingsw 65 F3
Kelston Rd. Bath 101 D4
Kelston Rd. Bris 49 E4
Kelston Rd. Keyn 81 E3
Kelston Rd. W-S-M 89 D3
Kelston View. Bath 101 D3
Kelston Wlk. Bris 51 E2
Kelting Gr. Cleve 57 F1
Kemble Cl. Kingsw 65 F3
Kemble Cl. Nail 60 A1
Kemble Gdns. Bris 47 F3
Kempe's Cl. Lo Ash 62 A1
Kemperleye Way. St Gif 36 B4
Kempton Cl. Mang 37 F1
Kempton Cl. Thorn 8 A2
Kencot Wlk. Bris 79 D2
Kendal Rd. Bris 50 A4
Kendall Gdns. Kingsw 51 E1
Kendall Rd. Kingsw 51 E1

Kendon Dr. Bris 49 E4
Kenilworth Cl. Keyn 81 E2
Kenilworth Dr. Kingsw 66 A1
Kenilworth Rd. Bris 49 E1
Kenilworth. Yate 27 F1
Kenmare Rd. Bris 63 F1
Kenmeade Cl. Ship 125 F4
Kenmore Cres. Bris 35 F1
Kenmore Dr. Bris 35 F1
Kenmore Gr. Bris 35 F1
Kenn Cl. W-S-M 105 D3
Kenn Est. Yatt 73 F3
Kenn Moor Dr. Cleve 57 F1
Kenn Rd. Bris 65 D4
Kenn Rd. Yatt 73 F4
Kenn St. Yatt 73 F4
Kennard Cl. Bris 65 E4
Kennard Rd. Bris 65 E4
Kennard Rise. Bris 65 E4
Kennaway Rd. Cleve 57 E1
Kennedy Way. Ch Sod 40 A4
Kennedy Way. Yate 27 F1
Kennel Dr. Gr Bad 30 C1
Kennel La. Co Bi 123 F2
Kennel Lodge Rd. Bris 62 C2
Kennet Park. Bath 85 F1
Kennet Rd. Keyn 82 A2
Kennet Way. Thorn 15 D2
Kenneth Rd. Bris 64 B1
Kennford. W-S-M 89 D1
Kennington Ave. Bris 49 E2
Kennington Ave. Kingsw .. 51 E1
Kennington Rd. Bath 101 D4
Kennion Rd. Bris 65 D4
Kennmoor Cl. Kingsw 66 A3
Kennmoor Rd. Yatt 74 A3
Kensal Ave. Bris 63 F2
Kensal Rd. Bris 63 F2
Kensington Cl. Thorn 8 A1
Kensington Ct. Bath 85 D1
Kensington Gdns. Bath 85 D1
Kensington Park Rd. Bris .. 64 B1
Kensington Park. Bris 50 A1
Kensington Pl. Bris 63 D4
Kensington Rd. Bris 49 E1
Kensington Rd. Bris 65 D4
Kensington Rd. Kingsw 51 E2
Kensington Rd. W-S-M 104 C3
Kent Ave. Yate 27 F2
Kent Rd. St Gif 36 B2
Kent Rd. Bris 49 F2
Kent Rd. Cong 91 E3
Kent St. Bris 63 E2
Kent Way. W-S-M 89 D2
Kenton Mews. Bris 49 E3
Kents Green. Kingsw 51 F1
Kentshare La. Win 95 D3
Keppel Cl. Keyn 82 B1
Kerry Rd. Bris 79 F4
Kersteman Rd. Bris 49 E2
Kestrel Cl. Bris 35 F4
Kestrel Cl. Ch Sod 39 F4
Kestrel Cl. Thorn 8 B1
Kestrel Dr. Puck 53 E2
Kestrel Dr. W-S-M 88 C1
Kestrel Pl. Rod 138 A4
Keswick Wlk. Bris 35 F1
Ketch Rd. Bris 63 F2
Ketley Hill. Mid No 132 B2
Kew Rd. W-S-M 87 F1
Kew Wlk. Bris 80 B4
Kewside. W-S-M 88 A2
Kewstoke Rd. Bath 102 A1
Kewstoke Rd. Bris 48 C2
Kewstoke Rd. W-S-M 88 B2
Keyes Path. W-S-M 88 C2
Keynsham By-pass. Keyn .. 81 F2
Keynsham Rd. Bitt 82 A4
Keys Ave. Bris 49 F4
Kielder Dr. W-S-M 88 C2
Kilbirnie Rd. Bris 80 A2
Kilburn St. Bris 64 A4
Kildare Rd. Bris 63 E1
Kilkenny La. Engl 118 A4
Kilkenny St. Bris 63 F3
Kilcott Rd. Hill 19 F4
Kilmersdon Hill. Kilm 139 D3
Kilmersdon Rd. Bris 79 D2
Kilmersdon Rd. Rad 138 C2
Kilminster Rd. Bris 47 E4
Kiln Cl. Bris 51 D1
Kiln Park. W-S-M 105 D3
Kilnhurst Cl. Kingsw 65 F1
Kilve. W-S-M 104 C1
Kilvert Cl. Bris 64 B3
Kimberley Ave. Bris 51 E3
Kimberley Cl. Mang 51 F4
Kimberley Cres. Bris 51 E3
Kimberley Rd. Bris 51 E3
Kimberley Rd. Cleve 57 E1
Kimberley Rd. Kingsw 51 E3
Kinber Cl. Bath 84 A2
King Alfred Way. Winsl 120 B4
King Dick's La. Bris 64 C4
King Edward Cl. Bris 80 A3
King Edward Rd. Bath 101 E3
King George V Pl. Bris 63 D3
King George's Rd. Bath 101 E3

King George's Rd. Bris 78 C3
King John's Rd. Bris 51 D1
King La. Clut 114 C2
King La. Hort 29 D4
King Rd. Bris 64 B1
King Road Ave. Avon 33 D1
King Sq. Bris 63 E4
King Square Ave. Bris 63 E4
King St. Avon 33 D1
King St. Bris 50 B1
King St. Bris 63 E3
King St. Bris 65 D4
King William Ave. Bris 63 E3
King William St. Bris 63 D2
King's Ave. Bris 49 E2
King's Dr. Bris 49 E2
King's Head La. Bris 78 C4
King's La. W-S-M 104 C4
King's Parade Ave. Bris 49 D1
King's Parade Mews. Bris .. 49 D1
King's Rd. Bris 64 B2
King's Rd. Cleve 57 E3
King's Rd. Portis 44 C2
Kingfisher Cl. Thorn 8 B1
Kingfisher Dr. Bris 50 C3
Kingfisher Dr. Rod 138 A4
Kingfisher Rd. Ch Sod 40 A4
Kingfisher Rd. W-S-M 105 F4
Kingrove Cres. Ch Sod 40 B4
Kingrove La. Ch Sod 40 B4
Kings Ave. Kingsw 65 D2
Kings Chase. Kingsw 65 E4
Kings Dr. Kingsw 65 D2
Kings Oak Meadow. Clut .. 114 C1
Kings Park Ave. Bris 64 B3
Kings Rd. Wring 92 B3
Kings Weston Ave. Bris 47 E4
Kings Weston La. Avon 33 F2
Kings Weston La. Bris 48 A4
Kings Weston Rd. Bris 34 B1
Kings Wlk. Bris 78 C4
Kingscote Park. Bris 65 D3
Kingscote. Yate 39 E3
Kingscourt Cl. Bris 80 A2
Kingsdown Gr. Box 86 C2
Kingsdown Par. Bris 63 E4
Kingsdown View. Bath 85 D1
Kingsfield La. Kingsw 65 F2
Kingsfield La. Kingsw 65 F3
Kingsfield. Bath 101 E2
Kingshill Gdns. Nail 59 E1
Kingshill House. Bris 64 A1
Kingshill La. Ch St 112 B3
Kingshill Rd. Bris 64 A1
Kingshill. Nail 59 E1
Kingsholm Rd. Bris 49 E4
Kingsholme Rd. Kingsw 51 E1
Kingsland Cl. Bris 64 A3
Kingsland Rd Br. Bris 64 A3
Kingsland Rd. Bris 64 A3
Kingsland Trading Est. Bris .. 64 A4
Kingsleigh Ct. Kingsw 65 F4
Kingsleigh Gdns. Kingsw .. 65 F4
Kingsleigh Park. Kingsw .. 65 F4
Kingsley Rd. Bris 49 E1
Kingsley Rd. Bris 50 B1
Kingsley Rd. Cleve 57 E1
Kingsley Rd. Rad 132 B1
Kingsley Rd. W-S-M 104 C2
Kingsmead N. Bath 101 F3
Kingsmead Rd. Bris 51 D1
Kingsmead Sq. Bath 101 F3
Kingsmead St. Bath 101 F3
Kingsmead W. Bath 101 F3
Kingsmead Wlk. Bris 51 D1
Kingsmead. Nail 59 E1
Kingsmill. Bris 48 B3
Kingston Ave. Cleve 57 F2
Kingston Ave. Keyn 82 B2
Kingston Cl. Mang 52 A4
Kingston Dr. Mang 52 A4
Kingston Dr. Nail 75 E4
Kingston La. Win 94 C4
Kingston Mead. Win 94 C4
Kingston Par. Bath 102 A3
Kingston Rd. Bath 102 A3
Kingston Rd. Bris 63 E2
Kingston Rd. Nail 75 E4
Kingston Way. Nail 75 E4
Kingstree St. Bris 64 A2
Kingsway Ave. Bris 65 D4
Kingsway Cres. Bris 65 E4
Kingsway. Bath 101 E2
Kingsway. Bris 65 D4
Kingsway. St Gif 36 B3
Kingswear Rd. Bris 63 E1
Kingswear. W-S-M 89 D1
Kingswood Rd. Hill 19 E4
Kingswood Trading Est.
Kingsw 51 E1
Kington La. Thorn 7 F1
Kington Rd. O-on-S 7 F2
Kington Rd. Thorn 7 F1
Kingwell View. Paul 115 F3
Kinsale Rd. Bris 80 B4
Kinsale Wlk. Bris 63 F1

Name	Page	Grid
Kinvara Rd. Bris	79	F4
Kipling Rd. Bris	36	A1
Kipling Rd. Rad	132	B1
Kipling Rd. W-S-M	105	D2
Kiplingave. Bath	101	F2
Kirkby Rd. Bris	34	A1
Kirkstone Gdns. Bris	35	E1
Kirtlington Rd. Bris	50	A2
Kite Hay Cl. Bris	50	C3
Kite Wlk. W-S-M	105	F4
Kites Cl. St Gif	24	B1
Kitland La. Chur	109	E4
Knapp La. Crom	10	A2
Knapp Rd. Thorn	8	C1
Knapps Cl. Wins	124	C4
Knapps Dr. Wins	124	C4
Knapps La. Bris	50	C1
Knightcott Gdns. Ban	106	C2
Knightcott Ind Est Ban	106	C2
Knightcott Park. Ban	107	D2
Knightcott Rd. Ab Lei	61	F4
Knightcott Rd. Ban	107	D2
Knighton Rd. Bris	35	F1
Knights Cl. W-S-M	89	D3
Knightstone Cl. Axb	125	E1
Knightstone Cl. P St J	133	D4
Knightstone Cswy. W-S-M	104	B4
Knightstone Ct. Bris	50	B1
Knightstone Pl. Bath	84	A1
Knightstone Pl. Kingsw	65	D2
Knightstone Rd. W-S-M	104	B4
Knightstone Sq. Bris	80	B3
Knightwood Rd. St Gif	36	C3
Knobsbury Hill. Kilm	139	E3
Knobsbury La. Kilm	139	E4
Knobsbury La. Rad	133	E1
Knole Cl. Alm	23	F2
Knole La. Bris	35	D2
Knole Park. Alm	23	F2
Knoll Hill. Bris	48	B2
Knoll The. Portis	45	D4
Knovill Cl. Bris	34	A1
Knowle Rd. Bris	63	F2
Knowles Rd. Cleve	57	E1
Knowsley Rd. Bris	50	C2
Kylross Ave. Bris	80	A3
Kynges Mill Cl. Bris	51	D4
Kyrle Gdns. Bathe	85	F2
Labbott The. Keyn	81	F3
Laburnham Wlk. Keyn	81	E2
Laburnum Cl. Mid No	137	F4
Laburnum Ct. W-S-M	105	D4
Laburnum Gr. Bris	51	D2
Laburnum Gr. Mid No	137	F4
Laburnum Rd. Kingsw	65	E3
Laburnum Rd. W-S-M	105	D4
Lacey Rd. Bris	80	C3
Lacock Dr. Kingsw	65	F3
Ladd Cl. Kingsw	65	F4
Ladden Ct. Thorn	15	E4
Ladies Mile. Bris	48	C1
Ladman Gr. Bris	80	C3
Ladman Rd. Bris	80	C3
Ladycroft. Cleve	57	D1
Ladye Bay. Cleve	57	E4
Ladye Wake. W-S-M	88	C2
Ladymead La. Chur	108	C3
Ladymeade. Back	76	A4
Ladysmith Rd. Bris	49	D2
Ladywell. Wring	92	B1
Laggan Gdns. Bath	84	C1
Lake Rd. Bris	49	E4
Lake Rd. Portis	45	D4
Lake View Rd. Bris	64	B4
Lakemead Gdns. Bris	78	C2
Lakemead Gr. Bris	78	C3
Lakeside. Bris	50	C2
Lakewood Cres. Bris	49	D4
Lakewood Rd. Bris	49	D4
Lamb St. Bris	63	F4
Lambert Pl. Bris	79	E3
Lambley Rd. Bris	64	C4
Lambourn Cl. Bris	63	E2
Lambourn Rd. Keyn	82	A2
Lambridge Mews. Bath	85	E1
Lambridge Pl. Bath	85	E1
Lambridge St. Bath	85	E1
Lambrook Rd. Bris	51	D2
Lamford Gate. St Gif	36	C3
Lampard's Bldgs. Bath	101	F4
Lampeter Rd. Bris	49	D4
Lampley Rd. K Sey	73	E1
Lampley Rd. Yatt	73	E1
Lampton Ave. Bris	79	F2
Lampton Gr. Bris	79	F2
Lampton Rd. Lo Ash	61	F1
Lanaway Rd. Bris	51	D3
Lancashire Rd. Bris	49	F2
Lancaster Cl. St Gif	36	B2
Lancaster Rd. Bris	50	A1
Lancaster Rd. Yate	27	F2
Lancaster St. Bris	64	B4
Land The. Fr Cot	38	B4
Landemann Cir. W-S-M	87	F1
Landowan View. Kingsw	65	F4
Landseer Ave. Bris	50	A4
Landseer Cl. W-S-M	88	C2
Landseer Rd. Bath	101	D3
Lane The. Alm	22	C1
Lanercost Rd. Bris	35	E1
Lanesborough Rise. Bris	80	B4
Laneys Dro. Lock	105	F3
Langdale Rd. Bris	50	C2
Langdon Rd. Bath	101	D2
Langdown Ct. Bris	80	C3
Langfield Cl. Bris	34	C2
Langford La. Blag	109	F3
Langford Rd. Bris	78	C4
Langford Rd. Chur	109	D3
Langford Rd. W-S-M	105	D4
Langford Way. Kingsw	65	F4
Langfords La. Paul	131	E4
Langham Pl. Rode	136	C1
Langham Rd. Bris	64	A1
Langhill Ave. Bris	79	E4
Langley Cres. Bris	62	C1
Langley's La. Ston E	131	E1
Langport Gdns. Nail	75	F4
Langport Rd. W-S-M	104	C3
Langridge La. Charl	84	B4
Langthorn Cl. Fr Cot	38	B4
Langton Court Rd. Bris	64	B3
Langton Park. Bris	63	E2
Langton Rd. Bris	64	B3
Langton Way. Bris	64	C3
Lansdown Cl. Kingsw	51	E1
Lansdown Cres. Bath	101	F4
Lansdown Cres. Tims	116	B1
Lansdown Gdns. W-S-M	89	D3
Lansdown Gr. Bath	101	F4
Lansdown La. Bath	84	A2
Lansdown La. Bitt	67	E1
Lansdown La. Charl	84	A2
Lansdown Park. Bath	84	C2
Lansdown Pl. Bris	63	D4
Lansdown Pl. Paul	115	E1
Lansdown Place W. Bath	84	C1
Lansdown Rd. Bath	84	C2
Lansdown Rd. Bris	49	E1
Lansdown Rd. Bris	63	D4
Lansdown Rd. Bris	64	A4
Lansdown Rd. Keyn	82	C2
Lansdown Rd. Kingsw	51	E1
Lansdown Rd. Puck	53	E3
Lansdown Terr. Bath	84	B1
Lansdown Terr. Bris	49	E3
Lansdown View. Bath	84	A1
Lansdown View. Bath	101	E3
Lansdown View. Faulk	134	B1
Lansdown View. Tims	116	B1
Lansdown. Yate	39	F4
Lansdowne. Bris	37	E1
Lapdown La. Tor	41	E1
Laphams Ct. Kingsw	65	F2
Lapwing Cl. St Gif	24	B1
Lapwing Gdns. Bris	50	C3
Lapwing Gdns. W-S-M	88	C1
Larch Cl. Chur	109	D3
Larch Cl. Nail	60	A1
Larch Ct. Rod	138	B4
Larch Rd. Col	70	C3
Larch Rd. Kingsw	51	E2
Larch Way. Bris	35	F4
Larches The. W-S-M	89	D1
Larchgrove Cres. W-S-M	88	C1
Larchgrove Wlk. Bris	89	D1
Lark Cl. Rod	138	A4
Lark Rd. W-S-M	88	C1
Lark's Field. Bris	50	C3
Lark's La. Ir Act	26	A4
Larkfield. Fr Cot	38	B4
Larkhall Pl. Bath	85	E1
Larksleaze Rd. Kingsw	65	F1
Larkspur Cl. Thorn	8	B1
Lasbury Gr. Bris	79	E3
Latchmoor House. Bris	79	D4
Late Broads. Winsl	120	B4
Latimer Cl. Bris	64	C2
Latteridge La. Ir Act	26	A4
Latteridge La. Tyth	26	A4
Latteridge Rd. Ir Act	26	B2
Latton Rd. Bris	49	F3
Launceston Ave. Kingsw	65	D3
Launceston Rd. Bris	51	D1
Laura Pl. Bath	102	A4
Laurel Dr. Col	70	C3
Laurel Dr. Nail	59	F1
Laurel Dr. Paul	131	F3
Laurel Dr. W-S-M	104	C1
Laurel Gdns. Yatt	74	A1
Laurel St. Kingsw	65	E2
Laurel Terr. Yatt	74	A1
Laurels The. Mang	52	A3
Laurels The. W-S-M	104	C1
Laurie Cres. Bris	49	E3
Laurie Lee Ct. Kingsw	66	A3
Lavender Cl. Thorn	8	B1
Lavers Cl. Kingsw	66	A3
Lavington Cl. Cleve	57	D1
Lavington Rd. Bris	65	D3
Lawford Ave. St Gif	36	B3
Lawford St. Bris	63	F4
Lawfords Gate. Bris	63	F4
Lawn Ave. Bris	51	D3
Lawn Rd. Bris	51	D3
Lawns Rd. Yate	27	F1
Lawns The. Bris	47	F4
Lawns The. W-S-M	89	D2
Lawns The. Yatt	74	A1
Lawnside. Back	76	A3
Lawnwood Rd. Bris	64	A4
Lawrence Ave. Bris	50	A1
Lawrence Cl. W-S-M	88	C1
Lawrence Dr. Yate	27	D1
Lawrence Gr. Bris	49	D3
Lawrence Hill Ind Pk. Bris	64	A4
Lawrence Hill Roundabout. Bris	64	A4
Lawrence Hill. Bris	64	A4
Lawrence Mews. W-S-M	88	C1
Lawrence Rd. W-S-M	88	C1
Lawrence Rd. Wring	92	C1
Lawrence Weston Rd. Avon	33	F3
Lawrence Weston Rd. Bris	34	A1
Lawrence Weston Rd. Bris	34	B1
Lawson Cl. Keyn	82	B1
Laxey Rd. Bris	49	F4
Laxton Cl. Olve	14	A2
Laxton Dr. Kings	11	F2
Laxton Way. P St J	133	E4
Lays Dr. Keyn	81	E3
Lays La. Blag	110	B2
Lea Croft. Bris	79	D2
Lea Grove Rd. Cleve	57	E2
Leach Cl. Cleve	57	E1
Leafy Way. Lock	106	A3
Leaholme Gdns. Bris	80	A2
Leaman Cl. Ch Sod	28	A1
Leap Vale. Mang	52	A4
Leap Valley Cres. Mang	52	A4
Leaze La. Priddy	126	C4
Leaze The. Rod	138	B4
Leaze The. Yate	27	E1
Leda Ave. Bris	80	A4
Ledbury Rd. Bris	51	E2
Lee Cl. Bris	35	F4
Leechpool Way. Yate	27	F3
Leeming Way. Avon	47	E4
Lees Hill. Kingsw	51	F1
Lees La. Kingsw	66	B3
Lees The. Cong	91	E2
Leeside. Portis	45	E3
Leewood Rd. W-S-M	87	F1
Leg La. Blag	110	A2
Leicester Sq. Kingsw	51	E2
Leicester St. Bris	63	E2
Leicester Wlk. Bris	64	C3
Leigh Cl. Bath	85	D1
Leigh La. Co Ash	69	D2
Leigh La. West	39	E1
Leigh Rd. Bris	63	D4
Leigh Rd. Bris	63	D2
Leigh View Rd. Portis	45	F4
Leighton Cres. W-S-M	122	A4
Leighton Rd. Bath	84	A2
Leighton Rd. Bris	63	D2
Leighton Rd. Bris	64	A1
Leighwood Dr. Nail	59	D1
Leighwood House. Lo Ash	62	B3
Leinster Ave. Bris	79	E4
Lemon La. Bris	63	F4
Lena Ave. Bris	50	B1
Lena St. Bris	50	B1
Lenover Gdns. Bris	79	D2
Leonard La. Bris	63	E4
Leonard Rd. Bris	64	A4
Leonards Ave. Bris	50	B1
Leopold Rd. Bris	49	F1
Lescren Way. Avon	33	E1
Leslie Rise. Westw	120	C2
Lester Dr. W-S-M	89	D2
Lewin St. Bris	64	B4
Lewington Rd. Bris	51	E2
Lewins Mead. Bris	63	E4
Lewis Cl. Kingsw	66	B3
Lewis Rd. Bris	79	D4
Lewis St. Bris	64	A3
Lewisham Gr. W-S-M	105	D4
Lewton La. Wint	37	F4
Ley La. Olve	13	F2
Leyland Wlk. Bris	78	C2
Leys The. Cleve	57	D1
Leyton Villas. Bris	49	D1
Liberty Ind Park. Bris	63	D1
Liberty La. Blag	110	C1
Lichfield Rd. Bris	64	C3
Lilac Cl. Bris	35	E1
Lilac Ct. Keyn	81	E2
Lilac Terr. Mid No	132	B1
Lilian Terr. Paul	131	F3
Lilian St. Bris	64	B4
Lillington Cl. Rad	133	D1
Lillington Rd. Rad	133	D1
Liliput Ave. Ch Sod	40	A4
Liliput Cl. Ch Sod	40	A4
Lilstock Ave. Bris	49	F2
Lilton Wlk. Bris	63	D1
Lilymead Ave. Bris	64	A2
Lime Cl. Bris	35	D2
Lime Cl. Col	70	C3
Lime Cl. W-S-M	89	D1
Lime Croft. Yate	27	F2
Lime Ct. Keyn	81	E2
Lime Gr. Alve	14	C3
Lime Gr. Bath	102	A3
Lime Grove Gdns. Bath	102	A3
Lime Kiln Gdns. St Gif	24	B2
Lime Rd. Bris	63	D2
Lime Rd. Kingsw	65	D3
Lime Terr. Rad	132	B1
Lime Tree Gr. E in G	47	E2
Limeburn Hill. Ch Mag	95	F3
Limekiln La. Bath	102	C2
Limekiln Rd. Yate	27	E4
Limerick Rd. Bris	49	E1
Limes The. Bris	37	D1
Limes The. Gr Bad	30	C1
Limpley Stoke Rd. Winsl	120	B3
Lincoln Cl. Keyn	81	E2
Lincoln St. Bris	64	A4
Lincombe Ave. Mang	51	E3
Lincombe Rd. Mang	51	E3
Lincombe Rd. Rod	138	B4
Lincott View. P St J	133	E4
Linden Ave. W-S-M	105	D4
Linden Cl. Bris	51	D1
Linden Cl. Bris	80	C3
Linden Cl. Col	70	C3
Linden Cl. Rod	138	C4
Linden Cl. Wint	37	F3
Linden Dr. St Gif	36	C4
Linden Gdns. Bath	101	E4
Linden Rd. Bris	49	D2
Linden Rd. Cleve	57	E2
Lindens The. W-S-M	88	C2
Lindrea St. Bris	63	D2
Lindsay Rd. Bris	50	A2
Lindsey Cl. Portis	44	C2
Linemere Cl. Back	76	B3
Lines Way. Whit	80	B2
Lingfield Park. Mang	37	F1
Link La. Blag	109	F2
Link Rd. Bris	36	A1
Link Rd. Nail	59	F1
Link Rd. Portis	45	E3
Link Rd. Yate	27	F1
Links Rd. W-S-M	104	B1
Linkside. Cleve	57	F3
Linley Cl. Bath	101	D3
Linleys The. Bath	101	E4
Linnell Cl. Bris	50	A3
Linnet Cl. Bris	35	F4
Linnet Cl. W-S-M	88	C1
Linnet Way. Rod	138	A4
Lintern Cres. Kingsw	66	A3
Lintham Dr. Kingsw	65	F3
Linton Rd. Bris	63	E1
Lion Cl. Nail	59	E1
Lippiatt Hill. Faulk	134	B2
Lippiatt La. Ship	125	F4
Lippiatt La. Tims	116	A2
Lisburn Rd. Bris	63	F1
Lisle Rd. W-S-M	89	D2
Lister Gr. Westw	120	C2
Litfield Rd. Bris	62	C4
Litt Hill. Litt	129	F1
Little Ann St. Bris	63	F4
Little Birch Croft. Bris	80	A2
Little Bishop St. Bris	63	F4
Little Bristol La. Char	11	D2
Little Caroline Pl. Bris	62	C3
Little Dowles. Kingsw	66	A2
Little George St. Bris	63	F4
Little George St. W-S-M	104	C4
Little Green La. Piln	22	A4
Little Halt. Portis	44	C2
Little Ham. Cleve	73	E4
Little Headley Cl. Bris	79	E4
Little King St. Bris	63	E3
Little La. Farm	116	A3
Little Mead Cl. Lock	105	F2
Little Mead. Bris	34	A1
Little Mead. Bris	34	A1
Little Meadow End. Nail	75	F4
Little Meadow. St Gif	37	D3
Little Orch. W-S-M	104	B1
Little Paradise. Bris	63	E2
Little Paul St. Bris	63	E4
Little Solsbury La. Bathe	85	F2
Little Stoke La. St Gif	36	B4
Little Stoke Rd. Bris	48	C2
Little Withey Mead. Bris	48	C3
Littlebrook. Paul	131	F3
Littledean. Yate	39	F4
Littlefields Ave. Ban	107	D2
Littlefields Rd. Ban	107	D2
Littleton Cl. Bris	23	F1
Littleton La. Ch Mag	95	E2
Littleton La. Dun	95	E4
Littleton La. Well	134	B4
Littleton La. Win	95	D4
Littleton St. Bris	64	B1
Littleton St. Bris	50	B1
Littlewood Cl. Bris	80	A2
Littlewood La. Brock	75	E1
Litton. Bris	105	D1
Livingstone Rd. Bath	101	E3
Llewellyn Ct. Bris	49	D4
Llewellyn Way. W-S-M	89	D2
Lock Gdns. Bris	78	C4
Lockemor Rd. Bris	79	F2
Locking Head Dro. Lock	106	A4
Locking Moor Rd. W-S-M	105	E4
Locking Rd. W-S-M	105	D4
Lockingwell Rd. Keyn	81	E3
Leckleaze Rd. Bris	50	A3
Locksbrook Rd. Bath	101	E3
Locksbrook Rd. W-S-M	89	D3
Lodge Causeway. Bris	51	D2
Lodge Cl. Yatt	91	D4
Lodge Dr. Kingsw	66	B3
Lodge Dr. Lo Ash	62	A1
Lodge Dr. W-S-M	88	A1
Lodge Gdns. Bath	101	E1
Lodge Hill. Bris	51	E1
Lodge La. Wrax	60	A1
Lodge Pl. Bris	63	E4
Lodge Rd. Bris	51	E1
Lodge Rd. Wick	53	D1
Lodge Rd. Yate	27	D2
Lodge St. Bris	63	E4
Lodge Wlk. Mang	51	E3
Lodgeside Ave. Bris	51	E1
Lodgeside Gdns. Bris	51	E1
Lodore Rd. Bris	50	C2
Lodway Cl. E in G	47	E3
Lodway Gdns. E in G	47	E2
Lodway Rd. Bris	64	B1
Lodway. E in G	47	E3
Logan Rd. Bris	49	E2
Logus Ct. Kingsw	65	F2
Lombard St. Bris	63	E2
Lomond Rd. Bris	35	F1
London Rd E. Bathe	86	A2
London Rd W. Bath	85	F1
London Rd. Bath	102	A4
London Rd. Bris	49	F1
London Rd. Sist	66	B4
London Rd. Wick	67	F3
London St. Bath	102	A4
London St. Kingsw	65	E4
Long Acres Cl. Bris	48	B4
Long Ave. Cleve	57	D1
Long Ashton Rd. Lo Ash	62	B1
Long Barnaby. Mid No	132	A1
Long Beach Rd. Kingsw	66	A2
Long Cl. Bris	51	E3
Long Cl. St Gif	36	C3
Long Croft. Yate	27	E2
Long Cross. Bris	34	A1
Long Cross. Win	94	B4
Long Eaton Dr. Bris	80	A4
Long Handstones. Kingsw	66	A2
Long Hay Cl. Bath	101	D3
Long La. Back	76	B2
Long La. But	94	A3
Long La. Wring	93	D1
Long Leaze. Burt	43	D1
Long Mead. Yate	27	F3
Long Meadow. Bris	50	B3
Long Rd. Mang	52	A3
Long Row. Bris	63	F3
Long Thorn La. Win	111	F4
Longacre Rd. Bris	80	A2
Longacre. Cleve	73	D4
Longbottom. Ched	125	F3
Longcross. Crom	10	A1
Longden Rd. Mang	51	F3
Longdown Dr. W-S-M	89	D2
Longfellow Ave. Bath	101	F2
Longfellow Rd. Rad	132	B1
Longfellow Rd. Rod	138	B4
Longfield Rd. Bris	49	E2
Longford Ave. Bris	49	E4
Longford. Yate	39	E4
Longleat Cl. Bris	49	E3
Longleaze Gdns. Lock	105	F2
Longmead Ave. Bris	49	E3
Longmead Croft. Bris	78	C2
Longmeadow Rd. Keyn	81	E2
Longmoor Rd. Bris	63	D1
Longney Pl. Bris	23	F1
Longreach Gr. Bris	80	B3
Longs Dr. Yate	27	E1
Longs View. Char	11	D3
Longton Grove Rd. W-S-M	104	C4
Longton Ind Est. W-S-M	104	C3
Longway Ave. Bris	79	F2
Longwell House. Kingsw	65	F2
Longwood La. Lo Ash	61	F2
Longwood. Bris	65	D1
Lonsdale Ave. W-S-M	104	C1
Lorain Wlk. Bris	34	C1
Lorne Rd. Bath	101	E3
Lorton Rd. Bris	35	D1
Lott's Ave. Back	76	A4
Louisa St. Bris	63	F3
Louise Ave. Kingsw	52	A3
Love La. Ch Sod	40	A4
Love La. Yate	28	A2
Love's La. Farm	115	F3
Lovelinch Gdns. Lo Ash	61	F1
Lovell Ave. Kingsw	66	B1
Lovells Mill. Bi Sut	113	E2
Loveringe Cl. Bris	34	C2
Lovers La. Paul	132	A3

Lovers' Wlk. W-S-M	104	B4
Loves Hill. Tims	116	A1
Lowbourne. Bris	79	F3
Lower Ashley Rd. Bris	49	F1
Lower Ashley Rd. Bris	50	A1
Lower Batch. Ch Mag	96	A2
Lower Borough Walls. Bath	101	F3
Lower Bristol Rd. Bath	101	E3
Lower Bristol Rd. Clut	114	C2
Lower Castle St. Bris	63	F4
Lower Chapel La. Fr Cot	38	B4
Lower Chapel Rd. Kingsw	65	E3
Lower Cheltenham Pl. Bris	49	F1
Lower Church La. Bris	63	E4
Lower Church Rd. W-S-M	104	B4
Lower Claverham. Yatt	74	C2
Lower Clifton Hill. Bris	63	D3
Lower Cock Rd. Kingsw	65	F4
Lower College St. Bris	63	E3
Lower Court Rd. Alm	24	A3
Lower Down Rd. Portis	45	D3
Lower Fallow Cl. Bris	79	F2
Lower Gay St. Bris	63	E4
Lower Grove Rd. Bris	50	C2
Lower Hanham Rd. Kingsw	65	E3
Lower High St. Bris	47	E4
Lower House Cres. Bris	36	A2
Lower Kingsdown Rd. Box	86	C2
Lower Knole La. Bris	35	D2
Lower Knowles Rd. Cleve	57	E1
Lower Lamb St. Bris	63	E3
Lower Linden Rd. Cleve	57	E2
Lower Maudlin St. Bris	63	E4
Lower Moor Rd. Yate	27	E1
Lower Northend Est. Bathe	85	F3
Lower Norton La. W St L	88	B2
Lower Norton La. W-S-M	88	C2
Lower Oldfield Park. Bath	101	F3
Lower Park Row. Bris	63	E4
Lower Queen's Rd. Cleve	57	E2
Lower Rd. Hin Ble	129	F3
Lower Redland Rd. Bris	49	D1
Lower Sidney St. Bris	63	D2
Lower St. Rode	136	C1
Lower Station Rd. Bris	51	D2
Lower Station Rd. Kingsw	51	E2
Lower Stoke. Bath	103	D1
Lower Stoke. Li St	120	A4
Lower Stone Cl. Fr Cot	38	B4
Lower Strode Rd. Cleve	73	D4
Lower Strode. Win	112	A4
Lower Thirlmere Rd. Bris	36	A4
Lower Tockington Rd. Olve	14	A1
Lower Whitelands. Mid No	133	D2
Lowlis Cl. Bris	34	C2
Lowther Rd. Bris	35	E1
Loxley Gdns. Bath	101	E2
Loxton Dr. Bath	101	D3
Loxton Rd. W-S-M	104	C1
Loxton Sq. Bris	80	A3
Lucas Cl. Bris	64	B1
Luccombe Hill. Bris	49	D1
Luckington Cross. Hol	139	D1
Luckington Rd. Bris	49	F4
Lucklands Rd. Bath	84	B1
Luckley Ave. Bris	79	E3
Luckwell Rd. Bris	63	D2
Lucky La. Bris	63	E2
Ludlow Cl. Bris	49	F1
Ludlow Cl. Keyn	81	E3
Ludlow Cl. Kingsw	66	A1
Ludlow Rd. Bris	50	A4
Ludwell Cl. Wint	37	E3
Ludwells Orch. Paul	131	F3
Lullington Rd. Bris	64	A1
Lulsgate Rd. Bris	79	D4
Lulworth Cres. Mang	51	F4
Lulworth Rd. Keyn	81	F2
Lurgan Wlk. Bris	63	E1
Luvers La. Blag	110	B1
Lux Furlong. Bris	48	A4
Luxton St. Bris	64	A4
Lychgate Park. Lock	106	A2
Lydbrook Cl. Yate	39	E4
Lyddington Rd. Bris	49	F4
Lyddon Rd. W-S-M	89	D2
Lydford Wlk. Bris	63	E1
Lydiard Croft. Kingsw	65	E2
Lydney Rd. Bris	49	E4
Lydney Rd. Bris	51	F2
Lydstep Terr. Bris	63	E2
Lye Cross Rd. Wring	93	E1
Lye Hole La. Wring	93	E1
Lyefield Rd. W-S-M	88	C2
Lyme Gdns. Bath	101	D4
Lyme Rd. Bath	101	D4
Lymore Ave. Bath	101	E3
Lymore Gdns. Bath	101	E3
Lymore Terr. Bath	101	E2
Lympsham Green. Bath	118	B4
Lympsham Rd. Lymp	122	A1
Lynbrook La. Bath	101	F2
Lynbrook. Lo Ash	61	F1
Lynch Cl. W-S-M	88	C2
Lynch Cres. Wins	124	C4
Lynch Ct. Kingsw	65	F2
Lynch Hill. Chil	137	D2
Lynch The. Wins	124	C4
Lynchmead. Wins	124	C4
Lyncombe Hill. Bath	102	A3
Lyncombe Vale Rd. Bath	102	A2
Lyncombe Vale. Bath	102	A2
Lyncombe Wlk. Bris	51	D1
Lyndale Ave. Bris	48	B3
Lyndale Rd. Bris	64	B4
Lyndale Rd. Yate	27	E1
Lynde Cl. Bris	79	D2
Lyndhurst Rd. Bath	101	E3
Lyndhurst Rd. Bris	48	C4
Lyndhurst Rd. Keyn	81	F2
Lyndhurst Rd. Rod	138	A4
Lyndhurst Rd. W-S-M	104	C2
Lynfield Park. Bath	84	B1
Lynmouth Cl. W-S-M	89	D1
Lynmouth Rd. Bris	50	A1
Lynn Rd. Bris	50	B3
Lynton Cl. Portis	45	F2
Lynton Pl. Bris	64	B4
Lynton Rd. Rod	138	A4
Lynton Way. Bris	37	D1
Lynton. Kingsw	66	A4
Lynwood Cl. Rod	138	A4
Lyons Court Rd. Bris	80	B4
Lyons Ct. W-S-M	104	C4
Lyppiatt Rd. Bris	64	B4
Lyppincourt Rd. Bris	35	D2
Lysander Rd. Bris	35	E3
Lysander Wlk. St Gif	36	C3
Lytchet Dr. Mang	51	F4
Lytes Cary Rd. Keyn	82	A2
Lytton Gdns. Bath	101	D2
Lytton Gr. Bris	50	A4
Lytton Gr. Keyn	82	A3
Lyveden Gdns. Bris	79	D3
Lyvedon Way. Lo Ash	62	A1
Macaulay Bldgs. Bath	102	B2
Macauley Rd. Bris	50	A4
Macey's Rd. Bris	79	E2
Machin Cl. Bris	34	C2
Machin Rd. Bris	34	C2
Machley La. N St P	135	F2
Macies The. Bath	84	A2
Mackie Ave. Bris	36	A1
Mackie Gr. Bris	36	A1
Mackie Rd. Bris	36	A1
Macleod Cl. Cleve	57	D1
Madam La. W-S-M	88	C1
Madam La. W-S-M	89	D2
Madam's Paddock. Ch Mag	96	A2
Madeira Rd. Cleve	57	E2
Madeira Rd. W-S-M	87	E1
Madeline Rd. Bris	50	C1
Madison Cl. Yate	27	E1
Maesbury Rd. Keyn	82	A1
Maesbury. Kingsw	65	F3
Maesknoll La. Whit	97	D4
Magdalen Ave. Bath	101	F3
Magdalen Rd. Bath	101	F3
Magdalen Way. W-S-M	89	D2
Magdalene Pl. Bris	49	F1
Magdalene Rd. Rad	133	E1
Magellan Cl. W-S-M	88	C2
Maggs Folly. Paul	115	E1
Maggs La. Whit	80	B2
Magnolia Ave. W-S-M	89	D1
Magnolia Rd. Rad	132	C1
Magpie Bottom La. Bris	65	E3
Magpie Bottom La. Kingsw	65	E3
Magpie Cl. W-S-M	105	F4
Maiden Way. Avon	47	E4
Maidenhead Rd. Bris	79	E2
Maidstone Gr. W-S-M	105	D1
Maidstone St. Bris	63	F2
Main Rd. Back	76	C4
Main Rd. Brock	75	F1
Main Rd. Lock	105	F1
Main Rd. Puck	52	B3
Main St. Paul	131	D2
Main View. Fr Cot	38	B4
Maisemore Ave. St Gif	24	A1
Maisemore. Yate	39	F3
Makin Cl. Kingsw	66	B3
Malago Rd. Bris	63	E2
Malago Vale Est. Bris	63	E2
Malago Wlk. Bris	78	C2
Maldowers La. Bris	65	D4
Mall The. Bath	102	A3
Mall The. Bris	62	C4
Mallard Cl. Bris	50	C1
Mallard Cl. Ch Sod	40	A4
Mallard Cl. St Gif	24	B1
Mallard Wlk. W-S-M	105	F4
Mallow Cl. Cleve	57	F1
Mallow Cl. Thorn	8	B1
Malmains Dr. Bris	37	D1
Malmesbury Cl. Bris	49	E2
Malmesbury Cl. Kingsw	65	F3
Maltings Ind Est The. Bath	101	D4
Maltings The. W-S-M	88	C1
Maltlands. W-S-M	105	E4
Maltravers Cl. St Gif	36	B4
Malvern Bldgs. Bath	85	D1

Malvern Ct. Bris	64	C4
Malvern Dr. Kingsw	66	B3
Malvern Dr. Thorn	15	E4
Malvern Rd. Bris	64	B2
Malvern Rd. Bris	64	C4
Malvern Rd. W-S-M	104	C3
Mancroft Ave. Bris	47	F4
Mandy Meadows. Mid No	131	F1
Mangotsfield Rd. Mang	52	A3
Manilla Pl. W-S-M	87	E1
Manilla Rd. Bris	63	D4
Manmoor La. Cleve	58	A1
Manor Cl. E in G	47	D2
Manor Cl. Fr Cot	38	B3
Manor Cl. Olve	14	B1
Manor Cl. Paul	131	D2
Manor Cl. Well	118	B1
Manor Copse Rd. Rad	133	E1
Manor Court Dr. Bris	49	F4
Manor Ct. Back	76	A3
Manor Ct. Bris	50	C2
Manor Dr. Bathf	86	A1
Manor Farm Cl. W-S-M	105	D1
Manor Farm Cres. W-S-M	105	D1
Manor Farm. St Gif	36	B4
Manor Gdns. Farm	115	F3
Manor Gdns. Lock	106	A2
Manor Gdns. Paul	131	D2
Manor Gdns. W-S-M	88	A2
Manor Gr. Kingsw	52	A2
Manor Gr. St Gif	24	A1
Manor Grange. Blea	122	A4
Manor La. Ab Lei	61	F4
Manor La. Char	11	D2
Manor La. Wint	37	F4
Manor Park. Bath	101	D4
Manor Park. Bris	49	D2
Manor Park. Olve	14	A1
Manor Park. Rad	133	E1
Manor Pl. Bris	37	E1
Manor Rd. Ab Lei	61	F4
Manor Rd. Bath	84	B1
Manor Rd. Bris	49	F2
Manor Rd. Bris	50	C3
Manor Rd. Bris	79	D3
Manor Rd. Ir Act	27	D4
Manor Rd. Keyn	82	A1
Manor Rd. Kingsw	52	A2
Manor Rd. Rad	133	E1
Manor Rd. W-S-M	105	D4
Manor Rd. Wick	67	E3
Manor Rd. Wickw	27	D4
Manor Terr. Rad	133	E1
Manor Valley. W-S-M	88	A1
Manor Villas. Bath	84	B1
Manor Way. Ch Sod	28	A1
Manor Way. Wrax	61	E2
Manor Wlk. Thorn	8	A3
Mansel Cl. Keyn	82	B2
Mansfield Ave. W-S-M	105	D4
Mansfield St. Bris	63	D1
Manston Cl. Bris	80	B4
Manvers St. Bath	102	A3
Manworthy Rd. Bris	64	B2
Manx Rd. Bris	49	F4
Maple Ave. Bris	51	E2
Maple Ave. Thorn	8	B1
Maple Cl. Bris	80	B2
Maple Cl. Kingsw	66	A2
Maple Cl. St Gif	36	B4
Maple Cl. W-S-M	105	D4
Maple Dr. Rad	132	C1
Maple Gdns. Bath	101	F2
Maple Gr. Bath	101	F2
Maple Leaf Ct. Bris	63	D4
Maple Rd. Bris	49	E3
Maple Rd. Bris	64	B3
Maple Wlk. Keyn	81	E2
Maple Wlk. Puck	53	E3
Mapleleaze. Bris	64	B2
Maplemeade. Bris	49	E2
Mapleridge La. Hort	28	B4
Mapleridge La. Yate	28	B4
Maples The. Nail	59	E1
Maplestone Rd. Bris	80	A2
Marbeck Rd. Bris	35	D1
Marchfields Way. W-S-M	105	D3
Marconi Rd. Portis	44	C3
Mardale Cl. Bris	35	E1
Marden Rd. Keyn	82	A2
Mardon Rd. Bris	64	B3
Mardyke Ferry Rd. Bris	63	D3
Marfield Wlk. Bris	78	C4
Margaret Rd. Bris	78	C2
Margaret's Bldgs. Bath	101	F4
Margaret's Hill. Bath	102	A4
Margate St. Bris	63	F2
Marguerite Rd. Bris	78	C4
Marigold Wlk. Bris	63	D1
Marina Gdns. Bris	50	C2
Marindin Dr. W-S-M	89	D2
Marine Hill. Cleve	57	E2
Marine Par. Cleve	57	E2
Marine Par. E in G	47	E3
Marine Par. W-S-M	104	B3
Mariner's Cl. W-S-M	88	B1
Mariner's Way. E in G	47	E3

Mariners Cl. Back	76	A3
Mariners Dr. Back	76	A3
Mariners Dr. Bris	48	B2
Marion Way. Kingsw	65	D2
Marion Wlk. Bris	65	D4
Marissal Cl. Bris	34	C2
Marissal Rd. Bris	34	C2
Mariston Way. Kingsw	66	B3
Mark La. Bris	63	E3
Market Ind Est. Yatt	74	A1
Market La. W-S-M	104	B4
Market Pl. Marsh	70	A4
Market Pl. Win	94	C4
Market Sq. Bris	51	E2
Markham Cl. Bris	47	E4
Marksbury Rd. Bris	63	E1
Marksbury. Marks	99	D1
Marlborough Ave. Bris	50	C2
Marlborough Bldgs. Bath	101	F4
Marlborough Dr. Bris	37	D1
Marlborough Dr. W-S-M	89	D1
Marlborough Hill Pl. Bris	63	E4
Marlborough Hill. Bris	63	E4
Marlborough La. Bath	101	F4
Marlborough St. Bath	101	F4
Marlborough St. Bris	50	C2
Marlborough St. Bris	63	E4
Marlepit Gr. Bris	78	C3
Marling Rd. Bris	64	C4
Marlwood Dr. Bris	35	D2
Marmaduke St. Bris	63	F2
Marmion Cres. Bris	34	C2
Marne Cl. Bris	80	B2
Marsden Rd. Bath	101	E2
Marsh Cl. Wint	37	F3
Marsh Comm. Piln	22	B3
Marsh La. Bris	63	D1
Marsh La. Bris	64	B3
Marsh La. Clut	115	D1
Marsh La. E in G	46	C3
Marsh La. Paul	131	D2
Marsh Rd. Bris	62	C2
Marsh Rd. Rode	136	C1
Marsh St. Avon	47	E4
Marsh St. Bris	63	E3
Marshacre La. Aust	13	F3
Marsham Way. Kingsw	65	F2
Marshfield La. Bitt	67	E1
Marshfield Rd. Bris	51	E2
Marshfield Rd. Mang	51	E4
Marshfield Rd. Tor	41	F1
Marshfield Way. Bath	85	D1
Marshwall La. Alm	23	F3
Marston Rd. Cleve	57	E2
Marston Rd. Bris	64	A2
Martin Cl. Bris	35	F4
Martin St. Bris	63	D2
Martin's Rd. Kingsw	65	E3
Martindale Ct. W-S-M	105	E4
Martindale Rd. W-S-M	105	E4
Martingale Rd. Bris	64	B2
Martins Cl. Kingsw	65	E3
Martins Gr. W-S-M	88	C1
Martock Cres. Bris	63	E1
Martock Rd. Bris	63	E1
Martock Rd. Keyn	82	A2
Martock. W-S-M	104	C1
Martor Ind Est. Marsh	56	A1
Marwood Rd. Bris	79	F4
Mary Carpenter Pl. Bris	49	F1
Mary St. Bris	64	B4
Marybush La. Bris	63	F4
Marygold Leaze. Kingsw	66	A2
Mascot Rd. Bris	63	E2
Masefield Way. Bris	50	A4
Maskelyne Ave. Bris	49	E4
Masons View. Wint	37	F4
Matchells Cl. Bris	64	C3
Materman Rd. Bris	80	C3
Matford Cl. Bris	35	E2
Matford Cl. Wint	37	F3
Matford La. Stone		
Matthew's Rd. Bris	64	B4
Matthews Cl. Bris	80	C3
Maules La. St Gif	36	C1
Maunsell Rd. Bris	34	A1
Maurice Rd. Bris	49	F1
Max Mill La. Wins	124	B4
Maxse Rd. Bris	64	A2
May St. Bris	51	E1
May Tree Cl. Nail	59	E1
May Tree Rd. Rad	132	C1
May Tree Wlk. Keyn	81	E2
May's La. Pux	90	B2
Maybank Rd. Yate	27	E1
Maybec Gdns. Bris	65	D3
Maybourne. Bris	65	D1
Maybrick Rd. Bath	101	E3
Maycliffe Park. Bris	49	F1
Mayfair Ave. Nail	59	E1
Mayfield Ave. Bris	51	D1
Mayfield Ave. W-S-M	88	C1
Mayfield Pk N. Bris	51	D1
Mayfield Pk S. Bris	51	D1
Mayfield Pk. Bris	51	D1
Mayfield Rd. Bath	101	E3
Mayfields. Keyn	81	F3

Mayflower Gdns. Nail	60	A1
Maynard Cl. Bris	79	E3
Maynard Cl. Cleve	57	F2
Maynard Rd. Bris	79	E3
Maynard Terr. Clut	115	D2
Maypole Cl. Clut	114	C2
Maysfield Cl. Portis	45	E2
Maysgreen Rd. Pux	90	A2
Maysmead La. Chur	109	E3
Maytree Ave. Bris	79	D4
Maytree Cl. Bris	79	D4
Mayville Ave. Bris	36	A2
Maywood Ave. Bris	51	D2
Maywood Cres. Bris	51	D2
Maywood Rd. Bris	51	D2
Maze St. Bris	64	A3
McAdam Way. Bris	62	C3
Mead Cl. Bath	101	F2
Mead Cl. Bris	47	F3
Mead La. Keyn	82	C2
Mead La. Keyn	83	D2
Mead La. Winsc	107	F2
Mead Lands. Cor	100	A4
Mead Rd. Ch Sod	28	A1
Mead Rd. Portis	45	E1
Mead Rd. St Gif	36	C3
Mead Rise. Bris	63	F2
Mead St. Bris	63	F3
Mead The. Alve	15	D3
Mead The. Bris	36	A2
Mead The. Chil	137	F1
Mead The. Clut	114	C2
Mead The. Dun	78	B1
Mead The. Farm	116	A3
Mead The. Ship	125	F4
Mead The. Tims	116	B2
Mead The. Win	95	D3
Mead The. Winsl	120	C4
Mead Vale. W-S-M	105	F4
Mead Way. Thorn	15	D4
Meadow Cl. Back	76	A3
Meadow Cl. Mang	51	F4
Meadow Cl. Nail	59	F2
Meadow Cl. Portis	44	C3
Meadow Court Dr. Kingsw	66	B2
Meadow Croft. W-S-M	105	D4
Meadow Dr. Lock	106	A2
Meadow Dr. W in G	44	C1
Meadow Gdns. Bath	84	A1
Meadow Gr. Bris	47	E4
Meadow La. Bath	85	E1
Meadow Mead. Fr Cot	38	A4
Meadow Park. Bathe	86	A2
Meadow Rd. Ch Sod	28	A1
Meadow Rd. Cleve	57	F2
Meadow Rd. Crom	10	A2
Meadow Rd. Paul	131	F2
Meadow St. Avon	33	D1
Meadow St. Axb	125	E1
Meadow St. Bris	63	F4
Meadow St. W-S-M	104	C4
Meadow Vale. Bris	51	D1
Meadow View. Fr Cot	38	B4
Meadow View. Rad	133	D1
Meadow Villas. W-S-M	104	C4
Meadow Way. St Gif	36	C4
Meadowbank. W-S-M	88	C2
Meadowland Rd. Bris	34	C2
Meadowland. Yatt	74	A1
Meadowlands. Lock	89	E1
Meadows The. Kingsw	65	E2
Meadowside Dr. Bris	80	A2
Meadowside. Thorn	15	E4
Meadowsweet Ave. Bris	36	A2
Meads The. Burt	43	D2
Meads The. Mang	51	F4
Meadway Ave. Nail	59	E1
Meadway. Bris	48	B3
Meadway. Clut	114	C1
Meadway. Farm	116	A3
Mearcombe La. Blea	122	C3
Meardon Rd. Bris	80	C3
Meare Rd. Bath	102	A1
Meare. W-S-M	104	C1
Mede Cl. Bris	63	F3
Medical Ave. Bris	63	E4
Medina Cl. Thorn	15	E4
Medway Cl. Keyn	82	A2
Medway Ct. Thorn	15	E4
Medway Dr. Fr Cot	38	A4
Medway Dr. Keyn	82	A2
Meere Bank. Bris	34	A1
Meeting House La. Brock	75	D1
Meetinghouse La. Yatt	75	D1
Meg Thatchers Cl. Bris	65	D4
Meg Thatchers Gdns. Bris	65	D4
Melbourne Dr. Ch Sod	28	A1
Melbourne Rd. Bris	49	E2
Melbourne Terr. Cleve	57	E1
Melbury Rd. Bris	64	A1
Melcombe Rd. Bath	101	E3
Melita Rd. Bris	49	F2
Mellent Ave. Bris	79	E4
Mells Cl. Keyn	82	A1
Mells La. Kilm	133	D1
Mells La. Rad	133	D1
Melrose Ave. Bris	63	D4
Melrose Ave. Yate	28	A1

Melrose Cl. Yate 28 A1
Melrose Gr. Bath 101 D2
Melrose Pl. Bris 63 D4
Melton Cres. Bris 50 A4
Melville Rd. Bris 49 D1
Melville Terr. Bris 63 E2
Memorial Cl. Kingsw 65 D2
Memorial Cotts. Bath 84 B1
Memorial Rd. Kingsw 65 D2
Memorial Rd. Wring 92 C1
Mendip Ave. W-S-M 88 C1
Mendip Cl. Axb 125 E1
Mendip Cl. Keyn 81 E3
Mendip Cl. Nail 59 F1
Mendip Cl. Paul 131 F2
Mendip Cl. Yatt 91 D4
Mendip Cres. Mang 52 A4
Mendip Edge. W-S-M 121 F4
Mendip Gdns. Bath 118 B4
Mendip Gdns. Yatt 91 D4
Mendip Rd. Bris 63 E2
Mendip Rd. Portis 45 D3
Mendip Rd. W-S-M 105 D4
Mendip Rd. Yatt 91 D4
Mendip Rise. Lock 106 A2
Mendip View Ave. Bris ... 51 D2
Mendip View. Wick 67 E4
Mendip Villas. Co Mar ... 127 F4
Mendip Way. 132 C2
Menlea. Blag 110 B2
Merchant St. Bris 63 F4
Merchants Ct. Bris 63 D3
Merchants Quay. Bris 63 E3
Merchants Rd. Bris 63 D3
Merchants Rd. Bris 63 E3
Mercia Dr. Bris 50 A1
Mercier Cl. Yate 27 F1
Meredith Ct. Bris 63 D3
Merfield Rd. Bris 64 A1
Meridian Pl. Bris 63 D4
Meridian Rd. Bris 49 E1
Meridian Vale. Bris 63 D4
Meriet Ave. Bris 79 D2
Merioneth St. Bris 63 F2
Meriton St. Bris 64 A3
Merlin Cl. Bris 48 C4
Merlin Cl. W-S-M 105 F4
Merlin Park. Portis 45 D2
Merlin Rd. Bris 35 E3
Merlin Ridge. Puck 53 E2
Merlin Way. Ch Sod 39 F4
Merrimans Rd. Bris 47 E4
Merryweathers. Bris 64 C1
Merrywood Cl. Bris 63 E2
Merrywood Rd. Bris 63 E2
Merstham Rd. Bris 50 A1
Merton Rd. Bris 49 F3
Mervyn Rd. Bris 49 F2
Metford Gr. Bris 49 D2
Metford Pl. Bris 49 E2
Metford Rd. Bris 49 E2
Methwyn Cl. W-S-M 105 E4
Mews The. Bath 101 D4
Michaels Mead. Bath 84 A1
Middle Ave. Bris 63 E3
Middle La. Bath 85 D1
Middle La. K Sey 73 D2
Middle Rd. Kingsw 51 F2
Middle St. E Harp 128 C2
Middle Stoke. Li St 120 A3
Middle Yeo Green. Nail ... 59 E2
Middledown Rd. Marsh 55 E1
Middleford House. Bris 79 E2
Middlemead. Chil 137 F2
Middlepiece La. Keyn 99 D4
Middleton Rd. Bris 47 F4
Midford Hill. Hin Cha 119 E2
Midford La. Hi Cha 120 A3
Midford La. Li St 119 F4
Midford Rd. Bath 101 F1
Midford Rd. Sosto 119 D4
Midford. W-S-M 104 C1
Midhaven Rise. W-S-M 88 C2
Midland Bridge Rd. Bath 101 F3
Midland Rd. Bath 101 E4
Midland Rd. Bris 63 F4
Midland Rd. Kingsw 51 E2
Midland Terr. Bris 50 C2
Midland Way. Thorn 15 D4
Midsomer Enterprise Park.
         Mid No 132 B1
Midsummer Bldgs. Bath ... 85 D1
Milbourn Cl. Winsl 120 B4
Milburn Rd. W-S-M 104 C4
Mildred St. Bris 64 B4
Mile Wlk. Bris 80 A3
Miles Ct. Kingsw 65 F2
Miles Rd. Bris 49 D1
Miles St. Bath 102 A3
Miles's Bldgs. Bath 101 F4
Milestone Ct. Lock 89 E1
Milford Ave. Wick 67 D4
Milford St. Bris 63 E3
Milk St. Bath 101 F3
Mill Ave. Bris 63 E4
Mill Cl. Fr Cot 38 B4
Mill Cl. Portb 46 B1
Mill Cres. West 39 D2

Mill Hill. Well 118 C1
Mill Hill. Bath 85 F1
Mill La. Bath 101 D3
Mill La. Bath 119 F4
Mill La. Bitt 66 C1
Mill La. Bitt 82 C4
Mill La. Bris 63 E2
Mill La. But 111 D4
Mill La. Ch Sod 28 A1
Mill La. Ch Sod 40 C3
Mill La. Ch St 112 B4
Mill La. Co Mar 128 A4
Mill La. Cong 91 E2
Mill La. Doyn 53 F1
Mill La. Falf 9 F4
Mill La. Fr Cot 26 A1
Mill La. Kingsw 66 B3
Mill La. Olve 14 A1
Mill La. Portb 46 C1
Mill La. Pris 117 D4
Mill La. Tims 116 A1
Mill La. Wring 109 F4
Mill Leg. Cong 91 F2
Mill Pool Ct. Bris 35 D1
Mill rd. Mid No 133 D1
Mill Rd. Wint 37 E2
Mill Stream Cl. Axb 125 D1
Millard's Hill. Mid No 132 A2
Millbank Cl. Bris 64 C2
Millbrook Ave. Bris 64 C2
Millbrook Pl. Bath 102 A3
Millbrook Rd. Yate 27 D1
Millcross. Cleve 73 E4
Millers Cl. E in G 47 E2
Millers Dr. Kingsw 66 B3
Millers Rise. W-S-M 89 E3
Millfield Dr. Kingsw 66 B3
Millfield. Mid No 137 F4
Millfield. Thorn 8 B1
Millground Rd. Bris 78 C3
Millier Rd. Brock 92 A4
Milliman Ct. Bris 79 E3
Millmead House. Bris 79 E2
Millmead Rd. Bath 101 E3
Millpond St. Bris 50 A1
Millward Gr. Bris 51 E2
Milner Green. Kingsw 66 A3
Milner Rd. Bris 49 F3
Milsom St. Bath 101 F4
Milsom St. Bris 64 A4
Milton Ave. Bath 101 F2
Milton Ave. W-S-M 105 D4
Milton Brow. W-S-M 88 A1
Milton Cl. Nail 59 E2
Milton Cl. Yate 27 E1
Milton Green. W-S-M 88 B1
Milton Hill. W-S-M 88 A1
Milton Park Rd. W-S-M ... 88 B1
Milton Pk. Bris 64 B4
Milton Rd. Bris 49 F3
Milton Rd. Rad 132 B1
Milton Rd. Yate 27 E1
Milton Rise. W-S-M 88 B1
Miltons Cl. Bris 79 E2
Milverton. W-S-M 104 C1
Milward Rd. Keyn 81 F3
Mina Rd. Bris 50 A1
Minehead Rd. Bris 64 A1
Minerva Gdns. Bath 101 E2
Minor's La. Avon 34 A4
Minsmere Rd. Keyn 82 A2
Minster Way. Bath 102 B4
Minto Rd. Bris 50 A1
Minto Road Ind Centre. Bris 49 F1
Mission Rd. Ir Act 27 D2
Mitchell Ct. Bris 63 F3
Mitchell La. Bris 63 F3
Mitford-Slade Ct. Yatt 91 E4
Mivart St. Bris 50 A1
Mizzymead Cl. Nail 59 E1
Mizzymead Rd. Nail 59 F1
Mizzymead Rise. Nail 59 E1
Modecombe Gr. Bris 34 C2
Mogg St. Bris 50 A1
Molesworth Cl. Bris 79 D2
Molesworth Dr. Bris 79 D2
Molesworth Dr. Bris 79 D2
Molly Cl. Clut 130 C4
Monger La. Mid No 132 A2
Monk Rd. Bris 49 E2
Monk's Park Ave. Bris 49 F4
Monks Ave. Bris 65 D4
Monks Hill. W-S-M 88 A2
Monksdale Rd. Bath 101 E2
Monkton Ave. W-S-M 105 D1
Monkton Farleigh, Mon Far 103 F4
Monkton Rd. Kingsw 65 D3
Monmouth Cl. Portis 44 C2
Monmouth Hill. Alm 23 F2
Monmouth Paddock. N St P 135 F2
Monmouth Pl. Bath 101 F3
Monmouth Rd. Bris 49 E2
Monmouth Rd. E in G 47 E2
Monmouth Rd. Keyn 81 E3
Monmouth St. Bath 101 F3
Monmouth St. Bris 63 F2
Monsdale Cl. Bris 35 D2

Monsdale Dr. Bris 35 D1
Montague Cl. St Gif 36 C3
Montague Hill S. Bris 63 E4
Montague Hill. Bris 63 E4
Montague Pl. Bris 63 E4
Montague Rd. Keyn 82 B1
Montague Rd. Well 133 F3
Montague St. Bris 63 E4
Montgomery St. Bris 63 F2
Montpelier E. W-S-M 87 F1
Montpelier. W-S-M 104 C4
Montreal Ave. Bris 50 A4
Montrose Ave. Bris 49 E1
Montrose Dr. Kingsw 66 A3
Montrose Pk. Bris 64 B1
Montroy Cl. Bris 49 E3
Moon St. Bris 63 F4
Moor Croft Dr. Kingsw 65 F2
Moor Croft Rd. Lock 105 F2
Moor End Spout. Nail 59 E1
Moor Gr. Bris 48 A4
Moor Green. Axb 125 E1
Moor La. Back 75 F3
Moor La. Cleve 58 A1
Moor La. Lock 105 E2
Moor La. Nail 58 C2
Moor La. Olve 14 A4
Moor La. Piln 23 F4
Moor La. W in G 45 F1
Moor La. W-S-M 105 F4
Moor Park. Cleve 57 F1
Moor Rd. Ban 107 D3
Moor Rd. Yatt 74 A1
Moordell Cl. Yate 27 E1
Moorend Gdns. Bris 47 F4
Moorend Rd. Wint 37 E2
Moorfield Rd. Back 76 A3
Moorfields Cl. Bath 101 E2
Moorfields Cl. Nail 59 E1
Moorfields Rd. Bath 101 E2
Moorfields Rd. Nail 59 E1
Moorham Rd. Wins 108 A1
Moorhill St. Bris 50 A1
Moorhouse La. Avon 34 A2
Moorings The. E in G 47 E2
Moorland Rd. Bath 101 E3
Moorland Rd. W-S-M 104 C2
Moorland Rd. Yate 27 E1
Moorland St. Axb 125 E1
Moorlands Cl. Nail 59 E1
Moorlands Rd. Bris 50 C2
Moorlands Rd. Bris 51 D1
Moorledge La. Ch Mag 96 B1
Moorledge La. Pens 113 F4
Moorledge Rd. Ch Mag 96 A1
Moorpark Ave. Yate 27 E1
Moorsfield. Clut 114 C2
Moorside Ct. Cleve 57 F1
Moorside Villas. Cleve 57 E1
Moorslade La. Falf 3 E1
Moorslade La. Stone 3 E1
Moravian Ct. Kingsw 65 E4
Moravian Rd. Kingsw 65 E4
Morden Wlk. Bris 80 B4
Moreton Cl. Bris 80 A2
Moreton St. Bris 63 F4
Morford St. Bath 101 F4
Morgan Cl. Keyn 82 B1
Morgan St. Bris 49 F1
Morgan's La. E Harp 128 C2
Morgans Hill Cl. Nail 75 E4
Morley Ave. Kingsw 52 A2
Morley Cl. Bris 51 E2
Morley Cl. Kingsw 51 E2
Morley Cl. St Gif 36 B4
Morley Rd. Bris 63 E2
Morley Rd. Kingsw 51 E2
Morley Sq. Bris 49 F2
Morley St. Bris 49 F1
Morley St. Bris 64 A4
Morley Terr. Kingsw 51 E1
Morley Terr. Mid No 133 D2
Mornington Rd. Bris 49 D1
Morpeth Rd. Bris 79 E4
Morris La. Bathe 86 A2
Morris Rd. Bris 50 B3
Morse Rd. Bris 64 B4
Mortimer Cl. Bath 84 A1
Mortimer Rd. Bris 36 A1
Mortimer Rd. Bris 63 D4
Morton St. Bris 64 A4
Morton St. Thorn 8 B2
Morton Way. Thorn 8 B1
Moseley Gr. W-S-M 104 C1
Mount Beacon Row. Bath .. 84 C1
Mount Beacon. Bath 85 D1
Mount Cl. Fr Cot 37 F4
Mount Cres. Wint 37 F3
Mount Gdns. Kingsw 65 E3
Mount Gr. Bath 101 D2
Mount Hill Rd. Kingsw 65 E3
Mount Pleasant Terr. Bris . 63 E2
Mount Pleasant. Bath 102 B1
Mount Pleasant. E in G 47 E2
Mount Pleasant. Rad 133 D1
Mount Rd. Bath 101 D2
Mount Rd. Bath 101 F4
Mount View. Bath 101 D2
Mountain Ash. Bath 84 B1

Mountain Wood. Bathf 86 B1
Mountbatten Cl. W-S-M ... 88 C2
Mountbatten Cl. Yate 27 E2
Mounteney's La. Kings 18 B4
Mow Barton. Bris 78 C3
Mow Barton. Yate 27 E1
Mowbray Rd. Bris 80 B4
Mowcroft Rd. Bris 79 E2
Moxham Dr. Bris 79 E2
Mud La. Yatt 74 C1
Muddy La. W ST L 89 D4
Muirfield. Kingsw 66 A3
Muirfield. Yate 39 F4
Mulberry Cl. Back 76 A3
Mulberry Cl. Kingsw 65 F4
Mulberry Dr. Kingsw 51 F1
Mulberry La. Blea 122 B3
Mulberry Rd. Cong 91 F2
Mulberry Wlk. Bris 48 B4
Mule St. N Nib 4 A2
Mullberry Cl. W-S-M 89 D1
Muller Ave. Bris 49 F3
Muller Rd. Bris 50 A2
Mulready Cl. Bris 50 B3
Mumbleys Hill. Thorn 14 C4
Mumbleys La. Thorn 14 C4
Murford Ave. Bris 79 D2
Murford Wlk. Bris 79 D2
Murray St. Bris 63 E2
Musgrove Cl. Bris 34 B1
Myrtle Dr. Bris 47 F3
Myrtle Hill. E in G 47 E2
Myrtle Rd. Bris 63 E4
Myrtle St. Bris 63 D2
Myrtles The. Lock 105 E1

Nags Head Hill. Bris 65 D4
Nailsea Cl. Bris 79 D4
Nailsea Park Cl. Nail 59 F1
Nailsea Park. Nail 59 F1
Nailsea Wall. Nail 74 B4
Nailsea Wall. Yatt 74 B4
Nailsworth Dr. Yate 27 F1
Naish Hill. Wrax 59 F4
Naish La. Ba Gu 77 E2
Naish's Cross. Chil 137 E2
Naishcombe Hill. Wick 67 E4
Naishes Ave. P St J 133 E4
Naite The. O-on-S 7 E3
Nanny Hurn's La. Bi Sut .. 114 A1
Nanny Hurn's La. Clut 130 A4
Napier Ct. Bris 63 D3
Napier Miles Rd. Bris 48 A4
Napier Rd. Avon 33 D1
Napier Rd. Bath 84 A2
Napier Rd. Bris 49 D1
Napier Rd. Bris 50 A2
Napier Sq. Avon 33 D1
Napier St. Bris 64 A3
Narrow La. Kingsw 51 F2
Narrow Plain. Bris 63 F3
Narrow Quay. Bris 63 E3
Narroways Rd. Bris 50 A2
Naseby Wlk. Bris 50 C1
Nash Cl. Keyn 82 A3
Nash Dr. Bris 50 B4
Nates La. Wring 92 C1
Naunton Way. W-S-M 88 A1
Neath Rd. Bris 64 B4
Nelson Ct. W-S-M 88 C2
Nelson Pl W. Bath 101 F3
Nelson Pl. Bath 102 A4
Nelson Rd. Mang 51 E2
Nelson St. Bris 63 D1
Nelson St. Bris 63 E4
Nelson Terr. Bath 102 A4
Nelson Villas. Bath 101 F3
Nempnett St. But 111 E3
Neston Wlk. Bris 79 F4
Netham Park Ind Est. Bris . 64 B3
Netham Rd. Bris 64 B4
Netham View Ind Park. Bris 64 B4
Netherways. Cleve 57 D1
Nettlestone Cl. Bris 34 C2
Nettleton Rd. Burt 43 D2
Neva Rd. W-S-M 104 C3
Nevalan Dr. Bris 65 D3
Nevil Rd. Bris 49 F2
Neville Rd. Kingsw 51 F1
New Bldgs. Bris 50 C2
New Bldgs. P St J 133 D4
New Bond St. Bath 102 A3
New Bond Street Pl. Bath . 102 A3
New Bristol Rd. W-S-M 88 C1
New Brunswick Ave. Bris .. 65 D4
New Charlotte St. Bris 63 E2
New Cheltenham Rd.
         Kingsw 51 F1
New Cut Bow. K Sey 73 D3
New Fosseway Rd. Bris 80 A3
New John St. Bris 63 E2
New King St. Bath 101 F3
New Kingsley Rd. Bris 63 F3
New La. Alve 15 E3
New Leaze. St Gif 24 B2
New Orchard St. Bath 102 A3
New Queen St. Bris 63 E2
New Queen St. Bris 65 D4

New Rd. Bathf 86 B1
New Rd. Bris 36 A2
New Rd. Bris 36 B2
New Rd. Chur 108 C2
New Rd. E in G 47 E2
New Rd. Farm 115 E2
New Rd. Hi Cha 120 A3
New Rd. Kilm 139 F2
New Rd. N Nib 5 F2
New Rd. Olve 14 A1
New Rd. Paul 115 E2
New Rd. Pens 97 E2
New Rd. Ship 108 C2
New Rd. Tyth 16 B3
New Rd. W-u-E 11 F3
New Rd. Wickw 27 D4
New Rd. Wring 93 D2
New Rd. Yate 17 E1
New Rock Ind Est. Chil ... 137 E1
New St. Bath 101 F3
New St. Bris 63 F4
New St. Char 11 D3
New Station Rd. Bris 51 D2
New Thomas St. Bris 63 F3
New Tyning La. Hort 29 E2
New Walls. Bris 63 F2
New Wlk. Kingsw 65 E3
Newark St. Bath 102 A3
Newbolt Cl. W-S-M 105 D2
Newbourne Rd. W-S-M .. 105 D1
Newbridge Cl. Bris 64 B3
Newbridge Ct. Bath 101 D4
Newbridge Gdns. Bath ... 101 D4
Newbridge Hill. Bath 101 D4
Newbridge Rd. Bath 101 D4
Newbridge Rd. Bris 64 C3
Newbury Rd. Bris 50 A4
Newchurch Rd. W-S-M .. 104 B1
Newclose La. Co Mar 128 B4
Newcombe Dr. Bris 48 B2
Newcombe Rd. Bris 48 C4
Newditch La. Ba Gu 77 E1
Newent Ave. Bris 65 D4
Newfields. Blag 126 B4
Newfoundland Rd. Bris 63 F4
Newfoundland St. Bris 63 F4
Newfoundland Way. Bris .. 49 F1
Newgate. Bris 63 F4
Newhaven Pl. Portis 44 C2
Newhaven Rd. Portis 44 B2
Newland Dr. Bris 79 D2
Newland Rd. Bris 79 D2
Newland Rd. W-S-M 104 C3
Newland Wlk. Bris 79 D2
Newlands Ave. Fr Cot 38 B4
Newlands Green. Cleve 57 F1
Newlands Hill. Portis 45 E2
Newlands Rd. Keyn 81 E2
Newlands The. Bris 51 D4
Newlyn Ave. Bris 48 B3
Newlyn Wlk. Bris 64 A1
Newman Cl. West 39 D2
Newmans La. Tims 116 A1
Newmarket Ave. Bris 63 E4
Newnham Cl. Bris 80 B4
Newnham Pl. Bris 23 F1
Newpit La. Bitt 66 C1
Newport Cl. Cleve 57 E1
Newport Cl. Portis 44 C2
Newport Rd. E in G 47 E3
Newport St. Bris 63 F2
Newquay Rd. Bris 63 F1
Newry Wlk. Bris 63 F1
Newsome Ave. E in G 47 E2
Newton Cl. E Harp 128 C3
Newton Cl. Kingsw 52 A1
Newton Dr. Kingsw 66 A3
Newton Green. Nail 75 E4
Newton Rd. Bath 100 C3
Newton Rd. Kingsw 66 A3
Newton Rd. W-S-M 104 C3
Newton St. Bris 64 A4
Newton's Rd. W-S-M 88 C2
Newtown. Char 11 D3
Niblett Cl. Kingsw 65 F3
Niblett's Hill. Bris 65 D3
Nibley La. Ir Act 26 C2
Nibley Rd. Bris 47 F3
Nichol's Rd. Portis 44 C3
Nicholas La. Bris 65 D3
Nicholas Rd. Bris 50 A1
Nicholas St. Bris 63 F2
Nicholettes. Kingsw 66 B3
Nicholls La. Wint 37 F3
Nigel Park. Bris 47 F4
Nightingale Cl. Fr Cot 38 A3
Nightingale Cl. Thorn 8 B1
Nightingale Cl. W-S-M 88 C1
Nightingale Gdns. Nail 59 E1
Nightingale La. Wint 38 A4
Nightingale Rise. Portis ... 44 C2
Nightingale Way. Rod 138 A4
Nine Tree Hill. Bris 49 F1
Ninth Ave. Bris 36 A1
Nippors Way. Wins 124 C4
Nithsdale Rd. W-S-M 104 C2
Noble Ave. Kingsw 66 B2

157

Nomis Park. Cong — Park Rd. Mang

Nomis Park. Cong 91 F1
Nore Gdns. Portis 45 E3
Nore Park Dr. Portis 44 C3
Nore Rd. Portis 45 D3
Norfolk Ave. Bris 49 F1
Norfolk Ave. Bris 63 F4
Norfolk Bldgs. Bath 101 F3
Norfolk Cres. Bath 101 F3
Norfolk Gr. Keyn 81 E2
Norfolk Pl. Bris 63 E2
Norfolk Rd. Portis 45 F2
Norland Rd. Bris 62 C4
Norley Rd. Bris 49 F4
Norman Gr. Bris 51 E1
Norman Rd. Bris 50 A1
Norman Rd. Keyn 82 C2
Norman Rd. Sist 66 A4
Normanby Rd. Bris 50 A1
Normans The. Bath 85 F1
Normanton Rd. Bris 49 D1
Norrisville Rd. Bris 49 F1
North Croft. Kingsw 66 B2
North Devon Rd. Bris 51 D3
North Down Cl. Ship 125 F4
North Down La. Ship 125 F4
North East Rd. Thorn 8 B1
North End Rd. Yatt 73 F2
North End. Yatt 74 A1
North Gr. E in G 47 E2
North Green St. Bris 62 C3
North Hills Cl. W-S-M 105 D1
North La. Bath 102 B3
North La. Nail 59 D1
North La. W-S-M 104 C4
North Leaze. Lo Ash 62 A1
North Meadows. P St J 133 F4
North Par. Bath 102 A3
North Par. Yate 27 F1
North Parade Bldgs. Bath . 102 A3
North Parade Pas. Bath 102 A3
North Parade Rd. Bath 102 A3
North Pk. Kingsw 51 F1
North Rd. Ban 107 D2
North Rd. Bath 102 B1
North Rd. Bath 102 B3
North Rd. Bris 49 F1
North Rd. Bris 62 B4
North Rd. Bris 63 D2
North Rd. Ir Act 27 D2
North Rd. Lymp 122 B1
North Rd. Mid No 132 A1
North Rd. St Gif 36 C2
North Rd. Thorn 8 B1
North Rd. Tims 116 A1
North Rd. Wint 37 F4
North Rd. Yate 27 D2
North Side Rd. Wring 94 A4
North St. Bris 63 D2
North St. Bris 63 F4
North St. Kingsw 66 B2
North St. Mang 51 F3
North St. N St P 135 F2
North St. Nail 59 D1
North St. W-S-M 104 C4
North St. Wickw 18 A3
North Stoke La. Bitt 83 D4
North View Cl. Bath 101 D3
North View Dr. Ban 107 D1
North View. Bris 49 D2
North View. Kingsw 51 E2
North View. Mang 51 F3
North View. Rad 133 D1
North Way. Bath 101 D3
North Way. Mid No 132 A1
North Wlk. Yate 27 F1
Northampton Bldgs. Bath .. 101 F4
Northampton House. Wrax .. 60 B2
Northampton St. Bath 101 F4
Northavon Bsns Centre.
Yate 27 E2
Northcote Rd. Bris 48 C1
Northcote Rd. Bris 64 C4
Northcote Rd. Mang 51 F3
Northcote St. Bris 50 A1
Northdown Rd. Paul 132 C3
Northend Ave. Kingsw 51 E1
Northend Gdns. Kingsw 51 E1
Northend Rd. Kingsw 51 F1
Northern Way. Cleve 57 F2
Northfield Ave. Kingsw 65 E3
Northfield Rd. Bris 65 D4
Northfield Rd. Portis 44 C2
Northfield. Mid No 133 D2
Northfield. Tims 116 B2
Northfield. Winsl 120 C4
Northfield. Yate 39 E4
Northfields Cl. Bath 84 C1
Northfields. Bath 84 C1
Northgate St. Bath 102 A3
Northleach Wlk. Bris 47 F3
Northleigh Ave. W-S-M 88 B1
Northmead Ave. Mid No 131 F1
Northmead Cl. Mid No 131 F1
Northmead La. Ir Act 26 B3
Northmead Rd. Mid No 131 F1
Northover Rd. Bris 35 D1
Northridge Bsns Centre.
Yate 27 E1
Northumberland Pl. Bath ... 102 A3
Northumberland Rd. Bris 49 E1
Northumbria Dr. Bris 49 D3
Northville Rd. Bris 36 A1
Northway. Bris 36 A2
Northwick Gdns. Bi Sut 113 E2
Northwick Rd. Bris 49 F4
Northwick Rd. Ch Mag 96 B4
Northwick Rd. Piln 22 B4
Northwick Rd. Whit 96 B4
Northwoods Wlk. Bris 35 E2
Norton Cl. Ch Mag 96 A2
Norton Cl. Kingsw 65 F4
Norton La. Ch Mag 96 B3
Norton La. Hin Cha 135 E4
Norton La. W St L 88 B2
Norton La. Well 135 E4
Norton La. Whit 80 B1
Norton La. Whit 96 B3
Norton Rd. Bris 64 C2
Nortons Wood La. Cleve 58 A3
Norwich Dr. Bris 64 C3
Norwood Ave. Bath 102 C3
Norwood Gr. Portis 44 C3
Notgrove Cl. W-S-M 88 A1
Nottingham Rd. Bris 49 F2
Nottingham St. Bris 63 F2
Nova Scotia Pl. Bris 63 D3
Novers Cres. Bris 79 E4
Novers Hill Trading Est. Bris 63 E1
Novers Hill. Bris 79 E4
Novers La. Bris 79 E4
Novers Park Dr. Bris 79 E4
Novers Park Rd. Bris 79 E4
Novers Rd. Bris 79 E4
Nugent Hill. Bris 49 E1
Nunney Cl. Keyn 82 A1
Nupdown Rd. O-0n-S 1 C3
Nupdown Rd. Rock 2 A2
Nursery Gdns. Bris 35 D2
Nursery The. Bris 63 D2
Nutfield Gr. Bris 36 A1
Nutgrove Ave. Bris 63 F2
Nutgrove La. Ch Mag 96 A2
Nuthatch Dr. Bris 50 C3
Nutwell Rd. W-S-M 88 C1
Nutwell Sq. W-S-M 88 C1
Nye Rd. Winsc 107 F3
Nympsfield. Kingsw 51 F1

Oak Ave. Bath 101 E2
Oak Cl. St Gif 36 B4
Oak Cl. Yate 27 E2
Oak Dr. Portis 45 D2
Oak Gr. E in G 47 E3
Oak La. Bris 50 C1
Oak Rd. Bris 49 F3
Oak Rd. Col 70 C3
Oak Rd. Wins 125 D4
Oak St. Bath 101 F3
Oak Terr. Rad 132 B1
Oak Tree Ave. Puck 53 D2
Oak Tree Cl. Kingsw 65 E2
Oak Tree Wlk. Keyn 81 E2
Oakdale Ave. Mang 51 E4
Oakdale Cl. Mang 51 F4
Oakdale Ct. Mang 51 F4
Oakdale Gdns. W-S-M 88 C1
Oakdale Rd. Bris 80 A4
Oakdale Rd. Mang 51 F4
Oakdene Ave. Bris 50 B2
Oakenhill Wlk. Bris 64 C1
Oakes La. Tor 42 A3
Oakfield Gr. Bris 63 D4
Oakfield Pl. Bris 63 D4
Oakfield Rd. Bath 101 E4
Oakfield Rd. Bris 63 D4
Oakfield Rd. Keyn 81 F1
Oakfield Rd. Kingsw 65 E4
Oakford Ave. W-S-M 104 C4
Oakford La. Marsh 70 A1
Oakhanger Dr. Bris 34 A1
Oakhill Ave. Kingsw 66 B1
Oakhill Cl. Nail 60 A1
Oakhill Rd. Bath 101 F1
Oakhill. Bris 34 B2
Oakhill. W-S-M 105 D1
Oakhurst Rd. Bris 48 C3
Oakland Dr. Lock 105 F2
Oakland Rd. Bris 49 D1
Oakland Rd. Bris 64 C4
Oaklands Cl. Mang 52 A3
Oaklands Dr. Alm 24 A2
Oaklands Dr. Bris 51 D4
Oaklands Dr. Kingsw 66 B1
Oaklands Rd. Mang 52 A3
Oaklands. Clut 114 C1
Oaklands. Paul 131 F2
Oakleaze Rd. Thorn 8 B1
Oakleaze. Fr Cot 38 B4
Oakleigh Ave. Bris 64 B4
Oakleigh Cl. Back 76 A3
Oakleigh Gdns. Kingsw 66 B1
Oakley Rd. Bris 49 F4
Oakley. Bath 102 C3
Oakley. Cleve 73 D4
Oakmead Pk. Bris 64 A1
Oakridge Cl. Kingsw 66 A4
Oakridge Cl. Wins 125 D4
Oakridge La. Wins 125 D4
Oaks The. Win 94 C4
Oaksey Gr. Nail 60 A1
Oaktree Cres. St Gif 24 B1
Oaktree Ct. Bris 47 F4
Oaktree Gdns. Bris 78 C3
Oakwood Ave. Bris 49 D3
Oakwood Rd. Bris 49 D3
Oatlands Ave. Bris 80 A3
Oberon Ave. Bris 50 C1
Oclite Rd. Bath 101 E1
Odins Rd. Bath 101 E1
Okebourne Cl. Bris 35 D2
Okebourne Rd. Bris 35 D2
Old Ashley Hill. Bris 49 F1
Old Aust Rd. Alm 24 B3
Old Banwell Rd. Lock 106 A2
Old Barn La. But 94 A3
Old Barrow Hill. Bris 47 E4
Old Bond St. Bath 101 F3
Old Bread St. Bris 63 F3
Old Bristol Rd. Priddy 128 A2
Old Bristol Rd. W-S-M 89 D1
Old Chelsea La. Wrax 61 E2
Old Church Rd. Axb 125 E1
Old Church Rd. Cleve 57 E2
Old Church Rd. Nail 75 E4
Old Church Rd. W-S-M 104 B1
Old Coach Rd. Co Bi 124 C2
Old Down Rd. Ch Sod 42 B4
Old Down Rd. Gr Bad 30 C1
Old England Way. P St J ... 133 F4
Old Farm La. Bris 65 D3
Old Ferry Rd. Bath 101 E3
Old Fosse Rd. Bath 101 E1
Old Fosse Way. Mid No 132 C3
Old Frome Rd. Bath 118 C4
Old Gloucester Rd. Alve 15 D3
Old Gloucester Rd. Alve 25 E2
Old Gloucester Rd. Bris 37 D1
Old Gloucester Rd. Fr Cot ... 25 E2
Old Gloucester Rd. St Gif 37 D2
Old Gloucester Rd. St Gif 37 D4
Old Gloucester Rd. Thorn 9 D1
Old Gloucester Rd. Wint 37 D4
Old Hill. Win 94 B3
Old Hill. Wring 92 C2
Old King St Ct. Bris 63 F4
Old King St. Bath 101 F4
Old La. Farm 116 A3
Old La. Nail 59 E3
Old Manor Cl. Char 11 D3
Old Market St. Bris 63 F4
Old Midford Rd. Sosto 119 D4
Old Mill Rd. Portis 45 E3
Old Millard's Hill. Mid No ... 132 A2
Old Mills Ind Est. Paul 131 F1
Old Mills La. Paul 131 E2
Old Newbridge Hill. Bath ... 101 D4
Old Orchard St. Bath 102 A3
Old Orchard. Bath 102 A4
Old Park Hill. Bris 63 E4
Old Park Rd. Bris 47 E4
Old Park Rd. Cleve 57 F2
Old Park. Bris 63 E4
Old Pit Terr. Mid No 132 C2
Old Post Office La. W-S-M 104 B4
Old Priory Rd. E in G 47 D2
Old Quarry Rd. Bris 47 F4
Old Quarry Rise. Bris 47 F4
Old Quarry. Bath 101 E1
Old Rd. Rad 133 E1
Old Rectory Rd. Kings 11 F2
Old School La. Blea 122 B3
Old Sneed Ave. Bris 48 B2
Old Sneed Park. Bris 48 B2
Old Sneed Rd. Bris 48 B2
Old St. Cleve 57 F2
Old Station Cl. Wring 92 B1
Old Tarnwell. Pens 97 D1
Old Track. Li St 119 F4
Old Vicarage Green. Keyn .. 81 F3
Old Wall. Blea 121 E3
Old Water Gdns The. Blag 110 C1
Old Wells Rd. Bath 101 F2
Old Weston Rd. Back 77 D4
Old Weston Rd. Cong 91 D3
Oldacre Rd. Bris 80 A2
Oldbridge Rd. Whit 80 B2
Oldbury Chase. Kingsw 66 A1
Oldbury Court Dr. Bris 51 D3
Oldbury Court Rd. Bris 51 D3
Oldbury La. Thorn 8 A2
Oldbury La. Wick 67 E3
Oldfield La. Bath 101 F2
Oldfield Pl. Bris 62 C3
Oldfield Rd. Bath 101 F3
Oldfield Rd. Bris 62 C3
Oldfield Rd. Bris 63 D3
Oldfield. Cleve 57 F1
Oldfields La. Alve 25 E4
Oldlands Ave. Fr Cot 38 B3
Oldmead Wlk. Bris 78 C4
Oldmixon Cres. W-S-M 105 D2
Oldmixon Rd. W-S-M 105 D1
Oldmixon Rd. W-S-M 105 D1
Oldown Hill. Olve 14 B1
Oldville Ave. Cleve 57 E1
Olive Gdns. Alve 14 C2
Olveston Rd. Bris 49 F3
Olympus Cl. St Gif 36 B3
Olympus Rd. Bris 35 E4
Oolite Gr. Bath 118 B4
Oram Ct. Kingsw 65 F2
Orange Gr. Bath 102 A3
Orange St. Bris 63 F4
Orchard Ave. Bris 63 E3
Orchard Ave. Mid No 131 F1
Orchard Ave. Nail 58 C2
Orchard Ave. Thorn 8 B1
Orchard Bvd. Kingsw 66 A2
Orchard Cl. Back 77 D4
Orchard Cl. Ban 107 D2
Orchard Cl. Bi Sut 113 E2
Orchard Cl. Bris 48 C3
Orchard Cl. Char 11 D3
Orchard Cl. Keyn 81 E3
Orchard Cl. Kingsw 65 F4
Orchard Cl. Portis 45 E3
Orchard Cl. W-S-M 88 A2
Orchard Cl. W-S-M 88 C1
Orchard Cl. Westw 120 C2
Orchard Cl. Win 94 B4
Orchard Cl. Wring 92 C1
Orchard Cl. Yate 27 F1
Orchard Cres. Bris 47 E4
Orchard Dr. Aust 13 D4
Orchard Dr. Bris 79 D3
Orchard Dr. Wins 108 A2
Orchard End. E Harp 128 C2
Orchard Gdns. Kingsw 65 F4
Orchard Grange. Thorn 8 A1
Orchard La. Bris 63 E3
Orchard Lea. Alve 15 D3
Orchard Lea. E in G 47 E2
Orchard Pl. W-S-M 104 C4
Orchard Rd. Axb 125 E1
Orchard Rd. Back 76 A3
Orchard Rd. Bris 49 F2
Orchard Rd. Bris 64 C4
Orchard Rd. Cleve 57 E1
Orchard Rd. Fr Cot 38 B4
Orchard Rd. Kingsw 65 F4
Orchard Rd. Lo Ash 61 F1
Orchard Rd. Lock 105 E1
Orchard Rd. Nail 59 E1
Orchard Rd. Paul 131 F3
Orchard Rd. Puck 53 D3
Orchard Rise. Olve 14 A2
Orchard St. Bris 63 E3
Orchard St. W-S-M 104 C4
Orchard Terr. Bath 101 D3
Orchard The. Ban 107 D2
Orchard The. E in G 47 E2
Orchard The. Fr Cot 38 B4
Orchard The. Hi Cha 120 B3
Orchard The. Lock 106 A3
Orchard The. Pens 97 D1
Orchard The. Pens 97 F2
Orchard The. St Gif 36 C3
Orchard The. Tyth 16 A3
Orchard Vale. Kingsw 65 F4
Orchard Vale. Mid No 131 F1
Orchard Wlk. Chur 108 C2
Orchard Wlk. Kings 11 F2
Orchards The. Kingsw 65 F4
Oriel Gdns. Bath 85 E1
Oriel Gr. Bath 101 D2
Orion Dr. St Gif 36 B3
Orland Way. Kingsw 66 A2
Orlebar Gdns. Bris 34 A1
Orme Dr. Cleve 57 E3
Ormerod Rd. Bris 48 C3
Ormonds Cl. St Gif 24 C1
Ormsley Cl. St Gif 36 B4
Orpen Gdns. Bris 50 A3
Orpen Park. St Gif 24 B2
Orpheus Ave. St Gif 36 B3
Orwell Dr. Keyn 81 F2
Orwell St. Bris 63 F2
Osborne Ave. Bris 49 F2
Osborne Ave. W-S-M 104 C4
Osborne Cl. St Gif 36 B2
Osborne Rd. Bath 101 D4
Osborne Rd. Bris 49 D1
Osborne Rd. Bris 63 E2
Osborne Rd. Piln 22 A4
Osborne Rd. W-S-M 104 C4
Osborne Terr. Bris 63 D1
Osborne Villas. Bris 63 E4
Oslings La. Bathf 86 A1
Osprey Ct. Bris 79 E3
Osprey Gdns. W-S-M 88 C1
Osprey Pk. Thorn 8 B2
Osprey Rd. Bris 64 B4
Ottawa Rd. W-S-M 104 C2
Otter Rd. Cleve 57 F1
Otterford Cl. Bris 80 A3
Ottery Cl. Bris 34 A1
Ottrells Mead. St Gif 24 B2
Oval The. Bath 101 E2
Over La. Alm 23 F1
Overdale. Mid No 132 C3
Overdale. Tims 116 C2
Overhill. E in G 47 E2
Overndale Rd. Mang 51 E3
Overnhill Ct. Mang 51 E3
Overnhill Rd. Mang 51 E3
Overnhurst Ct. Mang 51 E3
Overton Rd. Bris 49 F1
Owen Dr. Wrax 61 D2
Owen Gr. Bris 49 D3
Owen St. Bris 64 A4
Owls Head Rd. Kingsw 65 F3
Oxbarton. St Gif 36 C3
Oxen Leaze. St Gif 24 C1
Oxford Pl 102 B1
Oxford Pl. Bris 50 A1
Oxford Pl. Bris 62 C3
Oxford Pl. W-S-M 104 B4
Oxford St. Bris 63 E4
Oxford St. Bris 63 F2
Oxford St. Bris 64 A3
Oxford St. Bris 64 B4
Oxford St. W-S-M 104 B4
Oxhouse La. Win 94 B3
Oxhouse La. Wrax 61 D3
Oxlease. Bris 79 E2
Oxleaze La. Bris 78 C2
Ozleworth. Kingsw 66 A4

Pack Horse La. Sosto 119 D4
Paddock Cl. St Gif 24 B1
Paddock Gdn. Bris 79 F2
Paddock Gdns. Alve 15 D3
Paddock The. Ban 107 D2
Paddock The. Cleve 57 E1
Paddock The. Portis 45 E2
Paddock Woods. Bath 102 B1
Paddocks The. Bath 102 A1
Paddocks The. Chur 108 B2
Paddocks The. Thorn 8 B1
Paddocks The. W-S-M 104 B1
Padfield Cl. Bath 101 D3
Padleigh Hill. Bath 101 D1
Padmore Ct. Bris 64 B4
Padstow Rd. Bris 79 F4
Pagans Hill. Ch Mag 95 E1
Pagans Hill. Ch St 95 E1
Page Rd. Kingsw 51 E2
Page's Ct. Yatt 91 E4
Pages Mead. Avon 47 E4
Painswick Ave. St Gif 36 A4
Painswick Dr. Yate 27 F1
Palace Yd Mews. Bath 101 F3
Palmdale Cl. Kingsw 66 A2
Palmer Row. W-S-M 104 C4
Palmer St. W-S-M 104 C4
Palmers Cl. Kingsw 66 A3
Palmers Leaze. St Gif 37 D4
Palmers Way. Lock 105 E1
Palmerston Rd. Bris 49 E2
Palmerston St. Bris 63 E2
Palmyra Rd. Bris 63 D1
Par The. Bath 101 D3
Parade The. Bris 23 F1
Parade The. Bris 47 F3
Parade The. Ch Sod 28 A1
Paradise Row. Pens 98 A3
Paragon Rd. W-S-M 87 E1
Paragon The. Bris 62 C3
Parfitt's Hill. Bris 64 C3
Park Ave. Bath 101 F3
Park Ave. Bris 50 B2
Park Ave. Bris 63 F2
Park Ave. Bris 64 C4
Park Ave. Fr Cot 38 A4
Park Ave. St Gif 24 A1
Park Ave. Wint 37 F4
Park Ave. Yatt 74 A1
Park Batch. Blag 110 C2
Park Cl. Keyn 81 E3
Park Cl. Kingsw 65 F4
Park Cl. Kingsw 66 A3
Park Cres. Bris 37 E1
Park Cres. Bris 64 B4
Park Cres. Kingsw 66 A3
Park Farm Ct. Kingsw 65 F2
Park Gdns. Bath 101 E4
Park Gr. Bris 49 E3
Park Hill. Bris 47 F3
Park La. Bath 101 E4
Park La. Blag 110 C2
Park La. Bris 63 E4
Park La. Faulk 134 A1
Park La. Fr Cot 38 A3
Park La. N Nib 5 F4
Park Pl. Bath 101 F4
Park Pl. Bris 50 C2
Park Pl. Bris 63 D4
Park Pl. W-S-M 104 B4
Park Rd. Bath 101 D4
Park Rd. Bris 36 A1
Park Rd. Bris 47 F3
Park Rd. Bris 50 B3
Park Rd. Bris 63 D3
Park Rd. Cleve 57 E2
Park Rd. Cong 91 F2
Park Rd. Crom 10 A2
Park Rd. Keyn 81 F2
Park Rd. Kingsw 65 E4
Park Rd. Kingsw 66 A3
Park Rd. Mang 51 F3

Name	Page	Grid
Park Rd. Paul	131	E3
Park Rd. Thorn	8	A1
Park Row. Bris	63	E4
Park Row. Fr Cot	38	A4
Park St Ave. Bris	63	E4
Park St Mews. Bath	101	F4
Park St. Bath	101	F4
Park St. Bris	63	E4
Park St. Bris	64	A2
Park St. Bris	64	C4
Park St. H Up	20	A1
Park St. Ir Act	26	B2
Park The. Bitt	66	A1
Park The. Bris	37	D1
Park The. Keyn	81	F3
Park The. Kingsw	65	F4
Park The. St Gif	24	B2
Park The. Yatt	74	A1
Park View Ave. Thorn	8	B1
Park View Terr. Bris	64	C4
Park View. Kingsw	65	F4
Park View. Paul	131	E3
Park Way. Kingsw	66	A3
Park Way. Mid No	138	A4
Park Wood Cl. Bris	79	F2
Parker St. Bris	63	D2
Parkers Ave. Wick	67	E4
Parkers Barton. Bris	64	A3
Parkers Cl. Bris	35	E2
Parkfield Ave. Bris	64	B4
Parkfield Gdns. Bi Sut	113	E2
Parkfield Rd. Axb	125	E1
Parkfield Rd. Puck	53	D3
Parkhouse La. Keyn	81	E1
Parkhurst Ave. Bris	51	D2
Parkhurst Rd. W-S-M	105	D4
Parkland Way. Thorn	8	B2
Parklands Ave. W-S-M	88	C2
Parklands Rd. Bris	62	C2
Parklands. Kingsw	65	F4
Parklands. Paul	115	E1
Parkside Ave. Wint	37	F3
Parkside Gdns. Bris	50	A2
Parkstone Ave. Bris	49	F3
Parkwall Cres. Kingsw	66	A2
Parkwall Rd. Kingsw	66	A2
Parkway La. Tims	116	B2
Parkway. Tims	116	C1
Parliament St. Bris	64	C2
Parnall Cres. Yate	27	E2
Parnall Rd. Bris	51	D2
Parry Cl. Bath	101	D2
Parry's Cl. Bris	48	C3
Parry's La. Bris	48	C3
Parslow Barton. Bris	65	D4
Parson St. Bris	63	E1
Parsonage Cl. Win	94	C3
Parsonage La. Bath	101	F3
Parsonage La. Ched	125	F1
Parsonage La. Chil	137	E2
Parsonage La. Pens	97	E3
Parsonage La. Win	94	C3
Parsonage Rd. Lo Ash	62	B1
Parsons Ave. St Gif	36	C3
Parsons Gn. Cleve	73	E4
Parsons Green. W-S-M	89	D2
Parsons Mead. Back	76	C4
Parsons Paddock. Bris	80	A4
Parsons Way. Wins	124	B3
Partis College. Bath	101	D4
Partis Way. Bath	101	D4
Partition St. Bris	63	E3
Partridge Cl. W-S-M	88	C1
Partridge Cl. Yate	27	F2
Partridge Rd. Puck	53	E2
Passage Leaze. Bris	47	E3
Passage Rd. Bris	35	D1
Passage Rd. Bris	35	D2
Passage Rd. Bris	35	D3
Passage St. Bris	63	F3
Pastures The. Westw	120	C2
Patch Croft. Cleve	73	E4
Patch Elm La. Wickw	26	C4
Patch La. Wickw	27	D4
Patchway Trading Est. Bris	35	F4
Paul St. Bris	63	E4
Paul's Cswy. Cong	91	E2
Paulman Gdns. Lo Ash	77	F4
Paulmont Rise. Clut	114	C1
Paulto' Hill. Paul	132	A4
Paulton Dr. Bris	49	E2
Paulton La. Tims	132	B4
Paulton Rd. Mid No	131	F1
Paulton Rd. Paul	131	D4
Paulton Rd. Paul	131	E3
Paultow Ave. Bris	63	F2
Paultow Rd. Bris	63	F2
Paulwood Rd. Clut	114	C1
Pavey Cl. Bris	79	E2
Pavey Rd. Bris	79	E2
Pawlett Rd. Bris	79	E2
Pawlett Wlk. Bris	79	E2
Pawlett. W-S-M	105	D1
Paybridge Rd. Bris	78	C2
Payne Dr. Bris	64	A4
Payne Rd. Lock	105	E1
Peach La. Mang	51	F3
Peacock La. Kingsw	65	E4
Pear Tree Hey. Yate	27	F3
Pear Tree Rd. St Gif	24	B2
Pearces Hill. Bris	51	D4
Pearl St. Bris	63	D2
Pearsall Rd. Kingsw	65	F1
Pearse Cl. W-S-M	89	D3
Peart Cl. Bris	78	C3
Peart Dr. Bris	78	C2
Peartree La. Bris	65	D3
Peartree La. Bris	65	D3
Pedder Rd. Cleve	57	E1
Peel St. Bris	63	F4
Pegasus Rd. Bris	35	E4
Pelican Cl. W-S-M	105	F4
Pemberton Ct. Bris	51	E3
Pembery Rd. Bris	63	D2
Pembroke Ave. Bris	47	F3
Pembroke Gr. Bris	63	D4
Pembroke Pl. Bris	63	D3
Pembroke Rd. Bris	47	F3
Pembroke Rd. Bris	63	D4
Pembroke Rd. Bris	63	D4
Pembroke Rd. Kingsw	51	F1
Pembroke Rd. Portis	44	C2
Pembroke Rd. W-S-M	104	C2
Pembroke St. Bris	63	F4
Pembroke Vale. Bris	63	D4
Pen Park Rd. Bris	35	E1
Penard Way. Kingsw	66	A3
Penarth Dr. W-S-M	105	D1
Pendennis Ave. Mang	51	F2
Pendennis Pk. Bris	64	B1
Pendennis Rd. Mang	51	E3
Pendlesham Gdns. W-S-M	88	A1
Pendock Cl. Kingsw	66	B1
Pendock Rd. Bris	35	E1
Pendock Rd. Wint	37	F3
Penfield Rd. Bris	50	A1
Penlea Ct. Bris	47	E4
Penn Gdns. Bath	101	D4
Penn Hill Rd. Bath	84	A1
Penn Lea Rd. Bath	84	A1
Penn Lea Rd. Bath	101	D4
Penn St. Bris	63	F4
Penn Way. Axb	125	E1
Pennard Cl. Bris	80	A3
Pennard Green. Bath	101	D3
Pennard. W-S-M	105	D1
Penngrove. Kingsw	66	A2
Pennine Gdns. W-S-M	88	A1
Pennine Rd. Kingsw	66	B2
Pennlea. Bris	79	E4
Penns The. Cleve	57	F1
Pennycress. W-S-M	105	E4
Pennyquick View. Bath	100	C3
Pennyquick. Cor	100	B3
Pennyroyal Gr. Bris	50	C2
Pennywell Rd. Bris	64	A4
Penpole Ave. Bris	47	F3
Penpole Cl. Bris	47	E4
Penpole La. Bris	47	F4
Penpole Pl. Bris	47	F3
Penrice Cl. W-S-M	88	B1
Penrith Gdns. Bris	49	E4
Penrose. Bris	79	F4
Pensfield Park. Bris	35	E2
Pensford Ct. Bris	80	B3
Pensford Hill. Pens	97	E3
Pensford La. Pens	97	D1
Pensford Old Rd. Pens	97	F2
Pentagon The. Bris	48	A3
Pentire Ave. Bris	79	D4
Pentland Ave. Thorn	15	F4
Peppershells La. Co Dan	98	B3
Pepys Cl. Keyn	82	B1
Pera Pl. Bath	102	A4
Pera Rd. Bath	102	A4
Percival Rd. Bris	62	C4
Percy St. Bris	63	E2
Peregrine Cl. W-S-M	88	C1
Perrin Cl. Clut	130	C4
Perrings The. Nail	75	F4
Perrinpit Rd. Fr Cot	25	F1
Perrott Rd. Kingsw	52	A1
Perry Cl. Wint	37	E3
Perry Rd. Bris	63	E4
Perry St. Bris	64	A4
Perrycroft Ave. Bris	79	D3
Perrycroft Rd. Bris	79	D3
Perrymans Cl. Bris	51	D3
Perrymead. Bath	102	A2
Perrymead. W-S-M	89	D3
Perrys Lea. St Gif	24	B1
Pesley Cl. Bris	79	D2
Peter's Terr. Bris	64	A4
Petercole Dr. Bris	79	D3
Peterside. Clut	130	C4
Peterson Sq. Bris	79	E2
Petersway Gdns. Bris	65	D3
Petherton Cl. Kingsw	65	F4
Petherton Gdns. Bris	80	A4
Petherton Rd. Bris	80	A4
Peto Gr. Westw	120	C2
Pettigrove Gdns. Kingsw	65	F4
Pettigrove Rd. Kingsw	65	F4
Pevensey Wlk. Bris	79	E4
Peverell Cl. Bris	34	C2
Peverell Dr. Bris	34	C2
Philadelphia Ct. Bris	63	F4
Philip St. Bris	63	E2
Philip St. Bris	64	A3
Philippa Cl. Bris	80	A4
Phillips Rd. W-S-M	105	D3
Phillis Hill. Paul	131	F2
Phippen St. Bris	63	F3
Phipps St. Bris	63	D2
Phoenix Gr. Bris	49	E3
Piccadilly Pl. Bath	102	A4
Pickedmoor La. O-on-S	7	E3
Pickwick Rd. Bath	85	D1
Picton La. Bris	49	F1
Picton St. Bris	49	F1
Pier Rd. Portis	45	F4
Pierrepont Pl. Bath	102	A3
Pierrepont St. Bath	102	A3
Pigeon La. Wring	93	F1
Pigott Ave. Bris	79	D2
Pilgrims Way. Avon	47	E4
Pilgrims Way. Ch St	112	B4
Pilgrims Way. Mang	51	E4
Pilgrims Way. W-S-M	88	C2
Pilgrims Wharf. Bris	64	C4
Pilkington Cl. Bris	36	B1
Pill Rd. Ab Lei	47	F1
Pill St. E in G	47	E2
Pill Way. Cleve	57	D1
Pillingers Rd. Kingsw	65	E4
Pilning St. Piln	23	E4
Pimm's La. W-S-M	88	A1
Pinchay La. Win	95	D2
Pinckney Green. Mon Far	103	F3
Pincots La. Wickw	18	A2
Pine Cl. Thorn	8	B1
Pine Cl. W-S-M	88	B1
Pine Ct. Ch Mag	96	A2
Pine Ct. Keyn	81	E2
Pine Ct. Rad	133	D1
Pine Gr. Bris	36	A1
Pine Grove Pl. Bris	49	E2
Pine Hill. W-S-M	88	B1
Pine Lea. Blea	122	A4
Pine Rd. Bris	35	D2
Pine Ridge Cl. Bris	48	B2
Pine Wlk. Rad	132	C1
Pinecroft. Bris	79	F4
Pinecroft. Portis	44	C3
Pines Cl. Chil	137	E2
Pines La. Olve	14	B2
Pines Rd. Kingsw	66	B1
Pines Way. Bath	101	F3
Pines Way. Rad	133	D1
Pinewood Ave. Mid No	131	F1
Pinewood Cl. Bris	49	D4
Pinewood Gr. Mid No	131	F1
Pinewood Rd. Mid No	131	F1
Pinewood Way. Col	70	C4
Pinewood. Kingsw	51	F1
Pinhay Rd. Bris	79	D3
Pinkhams Twist. Bris	80	A3
Pioneer Ave. Bath	101	F1
Pipe La. Bris	63	E3
Pipe La. Bris	63	F3
Pipehouse La. Hi Cha	120	A2
Pipehouse La. Hin Cha	119	F2
Piper Rd. Yate	27	F2
Pippin Cl. P St J	133	E4
Pippin Cl. Kingsw	65	F2
Pit La. Back	76	A2
Pit La. Win	111	F3
Pit Rd. Mid No	132	A1
Pitch And Pay La. Bris	48	C2
Pitch And Pay Park. Bris	48	C2
Pitch La. Bris	49	E1
Pitchcombe Gdns. Bris	48	B4
Pitchcombe. Yate	39	E4
Pitcot La. Hol	138	A1
Pithay Ct. Bris	63	E4
Pithay The. Bris	63	E4
Pithay The. Paul	131	F3
Pitman Ct. Bath	85	E1
Pitman Rd. W-S-M	104	C3
Pitt Rd. Bris	49	F3
Pittville Cl. Thorn	8	B2
Pitville Pl. Bris	49	D1
Pitway Cl. Paul	130	C2
Pitway La. Paul	130	B2
Pixash Bsns Centre. Keyn	82	A3
Pixash La. Keyn	82	A3
Pizey Ave. Cleve	57	D1
Pizey Cl. Cleve	57	D1
Plain The. N St P	135	F2
Plain The. Thorn	8	A1
Players Cl. St Gif	37	D2
Playford Gdns. Bris	47	F4
Pleasant Pl. Bathf	86	B1
Pleasant Rd. Mang	51	E3
Pleshey Cl. W-S-M	88	B1
Ploughed Paddock. Nail	59	E1
Plover Cl. W-S-M	88	C1
Plover Cl. Yate	27	E1
Plovers Rise. Mid No	133	D2
Plumbers Hill. Bris	64	C4
Plumers Cl. Cleve	57	F1
Plumpton Ct. Mang	37	F1
Plumptre Cl. Paul	131	F3
Plumptre Rd. Paul	131	F3
Plumtree Cl. Wins	108	A1
Plunder St. Brock	92	A4
Podium The. Bath	102	A3
Poets Cnr. Rad	132	B1
Poets' Cl. Bris	64	B4
Polden Cl. Nail	59	F1
Polden Rd. Kingsw	51	F2
Polden Rd. W-S-M	104	C4
Police Station Hill. Puck	53	D2
Polly Barnes Cl. Kingsw	65	D3
Polly Barnes Hill. Kingsw	65	D3
Polygon Rd. Bris	63	D3
Polygon The. Bris	62	C3
Pomfret Gdns. Bris	80	C3
Pomfrett Gdns. Bris	80	C3
Pomphrey Hill. Mang	52	A2
Ponsford Rd. Bris	80	A4
Ponting Cl. Bris	51	D1
Pool La. Win	95	D1
Pool Rd. Kingsw	51	F2
Poole Court Dr. Yate	27	F1
Poole St. Avon	47	D4
Poolemead Rd. Bath	100	C3
Poor Hill. Farm	115	F3
Pope's Wlk. Bath	102	A2
Poplar Ave. Bris	48	B3
Poplar Cl. Bath	101	E2
Poplar Cl. Kingsw	66	B3
Poplar Dr. Puck	53	D3
Poplar La. Wickw	18	A2
Poplar Pl. Bris	51	D2
Poplar Pl. W-S-M	104	C1
Poplar Rd. Bris	50	C1
Poplar Rd. Bris	65	D3
Poplar Rd. Bris	78	C4
Poplar Rd. Kingsw	66	B3
Poplar Way. Col	70	C3
Poplar Wlk. Lock	105	F3
Poplars The. E in G	47	D2
Poplars The. W-S-M	89	D1
Pople's La. Kilm	139	F1
Popular Terr. Kingsw	65	F4
Porlock Cl. Cleve	57	F1
Porlock Cl. W-S-M	104	C1
Porlock Gdns. Nail	59	F1
Porlock Rd. Bath	102	A1
Porlock Rd. Bris	63	E2
Port Elizabeth House. Bris	35	D1
Port View. E in G	47	E3
Portbury Comm. Portis	45	F2
Portbury Gr. Bris	47	E3
Portbury Hundred The. Portb	46	B2
Portbury La. Wrax	60	C3
Portbury Way. Portb	46	C3
Portbury Wlk. Bris	47	E3
Portishead Rd. W-S-M	89	D2
Portishead Way. Bris	62	C2
Portland Cl. Nail	59	E1
Portland Ct. Bris	63	D3
Portland Dr. Portis	45	F2
Portland Pl. Bath	101	F4
Portland Pl. Bris	63	D4
Portland Sq. Bris	63	F4
Portland St. Bris	62	C4
Portland St. Bris	63	E4
Portland St. Kingsw	51	E2
Portmeade Dro. Axb	125	E1
Portmeirion Cl. Bris	80	A3
Portview Rd. Avon	47	D4
Portwall La E. Bris	63	F3
Portwall La. Bris	63	F3
Portway La. Ch Sod	29	D1
Portway. Bris	48	B2
Post Office La. Back	76	C4
Post Office La. Blag	110	B2
Poston Way. Winsl	120	C4
Pottery Cl. W-S-M	105	D3
Potts Cl. Bathe	85	F2
Pound Dr. Bris	50	C3
Pound La. Bris	50	C2
Pound La. Nail	59	E2
Pound Mead. Win	94	B4
Pound Rd. Kingsw	51	F1
Pound The. Alm	24	A3
Pound The. O-on-S	7	D3
Pound The. Wring	93	E2
Pountney Dr. Bris	64	A4
Powell Cl. Bris	44	A2
Pow's Hill. Paul	132	B3
Pow's Orch. Mid No	132	A1
Pow's Rd. Kingsw	65	E4
Powis Cl. W-S-M	88	B1
Powlett Rd. Bath	102	A4
Poyntz Ct. Kingsw	65	F2
Poyntz Rd. Bris	79	F4
Pratten's La. Mang	51	E2
Preanes Green. W-S-M	89	D1
Preddy's La. Bris	65	D3
Prescot Cl. W-S-M	88	A1
Prescott. Yate	39	E4
Press Moor Dr. Kingsw	65	F2
Prestbury. Yate	39	E4
Preston Wlk. Bris	64	A1
Prestwick Cl. Bris	64	B1
Pretoria Rd. Bris	35	F4
Prewett St. Bris	63	F3
Priddy Cl. Bath	101	D3
Priddy Ct. Bris	80	A3
Priddy Dr Bris	80	A3
Priests Way. W-S-M	88	B1
Priestwood Cl. Bris	35	D2
Primrose Cl. Bris	65	E4
Primrose Cl. St Gif	24	B1
Primrose Dr. Thorn	8	B1
Primrose Hill. Bath	84	B1
Primrose La. Bris	51	E1
Primrose La. Mid No	132	A1
Primrose Terr. Bris	51	E1
Prince St. Bris	63	E3
Prince's Pl. Bris	49	F2
Prince's Rd. Cleve	57	E2
Prince's St. Bris	63	F4
Prince's St. Mid No	132	C3
Princes Ct. Kingsw	65	F2
Princes St. Bath	101	F3
Princes' La. Bris	62	C3
Princess Cl. Keyn	81	F2
Princess Gdns. Bris	50	B3
Princess Row. Bris	63	E4
Princess St. Bris	63	F2
Princess St. Bris	64	A1
Princess Victoria St. Bris	62	C2
Priors Hill. Tims	116	A1
Priors Lea. Yate	27	F1
Priory Ave. Bris	49	D4
Priory Cl. Bath	102	A1
Priory Cl. Mid No	132	A1
Priory Court Rd. Bris	49	D4
Priory Ct. Kingsw	65	F4
Priory Dene. Bris	49	D4
Priory Gdns. Bris	47	E4
Priory Gdns. Bris	49	F4
Priory Gdns. E in G	47	D2
Priory Park Rd. Bath	102	A3
Priory Rd. Bris	47	E3
Priory Rd. Bris	49	D4
Priory Rd. Bris	64	A1
Priory Rd. E in G	47	D2
Priory Rd. Keyn	81	F4
Priory Rd. Portb	46	B2
Priory Rd. W-S-M	105	D4
Priory Wlk. Portb	46	B2
Priston Cl. W-S-M	89	D3
Priston La. Pris	117	D3
Priston Rd. Engl	117	E3
Priston Rd. Pris	117	E3
Pritchard St. Bris	63	F4
Probyn Cl. Bris	51	D4
Proctor Cl. Bris	64	B1
Prospect Ave. Bris	51	D1
Prospect Cl. Alm	22	C1
Prospect Cl. Alm	23	D1
Prospect Cl. Fr Cot	37	F4
Prospect Cl. Wint	37	F2
Prospect Cres. Kingsw	51	F1
Prospect Gdns. Bathe	85	F3
Prospect La. Fr Cot	37	F4
Prospect Pl. Bath	84	B1
Prospect Pl. Bathf	86	B1
Prospect Pl. Bris	63	E2
Prospect Pl. Bris	64	B4
Prospect Pl. W-S-M	104	C4
Prospect Rd. Bath	102	B2
Prospect Rd. Piln	22	A3
Providence La. Lo Ash	61	F1
Providence Pl. Bris	63	F3
Providence St. Bris	63	E2
Prowse's La. Axb	125	D1
Prudham St. Bris	50	B1
Publow La. Pens	97	F3
Pucklechurch Trading Est. Puck	53	D3
Pudding Pie Cl. Chur	109	D3
Pudding Pie La. Chur	109	D3
Puffin Cl. W-S-M	105	F4
Pullen's Green. Thorn	8	A1
Pullin Ct. Kingsw	65	F2
Pulteney Ave. Bath	102	A3
Pulteney Bridge. Bath	102	A3
Pulteney Gdns. Bath	102	A3
Pulteney Gr. Bath	102	A3
Pulteney Mews. Bath	102	A4
Pulteney Rd. Bath	102	A3
Pump La. Bathf	86	A1
Pump La. Bris	63	F3
Pump La. Olve	14	B2
Pump La. Wring	93	E1
Pump Sq. E in G	47	E3
Purcell Wlk. Bris	79	E4
Purdey Rd. Bris	50	C2
Purdue Cl. W-S-M	89	D2
Purn La. W-S-M	122	A4
Purn Rd. W-S-M	121	F4
Purn Way. Blea	122	A4
Purplewert Dr. Bath	84	B1
Pursey Dr. St Gif	37	D2
Purton Cl. Kingsw	65	F3
Purton Rd. Bris	49	E1
Purving Row La. Lymp	122	B1
Purving Row. Lymp	122	B1
Puttingthorpe Dr. W-S-M	105	E4
Puxley Cl. Bris	80	C3
Puxton La. Ban	90	B1
Puxton La. Pux	90	B2
Puxton Rd. Ban	90	B1
Puxton Rd. Pux	90	B1

Pye Cnr. Chur 108 B2
Pye Croft. St Gif 24 C2
Pyecroft Ave. Bris 49 E4
Pylewell La. Ship 108 B1
Pylle Hill Cres. Bris 63 F2
Pyne Point. Cleve 57 E2
Pynne Cl. Bris 80 C3
Pynne Rd. Bris 80 C3
Pyracantha Wlk. Bris 80 A3

Quadrangle The. West 39 E2
Quadrant E. Bris 51 E2
Quadrant The. Bris 49 D2
Quadrant The. St Gif 24 A2
Quadrant W. Bris 51 E2
Quadrant. St Gif 24 A2
Quaker La. Thorn 8 A1
Quantock Cl. Kingsw 66 B3
Quantock Rd. Bris 83 E2
Quantock Rd. Portis 45 D3
Quantock Rd. W-S-M 104 C3
Quantocks. Bath 102 A1
Quarries The. Alm 24 B3
Quarrington Rd. Bris 49 F3
Quarry Barton. Wint 37 E2
Quarry Cl. Bath 101 F1
Quarry Hay. Ch St 112 B4
Quarry Head. Alve 14 C3
Quarry Rd. Alve 14 C3
Quarry La. Wint 37 F2
Quarry Rd. Bath 102 B3
Quarry Rd. Bris 51 E4
Quarry Rd. Ch Sod 28 A1
Quarry Rd. Kingsw 65 E3
Quarry Rd. Wins 108 A1
Quarry Stps. Bris 49 D1
Quarry Way. Bris 50 C3
Quarry Way. Nail 59 E1
Quay St. Bris 63 E4
Quayside. Bris 64 C3
Quedgeley. Yate 39 E4
Queen Ann Rd. Bris 64 A3
Queen Charlotte St. Bris 63 E3
Queen Charlton La. Co Dan ... 80 C1
Queen Charlton La. Whit 80 C1
Queen Sq Ave. Bris 63 E3
Queen Sq. Bath 101 F4
Queen Sq. Bath 101 F4
Queen Sq. Bris 63 E3
Queen Sq. Keyn 82 C2
Queen St. Avon 33 D1
Queen St. Bath 101 F3
Queen St. Bris 50 B2
Queen St. Bris 63 F4
Queen St. Bris 65 D4
Queen Victoria Rd. Bris 49 D2
Queen Victoria St. Bris 64 A3
Queen's Ave. Bris 63 D4
Queen's Ave. Portis 45 E3
Queen's Dr. Bath 102 A1
Queen's Dr. Bris 49 E3
Queen's Par Pl. Bath 101 F4
Queen's Par. Bris 63 E3
Queen's Rd. Bris 49 F3
Queen's Rd. Bris 63 D4
Queen's Rd. Bris 64 C4
Queen's Rd. Bris 78 C3
Queen's Rd. Cleve 57 E2
Queen's Rd. Kingsw 66 A2
Queen's Rd. Nail 59 E1
Queen's Rd. Portis 44 C2
Queen's Rd. Puck 53 D3
Queen's Rd. Rad 133 D1
Queen's Rd. W-S-M 87 E1
Queen's Way. Portis 44 C2
Queen's Way. W-S-M 89 D2
Queens Down Gdns. Bris 64 B2
Queens Dr. Kingsw 65 D2
Queens Par. Bath 101 F4
Queens Rd. Ban 107 D2
Queens Rd. Bris 64 B1
Queens Rd. Keyn 81 E2
Queens Wlk. Thorn 8 A2
Queensdale Cres. Bris 64 A1
Queenshill Rd. Bris 64 A1
Queensholm Ave. Mang 37 F1
Queensholm Cl. Mang 37 F1
Queensholm Dr. Mang 37 F1
Queensway. St Gif 36 B3
Queenwood Ave. Bath 85 D1
Quickthorn Cl. Bris 80 A3
Quiet St. Bath 101 F3
Quilter Gr. Bris 79 E4

Raby Mews. Bath 102 A4
Rackfield Pl. Bath 101 D3
Rackham Cl. Bris 50 A3
Rackhay. Bris 63 E3
Rackley La. Co Bi 124 A1
Rackvernal Rd. Mid No 132 A1
Radford Hill. Paul 132 B4
Radford Hill. Tims 116 B1
Radnor Rd. Bris 51 D2
Radnor Rd. Bris 49 D3
Radnor Rd. Bris 49 F3

Radstock Rd. Mid No 132 B1
Raeburn Rd. Bris 65 D3
Rag Hill. P St J 133 E3
Rag La. Wickw 17 E3
Raglan Cl. Chil 137 E2
Raglan La. Bris 65 D4
Raglan La. Win 94 C4
Raglan Pl. Bris 49 E2
Raglan Pl. Thorn 15 D4
Raglan Pl. W-S-M 87 E1
Raglan Rd. Bris 49 E2
Raglan Wlk. Keyn 81 E2
Ragland St. Bath 85 D1
Railton Jones Cl. St Gif 36 C2
Railway Pl. Bath 102 A3
Railway St. Bath 102 A3
Railway Terr. Bris 51 E2
Railway View Pl. Mid No 132 A1
Rainham Ct. W-S-M 87 E1
Rains Batch. Priddy 126 C3
Raleigh Cl. Keyn 82 B1
Raleigh Rd. Bris 63 D2
Raleigh Rise. Portis 45 D3
Ralph Allen Dr. Bath 102 B2
Ralph Rd. Bris 49 F2
Ram Hill. West 38 B2
Ramscombe La. Bathe 85 F3
Ramsey Cl. W-S-M 88 C2
Ramsey Rd. Bris 49 F4
Ranchways. Portis 44 C2
Randall Cl. Kingsw 51 F1
Randall Rd. Bris 63 D3
Randolph Ave. Bris 79 D3
Randolph Ave. Yate 27 E3
Randolph Cl. Bris 79 D3
Rangers Wlk. Kingsw 65 E2
Rankers La. Co Dan 98 B3
Rannoch Rd. Bris 35 F1
Ransome Ave. W-S-M 88 B1
Ransford. Cleve 57 D1
Raphael Ct. Bris 63 F3
Ratcliffe Dr. St Gif 36 C3
Rathbone Cl. Fr Cot 38 B3
Raven Cl. W-S-M 88 C1
Ravendale Dr. Kingsw 66 A1
Ravenglass Cres. Bris 35 E1
Ravenhead Dr. Bris 80 A4
Ravenhill Ave. Bris 63 F1
Ravenhill Rd. Bris 63 F2
Ravens Wood. Kingsw 66 A2
Ravenscourt Rd. Bris 36 A4
Ravenswood Rd. Bris 49 E1
Rawlins Ave. W-S-M 89 D3
Rayens Cl. Lo Ash 61 F1
Rayens Cross Rd. Lo Ash 61 F1
Rayleigh Rd. Bris 48 C4
Raymend Rd. Bris 63 F1
Raymend Wlk. Bris 63 F1
Raymill. Bris 65 D1
Raymore Rise. Lo Ash 61 F1
Raynes Rd. Bris 63 D2
Reach Hill. Ch St 112 B3
Rector's Way. W-S-M 104 C3
Rectory Cl. Farm 116 A3
Rectory Cl. Yate 27 F2
Rectory Dr. Yatt 91 E4
Rectory La. Bris 36 A2
Rectory La. Co Mar 128 A3
Rectory La. Crom 17 D4
Rectory La. Tims 116 B1
Rectory Rd. E in G 47 D2
Rectory Rd. Fr Cot 38 A4
Rectory Way. Lymp 121 F1
Rectory Way. Yatt 91 E4
Red Hill. Tims 116 C1
Red Hill. Wring 93 E1
Red House La. Alm 24 A2
Red House La. Bris 48 C3
Red Rd. Berr 121 D1
Redacre. Wring 93 E2
Redcatch Rd. Bris 63 F1
Redcliff Backs. Bris 63 F3
Redcliff Hill. Bris 63 F3
Redcliff Mead La. Bris 63 F3
Redcliff St. Bris 63 F3
Redcliffe Cl. Portis 44 C2
Redcliffe Par E. Bris 63 F3
Redcliffe Par W. Bris 63 E3
Redcliffe Way. Bris 63 F3
Redcroft. Wring 93 E2
Redcross La. Bris 63 F4
Redcross St. Bris 63 F4
Redding Pit La. Win 94 C2
Reddings The. Co Mar 128 A4
Reddings The. Kingsw 51 F1
Redfield Gr. Mid No 138 A4
Redfield Hill. Bitt 66 C2
Redfield Rd. Bris 36 A4
Redfield Rd. Mid No 132 A1
Redford Cres. Bris 78 C2
Redford Wlk. Bris 78 C2
Redham La. Piln 23 D4
Redhill Cl. Bris 50 C2
Redhill Dr. Bris 50 C2
Redhill La. Aust 13 D4
Redland Ave. E in G 46 C3

Redland Court Rd. Bris 49 E1
Redland Gr. Bris 49 E1
Redland Green Rd. Bris 49 E2
Redland Hill. Bris 49 D1
Redland Park. Bath 100 C3
Redland Park. Bris 49 D1
Redland Rd. Bris 49 D1
Redland Terr. Bris 49 D1
Redlands Terr. Mid No 137 F4
Redlynch La. Co Dan 81 E1
Redshard La. Chur 109 D4
Redshelf Wlk. Bris 35 E2
Redwick Cl. Bris 34 B1
Redwick Gdns. Piln 22 B4
Redwick Rd. Piln 22 B4
Redwing Dr. W-S-M 88 C1
Redwood Cl. Kingsw 66 A2
Redwood Cl. Nail 60 A1
Redwood Cl. Rod 138 C4
Redwood La. Lo Ash 77 E4
Redwoods The. Keyn 81 E3
Reed Ct. Kingsw 65 F2
Reed's Row. Hill 19 E4
Reedley Rd. Bris 48 C3
Reedling Cl. Bris 50 C3
Regency Dr. Bris 65 D1
Regent Rd. Bris 63 E2
Regent St. Kingsw 65 E4
Regent St. W-S-M 104 B4
Regents Cl. Thorn 8 A1
Regents St. Bris 63 D4
Regil La. Win 94 C2
Regil La. Win 95 D3
Remenham Dr. Bris 49 D3
Remenham Park. Bris 49 D3
Rendcomb Cl. W-S-M 88 A1
Rene Rd. Bris 64 A1
Repton Rd. Bris 64 B2
Retort Rd. Avon 33 E2
Retreat The. Faulk 133 F2
Reubens Ct. W-S-M 88 C2
Reynold's Wlk. Bris 50 A4
Reynolds Cl. Keyn 82 A3
Rhode Cl. Keyn 82 A2
Rhodyate Hill. Cong 91 F3
Rhodyate La. Brock 92 A4
Rhodyate The. Ban 107 E1
Rhodyate. Blag 110 B1
Rhyne Terr. W-S-M 104 B3
Ribblesdale. Thorn 15 E4
Richards Cl. W-S-M 89 D2
Richeson Cl. Bris 34 C1
Richeson Wlk. Bris 34 C1
Richmond Ave. Bris 49 F1
Richmond Ave. St Gif 36 C3
Richmond Cl. Bath 84 C1
Richmond Cl. Keyn 81 E2
Richmond Cl. Portis 45 F3
Richmond Dale. Bris 49 D1
Richmond Green. Nail 59 F1
Richmond Hill Ave. Bris 63 D4
Richmond Hill. Bath 84 C1
Richmond Hill. Bris 63 D4
Richmond Hts. Bath 84 C1
Richmond La. Bath 84 C1
Richmond La. Bris 63 D4
Richmond Park Rd. Bris 63 D4
Richmond Pl. Bath 84 C1
Richmond Rd. Bath 84 C1
Richmond Rd. Bris 49 F1
Richmond Rd. Bris 64 C4
Richmond Rd. Mang 52 A3
Richmond St. Bris 63 F2
Richmond St. W-S-M 104 B4
Richmond Terr. Avon 33 D1
Richmond Terr. Bris 63 D4
Ricketts La. W-S-M 89 D1
Rickford La. Blag 110 A2
Rickford Rd. Nail 59 F1
Rickford Rise. Blag 110 A2
Rickyard Rd. Wring 92 C1
Ride The. Kingsw 52 A1
Ridge Cl. Portis 45 D2
Ridge Cres. E Harp 128 C3
Ridge La. E Harp 128 B3
Ridge The. Bris 47 F4
Ridge The. Fr Cot 38 B4
Ridge The. Yatt 91 D4
Ridge View. Lo Ash 62 A1
Ridgehill. Bris 49 E3
Ridgemeade. Bris 80 A2
Ridgeway Ave. W-S-M 104 C3
Ridgeway Cl. E Harp 128 C3
Ridgeway Ct. Bris 35 D1
Ridgeway Gdns. Bris 80 B3
Ridgeway La. Bris 80 B3
Ridgeway Par. Bris 50 C2
Ridgeway Rd. Bris 50 C2
Ridgeway Rd. Lo Ash 62 A1
Ridgeway The. Bris 35 D1
Ridgeway The. W-S-M 88 A1
Ridgeway. Fr Cot 38 B4
Ridgeway. Nail 59 E1
Ridgeway. Yate 27 F1
Riding Barn Hill. Wick 67 D3
Ridingleaze. Bris 34 A1
Ridings Cl. Ch Sod 28 A1

Ridings Rd. Fr Cot 38 B3
Ridings The. Bris 78 C2
Ridings The. Fr Cot 38 B3
Ringspit La. Pens 97 F4
Ringswell Gdns. Bath 85 E1
Ringwell La. N St P 135 F2
Ringwell. N St P 135 F2
Ringwood Cres. Bris 35 E1
Ringwood Gr. W-S-M 88 A1
Ringwood Rd. Bath 101 E3
Ripley Rd. Bris 51 D1
Ripon Ct. Mang 37 F1
Ripon Rd. Bris 64 C3
Ripple The. Nail 59 E2
Rippleside Rd. Cleve 57 F3
Rippleside. Portis 45 E3
Risdale Rd. Bris 62 C1
Risedale Rd. Wins 125 D4
Rivendell. W-S-M 89 D2
River Rd. Ch Sod 28 A1
River Rd. E in G 46 C4
River St. Bris 63 F4
River Terr. Keyn 81 F3
River View. Bris 50 C3
Riverland Dr. Bris 78 C3
Riverleaze. Bris 48 A3
Riverleaze. Portis 44 C3
Rivers Rd. Bath 85 D1
Rivers St Mews. Bath 101 F4
Rivers St. Bath 101 F4
Riverside Bsns Park. Bris 64 B3
Riverside Cl. Bris 47 F3
Riverside Cl. Cleve 57 D1
Riverside Cl. Mid No 137 F4
Riverside Cotts. Keyn 65 D1
Riverside Ct. Bath 101 F3
Riverside Ct. Bris 64 C3
Riverside Gdns. Mid No 137 F4
Riverside Mews. Bris 64 C3
Riverside Rd. Bath 101 F3
Riverside Rd. Mid No 137 F4
Riverside Way. Kingsw 65 E2
Riverside Wlk. Mid No 137 F4
Riverside. Ban 107 D3
Riverway. Nail 59 F2
Riverwood Rd. Bris 37 E1
Riviera Cres. Kingsw 51 F2
Roach's La. Gr Bad 30 B1
Road Hill. Col 70 B1
Road Two. Avon 22 A2
Roath Rd. Portis 45 E3
Robbins Cl. Marsh 69 F4
Robbins Cl. St Gif 36 C3
Robel Ave. Fr Cot 37 F4
Robert St. Bris 50 A1
Robert St. Bris 64 A4
Robertson Rd. Bris 50 B1
Robin Cl. Rod 138 A4
Robin Cl. W-S-M 105 F4
Robin Dr. Lock 105 F1
Robin La. Cleve 57 E3
Robin Way. Ch Sod 40 A4
Robinson Cl. Back 76 A3
Robinia Wlk. Bris 80 A4
Robinson Way. Back 76 A3
Rochester Cl. W-S-M 105 D1
Rochester Rd. Bris 64 C3
Rock Ave. Nail 59 E1
Rock Cl. Bris 64 C1
Rock Hall La. Bath 102 A1
Rock La. Bath 102 A1
Rock La. St Gif 36 C3
Rock Rd. Chil 137 E1
Rock Rd. Mid No 132 A1
Rock Rd. Wick 67 E4
Rock Rd. Yatt 91 E4
Rock St. Thorn 15 D4
Rock The. Bris 64 C2
Rockhall Est. Keyn 81 F2
Rockingham Gr. W-S-M 88 A1
Rockland Gr. Bris 50 B3
Rockland Rd. Mang 51 E4
Rockleaze Ave. Bris 48 C2
Rockleaze Rd. Bris 48 C2
Rockliffe Ave. Bath 102 A4
Rockliffe Rd. Bath 102 A4
Rocks La. Ba Gu 77 F1
Rocks La. Win 77 F1
Rockside Ave. Mang 51 F4
Rockside Dr. Bris 49 E3
Rockside Gdns. Fr Cot 38 B4
Rockside Gdns. Mang 51 F4
Rockstowes Way. Bris 35 E2
Rockwell Ave. Bris 34 A1
Rodborough Way. Kingsw 66 A4
Rodborough. Yate 39 E4
Rodbourne Rd. Bris 49 F3
Rode Hill. Rode 136 C1
Rodford Way. Yate 39 E4
Rodfords Mead. Bris 80 A3
Rodmead Wlk. Bris 79 D2
Rodmoor Rd. Portis 45 E3
Rodney Ave. Bris 65 D4
Rodney Cres. Bris 36 A2
Rodney Pl. Bris 63 D3
Rodney Rd. Back 76 A2
Rodney Rd. Bris 65 D4

Rodney Rd. Keyn 82 C1
Rodney Wlk. Bris 51 D1
Rodney. W-S-M 105 D1
Rodway Hill Rd. Kingsw 52 A2
Rodway Hill. Sist 52 A2
Rodway Rd. Bris 36 A4
Rodway Rd. Mang 52 A3
Rodway View. Kingsw 51 F2
Roebuck Cl. W-S-M 89 D2
Roegate Dr. Bris 64 C3
Rogers Cl. Clut 114 C2
Rogers Cl. Kingsw 66 A3
Rokeby Ave. Bris 49 E1
Roman Rd. Bris 64 A4
Roman Rd. Winsc 107 F2
Roman Way. Bris 48 B2
Roman Way. Paul 131 E3
Roman Wlk. Bris 64 B2
Roman Wlk. St Gif 36 C3
Romney Ave. Bris 50 A3
Ronald Rd. Bris 50 C3
Ronayne Wlk. Bris 51 E3
Rook Rd. Keyn 81 F3
Rookery Cl. W-S-M 88 C2
Rookery La. Doyn 53 F2
Rookery La. Piln 23 D3
Rookery Rd. Bris 64 A2
Rookery Way. Bris 79 F2
Rooksbridge Wlk. Bath 101 D3
Roper's La. Wring 92 C2
Rose Acre. Bris 35 D2
Rose Cl. Wint 37 F2
Rose Gdns. W-S-M 89 D2
Rose Green Cl. Bris 50 C1
Rose Green Rd. Bris 50 C1
Rose Hill. Bath 85 E2
Rose La. Fr Cot 38 B3
Rose Mead. Bris 50 A4
Rose Meare Gdns. Bris 78 C4
Rose Oak La. Fr Cot 38 B4
Rose Rd. Bris 64 C4
Rose St. Bris 63 F3
Rose Wlk. Bris 51 E2
Rosebay Mead. Bris 50 C2
Roseberry Pk. Bris 64 B4
Roseberry Rd. Bath 101 E3
Roseberry Rd. Bris 64 B4
Rosebery Ave. Bris 50 A1
Rosedale Ave. W-S-M 105 D4
Rosedale Rd. Bris 51 E2
Roselarge Gdns. Bris 35 D1
Rosemary La. Bris 50 B1
Rosemary La. Hi Cha 120 A2
Rosemont Terr. Bris 63 D3
Rosemount La. Bath 102 A2
Rosery Cl. Bris 49 D4
Rosery The. Bris 51 E2
Rosevear. Bris 64 A4
Roseville Ave. Kingsw 66 A1
Rosewarn Cl. Bath 101 D2
Rosewell Ct. Bath 101 F4
Rosewood Gdns. Alve 14 C3
Rosling Rd. Bris 49 F3
Roslyn Ave. W-S-M 88 B1
Roslyn Rd. Bris 49 E1
Rossall Ave. St Gif 36 B3
Rossall Rd. Bris 64 B2
Rossendale Cl. W-S-M 88 C2
Rossiter Rd. Bath 102 A3
Rossiter's La. Bris 65 D3
Rosslyn Rd. Bath 101 D4
Rosslyn Way. Thorn 8 B2
Rotcombe La. Paul 115 E1
Rotcombe Vale. Paul 115 E1
Rounceval St. Ch Sod 28 A1
Roundhill Gr. Bath 101 D2
Roundhill Park. Bath 101 D2
Roundmoor Cl. Keyn 82 B2
Roundmoor Gdns. Bris 80 B4
Roundways. Fr Cot 38 B3
Rousham Rd. Bris 50 A2
Row La. Faulk 135 E1
Row Of Ashes La. But 94 A2
Row Of Ashes La. Wring 93 F2
Row The. Aust 13 D4
Rowacres. Bath 101 D2
Rowacres. Bris 79 F3
Rowan Cl. Bris 51 D1
Rowan Cl. Nail 60 A1
Rowan Ct. Rad 132 C1
Rowan Way. Chur 109 D3
Rowan Way. Kingsw 65 D2
Rowan Wlk. Keyn 81 E2
Rowans The. Bris 37 D1
Rowans The. Portis 45 E2
Rowberrow La. Ship 108 C1
Rowberrow La. Ship 125 F4
Rowberrow Way. Nail 59 F1
Rowberrow. Bris 79 F4
Rowland Ave. Bris 50 B2
Rowlands Cl. Bathf 86 A1
Rowlandson Gdns. Bris 50 A3
Rowley St. Bris 63 E2
Rownham Cl. Bris 62 C2
Rownham Ct. Bris 63 D3
Rownham Hill. Lo Ash 62 C3
Rownham Mead. Bris 63 D3
Rows The. W-S-M 88 C1

Roy King Gdns. Kingsw 66 B3
Royal Albert Rd. Bris 49 D2
Royal Ave. Bath 101 F4
Royal Cl. Bris 34 B2
Royal Cres. Bath 101 F4
Royal Cres. W-S-M 104 B4
Royal Fort Rd. Bris 63 E4
Royal Park. Bris 63 D4
Royal Portbury Dock Rd.
  E in G 46 C3
Royal Prom. Bris 63 D4
Royal York Cres. Bris 62 C3
Royal York Cres. Bris 63 D3
Royate Hill. Bris 50 B1
Roycroft Rd. Bris 36 A1
Royston Wlk. Bris 35 E1
Rozel Rd. Bris 49 F3
Rubens Cl. Keyn 82 A3
Ruby St. Bris 63 D2
Ruddymead. Cleve 57 E1
Rudford Cl. St Gif 24 A1
Rudgeway Park. Alve 14 C1
Rudgeway Rd. Paul 131 F2
Rudgewood Cl. Bris 79 E2
Rudgleigh Ave. E in G 47 E2
Rudgleigh Rd. E in G 47 E2
Rudhall Gr. Bris 49 F4
Rudhall Green. W-S-M 89 D2
Rudmore Park. Bath 101 E2
Rudthorpe Rd. Bris 49 F3
Ruffet Rd. West 38 B2
Rugby Rd. Bris 64 B2
Runnymead Ave. Bris 64 B1
Runnymede. Kingsw 51 F1
Runswick Rd. Bris 64 B2
Rupert St. Bris 63 E4
Rupert St. Bris 64 B4
Rurdown Rd. Bris 49 F3
Rush Cl. St Gif 24 B1
Rush Hill. Bath 101 D1
Rush Hill. Paul 130 C2
Rush Hill. Paul 130 C2
Rushgrove Gdns. Bi Sut ... 113 E2
Rushmead La. Marsh 55 F1
Rushmoor Gr. Back 76 A3
Rushmoor La. Back 76 A3
Rushmoor. Cleve 57 D1
Rushton Dr. Fr Cot 38 B4
Rushway. Blag 110 A2
Rushy. Kingsw 66 A2
Ruskin Gr. Bris 50 A4
Ruskin Rd. Rad 132 B1
Russ St. Bris 63 F3
Russell Ave. Kingsw 65 F4
Russell Cl. Win 95 D3
Russell Gr. Bris 49 E3
Russell Rd. Bris 49 D2
Russell Rd. Bris 51 D1
Russell Rd. Cleve 57 E2
Russell St. Bath 101 F4
Russell Town Ave. Bris 64 A4
Russet Cl. Olve 14 A2
Russet Cl. Kings 11 F2
Russet Way. P St J 133 E4
Russett Cl. Back 76 A3
Russett Gr. Nail 75 E4
Rutherford Cl. Kingsw 66 A2
Ruthven Rd. Bris 79 F4
Rutland Ave. Kingsw 66 A1
Rutland Cl. W-S-M 105 E4
Rutland Rd. Bris 49 F2
Rydal Ave. Lock 106 A2
Rydal Rd. W-S-M 104 C2
Ryde Rd. Bris 64 A1
Rye Cl. Bris 78 C3
Ryecroft Ave. W-S-M 88 C1
Ryecroft Rd. Fr Cot 38 B4
Ryecroft Rise. Lo Ash 62 A1
Ryedown La. Bitt 66 B1
Ryland Pl. Bris 50 A1
Rylestone Cl. Fr Cot 37 F4
Rylestone Gr. Bris 48 C3
Rysdale Rd. Bris 48 C3

Sabrina Way. Bris 48 B2
Sadbury Cl. W-S-M 89 D2
Sadlier Cl. Bris 48 A4
Saffron Ct. Bath 102 A4
Saffrons The. W-S-M 89 D2
Sage Cl. Portis 44 C2
Sailsburt St. Bris 64 C4
Sailsbury Rd. Bris 64 B3
St John's Rd. Back 76 A3
St Agnes Ave. Bris 63 F1
St Agnes Cl. Nail 60 A1
St Agnes Wlk. Bris 63 F1
St Aidan's Cl. Bris 65 D3
St Aidan's Rd. Bris 65 D3
St Alban's Rd. Bris 49 D2
St Aldams Dr. Puck 53 D3
St Aldwyn's Cl. Bris 49 F4
St Andrew's Cl. Cong 91 E2
St Andrew's Dr. Cleve 57 D2
St Andrew's Par. W-S-M ... 104 C2
St Andrew's Rd. Avon 33 D2
St Andrew's Rd. Bris 49 F1
St Andrew's Terr. Bath 101 F4
St Andrews Cl. Nail 60 A1

St Andrews Cl. W-S-M 88 C2
St Andrews Rd. Back 76 A3
St Andrews Trading Est.
  Avon 33 E1
St Andrews. Kingsw 66 A3
St Andrews. Yate 27 F1
St Ann's Way. Bath 102 A3
St Anne's Ave. Keyn 81 E3
St Anne's Cl. Kingsw 66 A2
St Anne's Ct. Keyn 81 E3
St Anne's Dr. Fr Cot 38 B3
St Anne's Dr. Wick 67 D4
St Anne's Park Rd. Bris 64 C3
St Anne's Rd. Bris 64 B3
St Anne's Rd. Bris 65 D3
St Anne's Terr. Bris 64 C3
St Annes Dr. Kingsw 66 B2
St Anthony's Dr. Wick 67 D4
St Anthonys Cl. Mid No 132 A1
St Anway. Kingsw 66 B1
St Aubin's Ave. Bris 64 C2
St Aubyn's Ave. W-S-M 104 B1
St Augustine's Cl. Portis ... 44 C2
St Augustine's Par. Bris 63 E3
St Augustine's Pl. Bris 63 E3
St Austell Cl. Nail 76 A4
St Austell Rd. W-S-M 105 D4
St Barnabas Cl. Bris 63 F1
St Barnabas Cl. Mid No 132 A2
St Barnabas Cl. Sist 66 B4
St Bartholomew's Rd. Bris .. 49 F2
St Bede's Rd. Bris 51 E1
St Bernard's Rd. Bris 47 F3
St Brelades Gr. Bris 64 C3
St Brendan's Way. Avon 33 D1
St Briavels Dr. Yate 39 E4
St Bridges Cl. W St L 88 A3
St Catherine's Cl. Bath 102 B4
St Catherine's Ind Est. Bris . 63 E2
St Catherine's Mead.
  E in G 47 E2
St Catherine's Pl. Bris 63 E2
St Chad's Ave. Mid No 132 A1
St Chad's Green. Mid No .. 132 A1
St Charles Cl. Mid No 132 A1
St Christophers Cl. Bath .. 102 B4
St Clements Ct. Keyn 81 F2
St Clements Rd. Keyn 81 F2
St David's Ave. Kingsw 66 A3
St David's Cl. W-S-M 88 A1
St David's Cres. Bris 64 C3
St Dunstan's Rd. Bris 63 E1
St Edward's Rd. Bris 63 D3
St Edyth's Rd. Bris 48 B3
St Fagans Ct. Kingsw 66 A1
St Francis Dr. Wick 67 D4
St Francis Rd. Wint 37 F3
St Francis Rd. Bris 63 D2
St Francis Rd. Keyn 81 E3
St Gabriel's Rd. Bris 64 A4
St George's Hill. Bath 102 B4
St George's Hill. E in G 47 D2
St George's Rd. Bris 63 E3
St George's Rd. E in G 46 C4
St George's Rd. Keyn 81 E3
St Giles Barton. Hill 19 E4
St Gregory's Rd. Bris 49 F4
St Gregory's Wlk. Bris 49 F4
St Helen's Wlk. Bris 51 D1
St Helena Rd. Bris 49 D2
St Helens Dr. Kingsw 66 B1
St Helens Dr. Wick 67 E4
St Helier Ave. Bris 64 C2
St Hilary Cl. Bris 48 B3
St Ivel Way. Kingsw 66 B3
St Ives Cl. Nail 60 A1
St Ives Rd. W-S-M 105 D3
St James Cl. Thorn 8 B2
St James Cl. St Gif 24 B2
St James St. W-S-M 104 B4
St James' Barton. Bris 63 F4
St James's Par. Bath 101 F3
St James's Park. Bath 101 F4
St James's Pl. Mang 52 A3
St James's Sq. Bath 101 F4
St James's St. Mang 52 A3
St John St. H Up 20 A2
St John St. Thorn 8 A1
St John's Ave. Cleve 57 E2
St John's Bridge. Bris 63 E4
St John's Cl. P St J 133 D4
St John's Cl. W-S-M 87 E1
St John's Cres. Bris 63 F1
St John's Cres. Mid No 132 A1
St John's La. Bris 63 F1
St John's Pl. Bath 101 F3
St John's Rd. Bath 101 E4
St John's Rd. Bath 102 A4
St John's Rd. Bris 63 E2
St John's Rd. Cleve 57 E2
St John's Rd. Bris 63 E2
St John's Steep. Bris 63 E4
St Johns Ct. Keyn 81 F3
St Johns Way. Ch Sod 28 A1
St Jonhs Rd. Tims 116 A1
St Joseph's Rd. Bris 35 D2

St Joseph's Rd. W-S-M 87 F1
St Jude's Terr. W-S-M 88 B1
St Julian's Rd. Well 133 F3
St Kenya Ct. Keyn 81 F3
St Keyna Rd. Keyn 81 F3
St Kilda's Rd. Bath 101 E3
St Ladoc Rd. Keyn 81 E3
St Laud Cl. Bris 48 B3
St Leonard's Rd. Bris 49 F3
St Leonard's Rd. Bris 50 B1
St Lucia Cl. Bris 49 F4
St Lucia Cres. Bris 49 F4
St Luke St. Bris 64 A4
St Luke's Cres. Bris 63 F2
St Luke's Gdns. Bris 64 C1
St Luke's Rd. Bath 101 F2
St Luke's Rd. Bris 63 F2
St Luke's Rd. Mid No 131 F1
St Margaret's Cl. Back 76 A3
St Margaret's Cl. Keyn 81 E3
St Margaret's Dr. Bris 49 E3
St Margaret's La. Back 76 A3
St Margaret's Terr. W-S-M . 104 B4
St Mark's Gr. Bris 50 A1
St Mark's Rd. Bath 102 A3
St Mark's Rd. Bris 50 A1
St Mark's Rd. Mid No 132 A1
St Mark's Terr. Bris 50 A1
St Marks Cl. Keyn 81 F3
St Marks Rd. W-S-M 89 D2
St Martin's Cl. Bris 64 A1
St Martin's Ct. Bath 101 F1
St Martin's Gdns. Bris 64 A1
St Martin's La. Marsh 69 F4
St Martin's Park. Marsh 69 F4
St Martin's Rd. Bris 64 A1
St Martin's Wlk. Bris 64 A1
St Martins Ct. W-S-M 88 C2
St Mary St. Thorn 15 D4
St Mary's Bldgs. Bath 101 F3
St Mary's Cl. Bath 102 A3
St Mary's Cl. Tims 116 A1
St Mary's Cl. W-S-M 105 D1
St Mary's Gdns. Chur 109 D3
St Mary's Gr. Nail 75 E4
St Mary's Pk Rd. Portis 45 E2
St Mary's Park. Nail 75 E4
St Mary's Rd. Bris 47 E4
St Mary's Rd. Lo Ash 62 B3
St Mary's Rd. Lock 105 E1
St Mary's Rd. Portis 45 E2
St Mary's Rise. Rad 133 E1
St Mary's St. Axb 125 E1
St Mary's Way. Yate 27 F1
St Mary's Wlk. Bris 47 E3
St Marys Cl. Lock 105 E1
St Marys Way. Thorn 8 A1
St Matthew's Rd. Bath 87 E1
St Matthew's Rd. Bris 63 E4
St Matthias Park. Bris 63 F4
St Michael's Ave. Cleve 57 E1
St Michael's Cl. Wint 37 F4
St Michael's Hill. Bris 63 E4
St Michael's Park. Bris 63 E4
St Michael's Rd. Bath 101 E4
St Michaels Cl. Bris 65 D4
St Michaels Rd. Bath 101 D3
St Micheal's Ave. W-S-M .. 89 D2
St Nicholas Ct. Bath 85 F1
St Nicholas Park. Bris 50 A1
St Nicholas Rd. W-S-M ... 104 B1
St Nicholas Rd. Whit 80 B2
St Nicholas Rd. Bris 63 E3
St Nicholas' Rd. Bris 49 F1
St Oswald's Ct. Bris 49 D2
St Oswald's Rd. Bris 49 D2
St Patrick's Ct. Bath 102 A3
St Patricks Ct. Keyn 81 F3
St Paul St. Bris 63 F4
St Paul's Rd. Bris 63 D4
St Paul's-Rd. Bris 63 E4
St Paul's Rd. W-S-M 104 C3
St Pauls Pl. Bath 101 F3
St Pauls Pl. Mid No 132 A1
St Peter's Ave. W-S-M 87 E1
St Peter's Cres. Fr Cot 38 A4
St Peter's Rd. Rod 138 B4
St Peter's Rise. Bris 79 D4
St Peter's Wlk. Bris 49 D3
St Peters Rd. Portis 45 E2
St Phillips Causeway. Bris .. 64 A3
St Phillips Rd. Bris 64 A4
St Pierre Dr. Kingsw 66 A3
St Ronan's Ave. Bris 49 E1
St Saviour's Rd. Bath 85 E1
St Saviours Way. Bath 85 E1
St Silas St. Bris 64 A3
St Stephen's Ave. Bris 63 E3
St Stephen's Cl. Bath 101 E3
St Stephen's Cl. Bris 101 F4
St Stephen's Rd. Kingsw ... 51 E1
St Stephen's St. Bris 63 E3
St Stephens Bsns Centre.
  Kingsw 66 B3
St Stephens Cl. Kingsw 51 F2
St Stephens Rd. Bath 101 F4
St Swithin's Pl. Bath 102 A4

St Thomas Rd. Mid No 132 A1
St Thomas St E. Bris 63 F3
St Thomas St. Bris 63 F3
St Vincent's Hill. Bris 49 D1
St Vincent's Rd. Bris 63 D3
St Werburgh's Park. Bris ... 50 A1
St Werburgh's Rd. Bris 49 F1
St Whytes Rd. Bris 79 E4
St Winifreds Dr. Bath 102 B1
Salcombe Gdns. W-S-M 89 D1
Salcombe Rd. Bris 64 A1
Salem Rd. Wint 37 F4
Salisbury Ave. Bris 65 D4
Salisbury Gdns. Mang 51 F3
Salisbury Rd. Bath 85 D1
Salisbury Rd. Bris 49 E1
Salisbury Rd. Mang 51 F3
Salisbury Rd. Paul 131 F2
Salisbury Rd. W-S-M 105 E4
Salisbury St. Bris 64 A3
Salisbury Terr. W-S-M 104 B4
Sally In The Wood Rd.
  Bathf 103 E3
Sallybarn Cl. Kingsw 65 F1
Sallys Way. Wint 37 F4
Sallysmead Cl. Bris 79 D2
Saltford Ct. Keyn 82 C2
Salthouse Ct. Cleve 57 D1
Salthouse Rd. Cleve 57 D1
Salthrop Rd. Bris 49 F2
Saltings Cl. Cleve 57 D1
Saltmarsh Dr. Bris 34 A1
Saltwell Ave. Whit 80 B3
Sambourne La. E in G 47 E2
Samian Way. St Gif 36 C3
Sampsons Rd. Bris 79 E2
Samuel St. Bris 64 B4
Samuel White Rd. Kingsw .. 65 E2
Samuel Wright Cl. Kingsw .. 66 B3
Sanctuary Gdns. Bris 48 B2
Sand Farm La. W St L 88 A3
Sand Hill. Bris 64 B2
Sand Rd. W St L 88 A3
Sandbach Rd. Bris 64 B2
Sandbed Rd. Bris 50 A1
Sandburrows Rd. Bris 78 C3
Sandburrows Wlk. Bris 78 C3
Sandcroft Ave. W-S-M 104 B1
Sandcroft. Bris 79 F3
Sandford Cl. Cleve 57 D1
Sandford Rd. Bris 63 D3
Sandford Rd. W-S-M 105 D4
Sandgate Rd. Bris 64 B2
Sandholm Rd. Bris 64 B2
Sandholme Cl. Mang 51 F4
Sandhurst Cl. St Gif 24 A1
Sandhurst Rd. Bris 64 B2
Sandhurst. Yate 39 E4
Sandling Ave. Bris 50 A4
Sandmead Rd. Wins 108 A2
Sandown Cl. Mang 51 F4
Sandown Rd. Bris 36 B2
Sandown Rd. Bris 64 B2
Sandpiper Dr. W-S-M 88 C1
Sandpits La. H Up 19 F1
Sandringham Ave. Mang ... 51 F4
Sandringham Park. Mang .. 51 F4
Sandringham Rd. Bris 64 B2
Sandringham Rd. Kingsw ... 65 F1
Sandringham Rd. St Gif 36 B2
Sandringham Rd. W-S-M .. 104 C3
Sands Hill. Dyrh 54 C2
Sandwich Rd. Bris 64 B2
Sandy Cl. St Gif 36 C3
Sandy La. Ab Lei 61 E4
Sandy La. Aust 13 D4
Sandy La. Bris 50 B2
Sandy La. Pens 96 C2
Sandy La. Wrax 47 D1
Sandy La. Wrax 61 E4
Sandy Lodge. Yate 39 F4
Sandy Park Rd. Bris 64 B2
Sandyleaze. Bris 48 C4
Sarabeth Dr. Pris 117 D2
Saracen Cl. Bath 102 A4
Sarah St. Bris 64 A4
Sargent St. Bris 63 F2
Sarum Cres. Bris 35 E1
Sassoon Ct. Kingsw 65 F3
Satchfield Cl. Bris 34 C1
Satchfield Cres. Bris 34 C1
Sates Way. Bris 49 E3
Saunders Rd. Kingsw 51 F2
Saunton Wlk. Bris 79 F4
Savages Wood Rd. St Gif .. 36 C4
Savages Wood Rd. St Gif .. 36 C4
Savernake Rd. W-S-M 88 C2
Saville Cres. W-S-M 105 E4
Saville Gate Cl. Bris 48 C2
Saville Pl. Bris 63 D3
Saville Rd. Bris 48 C2
Saville Rd. W-S-M 105 E4
Saville Row. Bath 101 F4
Saw Cl. Bath 101 F3
Saw Mill La. Thorn 8 A1

Sawyers Ct. Cleve 57 F2
Saxby Cl. Cleve 57 D1
Saxby Cl. W-S-M 89 D2
Saxon Rd. Bris 50 A1
Saxon Rd. W-S-M 105 E4
Saxon Way. St Gif 24 B1
Saxon Way. Winsl 120 C4
Says La. Chur 109 D2
Sbi Centre. Kingsw 65 D3
Scandrett Cl. Bris 34 C1
Scaurs The. W-S-M 88 C1
School Cl. Bris 79 F2
School Cl. Hill 19 F4
School Cl. St Gif 36 B4
School La. Ba Gu 77 E3
School La. Bathe 85 F2
School La. Bris 50 C3
School La. Ch St 112 B4
School La. Paul 131 D2
School La. Ship 109 D1
School La. Wring 94 A4
School Rd. Bris 64 A2
School Rd. Bris 64 C2
School Rd. Fr Cot 38 A4
School Rd. Kingsw 65 E4
School Rd. Kingsw 66 B2
School Rd. Wring 92 C1
School Way. Piln 22 A3
School Wlk. Bris 50 B1
Scobell Rise. Paul 115 E1
Scop La. Alm 24 A3
Score La. Blag 110 C1
Score The. Blag 110 C1
Scot La. Ch St 95 E1
Scotch Horn Cl. Nail 59 F1
Scotch Horn Way. Nail 59 F1
Scots Pine Ave. Nail 60 A1
Scott Cl. Kingsw 65 F3
Scott Lawrence Cl. Bris 51 D4
Scott Rd. W-S-M 105 D2
Scott Way. Ch Sod 39 F4
Scumbrum La. Farm 115 E1
Scumbrum La. Paul 115 E1
Sea Bank Rd. E in G 32 C1
Sea Mills La. Bris 48 B3
Seabrook Rd. W-S-M 88 B1
Seagry Cl. Bris 35 F1
Searl Court Ave. Bris 64 C2
Searle Cres. W-S-M 105 D3
Seaton Rd. Bris 50 B1
Seavale Rd. Cleve 57 E2
Seaview Rd. Portis 44 C2
Seaview Rd. Portis 44 C3
Seawalls Rd. Bris 48 B1
Seawalls. Bris 48 B1
Second Ave. Bath 101 E3
Second Ave. Rod 138 C4
Second Way. Avon 33 E1
Seddon Rd. Bris 50 A1
Sedgefield Gdns. Mang 37 F1
Sedgemoor Cl. Nail 75 F4
Sedgemoor Rd. Bath 101 F1
Sedgemoor Rd. W-S-M 87 F1
Sefton Park Rd. Bris 49 F2
Selbourne Cl. Bath 101 D4
Selbourne Rd. Bris 49 F3
Selbourne Rd. W-S-M 104 C2
Selbrooke Cres. Bris 51 E3
Selby Rd. Bris 50 C1
Selden Rd. Bris 80 C3
Selkirk Rd. Bris 51 E1
Selley Wlk. Bris 79 D3
Selwood Cl. W-S-M 105 E4
Selworthy Cl. Keyn 81 E3
Selworthy Gdns. Nail 59 F1
Selworthy Rd. Bris 64 A1
Selworthy Rd. W-S-M 105 D2
Selworthy. Kingsw 66 B4
Seneca Pl. Bris 64 B4
Seneca St. Bris 64 B4
Sercombe Park. Cleve 57 F1
Serlo Ct. W-S-M 88 C2
Seven Acres La. Bathe 85 F3
Seventh Ave. Bris 36 A1
Severn Ave. W-S-M 104 C3
Severn Cl. Char 11 D2
Severn Dr. Thorn 8 A1
Severn Grange. Bris 34 B2
Severn Rd. Avon 33 E2
Severn Rd. Avon 33 F4
Severn Rd. Bris 47 E3
Severn Rd. E in G 47 E3
Severn Rd. Piln 22 A3
Severn Rd. Portis 45 E3
Severn View Rd. Thorn 8 B1
Severn Way. Bris 23 F1
Severn Way. Keyn 81 F2
Severnmeade. Portis 44 C3
Severnwood Gdns. Piln 22 A3
Sevier Rd. Blea 123 E2
Sevier St. Bris 50 A1
Seville Rd. Portis 45 F4
Seward Terr. Rad 133 E1
Seymour Ave. Bris 49 F2
Seymour Cl. Cleve 57 D1
Seymour Cl. W-S-M 88 C2
Seymour Rd. Bath 102 A4

161
Seymour Rd. Bris
Station Rd. Axb

Seymour Rd. Bris 49 F2
Seymour Rd. Bris 50 A1
Seymour Rd. Kingsw 51 E1
Seymour Rd. Kingsw 51 F2
Seyton Wlk. St Gif 36 C3
Shackleton Ave. Yate 39 F4
Shadwell Rd. Bris 49 E2
Shaft Rd. Bath 102 B1
Shaft Rd. Piln 22 A4
Shaftesbury Ave. Bris 49 F1
Shaftesbury Rd. Bath 101 E3
Shaftesbury Rd. W-S-M 105 D4
Shaftesbury Terr. Bris 64 B4
Shaftesbury Terr. Mid No 133 D2
Shaftsbury Ave. Bath 101 E4
Shaftsbury Cl. Nail 75 E4
Shakespeare Ave. Bath 101 F2
Shakespeare Ave. Bris 50 A4
Shakespeare Rd. Rad 132 B1
Shaldon Rd. Bris 50 A2
Shallows The. Keyn 82 C2
Sham Castle La. Bath 102 B4
Shamrock Rd. Bris 50 B2
Shanklin Dr. Bris 36 A2
Shannon Ct. Thorn 15 E4
Shapcott Cl. Bris 64 A1
Shaplands. Bris 48 C3
Sharland Cl. Bris 48 C2
Shaw Cl. Bris 64 A4
Shaws Way. Bath 101 D3
Shaymoor La. Alm 23 D2
Sheene La. Bris 63 E2
Sheep Fair La. Marsh 69 F4
Sheeps Croft. Bris 79 D3
Sheepway. Portb 46 B3
Sheepwood Cl. Bris 35 D1
Sheepwood Rd. Bris 35 D1
Sheldare Barton. Bris 65 D4
Sheldon Cl. Cleve 57 F1
Sheldrake Dr. Bris 50 C3
Shellard Rd. Bris 36 A1
Shellards La. Alve 15 E2
Shellards Rd. Kingsw 65 F2
Shelley Ave. Cleve 57 E1
Shelley Cl. Bris 64 C4
Shelley Rd. Bath 101 F2
Shelley Rd. Rad 132 B1
Shelley Rd. W-S-M 105 D2
Shellmor Ave. St Gif 24 A1
Shellmor Cl. St Gif 24 B1
Shelly Way. Bris 50 A4
Shepherds Cl. Mang 51 F3
Sheppard Rd. Bris 51 E3
Sheppards Gdns. Bath 84 A1
Shepperdine Rd. O-On-S 1 B1
Sheppy's Mill. Cong 91 E3
Shepton Wlk. Bris 63 E1
Shepton. W-S-M 105 D1
Sherbourne Ave. St Gif 36 C4
Sherbourne Cl. Kingsw 51 F1
Sherbourne St. Bris 64 C4
Sherbourne's Brake. St Gif 36 C3
Sheridan Rd. Bath 100 C3
Sheridan Rd. Bris 50 A4
Sheridan Way. Kingsw 66 A1
Sherrin Way. Bris 78 C2
Sherrings The. St Gif 36 A4
Sherston Cl. Bris 51 D3
Sherston Cl. Nail 60 A1
Sherston Rd. Bris 49 F4
Sherston Rd. Luck 31 F3
Sherwell Rd. Bris 64 B2
Sherwood Cl. Keyn 81 F3
Sherwood Cres. W-S-M 88 C2
Sherwood Rd. Bris 51 D1
Sherwood Rd. Keyn 81 F3
Shetland Rd. Bris 35 E1
Shetland Way. Nail 60 A1
Shickle Gr. Bath 101 E1
Shields Ave. Bris 36 A1
Shiels Dr. St Gif 36 B4
Shilton Cl. Kingsw 65 F4
Shimsey Cl. Bris 51 E3
Shiners Elms. Yatt 91 D4
Ship La. Bris 63 F3
Shipham Cl. Bris 80 A3
Shipham Cl. Nail 75 F4
Shipham La. Ship 108 A2
Shipham La. Wins 108 A1
Shipham Rd. Ched 125 F3
Shiplate Rd. Blea 122 C3
Shipley Rd. Bris 49 D4
Shire Gdns. Bris 47 E4
Shire Hill. Tor 56 A3
Shire Way. Yate 39 E3
Shirehampton Rd. Bris 48 B3
Shockerwick La. Bathf 86 B3
Shop La. Gr Bad 30 C1
Shophouse Rd. Bath 101 D3
Shoreditch. Ch St 112 B4
Short La. Litt 129 F1
Short La. Lo Ash 62 A1
Short St. Bris 64 A3
Short Way. Thorn 15 D4
Short Way. Wrax 61 D2
Shorthill Rd. West 39 E2
Shortlands Rd. Bris 34 A1
Shortwood Hill. Puck 52 C2
Shortwood Rd. Bris 79 F2
Shortwood Rd. Puck 53 D3
Shortwood View. Kingsw 65 F4
Shortwood Wlk. Bris 79 F2
Showering Rd. Bris 80 B3
Shrubbery Ave. W-S-M 87 E1
Shrubbery Cotts. Bris 49 D1
Shrubbery Rd. Mang 51 E3
Shrubbery Rd. W-S-M 87 E1
Shrubbery Terr. W-S-M 87 E1
Shrubbery Wlk W. W-S-M 87 E1
Shrubbery Wlk. W-S-M 87 E1
Shuter Rd. Bris 78 C3
Sibland Cl. Thorn 15 E4
Sibland Rd. Thorn 15 E4
Sibland Way. Thorn 15 E4
Sibland. Thorn 15 E4
Sidcot La. Wins 125 D4
Sidcot. Bris 65 D1
Sideland Cl. Bris 80 C3
Sidelands Rd. Bris 51 E3
Sidings The. Char 11 D3
Sidlings The. Co Mar 127 E4
Sidmouth Gdns. Bris 63 E1
Sidmouth Rd. Bris 63 F1
Sidney Hill Cottage Homes. Chur 108 C2
Signal Rd. Kingsw 51 F2
Silbury Rd. Bris 62 C1
Silbury Rise. Keyn 82 A1
Silcox Rd. Bris 79 E2
Silklands Gr. Bris 48 B4
Silver Birch Cl. St Gif 36 B4
Silver Ct. Nail 59 E1
Silver Mead. Cong 91 E1
Silver Moor La. Ban 106 C4
Silver St. Bris 63 E4
Silver St. Ch Mag 96 A2
Silver St. Cong 91 E1
Silver St. Hol 138 B1
Silver St. Kilm 139 D3
Silver St. Mid No 138 A4
Silver St. Nail 59 E1
Silver St. Rod 138 A4
Silver St. W in G 44 C1
Silver St. Wring 92 C1
Silverberry Rd. W-S-M 89 D1
Silverhill Rd. Bris 34 C2
Silverlow Rd. Nail 59 E1
Silverstone Way. Cong 91 E2
Silverthorne La. Bris 64 A3
Silverthorne Wharf. Bris 64 A3
Silverton Ct. Bris 63 F1
Simon's Cl. Paul 131 F3
Simons Cl. W-S-M 89 D1
Simplex Ind Est The. Kingsw 66 B2
Singapore Rd. W-S-M 104 C2
Single Hill. Well 134 A3
Sion Hill Pl. Bath 84 C1
Sion Hill. Bath 84 C1
Sion Hill. Bath 101 E4
Sion Hill. Bris 62 C4
Sion La. Bris 62 C4
Sion Pl. Bris 62 C4
Sion Rd. Bath 84 C1
Sion Rd. Bris 63 E2
Sir John's La. Bris 50 A3
Siskin Wlk. W-S-M 105 F4
Siston Centre The. Kingsw 52 A1
Siston Cl. Sist 52 A1
Siston Comm. Sist 52 A1
Siston La. Puck 52 C1
Siston Park. Sist 52 A1
Six Ways. Cleve 57 E2
Sixpence. Paul 115 E1
Sixth Ave. Bris 36 A1
Sixty Acres Cl. Wrax 61 D2
Skinner's Hill. Tims 132 C4
Skinners La. Chur 108 C2
Skippon Ct. Kingsw 65 F3
Sladacre La. Blag 110 C1
Slade La. Ba Gu 77 E2
Slade La. Lymp 122 A1
Slade Rd. Portis 45 E3
Sladebrook Ave. Bath 101 E2
Sladebrook Rd. Bath 101 D2
Slate La. Co Dan 98 A4
Sleep La. Whit 80 B2
Slimbridge Cl. Ch Sod 39 F4
Sloan St. Bris 64 B4
Slough La. Co Ash 68 C3
Slymbridge Ave. Bris 35 D2
Small Down End. Winsc 107 F1
Small La. Bris 50 C3
Small St. Bris 63 E4
Small St. Bris 64 A3
Smallbrook La. Co Dan 98 A3
Smallcombe Cl. Mid No 132 C3
Smallcombe Rd. Mid No 132 C2
Smallway. Cong 91 E3
Smarts Green. Ch Sod 40 B4
Smeaton Rd. Bris 62 C3
Smithcourt Dr. St Gif 36 B3
Smithmead. Bris 79 D3
Smoke La. Avon 33 E4
Smyth Rd. Bris 63 D2
Smythe Croft. Bris 80 A2
Smyths Cl. Avon 33 D1
Snow Hill. Bath 85 D1
Snowberry Cl. W-S-M 89 D1
Snowberry Wlk. Bris 50 C1
Snowdon Cl. Bris 50 C2
Snowdon Rd. Bris 50 C2
Snowdon Vale. W-S-M 88 A1
Sodbury Rd. Wickw 18 A2
Solent Way. Thorn 15 E4
Solsbury Ct. Bathe 85 F2
Solsbury Way. Bath 85 D1
Somer Ave. Mid No 131 F1
Somer Lea. Chil 137 E3
Somer Rd. Mid No 131 F1
Somerby Cl. St Gif 36 B4
Somerdale Ave. Bath 101 E1
Somerdale Ave. Bris 64 A1
Somerdale Ave. W-S-M 105 E4
Somerdale Cl. W-S-M 105 E4
Somerdale Rd N. Keyn 81 F4
Somerdale Rd. Keyn 81 F4
Somerdale View. Bath 101 E1
Somermead. Bris 63 E1
Somerset Ave. Yate 27 F2
Somerset Cl. Kings 11 F2
Somerset Cres. St Gif 36 C3
Somerset Folly. Tims 116 A1
Somerset La. Bath 84 C1
Somerset Mews. W-S-M 104 C3
Somerset Pl. Bath 84 C1
Somerset Rd. Bris 64 A2
Somerset Rd. Cleve 57 F2
Somerset Rd. Portis 44 C3
Somerset Sq. Bris 63 F3
Somerset Sq. Nail 59 F1
Somerset St. Bris 63 E4
Somerset St. Bris 63 F3
Somerset Terr. Bris 63 E2
Somerset Way. Paul 131 F3
Somerton Cl. Kingsw 65 F4
Somerton Rd. Bris 49 F3
Somerton Rd. Cleve 57 F1
Somerton. W-S-M 105 D1
Somervale Rd. Rad 132 C1
Somerville Cl. Keyn 82 C1
Somerville Rd. Wins 108 A2
Sommerville Rd S. Bris 49 F1
Sommerville Rd. Bris 49 F2
Sophia Gdns. W-S-M 89 D2
Sorrel Cl. Thorn 8 B1
Soundwell Rd. Bris 65 E4
Soundwell Rd. Kingsw 51 E1
South Ave. Bath 101 E3
South Ave. Portis 45 E3
South Ave. Yate 27 D1
South Combe. Blea 122 A3
South Croft. Bris 49 E4
South Croft. Winsc 107 F1
South Dene. Bris 48 C3
South Gr. Bris 49 E3
South Gr. E in G 47 E2
South Green St. Bris 62 C3
South Hayes. Bris 50 A2
South Hill. Winsc 107 F1
South Lawn Cl. Lock 105 F2
South Lawn. Lock 105 F2
South Lea Rd. Bath 101 D4
South Liberty La. Bris 62 C1
South Meadows. Wring 92 C1
South Par. Bath 102 A3
South Par. Ch Mag 96 A2
South Par. W-S-M 104 B4
South Par. Yate 27 F1
South Rd. Alve 24 C3
South Rd. Bris 49 E1
South Rd. Bris 63 E2
South Rd. Kingsw 65 E4
South Rd. Lymp 122 A1
South Rd. Mid No 132 A1
South Rd. Portis 45 D4
South Rd. Tims 116 A1
South Rd. W-S-M 87 E1
South Rock Ind Est. Chil 137 E1
South Side. Cong 91 F3
South St. Bris 63 D2
South St. Chil 137 F1
South Terr. Bris 49 D1
South Terr. W-S-M 104 B4
South View Cres. Fr Cot 38 B3
South View Pl. Mid No 132 A1
South View Rd. Bath 101 E3
South View Rise. Fr Cot 38 B3
South View Terr. Yatt 74 A1
South View. Fr Cot 38 A4
South View. Kilm 139 D2
South View. Mang 51 F3
South View. Mid No 132 C3
South View. Portis 45 D4
South View. Tims 116 A1
South Wlk. Yate 27 F1
Southbourne Gdns. Bath 85 D1
Southcot Pl. Bath 102 A3
Southdown Ave. Bath 101 D2
Southdown Rd. Bath 101 D2
Southdown Rd. Bris 48 C4
Southdown. W-S-M 88 C2
Southend Rd. W-S-M 104 C2
Southern Way. Cleve 57 D1
Southernhay Ave. Bris 63 D3
Southernhay. Bris 63 D3
Southernhay. Kingsw 51 E2
Southey Ave. Kingsw 51 F1
Southey Ct. Kingsw 51 E1
Southey Rd. Cleve 57 E1
Southey St. Bris 49 F1
Southfield Ave. Kingsw 51 F1
Southfield Cl. Nail 59 F2
Southfield Cl. W-S-M 104 B1
Southfield Ct. Bris 49 D4
Southfield Pl. Bris 63 E2
Southfield Rd. Bris 49 D4
Southfield Rd. Bris 49 E1
Southfield Rd. Nail 59 F2
Southfield Road Trading Est. Nail 59 F2
Southfield. N St P 135 F2
Southfield. Rad 133 D1
Southgate. Bath 102 A3
Southlands Dr. Tims 116 A1
Southlands Way. Cong 91 F3
Southlands. Bath 84 A1
Southlands. Tyth 16 A2
Southleaze. Wins 125 D3
Southleigh Rd. Bris 63 D4
Southmead Rd. Bris 35 F1
Southmead Rd. W-S-M 105 D4
Southmead. Wins 125 D4
Southover Cl. Bris 49 D4
Southover Rd. Paul 115 E1
Southridge Hts. W-S-M 122 A4
Southsea Rd. Bris 36 A4
Southside Cl. Bris 48 A4
Southside Cres. W St L 88 A2
Southside. W-S-M 104 C4
Southstoke La. Sosto 118 C4
Southstoke Rd. Bath 101 F1
Southview Cl. Lock 105 F1
Southville Rd. Bris 63 E2
Southville Rd. W-S-M 104 C2
Southway Dr. Kingsw 66 B3
Southwell St. Bris 63 E4
Southwood Ave. Bris 48 B4
Southwood Dr E. Bris 48 B4
Southwood Dr. Bris 48 A4
Sovereign Gdns. Bris 48 C2
Spa La. Bath 85 E1
Spalding Cl. Bris 50 A2
Spaniorum View. Alm 22 C1
Spar Rd. Avon 33 E2
Spar Rd. Yate 27 E1
Spartley Dr. Bris 78 C3
Spartley Wlk. Bris 78 C3
Specklemead. Paul 131 E3
Speedwell Ave. Bris 64 B4
Speedwell Cl. Thorn 8 B1
Speedwell Rd. Bris 51 D1
Spencer Dr. W-S-M 89 D2
Spey Cl. Thorn 15 E4
Spider La. W-S-M 104 B4
Spindleberry Gr. Nail 60 A1
Spinners End. W-S-M 89 D2
Spinney Croft. Bris 78 C3
Spinney The. Fr Cot 38 A4
Spinney The. W-S-M 104 C1
Spires View. Bris 50 C3
Spratts Bridge. Ch Mag 96 A2
Spring Cres. Bath 102 A3
Spring Gardens Rd. Bath 102 A3
Spring Gardens Rd. Bath 102 A4
Spring Gdns. Bris 64 A1
Spring Ground Rd. Paul 131 F3
Spring Hill Dr. W-S-M 88 C1
Spring Hill. Bris 63 E4
Spring Hill. Kingsw 51 F1
Spring Hill. W-S-M 88 B1
Spring La. Bath 85 D1
Spring Rise. Portis 45 E2
Spring St Pl. Bris 63 F2
Spring St. Bris 63 F2
Spring Terr. W-S-M 88 B1
Spring Valley. W-S-M 88 B1
Springfield Ave. Bris 47 E3
Springfield Ave. Bris 49 F3
Springfield Ave. Mang 52 A4
Springfield Ave. W-S-M 88 B1
Springfield Bldgs. Mid No 133 D2
Springfield Bldgs. Paul 131 E1
Springfield Cl. Bath 101 D3
Springfield Cl. Mang 52 A4
Springfield Cres. Mid No 133 D2
Springfield Gdns. Ban 107 D2
Springfield Gr. Bris 49 E3
Springfield Hts. Mid No 132 C2
Springfield Lawns. Bris 47 E3
Springfield Pl. Mid No 132 C2
Springfield Rd. Bris 49 E1
Springfield Rd. E in G 47 E2
Springfield Rd. Mang 52 A4
Springfield Rd. Portis 45 D3
Springfield. P St J 133 E4
Springfield. Thorn 15 E4
Springfields. Bris 36 A1
Springhill Cl. Paul 131 E3
Springleaze. Bris 64 A1
Springleaze. Mang 52 A4
Springville Cl. Kingsw 66 A2
Springwater Park Ind Est. Bris 64 C4
Springwell. N St P 135 F2
Springwood Dr. Bris 34 B2
Spruce Way. Bris 35 F4
Square The. Alve 15 D2
Square The. Axb 125 E1
Square The. Ban 107 D2
Square The. Blag 109 F2
Square The. Bris 64 A1
Square The. Clut 114 C1
Square The. Mang 51 F2
Square The. Ship 125 F4
Square The. Tims 116 A1
Square The. Well 118 B1
Square The. Wins 124 C3
Squire La. Co Mar 111 E1
Squires Ct. Kingsw 65 F2
Squires Leaze. Thorn 8 B1
Stabbins Cl. W-S-M 89 D3
Stable Yd. Bath 101 E3
Stackpool Rd. Bris 63 E2
Staddlestones. Mid No 137 F4
Stadium Rd. Bris 49 E3
Stafford Cres. Thorn 8 A1
Stafford Pl. W-S-M 104 C4
Stafford Rd. Bris 50 A1
Stafford Rd. Portis 45 F2
Stafford Rd. W-S-M 104 C4
Stafford St. Bris 63 E2
Staffords Ct. Kingsw 66 A3
Stainer Cl. Bris 79 E4
Stalcombe La. Co Dan 99 D2
Stall St. Bath 102 A3
Stambrook Park. Bathe 85 F3
Stanbridge Cl. Mang 51 F3
Stanbridge Rd. Mang 51 F3
Stanbury Ave. Bris 51 E3
Stanbury Rd. Bris 63 F2
Stancombe La. Back 76 C4
Standfast Rd. Bris 34 C2
Standish Ave. St Gif 24 B1
Standish Cl. Bris 34 C1
Standon Way. Bris 35 E1
Stane Way. Avon 47 E4
Stanfield Cl. Bris 50 B3
Stanford Cl. Fr Cot 37 F4
Stanford Pl. Bris 79 E4
Stanhope Pl. Bath 101 F3
Stanhope Rd. Kingsw 65 F1
Stanhope Rd. W-S-M 104 C2
Stanhope St. Bris 64 A3
Stanier Rd. Bath 101 F3
Stanle Hill. Bris 64 A2
Stanley Ave. Bris 36 A1
Stanley Ave. Bris 49 F2
Stanley Chase. Bris 50 C1
Stanley Cres. Bris 36 A1
Stanley Ct. Mid No 132 A1
Stanley Gdns. Kingsw 66 A2
Stanley Gr. W-S-M 104 C4
Stanley Mead. St Gif 24 C1
Stanley Park Rd. Kingsw 51 F2
Stanley Park. Bris 50 B1
Stanley Rd W. Bath 101 E3
Stanley Rd. Bris 49 E1
Stanley Rd. Kingsw 66 A4
Stanley St N. Bris 63 E2
Stanley St S. Bris 63 E1
Stanley St. Bris 63 E2
Stanley Terr. Bris 63 E1
Stanley Terr. Mid No 133 D2
Stanshalls Cl. Win 94 B4
Stanshalls Dr. Win 94 B4
Stanshalls Rd. Win 94 B4
Stanshaw Cl. Bris 51 D4
Stanshaw Rd. Bris 51 D4
Stanshawe Cres. Yate 27 F1
Stanshawes Dr. Yate 27 E1
Stanshaws Cl. St Gif 24 B1
Stanton Cl. Kingsw 51 F1
Stanton La. Pens 97 E2
Stanton Rd. Bris 35 F1
Stanton Wick La. Pens 97 D1
Stanway Cl. Bath 101 E1
Staple Gr. Keyn 81 E3
Staple Grove Cres. Bris 65 D4
Staplehill Rd. Bris 51 E2
Staples Cl. Cleve 57 F1
Staples Green. W-S-M 89 D2
Staples Hill. Hi Cha 120 B2
Staples Rd. Yate 27 E1
Stapleton Cl. Bris 50 B3
Stapleton Rd. Bris 50 A1
Stapleton Rd. Bris 50 B2
Star Barn Rd. Wint 37 F4
Star La. Bris 50 C2
Starcross Rd. W-S-M 89 D1
Starling Cl. W-S-M 105 F4
Starrs Cl. Axb 125 D1
Station App. Pens 97 E3
Station App. W-S-M 104 C4
Station Ave. Bris 51 D2
Station Cl. Ch Sod 40 B4
Station Cl. Kingsw 66 B4
Station La. Bris 50 A2
Station Rd. Alm 22 C2
Station Rd. Axb 125 E1

Station Rd. Back

Station Rd. Back 76 A3
Station Rd. Back 77 D4
Station Rd. Bath 101 E4
Station Rd. Blag 110 C2
Station Rd. Bris 34 C2
Station Rd. Bris 36 A1
Station Rd. Bris 36 A2
Station Rd. Bris 47 E3
Station Rd. Bris 49 F1
Station Rd. Bris 49 F2
Station Rd. Bris 51 D2
Station Rd. Bris 64 B1
Station Rd. Char 11 D3
Station Rd. Cleve 57 E2
Station Rd. Clut 114 C2
Station Rd. Cong 91 E2
Station Rd. E in G 47 E2
Station Rd. Fr Cot 38 B3
Station Rd. Gr Bad 30 C1
Station Rd. Hi Cha 120 B3
Station Rd. Ir Act 26 B2
Station Rd. Keyn 81 F3
Station Rd. Kingsw 51 F2
Station Rd. Kingsw 66 B4
Station Rd. Lock 89 E1
Station Rd. Mid No 132 A1
Station Rd. Nail 59 F1
Station Rd. Piln 22 C2
Station Rd. Portb 46 B2
Station Rd. Portis 45 E3
Station Rd. St Gif 36 B4
Station Rd. W-S-M 88 C1
Station Rd. W-S-M 104 C4
Station Rd. Winsc 107 F2
Station Rd. Wint 37 F2
Station Rd. Wring 92 B1
Station Rd. Yate 27 E1
Station R d. Yatt 74 A1
Station R d. Wickw 18 A4
Staunton Fields. Whit 80 B2
Staunton La. Whit 80 B2
Staunton Rd. Ch Mag 96 A2
Staunton Way. Whit 80 B2
Staveley Cres. Bris 35 E1
Staverton Cl. St Gif 24 B1
Staverton Way. Kingsw 66 A4
Stavordale Gr. Bris 80 A3
Steam Mills. Mid No 137 F4
Stean Bridge Rd. St Gif 36 C3
Steel Ct. Kingsw 65 F2
Steel Mills. Keyn 81 F2
Stella Gr. Bris 63 D1
Stephen St. Bris 64 B4
Stephens Dr. Kingsw 65 F3
Stepney Rd. Bris 50 B1
Stepney Wlk. Bris 50 B1
Stepping Stones The. Bris .. 64 C3
Sterncourt Rd. Bris 51 D4
Stevens Cres. Bris 63 F2
Stevens La. Lymp 122 B2
Steway La. Bathe 86 A3
Stibbs Ct. Kingsw 65 F2
Stibbs Hill. Bris 65 D4
Stickland. Cleve 57 E1
Stidcot La. Tyth 16 B3
Stidcote La. Wickw 16 C3
Stile Acres. Bris 34 A1
Stilemead La. Co Mar 111 E2
Stillhouse La. Bris 63 E2
Stillingfleet Rd. Bris 79 E3
Stillman Cl. Bris 78 C2
Stinchcombe. Yate 27 F1
Stirling Cl. Yate 27 E2
Stirling Rd. Bris 64 B2
Stirling Way. Keyn 81 F2
Stirtingale Ave. Bath 101 E2
Stirtingale Rd. Bath 101 E2
Stitchings La. Engl 117 E4
Stitchings Shord La. Bi Sut 113 E2
Stock Hill. Thorn 7 E1
Stock La. Chur 109 D4
Stock La. Cong 91 F1
Stock Way N. Nail 59 F1
Stock Way S. Nail 59 F1
Stockhill Cl. Chil 137 E2
Stockhill Rd. Chil 137 E1
Stockmead. Chur 109 D3
Stockton Cl. Bris 79 F2
Stockton Cl. Kingsw 66 A2
Stockwell Ave. Mang 52 A3
Stockwell Cl. Mang 52 A3
Stockwell Dr. Mang 52 A3
Stockwell Glen. Mang 52 A3
Stockwood Cres. Bris 63 F1
Stockwood Hill. Keyn 81 E4
Stockwood La. Bris 80 C3
Stockwood La. Whit 80 C3
Stockwood Rd. Bris 81 D4
Stodelegh Cl. W-S-M 89 D2
Stoke Bridge Ave. St Gif 36 B3
Stoke Hamlet. Bris 48 C3
Stoke Hill. Bris 48 C2
Stoke Hill. Ch St 112 B4
Stoke La. Bris 48 C3
Stoke La. Bris 50 C4
Stoke La. St Gif 36 B4
Stoke Mead. Li St 119 F4
Stoke Meadows. St Gif 24 B1

Stoke Paddock Rd. Bris 48 B3
Stoke Park Rd S. Bris 48 C2
Stoke Park Rd. Bris 48 C2
Stoke Rd. Bris 49 D1
Stoke Rd. Portis 45 C3
Stoke View Rd. Bris 50 C2
Stoke View. Bris 36 A2
Stokefield Cl. Thorn 8 A1
Stokeleigh Wlk. Bris 48 B3
Stokemead. St Gif 36 B4
Stokes Croft. Bris 63 F4
Stokes Ct. Kingsw 66 A2
Stone La. Wint 37 F2
Stone's Cross. Mid No 132 A1
Stoneable Rd. Mid No 133 D2
Stoneage La. P St J 117 D1
Stoneberry Rd. Bris 80 A2
Stonebridge Park. Bris 50 C1
Stonebridge Rd. W-S-M 104 C2
Stonebridge. Cleve 57 E1
Stonechat Gdns. Bris 50 C3
Stonehenge La. Nail 59 F2
Stonehill. Kingsw 65 F2
Stonehouse Cl. Bath 102 A1
Stonehouse La. Bath 102 A1
Stoneleigh Cres. Bris 64 A1
Stoneleigh Rd. Bris 64 A1
Stoneleigh Wlk. Bris 64 A1
Stoneleigh. Ch Mag 96 A2
Stonewell Dr. Cong 91 E2
Stonewell Gr. Cong 91 E2
Stonewell La. Cong 91 E2
Stonewell Park Rd. Cong ... 91 E2
Stoney Steep. Wrax 60 A2
Stoney Stile Rd. Alve 15 D3
Stoneyard Cl. Litt 129 E1
Stoneyfield Cl. E in G 47 D3
Stoneyfields. E in G 47 D2
Stores Rd. Avon 33 E2
Stormont Cl. W-S-M 104 C2
Stothard Rd. Bris 50 A4
Stottbury Rd. Bris 50 A2
Stoulton Gr. Bris 35 D2
Stourden Cl. Bris 51 D4
Stourton Dr. Kingsw 65 F2
Stover Rd. Yate 27 D1
Stover Trading Est. Yate 27 D1
Stowel Hill Rd. Tyth 16 A3
Stowey Bottom. Bi Sut 113 F3
Stowey Park. Yatt 91 E4
Stowey Rd. Yatt 91 E4
Stowick Cres. Bris 34 B1
Stradbrook Ave. Bris 65 D4
Stradling Ave. W-S-M 104 C3
Stradling Rd. Bris 34 B1
Straight St. Bris 63 F3
Straits Par. Bris 51 D3
Stratford Cl. Bris 79 F2
Stratford La. Co Mar 112 C1
Strathmore Rd. Bris 49 F3
Stratton Cl. St Gif 36 B4
Stratton Rd. Keyn 82 C2
Stratton St. Bris 63 F4
Strawberry Cl. Nail 59 E1
Strawberry Gdns. Nail 75 E4
Strawberry Hill. Cleve 57 F2
Strawberry La. Dun 78 C2
Strawbridge Rd. Bris 64 A4
Stream Cl. Bris 35 E2
Stream Side. Mang 51 F3
Stream The. Bris 37 D1
Streamcross. Yatt 74 C1
Streamleaze La. Thorn 15 D4
Streamleaze. Ch Mag 96 A2
Streamleaze. Thorn 15 E4
Streamside Rd. Ch Sod 28 A1
Streamside. Ch Mag 96 A2
Streamside. Cleve 57 F2
Street End La. Blag 110 B1
Street End. Blag 110 B1
Street The. Alve 15 D3
Street The. Bi Sut 113 F2
Street The. Ch St 112 B4
Street The. Chil 137 E3
Street The. Co Mar 111 E1
Street The. Co Mar 128 A4
Street The. Farm 115 F3
Street The. Luck 31 F2
Street The. N Nib 5 E2
Street The. Olve 14 A2
Street The. Rad 132 B1
Street The. Win 94 C1
Stretford Ave. Bris 64 B4
Stretford Rd. Bris 64 B4
Stride Cl. Piln 22 A3
Strode Comm. Alve 14 C3
Strode Gdns. Alve 14 C3
Strode Rd. Cleve 57 E1
Stroud Rd. Bris 35 F4
Stroud Rd. Bris 47 F3
Stuart Pl. Bath 101 E3
Stuart Rd. W-S-M 105 D3
Stuart St. Bris 64 B4
Stumpwell La. N Nib 5 F1
Sturden La. Bris 37 E2
Sturdon Rd. Bris 63 D2
Sturmer Cl. Yate 27 F2
Sturminster Cl. Bris 80 B3

Sturminster Rd. Bris 80 B4
Sullivan Cl. Bris 79 E3
Sumerlin Dr. Cleve 57 F2
Summer Hill. Bris 64 A2
Summer La N. W-S-M 89 D1
Summer La. Ban 106 C2
Summer La. Bath 102 B1
Summer La. Lock 89 D1
Summer La. W-S-M 89 D1
Summer St. Bris 63 E2
Summerfield Rd. Bath 85 D1
Summerfield. W-S-M 89 D2
Summerhayes. Kingsw 66 B3
Summerhill Rd. Bath 84 B1
Summerhill Rd. Bris 64 C4
Summerhill Terr. Bris 64 C4
Summerhouse. Nail 59 E2
Summerlands Rd. W-S-M .. 105 E4
Summerlands. Back 76 A3
Summerlea. Pris 117 D3
Summerleaze. Bris 51 E2
Summerleaze. Keyn 81 F4
Summers Dr. Doyn 54 A1
Summers Mead. Yate 27 F2
Summers Rd. Bris 50 A1
Summers Terr. Bris 50 A1
Sundays Hill. Alm 24 A2
Sundayshill La. Falf 9 E4
Sundayshill La. Rock 9 E4
Sunderland Pl. Bris 63 D4
Sunderland St. Bath 102 A4
Sundridge Park. Yate 39 F4
Sunfield Rd. Lock 105 F2
Sunningdale Cl. Nail 60 A1
Sunningdale Dr. Kingsw 66 A3
Sunningdale Rd. W-S-M 88 C2
Sunningdale. Bris 63 D4
Sunningdale. Yate 39 F4
Sunny Bank. Bris 51 D1
Sunny Hill. Bris 48 B4
Sunny Wlk. Bris 51 D1
Sunnybank. Mang 51 F3
Sunnydene. Bris 64 B2
Sunnyhill Dr. Bris 47 F3
Sunnymead. Keyn 81 F2
Sunnymead. Mid No 131 F1
Sunnymeade Rd. Nail 59 E2
Sunnyside La. Yate 27 E1
Sunnyside Rd N. W-S-M ... 104 C3
Sunnyside Rd. Cleve 57 E2
Sunnyside Rd. W-S-M 104 C3
Sunnyside View. P St J 133 E4
Sunnyside. Bris 48 C3
Sunnyside. Clut 115 D2
Sunnyside. Fr Cot 38 A4
Sunnyvale Dr. Kingsw 66 A2
Sunnyvale. Cleve 57 D1
Sunnyvale. Tims 132 C4
Sunridge Cl. Mid No 137 F4
Sunridge Park. Mid No 137 F4
Sunridge. Mang 51 E3
Sunrise Gr. Bris 64 B2
Surrey Rd. Bris 49 F2
Surrey St. Bris 63 F4
Sussex Pl. Bris 49 F1
Sussex St. Bris 64 A3
Sutherland Ave. Mang 51 F4
Sutherland Ave. Yate 27 F4
Sutherland Dr. Lock 105 E1
Sutherland Pl. Bris 49 D1
Sutton Ave. Bris 64 B2
Sutton Hill Rd. Bi Sut 113 E2
Sutton La. Wring 93 F1
Sutton Park. Bi Sut 113 E2
Sutton St. Bath 102 A4
Swainswick Gdns. Bath 85 E1
Swainswick La. Bathe 85 E2
Swainswick. Bris 79 F3
Swaish Dr. Kingsw 66 A2
Swallow Cl. Bris 35 F4
Swallow Dr. Bris 49 D4
Swallow Gdns. W-S-M 105 F4
Swallow Park. Thorn 8 B2
Swallow St. Bath 102 A3
Swallows Ct. St Gif 36 C2
Swan Cl. W-S-M 105 F4
Swan La. Fr Cot 25 D1
Swan La. Wint 37 E4
Swancombe. Blag 110 C1
Swancombe. W in G 59 F4
Swane Rd. Bris 80 C3
Swangrove. Wint 37 F3
Swanley La. Newp 4 A3
Swanmoor Cres. Bris 35 D2
Sweets Cl. Kingsw 51 F1
Sweets Rd. Kingsw 51 F1
Swift Cl. W-S-M 88 C1
Swinhay La. N Nib 5 E1
Swiss Dr. Bris 62 C1
Swiss Rd. Bris 62 C1
Swiss Rd. W-S-M 104 C4
Sycamore Cl. Bris 50 C1
Sycamore Cl. Kingsw 65 D2
Sycamore Cl. Nail 59 F1
Sycamore Cl. Ship 125 F4
Sycamore Cl. W-S-M 105 D4
Sycamore Dr. Bris 35 F4

Sycamore Rd. Rad 133 D1
Sydenham Bldgs. Bath 101 F3
Sydenham Hill. Bris 49 E1
Sydenham La. Bris 49 F1
Sydenham Rd. Bath 101 F3
Sydenham Rd. Bris 49 E1
Sydenham Rd. Bris 64 A2
Sydenham Way. Kingsw 65 E2
Sydney Bldgs. Bath 102 A3
Sydney House. E in G 47 E2
Sydney Mews. Bath 102 A4
Sydney Pl. Bath 102 A4
Sydney Rd. Bath 102 A4
Sydney Row. Bris 63 D3
Sydney Wharf. Bath 102 A4
Sylvan Way. Bris 48 B4
Sylvia Ave. Bris 63 F2
Symes Ave. Bris 79 E2
Symington Rd. Bris 51 D3
Syston Way. Kingsw 51 E1

Tabernacle Rd. Kingsw 65 E3
Tackley Rd. Bris 50 A2
Tadwick La. Bathe 84 C4
Tailor's Ct. Bris 63 E4
Talbot Ave. Bris 51 E1
Talbot Rd. Bris 64 B1
Talgarth Rd. Bris 49 F2
Tallis Gr. Bris 79 E3
Tamar Cl. Thorn 15 E4
Tamar Dr. Keyn 82 A2
Tamar Rd. Bris 64 B3
Tamar Rd. W-S-M 89 D1
Tamblyn Cl. Mid No 133 D2
Tamsin Ct. Keyn 81 F3
Tamworth Rd. Keyn 81 F2
Tanhouse La. Ir Act 27 E4
Tanhouse La. Yate 27 E4
Tankard's Cl. Bris 63 E4
Tanner Cl. Kingsw 65 F3
Tanners Ct. Bris 37 D1
Tanners Ct. Thorn 15 D4
Tanners La. Marsh 69 F4
Tanorth Cl. Bris 80 A2
Tanorth Rd. Bris 79 F2
Tanyard The. Kingsw 66 A1
Tapsters. Kingsw 66 A2
Tarnock Ave. Bris 80 A4
Tarnwell. Pens 97 D1
Taunton Rd. W-S-M 89 D2
Taunton Wlk. Bris 50 A4
Taveners Ind Est. Nail 59 F2
Taverner Cl. Bris 79 E4
Tavistock Rd. Bris 63 F1
Tavistock Rd. W-S-M 89 D1
Tavistock Wlk. Bris 63 F1
Tawny Way. W-S-M 105 F4
Taylor Cl. Kingsw 65 F4
Taylor Ct. W-S-M 89 D2
Taylor Gdns. Bris 78 C2
Tayman Cl. Bris 49 F3
Tayman Ridge. Bitt 82 B4
Taynton Cl. Kingsw 66 B1
Teal Cl. St Gif 24 B1
Teal Cl. W-S-M 88 C1
Teddington Cl. Bath 101 E2
Teesdale Cl. W-S-M 105 E4
Teewell Ave. Kingsw 51 F2
Teewell Cl. Kingsw 51 F2
Teewell Hill. Kingsw 51 F2
Teignmouth Rd. Bris 63 F1
Teignmouth Rd. Cleve 57 F1
Telephone Ave. Bris 63 E3
Telford Wlk. Bris 51 D1
Tellisford La. N St P 135 F2
Templar Rd. Yate 27 F1
Temple Back. Bris 63 F3
Temple Gate. Bris 63 F3
Temple St. Bris 63 D1
Temple St. Bris 63 F3
Temple St. Keyn 81 F3
Temple Way Underpass.
    Bris 63 F4
Temple Way. Bris 63 F3
Templeland Rd. Bris 78 C3
Tenby Rd. Keyn 81 F2
Tenby St. Bris 64 A4
Tennessee Gr. Bris 49 E3
Tennis Court Ave. Paul 131 E3
Tennis Court Rd. Paul 131 E3
Tennis Rd. Bris 64 A1
Tenniscourt Rd. Kingsw 52 A1
Tennyson Ave. Cleve 57 D1
Tennyson Cl. Keyn 81 F3
Tennyson Rd. Bath 101 E4
Tennyson Rd. Bris 49 F3
Tennyson Rd. W-S-M 105 D2
Tenterk Cl. Blea 122 A3
Tenth Ave. Bris 36 A1
Tereslake Green. Bris 35 E2
Terrace Wlk. Bath 102 A3
Terrell Gdns. Bris 64 B4
Terrell St. Bris 63 E4
Terry Hill. Kilm 139 E4
Tetbury Cl. St Gif 36 B4
Tetbury Gdns. Nail 60 A1
Tetbury Rd. Bris 65 D4
Teviot Rd. Keyn 82 A2

Tewkesbury Rd. Bris 50 A1
Tewther Rd. Bris 79 E2
Teyfant Rd. Bris 79 F2
Teyfant Wlk. Bris 79 F2
Thackeray Ave. Cleve 57 F2
Thackeray Rd. Cleve 57 F2
Thackeray Wlk. Bris 50 A4
Thames Cl. Char 11 D2
Thanet Rd. Bris 63 D1
Thatcher Cl. Portis 45 C2
Thatchers Cl. Bris 65 D4
The Timbers. Rod 138 A4
The Triangle. Wring 92 B1
The Tyning. Hi Cha 120 A2
The Weal. Bath 84 B1
There-and-back-again La.
    Bris 63 E4
Theresa Ave. Bris 49 E3
Theynes Croft. Lo Ash 62 A1
Thicket Ave. Bris 51 E2
Thicket Rd. Bris 51 E2
Thicket Wlk. Thorn 8 B1
Thiery Rd. Bris 64 B1
Thingwall Park. Bris 50 C2
Third Ave. Bath 101 E3
Third Ave. Bris 36 A1
Third Ave. Rod 138 B4
Third Way. Avon 33 E1
Thirlmere Ct. Kingsw 66 B3
Thirlmere Rd. Bris 36 A4
Thirlmere Rd. W-S-M 105 D2
Thistle St. Bris 63 D2
Thomas Cl. Ban 107 D2
Thomas La. Bris 63 F3
Thomas Pring Wlk. Bris 51 D1
Thomas St N. Bris 49 E1
Thomas St. Bath 102 A4
Thomas St. Bris 49 F1
Thomas St. Bris 63 F4
Thomas St. Bris 64 A4
Thompson Rd. Bris 80 C3
Thomson Rd. Bris 64 A4
Thorn Cl. W-S-M 89 D1
Thorn Cl. Yate 27 E1
Thornbank Pl. Bath 101 F3
Thornbury Dr. W-S-M 104 B3
Thornbury Rd. Alve 15 D3
Thornbury Rd. W-S-M 104 B1
Thorndale Cl. W-S-M 105 E4
Thorndale. Bris 63 D4
Thornhayes Cl. Fr Cot 38 A4
Thornleigh Rd. Bris 49 F3
Thornmead Gr. Bris 35 D1
Thornycroft Cl. Bris 50 A4
Three Queens' La. Bris 63 F3
Three Wells Rd. Bris 78 C2
Thrissell St. Bris 64 A4
Throgmorton Rd. Bris 79 F4
Thrubwell La. But 94 A2
Thrush Cl. W-S-M 105 F4
Thurlestone. Bris 80 A3
Thurlow Rd. Bris 50 B1
Thurston's Barton. Bris 50 B1
Tibberton. Kingsw 66 A4
Tibbott Rd. Bris 80 B3
Tibbott Wlk. Bris 80 B3
Tichborne Rd. Bris 64 B4
Tichborne Rd. W-S-M 87 F1
Tickenham Hill. Nail 59 F3
Tickenham Rd. Cleve 58 A2
Tide Gr. Bris 48 A4
Tidenham Way. Bris 23 F1
Tiffany Ct. Bris 63 F3
Tiledown Cl. Clut 114 C1
Tiledown. Clut 114 C1
Tilley Cl. Farm 116 A3
Tilley Cl. Keyn 82 A1
Tilley La. Farm 115 F3
Tilling Rd. Bris 49 F4
Tilling Wlk. Bris 49 F4
Tilting Rd. Thorn 8 A1
Timber Dene. Bris 50 B2
Timberscombe Wlk. Bris 80 B3
Timsbury Rd. Bris 63 F1
Timsbury Rd. Farm 116 A3
Timsbury Rd. Paul 115 E1
Timsbury Wlk. Bris 63 F1
Tindell Ct. Kingsw 65 F2
Tinker's La. Co Mar 128 A4
Tinker's La. Hol 139 D1
Tintagel Cl. Keyn 81 E2
Tintern Ave. Bris 64 B4
Tintern Cl. Kingsw 65 E3
Tippetts Rd. Kingsw 65 E3
Tirley Way. W-S-M 88 A1
Titan Barrow. Bathf 86 B1
Tiverton Gdns. W-S-M 89 D1
Tiverton Rd. Cleve 57 F1
Tiverton Wlk. Bris 51 D1
Tockington La. Alm 24 A4
Tockington La. Olve 24 A4
Tockington La. Piln 24 A4
Tockington Park La. Alve ... 24 C4
Toddington Cl. Yate 39 E4
Toghill La. Doyn 68 A4
Toll Down Way. Burt 43 D2
Toll Rd. W-S-M 121 D4

Tolland. W-S-M

Tolland. W-S-M 105 D1

Tollbridge Rd. Bath 85 F2
Tone Rd. Cleve 57 E1
Top Rd. Ship 125 F4
Tor Cl. W-S-M 89 D1
Tormarton Cres. Bris 34 C2
Tormarton Rd. A Tur 42 C3
Tormarton Rd. Marsh 56 A2
Tormarton Rd. Marsh 70 A4
Tormynton Rd. W-S-M 88 C2
Toronto Rd. Bris 50 A4
Torpoint Rd. Bris 63 E1
Torrance Cl. Kingsw 66 B3
Torridge Rd. Keyn 82 A2
Torrington Ave. Bris 79 F4
Torrington Cres. W-S-M 89 D2
Tortworth Rd. Bris 49 F3
Totnes Cl. W-S-M 89 D1
Totshill Dr. Bris 79 F2
Totshill Gr. Bris 79 F2
Totterdown La. W-S-M 105 D1
Totterdown Rd. W-S-M 104 C2
Touching End La. Marsh 69 F4
Touchstone Ave. St Gif 36 C3
Tovey Cl. W-S-M 88 C2
Tower Hill. Bris 63 F4
Tower House La. Wrax 60 A2
Tower La. Bris 63 E4
Tower La. Kingsw 66 A3
Tower Rd N. Kingsw 66 A4
Tower Rd S. Kingsw 66 A3
Tower Rd. Bris 51 E1
Tower Rd. Portis 45 D2
Tower St. Bris 63 F3
Tower Wlk. W-S-M 87 E1
Towerhead Rd. Ban 107 E2
Town Barton. N St P 135 F2
Town End. N St P 135 F2
Townsend Cl. Bris 80 C3
Townsend La. Alm 24 A3
Townsend Rd. Bris 80 C3
Townsend Rd. W-S-M 89 D3
Townsend. Alm 23 F2
Townsend. E Harp 129 D3
Townwell. Crom 10 A1
Tracy Wlk. Bris 79 F4
Trafalgar Rd. Bath 84 A1
Trafalgar Terr. Bris 63 D1
Tralee Wlk. Bris 63 E1
Tramway Rd. Bris 64 B2
Tranmere Ave. Bris 35 D2
Tranmere Gr. Bris 35 D2
Tranton La. Rock 2 B2
Tratman Rd. Bris 34 C2
Travers Cl. Bris 79 E3
Travers Wlk. St Gif 36 C3
Trawden Cl. W-S-M 88 A1
Tredegar Rd. Bris 51 D2
Tree Leaze. Yate 27 F1
Treefield Pl. Bris 50 A1
Treefield Rd. Cleve 57 E1
Tregarth Rd. Bris 62 C1
Trelawn Cl. Lock 89 E1
Trelawney Ave. Bris 64 B4
Trelawney Park. Bris 64 B2
Trelawney Rd. Bris 49 E1
Tremlett Mews. W-S-M 89 D2
Trench La. St Gif 25 D1
Trenchard Rd. Keyn 82 B2
Trenchard St. Bris 63 E4
Trendlewood Park. Bris 50 C3
Trendlewood Way. Nail 60 A1
Trenleigh Dr. W-S-M 89 D1
Trent Dr. Thorn 15 E4
Trent Gr. Keyn 82 A2
Trentham Cl. Bris 50 A1
Tresham Cl. St Gif 24 B1
Trevanna Rd. Bris 62 C1
Trevelyan Rd. W-S-M 104 C4
Trevelyan Wlk. Bris 34 C2
Treverdowe Wlk. Bris 34 B2
Trevethin Cl. Kingsw 65 E4
Trevisa Gr. Bris 35 E2
Trewartha Cl. W-S-M 104 C4
Trewartha Park. W-S-M 104 C4
Trewint Gdns. Bris 79 F4
Triangle Centre The. Cleve . 57 E2
Triangle E. Bath 101 E3
Triangle N. Bath 101 E3
Triangle South. Bris 63 D4
Triangle The. Cleve 57 E2
Triangle W. Bath 101 E3
Triangle West. Bris 63 D4
Trident Rd. Mang 38 A1
Trim Bridge. Bath 101 F3
Trim St. Bath 101 F3
Trin Mills. Bris 63 E3
Trinder Rd. E in G 47 D2
Trinity Cl. Bath 101 F3
Trinity Ct. Nail 59 E1
Trinity Pl. W-S-M 87 E1
Trinity Rd. Bath 102 A1
Trinity Rd. Bris 64 A4
Trinity Rd. Nail 59 F1
Trinity Rd. W-S-M 87 E1
Trinity St. Bath 101 F3
Trinity St. Bris 64 A4
Trinity Wlk. Bris 64 A4
Tripps Cnr. Yatt 91 E4

Troon Dr. Kingsw 66 A3
Troon. Yate 39 F4
Troopers Hill Rd. Bris 65 D4
Trossachs Dr. Bath 102 B4
Trowbridge Rd. Bris 35 E1
Trowbridge Wlk. Bris 35 E1
Truro Rd. Bris 63 D2
Truro Rd. Nail 60 A1
Trym Cross Rd. Bris 48 B3
Trym Rd. Bris 49 D4
Trym Side. Bris 48 B3
Trymleaze. Bris 48 B3
Trymwood Cl. Bris 34 C1
Tucker St. Bris 63 F4
Tucker's La. Co Mar 127 F4
Tuckett La. Bris 51 E4
Tuckingmill La. Co Dan 98 C3
Tuckmill. Cleve 57 D1
Tudor Cl. Kingsw 66 B2
Tudor Mews. W-S-M 104 C4
Tudor Rd. Bris 49 F1
Tudor Rd. Bris 50 B1
Tudor Rd. Kingsw 65 E3
Tudor Rd. Portis 45 F2
Tudor Rd. W-S-M 89 D2
Tuffley Rd. Bris 49 E4
Tugela Rd. Bris 78 C4
Tuggy's La. Hin Cha 119 F1
Tunbridge Cl. Ch Mag 96 A1
Tunbridge Rd. Ch Mag 96 A1
Tunley Hill. Tims 116 C1
Tunley Rd. Pris 117 E2
Tunnel La. Chil 137 F3
Tunstall Cl. Bris 48 C2
Turley Rd. Bris 50 B1
Turnberry Wlk. Bris 64 B1
Turnberry. Kingsw 66 A3
Turnbridge Rd. Bris 35 E2
Turnbury Ave. Nail 60 A1
Turnbury Cl. W-S-M 88 C2
Turnbury. Yate 39 F4
Turner Ct. Keyn 82 A3
Turner Ct. W-S-M 88 C2
Turner Gdns. Bris 50 A3
Turner Way. Cleve 57 D1
Turner's Terr. Faulk 134 A1
Turners Ct. Kingsw 65 F2
Turnpike Gate. Wickw 18 A3
Turnpike Rd. Co Bi 124 C2
Turnpike Rd. Ship 125 F4
Turtlegate Ave. Bris 78 C2
Turtlegate Wlk. Bris 78 C2
Turville Dr. Bris 50 A3
Tutton Way. Cleve 57 F1
Tweed Cl. Thorn 15 E4
Tweed Rd. Cleve 57 E1
Tweeny La. Kingsw 66 B3
Twenty Acres Rd. Bris 35 D1
Twerton Farm Cl. Bath 101 D3
Twickenham Rd. Bris 49 E3
Twinhoe La. Well 118 C1
Two Acres Rd. Bris 80 A4
Two Mile Ct. Kingsw 65 E4
Two Stones La. Ch Sod 40 B4
Two Trees. Priddy 126 C4
Twomile Hill Rd. Bris 65 D4
Twynings The. Kingsw 51 F1
Tybalt Way. St Gif 36 C3
Tyler Cl. Kingsw 65 F3
Tyler Green. W-S-M 89 D2
Tyler St. Bris 64 A3
Tyler's La. Mang 51 E3
Tyndale Ave. Bris 51 D2
Tyndale Ave. Yate 27 E2
Tyndale Cl. N Nib 5 F2
Tyndale Rd. Kingsw 51 F1
Tyndale View. Thorn 15 D4
Tyndall Ave. Bris 63 E4
Tyndall Rd. Bris 64 A4
Tyndall's Park Mews. Bris 63 E4
Tyndall's Park Rd. Bris 63 E4
Tyne Rd. Bris 49 E2
Tyne St. Bris 50 A1
Tyning Cl. Bris 80 A4
Tyning Cl. Yate 27 F1
Tyning End. Bath 102 A3
Tyning Hill. Mid No 133 D2
Tyning La. Bath 85 D1
Tyning Rd. Bath 85 F1
Tyning Rd. Bath 102 B1
Tyning Rd. Bris 63 F2
Tyning Rd. Keyn 82 C1
Tyning Rd. P St J 133 E4
Tyning Rd. Winsl 120 C4
Tyning The. Bath 102 A3
Tynings The. Cleve 57 D1
Tynings Way. Clut 114 C2
Tynings Way. Westw 120 C2
Tynte Ave. Bris 79 E2
Tyntesfield Rd. Bris 79 D4
Tyrone Wlk. Bris 79 F4
Tyrrel Way. St Gif 36 C3
Tytherington Rd. Alve 16 A3

Ubley Dr. Priddy 127 D4
Ullswater Cl. Kingsw 66 B3
Ullswater Cl. Yate 27 F2
Ullswater Dr. Bath 85 D1

Ulswater Rd. Bris 35 E1
Uncombe Cl. Back 76 B4
Under La. Wring 93 E1
Underbanks. E in G 47 E2
Underhill Ave. Mid No 131 F1
Underhill Dr. W-S-M 104 B1
Underhill La. Mid No 131 F1
Underhill Rd. Char 11 D3
Underleaf Way. P St J 133 E4
Undertown La. Co Mar 128 A4
Undertown. Co Mar 128 A4
Underwood Ave. W-S-M 88 A1
Underwood Cl. Alve 15 D2
Underwood End. Wins 108 A2
Underwood Rd. Portis 45 E2
Union Pas. Bath 102 A3
Union Pl. W-S-M 104 B4
Union Rd. Bris 64 A3
Union St. Bath 102 A3
Union St. Bris 63 F4
Union St. Nail 59 E1
Union St. W-S-M 104 B4
Unity Ct. Keyn 82 A3
Unity Rd. Keyn 82 A3
Unity St. Bris 63 E3
Unity St. Bris 63 F4
Unity St. Bris 65 E4
University Cl. Bris 48 C2
University Rd. Bris 63 E4
University Wlk. Bris 63 E4
Uphill Dr. Bath 85 D1
Uphill Rd N. W-S-M 104 B2
Uphill Rd S. W-S-M 104 C1
Uphill Rd. Bris 49 F3
Uphill Way. W-S-M 104 B1
Upjohn Cres. Bris 79 E2
Uplands Cl. Li St 119 F4
Uplands Dr. Keyn 82 C1
Uplands Rd. Bris 51 E2
Uplands Rd. Keyn 82 C1
Uplands The. Nail 75 E4
Upper Bath Rd. Thorn 15 D4
Upper Belgrave Rd. Bris 49 D1
Upper Belmont Rd. Bris 49 F2
Upper Berkeley Pl. Bris 63 D4
Upper Bloomfield Rd.
    Bath 101 E1
Upper Borough Walls.
    Bath 101 F3
Upper Bristol Rd. Bath 101 E4
Upper Bristol Rd. Clut 114 B2
Upper Bristol Rd. W-S-M 88 A1
Upper Byron Pl. Bris 63 D4
Upper Chapel La. Fr Cot 38 B4
Upper Cheltenham Pl. Bris .. 49 F1
Upper Church La. Bris 63 E4
Upper Church La. Lock 105 E1
Upper Church Rd. W-S-M 87 E1
Upper Church St. Bath 101 F4
Upper Cranbrook Rd. Bris 49 D2
Upper East Hayes. Bath 85 D1
Upper Farm Cl. N St P 135 F2
Upper Hedgemead Rd.
    Bath 102 A4
Upper Lambridge St. Bath 85 E1
Upper Lansdown Mews.
    Bath 84 C1
Upper Maudlin St. Bris 63 E4
Upper Mount Pleasant.
    Hi Cha 120 A2
Upper Myrtle Hill. E in G 47 E2
Upper New Rd. Ched 125 E1
Upper Oldfield Park. Bath .. 101 F3
Upper Perry Hill. Bris 63 E2
Upper Pitching. Chil 137 E3
Upper Rd. Hin Ble 129 D4
Upper Sandhurst Rd. Bris 64 B2
Upper St. Bris 64 A2
Upper St. Dyrh 54 C2
Upper Stanton. Pens 97 D1
Upper Station Rd. Kingsw 51 E2
Upper Stone Cl. Fr Cot 38 B4
Upper Strode. Win 111 F4
Upper Sydney St. Bris 63 D2
Upper Tockington Rd. Olve ... 14 A1
Upper Town La. Win 94 B4
Upper Wells St. Bris 63 E4
Upper York St. Bris 63 F4
Upton La. Ch Mag 95 F4
Upton La. Dun 85 D2
Upton Rd. Bris 63 D2
Upton. W-S-M 105 D1
Urchinwood La. Cong 91 F2
Urfords Dr. Bris 51 E3

Vain End. W-S-M 88 C2
Valda Rd. W-S-M 88 B1
Vale Cres. Lock 89 E1
Vale End. Nail 59 E1
Vale La. Bris 79 E4
Vale St. Bris 64 A2
Vale The. Puck 52 C3
Vale View Terr. Bathe 85 F2
Vale View. Rad 133 D4
Valentine Cl. Bris 80 A3
Valerian Cl. Bris 47 F3
Valetta Cl. W-S-M 104 C2

Valley Cl. Nail 59 F1
Valley Gdns. Mang 51 F4
Valley Gdns. Nail 59 F1
Valley Rd. Bris 79 D4
Valley Rd. Cleve 57 F3
Valley Rd. Kingsw 66 B3
Valley Rd. Lo Ash 62 B4
Valley Rd. Mang 52 A3
Valley Rd. Portis 44 C2
Valley Rd. W in G 45 D1
Valley View Cl. Bath 85 D2
Valley View Rd. Bath 85 E2
Valley View Rd. Paul 131 F3
Valley View. Clut 114 C2
Valley Way Rd. Nail 59 F2
Valley Wlk. Mid No 132 A1
Valls The. St Gif 36 C3
Valma Rocks. Bris 65 D3
Van Diemen's La. Bath 84 C1
Vandyke Ave. Keyn 81 F3
Vane St. Bath 102 A4
Vassall Ct. Bris 51 D3
Vassall Rd. Bris 51 D3
Vattingstone La. Alve 14 C3
Vaughan Cl. Bris 34 C2
Vayre Cl. Ch Sod 28 A1
Veale The. Blea 122 B3
Vee La. Win 94 B4
Vellore La. Bath 102 A4
Ventnor Ave. Bris 64 C4
Ventnor Rd. Bris 36 A2
Ventnor Rd. Bris 50 C1
Venus La. Clut 114 C2
Venus St. Cong 91 F1
Vera Rd. Bris 50 C1
Verbena Way. W-S-M 89 D1
Vereland Rd. Lock 105 F2
Verlands. Cong 91 F3
Vernham Gr. Bath 101 E1
Vernon Cl. Keyn 82 B2
Vernon La. Co Bi 124 A2
Vernon Park. Bath 101 E3
Vernon St. Bris 63 F2
Vernon Terr. Bath 101 E3
Vernslade. Bath 84 A1
Verrier Rd. Bris 64 B4
Verwood Dr. Kingsw 66 B1
Vicarage Cl. W-S-M 89 D2
Vicarage Gdns. P St J 133 D4
Vicarage La. Ba Gu 77 E3
Vicarage La. Co Bi 124 A2
Vicarage La. Co Dan 98 B3
Vicarage La. Hill 19 E4
Vicarage La. N St P 135 F2
Vicarage La. Olve 14 A2
Vicarage Rd. Bris 63 D2
Vicarage Rd. Bris 64 B4
Vicarage Rd. Bris 79 D3
Vicarage Rd. Fr Cot 38 B3
Vicarage Rd. Kingsw 65 D2
Vicarage Rd. Lo Ash 62 B3
Vicarage Rd. Piln 22 B4
Vicars Cl. Bris 51 D2
Victor Rd. Bris 63 E2
Victor St. Bris 64 A3
Victoria Ave. Bris 64 B4
Victoria Bldgs. Bath 101 E3
Victoria Bridge Rd. Bath 101 F3
Victoria Cl. Bath 101 E3
Victoria Cl. Portis 45 E3
Victoria Cl. Thorn 8 A2
Victoria Cotts. Sosto 118 C4
Victoria Cres. Piln 22 A3
Victoria Ct. Portis 45 E3
Victoria Gdns. Bathe 85 F2
Victoria Gdns. Bris 61 E1
Victoria Gr. Bris 63 F2
Victoria Parade. Bris 64 B4
Victoria Park. Bris 51 D3
Victoria Park. Bris 51 E1
Victoria Park. W-S-M 87 E1
Victoria Pl. Bris 63 E2
Victoria Pl. Paul 131 E3
Victoria Quadrant. W-S-M . 104 C4
Victoria Rd. Avon 47 D4
Victoria Rd. Bath 101 E3
Victoria Rd. Bris 64 B4
Victoria Rd. Cleve 57 E2
Victoria Rd. Keyn 82 B2
Victoria Rd. Kingsw 65 E3
Victoria Rd. Kingsw 66 B3
Victoria Sq. Bris 63 D4
Victoria Sq. Portis 45 E3
Victoria Sq. W-S-M 104 B4
Victoria St. Bris 63 F3
Victoria St. Mang 51 E3
Victoria Terr. Bath 101 E3
Victoria Terr. Bris 62 C3
Victoria Terr. Bris 64 A3
Victoria Terr. Paul 131 F3
Victoria Wlk. Bris 49 E1
Vigor Rd. Bris 79 D3
Village Cl. Yate 27 E1
Villice La. Co Mar 128 A4
Villiers Rd. Bris 50 A1

Vilner La. Thorn 15 D4
Vimpany Cl. Bris 34 C2
Vimpennys La. Alm 22 C1
Vincent Cl. Bris 34 B1
Vine Gdns. W-S-M 89 D1
Viner's La. A Tur 43 D3
Vinery The. Wins 125 D4
Vineyard La. Kings 11 F3
Vining Wlk. Bris 64 A4
Vinney Ave. Mang 52 A4
Vinney Cl. Bris 28 C4
Vintery Leys. Bris 49 D4
Virginia Cl. Ch Sod 28 A1
Vivian St. Bris 63 E2
Vivien Ave. Mid No 132 A1
Vowell Cl. Bris 79 D2
Vynes Cl. Nail 60 A1
Vynes Way. Nail 60 A1
Vyvyan Rd. Bris 63 D4
Vyvyan Terr. Bris 63 D4

Wade Rd. Yate 27 D2
Wade St. Bris 63 F4
Wadehurst Ind Pk. Bris 64 A4
Wades Rd. Bris 36 A2
Wadham Dr. Bris 37 D1
Wadham St. W-S-M 104 B4
Wagtail Gdns. W-S-M 105 F4
Wainbridge Cres. Piln 22 B4
Wainbrook Dr. Bris 50 B1
Wains Cl. Cleve 57 E1
Wainwright Cl. W-S-M 89 D2
Waits Cl. Ban 106 C2
Wakedean Gdns. Yatt 74 A1
Wakeford Rd. Mang 52 A4
Walcot Gate. Bath 102 A4
Walcot St. Bath 102 A4
Waldegrave House. Bris 79 E2
Waldegrave Rd. Bath 84 C1
Waldegrave Terr. Mid No 133 D2
Walden Rd. Keyn 82 A2
Walford Ave. Lock 89 D2
Walk Mill La. Kings 11 F2
Walk The. Kings 11 F3
Walker Cl. Bris 64 A4
Walker Cl. Mang 52 A4
Walker St. Bris 63 E4
Walker Way. Thorn 15 D4
Wall Green. Axb 125 E1
Wallace La. E Harp 128 C2
Wallace Rd. Bath 85 D1
Wallenge Cl. Paul 131 F3
Wallenge Dr. Paul 131 F3
Walley La. Ch Mag 113 D4
Wallingford Rd. Bris 79 E4
Walliscote Ave. Bris 49 E3
Walliscote Grove Rd.
    W-S-M 104 C4
Walliscote Rd S. W-S-M 104 B2
Walliscote Rd. Bris 49 E3
Walliscote Rd. W-S-M 104 B3
Wallscourt Rd S. Bris 36 A1
Wallscourt Rd. Bris 36 A1
Wallsend La. Tor 55 E3
Wallycourt Rd. Ch St 112 C4
Walnut Ave. Yate 28 A1
Walnut Cl. Axb 125 D1
Walnut Cl. E in G 47 D2
Walnut Cl. Keyn 81 E2
Walnut Cl. Kingsw 51 F1
Walnut Cl. Nail 75 F4
Walnut Cl. Thorn 8 B1
Walnut Cl. W-S-M 105 D1
Walnut Cres. Kingsw 65 F4
Walnut Dr. Bath 101 F2
Walnut Dr. Col 70 C3
Walnut La. Kingsw 66 A4
Walnut Tree Cl. Alm 24 A3
Walnut Wlk. Bris 79 D3
Walnut Wlk. Keyn 81 E2
Walsh Ave. Bris 80 A4
Walsh Cl. W-S-M 105 D1
Walshe Ave. Ch Sod 28 A1
Walsingham Rd. Bris 49 F1
Walter St. Bris 63 D2
Walton Ave. Bris 64 B3
Walton Cl. Keyn 81 E2
Walton Cl. Kingsw 66 B1
Walton Dro. W in G 58 B3
Walton Heath. Yate 27 F1
Walton Rd. Bris 47 E3
Walton Rd. Cleve 57 F2
Walton Rise. Bris 49 D4
Walton St. Bris 50 A1
Walton. W-S-M 105 D1
Walwyn Cl. Bath 101 D3
Walwyn Gdns. Bris 79 E2
Wansbeck Rd. Keyn 82 A2
Wansbrough Rd. W-S-M 89 D2
Wanscow Wlk. Bris 49 D3
Wansdyke Cl. Bris 80 A3
Wansdyke Rd. Bath 101 E1
Wapley Hill. West 39 F2
Wapley Rd. Dod 40 A2
Wapping Rd. Bris 63 E3
Warden Rd. Bris 63 E2
Wardour Rd. Bris 79 E4

Wareham Cl. Nail

Wareham Cl. Nail 59 E1
Warleigh Dr. Bathe 86 A2
Warleigh La. Bathf 103 E3
Warleigh La. Mon Far 103 E3
Warman Cl. Bris 80 C3
Warman Rd. Bris 80 C3
Warmington Rd. Bris 80 B4
Warminster Rd. Bath 103 D3
Warminster Rd. Bris 50 A1
Warminster Rd. Hin Cha 119 F3
Warminster Rd. Li St 120 A4
Warne Park. W-S-M 105 D3
Warne Rd. W-S-M 105 D3
Warner Cl. Brock 92 A4
Warner Cl. Kingsw 65 F3
Warns The. Kingsw 66 A2
Warren Cl. Lock 105 E1
Warren Cl. St Gif 24 B2
Warren Croft. N Nib 5 F2
Warren Gdns. Bris 80 C3
Warren La. Lo Ash 61 F1
Warren Rd. Bris 36 A2
Warren Way. Yate 27 F2
Warrilow Cl. W-S-M 89 D3
Warrington Rd. Bris 64 B1
Warth La. W ST L 89 D4
Warwick Ave. Bris 50 A1
Warwick Cl. Kingsw 66 A1
Warwick Cl. Thorn 8 A1
Warwick Cl. W-S-M 105 E4
Warwick Gdns. Clut 114 B2
Warwick Rd. Bath 101 D4
Warwick Rd. Bris 49 D1
Warwick Rd. Bris 50 A1
Warwick Rd. Keyn 81 E2
Washing Pound La. Nail 59 D2
Washing Pound La. Whit 80 A2
Washingpool Hill Rd. Olve 14 B3
Washingpool La. Avon 33 F4
Washington Ave. Bris 50 B1
Washpool La. Engl 100 C1
Watch Elm Cl. St Gif 36 C3
Watchhouse Rd. E in G 47 E2
Watchill Ave. Bris 78 C3
Watchill Cl. Bris 78 C3
Water La. Bris 63 F2
Water La. Bris 63 F3
Water La. Bris 64 B1
Water La. E in G 47 E2
Water La. Kingsw 65 D1
Water La. Mid No 132 A2
Water La. S E Harp 128 C2
Water's La. Bris 49 D4
Waterbridge Rd. Bris 78 C3
Watercress Rd. Bris 49 F2
Waterdale Cl. Bris 49 E4
Waterdale Gdns. Bris 49 E4
Waterford Cl. Thorn 15 E4
Waterford Park. Rad 132 C1
Waterford Rd. Bris 49 D3
Waterloo Bldgs. Bath 101 D3
Waterloo Pl. Bris 64 A4
Waterloo Rd. Bris 63 F4
Waterloo Rd. Rad 133 D1
Waterloo St. Bris 62 C4
Waterloo St. Bris 63 F4
Waterloo St. W-S-M 104 B4
Watermore Cl. Fr Cot 38 B4
Waters Rd. Bris 65 E4
Waters Rd. Kingsw 65 E4
Waterside Cres. Rad 132 B1
Waterside Dr. St Gif 24 A1
Waterside La. W-S-M 138 C3
Waterside Park. Portis 44 B2
Waterside Rd. Rad 132 B1
Waterside Way. Rod 138 B4
Watery La. Bath 101 D3
Watery La. Chil 138 A2
Watery La. Doyn 68 A4
Watery La. Nail 59 E1
Watery La. Win 95 D2
Wathen Rd. Bris 49 F2
Watkins Yd. Bris 49 D4
Watley's End Rd. Wint 37 F4
Watling Way. Bris 47 E4
Watson Ave. Bris 64 B2
Watson's Rd. Kingsw 65 F2
Watters Cl. Fr Cot 38 B3
Wavell Cl. Yate 27 E2
Waveney Rd. Keyn 82 A2
Waverley Rd. Back 76 A4
Waverley Rd. Bris 47 F3
Waverley Rd. Bris 49 E1
Waverley Rd. Ir Act 27 D1
Waverley Rd. W-S-M 104 C2
Waverley St. Bris 50 A1
Wayacre Dro. Blea 121 F3
Wayfield Gdns. Bathe 85 F2
Wayford Cl. Keyn 82 A2
Wayland Rd. W-S-M 88 C2
Wayleaze. Fr Cot 38 B4
Wayside Cl. Fr Cot 38 A4
Wayside Dr. Cleve 57 F3
Wayside. W-S-M 88 B1
Weare Ct. Bris 63 D3
Weatherley Ave. Bath 101 E1
Weavers St. Kings 11 F2
Webb St. Bris 64 A4

Webbington Rd. Co Bi 124 B2
Webbs Heath. Sist 66 C4
Webbs Wood Rd. St Gif 36 C3
Webbs Wood. St Gif 36 C4
Wedgewood Rd. Mang 37 E1
Wedgwood Cl. Bris 80 A3
Wedgwood Rd. Bath 101 D3
Wedmore Cl. Kingsw 65 E4
Wedmore Cl. W-S-M 104 C1
Wedmore Park. Bath 101 D2
Wedmore Rd. Cleve 57 D1
Wedmore Rd. Keyn 82 B2
Wedmore Rd. Nail 75 F4
Wedmore Vale. Bris 63 F1
Weedon Cl. Bris 50 A1
Weekesley La. Tims 116 B1
Weetwood Rd. Cong 91 F3
Weight Rd. Bris 64 B4
Weind The. W-S-M 88 B1
Weir Cl. W-S-M 105 D1
Weir La. Ab Lei 61 F3
Weir La. Marsh 69 F4
Weir Rd. Cong 91 F2
Well Cl. W-S-M 105 D1
Well Cl. Wins 125 D4
Well House Cl. Bris 48 C2
Well La. Yatt 91 E4
Well Park. Cong 91 F2
Welland Rd. Keyn 81 F2
Wellard Cl. W-S-M 89 D2
Wellgarth Rd. Bris 64 A1
Wellgarth Wlk. Bris 64 A1
Wellington Ave. Bris 49 F1
Wellington Bldgs. Bath 84 A1
Wellington Cres. Bris 49 F3
Wellington Dr. Bris 49 E3
Wellington Dr. Yate 27 D1
Wellington Hill W. Bris 49 E4
Wellington Hill. Bris 49 E4
Wellington La. Bris 49 F1
Wellington Mews. Bris 47 E3
Wellington Park. Bris 49 D1
Wellington Pl. Bris 37 D1
Wellington Pl. W-S-M 104 B4
Wellington Rd. Bris 63 F4
Wellington Rd. Kingsw 51 E1
Wellington Rd. Yate 27 F2
Wellington Terr. Cleve 57 E2
Wellington Wlk. Bris 49 E4
Wellow La. Hin Cha 119 E1
Wellow La. N St P 135 E3
Wellow La. P St J 133 E3
Wellow Mead. P St J 133 D4
Wellow Rd. Well 134 A4
Wellow Tyning. P St J 133 E4
Wells Cl. Bris 80 B3
Wells Cl. Nail 60 A1
Wells Rd. Bath 101 F3
Wells Rd. Bris 64 A1
Wells Rd. Bris 80 B4
Wells Rd. Ch Mag 95 F4
Wells Rd. Chil 137 F2
Wells Rd. Cleve 57 E1
Wells Rd. Dun 95 F4
Wells Rd. Mid No 132 B1
Wells Rd. N St P 135 E2
Wells Rd. Paul 131 D3
Wells Sq. Rad 132 B1
Wells St. Bris 63 D2
Wellsea Gr. W-S-M 105 D4
Wellstead Ave. Yate 27 E1
Wellsway. Bath 101 F1
Wellsway. Keyn 81 F2
Welsford Ave. Bris 50 B2
Welsford Rd. Bris 50 B2
Welsh Back. Bris 63 E3
Welton Gr. Mid No 132 A2
Welton Rd. Rad 132 C1
Welton Vale. Mid No 132 A1
Welton Wlk. Bris 51 E1
Wemberham Cres. Yatt 74 A1
Wemberham La. Yalt 90 C4
Wenmore Cl. Mang 37 E1
Wentforth Dr. Bris 51 E1
Wentwood Dr. W-S-M 105 D1
Wentworth Rd. Bris 49 E2
Wentworth. Kingsw 66 A3
Wentworth. Yate 27 F1
Wesley Ave. Kingsw 65 E3
Wesley Ave. Rad 132 B1
Wesley Cl. Kingsw 51 E2
Wesley Dr. W-S-M 89 D2
Wesley Hill. Kingsw 51 E1
Wesley La. Kingsw 66 A3
Wesley Pl. Bris 49 D1
Wesley Rd. Bris 49 F2
Wesley St. Bris 63 E2
Wessex Ave. Bris 49 F4
Wessex Rd. W-S-M 105 D1
West Ave. Bath 101 E3
West Broadway. Bris 49 E3
West Cl. Bath 101 D3
West Coombe. Bris 48 B3
West Croft. Bris 49 E4
West Croft. Cleve 57 D1
West Dene. Bris 48 C3
West Dundry La. Dun 78 C1
West End. Bris 63 E3

West End. Bris 63 E4
West Garston. Ban 107 D2
West Gr. Bris 49 F1
West Hay Rd. Wring 92 B2
West Hill Gdns. Portis 45 E3
West Hill Gdns. Rad 132 C1
West Hill Rd. Rad 132 B1
West Hill. Portis 45 E3
West Hill. Wrax 60 A3
West La. Win 94 A4
West Lea Rd. Bath 84 A1
West Leaze Pl. St Gif 36 C3
West Links Cl. W-S-M 88 A2
West Littleton Rd. Marsh 55 F1
West Mall. Bris 62 C4
West Par. Bris 48 B4
West Park Rd. Mang 51 F3
West Park. Bris 63 D4
West Point Row. St Gif 24 B2
West Priory Cl. Bris 49 D4
West Rd. Lymp 122 A1
West Rd. Mid No 132 A2
West Rd. Yatt 91 D4
West Ridge. Fr Cot 38 B4
West Rocke Ave. Bris 48 B3
West Rolstone Rd. Ban 89 F1
West Shrubbery. Bris 49 D1
West St. Axb 125 D1
West St. Ban 107 D2
West St. Bris 63 E2
West St. Bris 63 F4
West St. Kingsw 65 E4
West St. Kingsw 66 B2
West St. Tyth 16 A3
West St. W-S-M 104 B4
West Town Ave. Bris 64 B1
West Town Gr. Bris 80 B4
West Town La. Bris 64 B1
West Town Park. Bris 80 B4
West Town Rd. Back 76 A3
West Town Rd. Bris 47 E4
West Tyning. Marks 99 D1
West View Rd. Bathe 86 A2
West View Rd. Bris 63 D2
West View Rd. Keyn 81 F3
West View. Alve 14 C2
West Way. Bris 35 F2
West Way. Cleve 57 E2
West Wick. Lock 89 E1
West Wlk. Yate 27 F1
West. St Gif 24 A1
Westacre Cl. Bris 35 D1
Westaway Cl. Yatt 91 E4
Westaway Park. Yatt 91 E4
Westbourn Rd. Bris 64 A4
Westbourne Ave. Cleve 57 D1
Westbourne Ave. Keyn 81 F3
Westbourne Cres. Cleve 57 D1
Westbourne Gr. Bris 63 E2
Westbourne Pl. Bris 63 D4
Westbourne Rd. Mang 51 F4
Westbourne Terr. Bris 51 D4
Westbrook Park. Charl 84 A1
Westbrook Rd. Bris 80 B4
Westbrook Rd. W-S-M 88 B1
Westbrooke Ct. Bris 63 D3
Westbury Court Rd. Bris 49 D4
Westbury Cres. W-S-M 104 C1
Westbury Ct. Bris 49 D4
Westbury Hill. Bris 49 D4
Westbury La. Bris 48 B4
Westbury Park. Bris 49 D2
Westbury Rd. Bris 49 D2
Westcourt Dr. Kingsw 66 A2
Westcroft. Blag 110 C1
Westend La. O-on-S 7 D3
Westend Rd. Wickw 17 F3
Westend Rd. Yate 17 F3
Westering Cl. Mang 52 A3
Westerleigh Cl. Mang 51 F4
Westerleigh Rd. Bath 102 A1
Westerleigh Rd. Cleve 57 D1
Westerleigh Rd. Mang 52 A4
Westerleigh Rd. Puck 53 E4
Westerleigh Rd. West 39 E2
Westerleigh Rd. Yate 39 E4
Western Ave. Fr Cot 26 A1
Western Ct. Cleve 57 E2
Western Dr. Bris 79 F3
Western La. E Harp 128 A2
Western La. Priddy 128 B2
Western Rd. Bris 49 F3
Westfield Cl. Back 76 A3
Westfield Cl. Bath 101 F2
Westfield Cl. Keyn 81 E3
Westfield Cl. Kingsw 65 E3
Westfield Cl. W-S-M 104 B1
Westfield Cres. Ban 107 D2
Westfield Dr. Back 76 A3
Westfield Ind and Trading Est.
   Rod 138 B4
Westfield La. W-S-M 36 C2
Westfield Park S. Bath 101 D4
Westfield Park. Bath 101 D4
Westfield Park. Bris 49 D1
Westfield Pl. Bris 62 C4
Westfield Rd. Back 76 A3
Westfield Rd. Ban 107 D2

Westfield Rd. Bris 49 D4
Westfield Rd. W-S-M 104 B1
Westfield Terr. Rad 132 B1
Westfield Way. St Gif 24 B1
Westfield. Cleve 73 E4
Westgate Bldgs. Bath 101 F3
Westgate St. Bath 101 F3
Westhall Rd. Bath 101 E4
Westland Ave. Kingsw 66 B2
Westleigh Cl. Yate 27 E1
Westleigh Park. Bris 80 A4
Westleigh Rd. Bris 35 E1
Westmarch Way. W-S-M 89 D2
Westmarsh La. O-on-S 7 D3
Westmarsh. O-on-S 7 D3
Westmead Gdns. Charl 84 A1
Westmead Rd. Bris 65 D4
Westminster Cl. Bris 49 D4
Westminster Rd. Bris 64 B4
Westmoreland Dr. Bath 101 F3
Westmoreland Rd. Bath 101 F3
Westmoreland Rd. Bris 49 D2
Westmoreland St. Bath 101 F3
Westmoreland Station Rd.
   Bath 101 F3
Westmorland Terr. Ch Sod .. 41 E4
Weston Ave. Bris 64 B4
Weston Cl. Bris 48 B4
Weston Cres. Bris 49 F3
Weston Dro. W in G 58 C4
Weston Farm La. Bath 84 A1
Weston Ind Est. W-S-M 105 D2
Weston La. Bath 101 E4
Weston Park Court. Bath 84 B1
Weston Park E. Bath 84 B1
Weston Park W. Bath 84 B1
Weston Park. Bath 84 B1
Weston Rd. Bath 101 E4
Weston Rd. Berr 121 D3
Weston Rd. Cong 91 D3
Weston Rd. Lo Ash 77 E4
Weston Rd. Wrax 61 E2
Weston Way. Lock 105 F1
Weston Wood Rd. Portis 45 E2
Westons Way. Kingsw 65 F4
Westover Cl. Bris 34 C1
Westover Dr. Bris 35 D1
Westover Gdns. Bris 48 C4
Westover Rd. Bris 35 D1
Westover Rise. Bris 35 D1
Westview Orchard. Hi Cha . 120 A3
Westview. Paul 131 E3
Westward Cl. Wring 92 B1
Westward Dr. E in G 47 E2
Westward Gdns. Lo Ash 62 A1
Westward Rd. Bris 78 C4
Westway. Nail 59 F1
Westwood Ave. Paul 115 E1
Westwood Cl. W-S-M 88 C1
Westwood Cres. Bris 64 B3
Westwood Rd. Bris 80 B4
Westwood Rd. Westw 120 C2
Westwoods. Bathe 86 A2
Wetherby Cl. Mang 37 F1
Wetherell Pl. Bris 63 D4
Wetlands La. Portis 45 E2
Wexford Rd. Bris 79 E4
Weymouth Rd. Bris 63 F1
Weymouth St. Bath 102 A4
Wharf La. Portb 46 A3
Wharf Rd. Bris 50 C1
Wharfedale. Thorn 15 E4
Wharfside. Lymp 121 F2
Wharnecliffe Cl. Bris 80 A3
Wharnecliffe Gdns. Bris 80 A3
Whatley Rd. Bris 49 D1
Wheatfield Dr. St Gif 24 B1
Wheathill Cl. Keyn 81 E3
Wheelers Cl. Mid No 132 B1
Wheelers Dr. Mid No 132 B1
Wheelers Rd. Mid No 132 B1
Whinchat Gdns. Bris 50 C3
Whippington Ct. Bris 63 F4
Whistley La. E Harp 128 C3
Whitby Rd. Bris 64 B4
Whitchurch La. Bris 79 F3
Whitchurch La. Bris 80 A2
Whitchurch La. Dun 79 E1
Whitchurch Rd. Bris 79 D3
White Cross Gate. Paul 130 C3
White Hill. Well 133 F3
White Horse Rd. Winsl 120 C1
White House La. Badg 123 D2
White House Rd. Yatt 91 F4
White Lodge Park. Portis 45 E3
White Lodge Rd. Kingsw 51 D2
White Ox Mead La. Well 117 F1
White St. Bris 63 F4
White Tree Rd. Bris 49 D2
Whitebrook La. P St J 133 D4
Whitebrook La. Tims 132 C1
Whitecroft Way. Kingsw 66 A4
Whitecross Ave. Bris 80 B3
Whitecross La. Ban 107 D2
Whitecross Rd. E Harp 128 C2
Whitecross Rd. W-S-M 104 C3
Whitefield Ave. Bris 51 D1
Whitefield Ave. Kingsw 65 E3

Willoughby Cl. Bris

Whitefield Cl. Bathe 86 A2
Whitefield Cl. Kingsw 51 E2
Whitefield Rd. Bris 51 D1
Whitefields. Ch Sod 28 A1
Whitegate Cl. Blea 122 A3
Whitehall Ave. Bris 50 C1
Whitehall Gdns. Bris 64 B4
Whitehall Rd. Bris 64 B4
Whitehall Trading Est. Bris .. 64 B4
Whitehouse La. Bris 63 E2
Whitehouse La. Litt 129 F1
Whitehouse La. Wrax 60 A3
Whitehouse Pl. Bris 63 F2
Whitehouse Rd. Piln 22 B4
Whitehouse St. Bris 63 F2
Whiteladies Rd. Bris 49 D1
Whitelands Hill. Mid No 133 D2
Whiteleaze. Bris 49 E4
Whiteoak Way. Nail 75 E4
Whites Hill. Bris 65 D3
Whitesfield Rd. Nail 59 E1
Whitewall La. Thorn 8 C1
Whiteway Ave. Bath 101 D2
Whiteway Cl. Bris 64 C3
Whiteway Ct. Bris 65 D4
Whiteway Mews. Bris 65 D4
Whiteway Rd. Bath 101 D2
Whiteway Rd. Bris 51 D1
Whitewells Rd. Bath 85 D1
Whitewood Rd. Bris 50 C1
Whitfield Rd. Thorn 8 C1
Whiting Rd. Bris 79 D2
Whitland Ave. Bris 79 D3
Whitland Rd. Bris 79 D3
Whitley Cl. Yate 27 E2
Whitley Mead. St Gif 36 C2
Whitling St. Win 95 D1
Whitmead Gdns. Bris 79 E2
Whitmore Ave. Bris 65 D2
Whitson St. Bris 63 E4
Whitting Rd. W-S-M 104 C1
Whittington Dr. W-S-M 88 C1
Whittington Rd. Bris 51 E3
Whittock Rd. Bris 80 B3
Whittock Sq. Bris 80 B4
Whittucks Cl. Kingsw 65 E2
Whittucks Rd. Kingsw 65 E2
Whitwell Rd. Bris 80 A4
Whytes Cl. Bris 49 D4
Wick Cres. Bris 64 B2
Wick Ct. W-S-M 89 D1
Wick House Cl. Keyn 82 B2
Wick La. Bitt 67 D1
Wick La. Lymp 121 F1
Wick La. Pens 97 C2
Wick La. Tims 116 C1
Wick Rd. Berr 121 E1
Wick Rd. Bi Sut 113 C2
Wick Rd. Bris 64 B2
Wick Rd. Bris 64 C3
Wick Rd. Lymp 121 E1
Wick Rd. Piln 22 B4
Wickets The. Bris 35 F1
Wickets The. Kingsw 51 E1
Wickfield. Cleve 57 E1
Wickham Cl. Ch Sod 40 B4
Wickham Ct. Bris 50 B3
Wickham Glen. Bris 50 B3
Wickham Hill. Bris 50 B3
Wickham View. Bris 50 B3
Wicklow Rd. Bris 79 F4
Wickwar Rd. Ch Sod 28 A3
Wickwar Rd. Kings 11 F2
Wickwar Rd. Wickw 17 D1
Wickwar Rd. Yate 28 A3
Widcombe Cl. Bris 65 D2
Widcombe Cres. Bath 102 A3
Widcombe Hill. Bath 102 B2
Widcombe Rise. Bath 102 A3
Widcombe. Bris 80 A3
Wigmore Gdns. W-S-M 88 B1
Wigton Cres. Bris 35 E1
Wilbye Gr. Bris 79 E3
Wilcox Cl. Kingsw 65 E3
WildCountry La. Ba Gu 77 F3
Wildcountry La. Lo Ash 77 F3
Wildcroft Rd. Bris 49 D2
Wilder St. Bris 63 F4
Willada Cl. Bris 63 D1
William Daw Cl. Ban 106 C2
William Mason Cl. Bris 64 A4
William St. Bath 102 A4
William St. Bris 49 E1
William St. Bris 51 D2
William St. Bris 63 F2
William St. Bris 64 A3
William St. Bris 84 B4
Williams Cl. Kingsw 65 F2
Williamson Rd. Bris 49 F2
Williamstowe. Bath 102 B1
Willinton Rd. Bris 79 F4
Willis Rd. Kingsw 51 F1
Williton Cres. W-S-M 104 C2
Willment Way. Avon 33 E1
Willmott Cl. Bris 79 F2
Willoughby Cl. Alve 15 D2
Willoughby Cl. Bris 79 D4

Willoughby Rd. Bris ... 49 F3
Willow Cl. Bris ... 35 F4
Willow Cl. Char ... 11 D2
Willow Cl. Cleve ... 57 F2
Willow Cl. Kingsw ... 66 B3
Willow Cl. Lo Ash ... 61 F1
Willow Cl. Lock ... 89 E1
Willow Cl. Portis ... 45 E2
Willow Cl. Rad ... 132 C1
Willow Cl. W-S-M ... 104 C1
Willow Cl. Wick ... 67 D3
Willow Dr. Blea ... 122 B3
Willow Dr. Lock ... 105 F1
Willow Dr. Lock ... 105 F3
Willow Gdns. Lock ... 89 E1
Willow Gr. Bris ... 51 E1
Willow Green. Bath ... 101 F2
Willow Rd. Kingsw ... 65 E2
Willow Way. Fr Cot ... 38 B3
Willow Wlk. Bris ... 35 D2
Willow Wlk. Keyn ... 81 E2
Willowdown. W-S-M ... 88 C2
Willowfalls The. Bath ... 85 F2
Willows Shopping Centre The.
  Mang ... 51 F3
Willows The. Bris ... 37 D1
Willows The. Nail ... 59 F2
Willows The. St Gif ... 36 B4
Willows The. Yate ... 27 E1
Wills Dr. Bris ... 64 A4
Willsbridge Hill. Kingsw ... 66 A1
Willway St. Bris ... 63 E2
Willway St. Bris ... 63 F4
Wilmot Ct. Kingsw ... 66 A3
Wilmots Way. E in G ... 47 E2
Wilmott House. E in G ... 47 E2
Wilson Pl. Bris ... 63 F4
Wilson St. Bris ... 63 F4
Wilton Cl. Bris ... 35 E1
Wilton Gdns. W-S-M ... 104 B4
Wiltons. Wring ... 92 B1
Wiltshire Ave. Kingsw ... 65 E3
Wiltshire Ave. Yate ... 28 A2
Wiltshire Pl. Kingsw ... 51 F2
Wiltshire Way. Bath ... 85 D1
Wilverley Ind Est. Bris ... 64 C1
Wimbledon Rd. Bris ... 49 E3
Wimblestone Rd. Winsc ... 107 F1
Wimborne Rd. Bris ... 63 E1
Winash Cl. Bris ... 80 B4
Wincanton Cl. Nail ... 60 A1
Winchcombe Cl. Nail ... 76 A4
Winchcombe Gr. Bris ... 47 F3
Winchcombe Rd. Fr Cot ... 38 A4
Winchester Ave. Bris ... 64 B2
Winchester Rd. Bath ... 101 E3
Winchester Rd. Bris ... 64 B2
Wincroft. Kingsw ... 66 B2
Windcliff Cres. Bris ... 47 F4
Windermere Rd. Bris ... 36 A4
Windermere Way. Kingsw ... 66 B3
Windmill Cl. Bris ... 63 F2
Windmill Farm Bsns Cen.
  Bris ... 63 E2
Windmill Hill. Bris ... 63 E2
Windmill Hill. Lock ... 106 A1
Windmill La. Bris ... 34 B2
Windrush Cl. Bath ... 100 C2
Windrush Ct. Thorn ... 15 E4
Windrush Green. Keyn ... 82 A2
Windrush Rd. Keyn ... 82 A2
Windsor Ave. Bris ... 65 D3
Windsor Ave. Keyn ... 81 F2
Windsor Bridge Rd. Bath ... 101 E4
Windsor Cl. Cleve ... 57 E1
Windsor Cl. St Gif ... 36 C2
Windsor Cres. Bris ... 34 B2
Windsor Ct. Bath ... 101 E4
Windsor Ct. Bris ... 62 C3
Windsor Ct. Mang ... 51 F4
Windsor Ct. Wick ... 67 E4
Windsor Dr. Yate ... 27 E1
Windsor Gr. Bris ... 64 A4
Windsor Pl. Bris ... 62 C3
Windsor Pl. Mang ... 52 A3
Windsor Rd. Bris ... 49 F1
Windsor Rd. Kingsw ... 65 F1
Windsor Rd. W-S-M ... 88 B1
Windsor Terr. Bris ... 62 C3
Windsor Terr. Bris ... 63 F2
Windwhistle Circ. W-S-M .. 104 C2
Windwhistle La. W-S-M ... 104 C2
Windwhistle Rd. W-S-M ... 104 B2
Wine St. Bath ... 102 A3
Wine St. Bris ... 63 E4
Wineberry Cl. Bris ... 50 B1
Winfield Rd. Sist ... 66 B4
Winford Cl. Portis ... 45 F2
Winford Gr. Bris ... 79 D4
Winford La. Dun ... 78 B1
Winford Rd. Ch Mag ... 95 F2
Wingard Cl. W-S-M ... 104 B1
Wingfield Rd. Bris ... 63 F1
Winifred's La. Bath ... 84 C1
Winkworth Pl. Bris ... 49 F1
Winnowing End. Wins ... 108 A2
Winsbury Way. St Gif ... 24 B1
Winscombe Cl. Keyn ... 81 E3

Winscombe Dro. Ship ... 125 E3
Winscombe Dro. Wins ... 125 E3
Winscombe Hill. Wins ... 124 C3
Winscombe Rd. W-S-M ... 105 D4
Winsford St. Bris ... 64 A4
Winsham Cl. Bris ... 80 A3
Winsley Hill. Winsl ... 120 A3
Winsley Rd. Bris ... 49 E1
Wint Hill. Ban ... 107 D1
Winterbourne Hill. Wint ... 37 E3
Winterbourne Rd. St Gif ... 36 C3
Winterfield Park. Paul ... 131 F2
Winterfield Rd. Paul ... 131 F3
Winterstoke Cl. Bris ... 63 D1
Winterstoke Rd. Bris ... 62 C2
Winterstoke Rd. W-S-M ... 105 D2
Winterstoke Underpass. Bris 62 C2
Winton St. Bris ... 63 F2
Wistaria Ave. Ch Sod ... 28 A1
Wisteria Ave. Lock ... 105 E1
Witch Hazel Rd. Bris ... 79 F2
Witchell Rd. Bris ... 64 B4
Witcombe Cl. Kingsw ... 51 F1
Witcombe. Yate ... 39 E4
Witherlies Rd. Bris ... 50 C3
Withey Cl E. Bris ... 48 C3
Withey Cl W. Bris ... 48 C3
Witheys The. Whit ... 80 B2
Withies La. Mid No ... 138 A4
Withies Park. Mid No ... 137 F4
Withington Cl. Kingsw ... 66 B1
Withleigh Rd. Bris ... 64 A1
Withyditch La. Pris ... 117 E2
Withymead Rd. Marsh ... 70 A4
Withypool Gdns. Bris ... 80 A3
Withywood Gdns. Bris ... 78 C2
Withywood Rd. Bris ... 78 C2
Witney Cl. Keyn ... 82 B2
Woburn Cl. Kingsw ... 65 F3
Woburn Rd. Bris ... 50 A2
Wolferton Rd. Bris ... 49 F1
Wolfridge Gdns. Bris ... 35 D2
Wolfridge La. Alve ... 14 C2
Wolfridge Ride. Alve ... 14 C2
Wolseley Rd. Bris ... 49 E2
Wolvers Hill Rd. Ban ... 106 C3
Wolvers Hill Rd. Lock ... 106 C3
Wolvershill Park. Ban ... 107 D2
Wood End Wlk. Bris ... 48 B3
Wood Hill Park. Portis ... 45 D4
Wood Hill. Cong ... 91 F3
Wood Kilns The. Yatt ... 74 A1
Wood La. Axb ... 125 E1
Wood La. Hork ... 19 D1
Wood La. W in G ... 59 F4
Wood La. W-S-M ... 87 F1
Wood Rd. Kingsw ... 65 E4
Wood St. Bath ... 101 F3
Wood St. Bath ... 101 F3
Wood St. Bris ... 50 A1
Woodbine Rd. Bris ... 64 B4
Woodborough Cres. Wins . 125 D4
Woodborough Dr. Wins ... 125 D4
Woodborough La. Mid No . 133 D2
Woodborough Rd. Mid No . 133 D2
Woodborough Rd. Wins ... 124 C4
Woodborough Rd. Wins ... 125 D4
Woodborough St. Bris ... 50 A1
Woodbridge Rd. Bris ... 64 A1
Woodbury La. Bris ... 49 D1
Woodchester Rd. Bris ... 49 E4
Woodchester. Kingsw ... 51 F2
Woodchester. Yate ... 39 F4
Woodcliff Ave. W-S-M ... 88 B1
Woodcliff Rd. W-S-M ... 88 B1
Woodcote Rd. Bris ... 51 D2
Woodcote Wlk. Bris ... 51 D1
Woodcote. Kingsw ... 65 E3
Woodcroft Ave. Bris ... 50 B1
Woodcroft Cl. Bris ... 64 C2
Woodcroft Rd. Bris ... 64 C2
Woodcroft. Bi Sut ... 113 E2
Woodend La. Rock ... 2 C1
Woodend Rd. Fr Cot ... 38 B4
Woodend. Kingsw ... 65 E3
Woodfield Rd. Bris ... 49 D1
Woodfinch Cres. Puck ... 53 E2
Woodford Cl. Nail ... 60 A1
Woodgrove Rd. Bris ... 34 B1
Woodhall Cl. Mang ... 51 F3
Woodhill Ave. Portis ... 45 E3
Woodhill Rd. Portis ... 45 D4
Woodhill Views. Nail ... 59 F2
Woodhouse Ave. Alve ... 24 B4
Woodhouse Cl. Alve ... 24 B3
Woodhouse Gr. Bris ... 49 F3
Woodhouse Rd. Bath ... 101 D3
Woodhurst Rd. W-S-M ... 105 D4
Woodington Ct. Kingsw ... 65 F3
Woodington Rd. Cleve ... 57 E1
Woodland Ave. Kingsw ... 51 E1
Woodland Cl. Wrax ... 61 D2
Woodland Cotts Winsl ... 120 B3
Woodland Glade. Cleve ... 57 F3
Woodland Gr. Bath ... 102 C3
Woodland Gr. Bris ... 48 B3
Woodland Rd. Bris ... 63 D4
Woodland Rd. Crom ... 10 A2

Woodland Rd. Nail ... 59 F2
Woodland Rd. W-S-M ... 104 B2
Woodland Terr. Bris ... 49 D1
Woodland Terr. Kingsw ... 65 F4
Woodland Way. Bris ... 51 E1
Woodland Way. Wrax ... 61 D2
Woodlands Ct. St Gif ... 24 A2
Woodlands Dr. Winsl ... 120 A3
Woodlands La. Alve ... 24 C3
Woodlands La. St Gif ... 24 B2
Woodlands Park. Bath ... 85 E1
Woodlands Park. St Gif ... 24 B2
Woodlands Rd. Char ... 11 D2
Woodlands Rd. Cleve ... 57 E2
Woodlands Rd. Portis ... 45 F4
Woodlands Rd. Tyth ... 16 A3
Woodlands Rise. Mang ... 51 E3
Woodlands The. Pris ... 116 C2
Woodlands. Mang ... 51 F3
Woodlands. St Gif ... 24 B2
Woodlands. Tyth ... 16 A3
Woodleaze. Bris ... 48 A3
Woodleigh Gdns. Bris ... 80 B3
Woodleigh. Thorn ... 8 B1
Woodmancote Rd. Bris ... 49 F1
Woodmancote. Yate ... 39 E4
Woodmans Cl. Ch Sod ... 40 A4
Woodmans Rd. Ch Sod ... 40 A4
Woodmans Vale. Ch Sod ... 40 B4
Woodmarsh Cl. Bris ... 80 A2
Woodmead Gdns. Bris ... 79 E2
Woodmead La. Doyn ... 54 A1
Woodmill. Yatt ... 74 A1
Woodpecker Ave. Rod ... 138 A4
Woodpecker Dr. W-S-M ... 105 F4
Woods Hill. Li St ... 120 A4
Woodside Ave. W-S-M ... 105 D1
Woodside Gdns. Portis ... 44 C3
Woodside Gr. Bris ... 34 B2
Woodside Rd. Bris ... 64 C3
Woodside Rd. Cleve ... 57 F3
Woodside Rd. Fr Cot ... 38 B4
Woodside Rd. Kingsw ... 65 E4
Woodside Rd. Mang ... 51 E4
Woodside. Bris ... 48 B2
Woodside. Mid No ... 131 F1
Woodspring Ave. W-S-M ... 88 A2
Woodspring Cres. W-S-M ... 88 A2
Woodstock Ave. Bris ... 49 E1
Woodstock Cl. Kingsw ... 65 F4
Woodstock Rd. Bris ... 49 E1
Woodstock Rd. Kingsw ... 65 F4
Woodstock Rd. W-S-M ... 105 D4
Woodview Cl. Bris ... 47 F4
Woodview Dr. Brock ... 92 A4
Woodview Terr. Nail ... 59 F1
Woodview Terr. W-S-M ... 105 D3
Woodview. Chil ... 137 F3
Woodview. Cleve ... 57 F2
Woodview. Paul ... 131 E3
Woodward Dr. Kingsw ... 65 F2
Woodwell Rd. Bris ... 47 F3
Woodyleaze Dr. Kingsw ... 65 E3
Wookey Cl. Nail ... 75 F4
Woolcot St. Bris ... 49 D1
Wooler Rd. W-S-M ... 104 C4
Woollard La. Pens ... 80 B1
Woollard La. Whit ... 80 B1
Woolley La. Charl ... 85 D2
Woolley Rd. Bris ... 80 C3
Wootton Cres. Bris ... 64 C3
Wootton Pk. Bris ... 64 A1
Wootton Rd. Bris ... 64 C3
Worcester Bldgs. Bath ... 85 D1
Worcester Cl. Bris ... 51 D1
Worcester Cres. Bris ... 63 D4
Worcester Gdns. Nail ... 75 E4
Worcester Park. Bath ... 85 D1
Worcester Pl. Bath ... 85 D1
Worcester Rd. Bris ... 63 D4
Worcester Rd. Kingsw ... 51 E1
Worcester Terr. Bris ... 63 D4
Worcester Villas. Bath ... 85 D1
Wordsworth Rd. Bris ... 50 A4
Wordsworth Rd. Cleve ... 57 E1
Wordsworth Rd. W-S-M ... 105 D2
Workshop Rd. Avon ... 33 E2
World's End La. Keyn ... 82 B3
Worldsend La. Stone ... 2 C4
Worle Ct. W-S-M ... 88 C2
Worle Parkway. W-S-M ... 89 D1
Worlebury Cl. W-S-M ... 88 A2
Worlebury Hill Rd. W-S-M ... 88 B2
Worlebury Park Rd. W-S-M . 88 A1
Wormcliffe La. Box ... 86 C2
Worrall Rd. Bris ... 49 D1
Worrel's La. Wint ... 37 E2
Worsley St. Bris ... 64 B4
Worth Cl. Kingsw ... 65 F3
Worthies The. Lymp ... 122 A1
Worthing Rd. Bris ... 35 F4
Worthy Cres. Lymp ... 122 A1
Worthy La. W-S-M ... 104 C4
Worthy Pl. W-S-M ... 104 B4
Worthy Rd. Avon ... 33 F4
Worthys The. St Gif ... 37 D3
Wotton Rd. Char ... 11 D3
Wotton Rd. Ir Act ... 26 C3

Wotton Rd. W-u-E ... 11 F3
Wotton Rd. Wickw ... 27 D4
Wrangle Farm Green. Cleve 57 F1
Wraxall Gr. Bris ... 79 D4
Wraxall Hill. Wrax ... 60 B3
Wraxall Rd. Kingsw ... 66 A3
Wren Cl. W-S-M ... 105 E4
Wren Dr. Bris ... 51 D3
Wrenbert Rd. Mang ... 51 E3
Wrington Cl. St Gif ... 36 B4
Wrington Cres. Bris ... 79 D4
Wrington Hill. Cong ... 92 C3
Wrington Hill. Wring ... 92 C3
Wrington La. Cong ... 91 F3
Wrington Mead. Cong ... 91 F3
Wrington Rd. Cong ... 91 F3
Wroughton Dr. Bris ... 79 E2
Wroughton Gdns. Bris ... 79 E2
Wroxham Dr. St Gif ... 36 B4
Wyatt Ave. Bris ... 78 C3
Wyatt Cl. Bris ... 78 C3
Wyatt's Cl. Nail ... 59 E1
Wychwood. Kingsw ... 65 F3
Wyck Beck Rd. Bris ... 35 D2
Wycliffe Rd. Bris ... 49 D4
Wycombe Gr. Bris ... 64 B1
Wye Croft Cl. Bris ... 35 E2
Wye Ct. Thorn ... 15 E4
Wyedale Ave. Bris ... 48 A4
Wykis Ct. Kingsw ... 65 F3
Wyllie Ct. W-S-M ... 89 D3
Wymbush Cres. Bris ... 79 E3
Wymbush Gdns. Bris ... 79 E3
Wyndham Cres. Bris ... 65 D2
Wyndham Cres. E in G ... 47 D2
Wyndham Way. Portis ... 45 F3
Wynstones The. Kingsw ... 65 E4
Wynter Cl. W-S-M ... 89 D2
Wytham Rd. Keyn ... 82 A2

Yadley Cl. Wins ... 125 D4
Yadley La. Wins ... 125 D3
Yadley Way. Wins ... 125 D4
Yanleigh Cl. Dun ... 78 B3
Yanley La. Lo Ash ... 78 B4
Yarbury Way. W-S-M ... 89 D1
Yate Rd. Ir Act ... 26 C2
Yate Rocks. Yate ... 27 F4
Yelverton Rd. Bris ... 64 C1
Yeo Bank La. K Sey ... 72 C1
Yeo Cl. Cong ... 91 E2
Yeo Cl. W-S-M ... 105 D3
Yeo La. Lo Ash ... 61 F1
Yeo Moor. Cleve ... 57 F1
Yeo Way. Cleve ... 57 D1
Yeolands Dr. Cleve ... 57 D1
Yeoman's Cl. Bris ... 48 B3
Yeomans Orch. Wring ... 92 C2
Yeomanside Cl. Bris ... 80 B3
Yeomead. Nail ... 59 F2
Yeomeads. Lo Ash ... 61 F1
Yeoward Rd. Cleve ... 57 F1
Yew Tree Cl. Bi Sut ... 113 E2
Yew Tree Cl. Blag ... 109 F3
Yew Tree Cl. Nail ... 59 E1
Yew Tree Dr. Kingsw ... 51 F2
Yew Tree Gdns. E in G ... 47 E2
Yew Tree Gdns. Nail ... 59 E1
Yew Tree Gdns. Wins ... 108 A2
Yew Tree La. Co Mar ... 128 A4
Yew Tree La. K Sey ... 73 D1
Yew Tree Park. Cong ... 91 E2
Yewcroft Cl. Bris ... 80 A2
Yewtree Batch. But ... 94 A1
Yomede Park. Bath ... 101 D4
York Ave. Bris ... 49 F2
York Cl. Mang ... 37 F1
York Cl. St Gif ... 36 B2
York Cl. W-S-M ... 89 D2
York Cl. Yate ... 27 F2
York Gdns. Bris ... 62 C3
York Gdns. Bris ... 63 D3
York Gdns. Wint ... 37 F4
York Pl. Bris ... 63 D4
York Pl. Bris ... 63 E1
York Rd. Bris ... 49 F1
York Rd. Bris ... 50 B1
York Rd. Bris ... 63 F2
York Rd. Kingsw ... 51 F2
York St. Bath ... 102 A3
York St. Bris ... 49 D1
York St. Bris ... 50 A1
York St. Bris ... 63 F4
York St. Bris ... 64 B4
York St. W-S-M ... 104 B4

Zetland Rd. Bris ... 49 E1
Zig Zag. Cleve ... 57 E2
Zinc Rd. Avon ... 33 E2
Zion Hill. Ston E ... 137 D4